Economy of Traces

Economy of Traces

Traceability, Tracking, and the Accounts We Live By

MICHAEL POWER

OXFORD
UNIVERSITY PRESS

OXFORD
UNIVERSITY PRESS

Oxford University Press is a department of the University of Oxford.
It furthers the University's objective of excellence in research, scholarship,
and education by publishing worldwide. Oxford is a registered trade mark of
Oxford University Press in the UK and in certain other countries.

Published in the United States of America by Oxford University Press
198 Madison Avenue, New York, NY 10016, United States of America.

Library of Congress Cataloging-in-Publication Data
Names: Power, Michael (Professor of Accounting) author
Title: Economy of traces : traceability, tracking, and the accounts we live by / Michael Power.
Description: New York, NY : Oxford University, [2026] |
Includes bibliographical references and index.
Identifiers: LCCN 2026003301 | ISBN 9780197853535 paperback |
ISBN 9780197681497 hardback | ISBN 9780197681510 epub | ISBN 9780197681527
Subjects: LCSH: Accounting—Social aspects
Classification: LCC HF5625 .P76 2026 | DDC 657—dc23/eng/20260403
LC record available at https://lccn.loc.gov/2026003301ss

DOI: 10.1093/9780197681527.001.0001

The manufacturer's authorized representative in the EU for product safety is
Oxford University Press España S.A. of Parque Empresarial San Fernando de Henares,
Avenida de Castilla, 2 – 28830 Madrid (www.oup.es/en or product.safety@oup.com).
OUP España S.A. also acts as importer into Spain of products made by the manufacturer.

For Caroline

Preface

In one of his rich and typically elusive interviews, the French philosopher Michel Foucault stated that when you start to write a book, you *should never* know how it will end. This imperative seems a little too strong, especially as the value of careful planning is deeply ingrained in academia and beyond. Yet he believed that writing is itself a process of discovery, of experimentation with ideas, with sources, and with the very formulation of sentences. There can be many twists and turns in the movement of thought during the process of writing. Understood thus, writing can even be a form of risk-taking, of reaching for something beyond our immediate grasp and bringing it out of the shadows, of proposing new and unlikely connections. It can be a critical project of struggle, which may, depending on the subject matter, be both necessary and impossible, and in which failure is normal, even when it seems to succeed on some "output-based" register of performance. In this spirit, the impossible but necessary project represented in this book is an analysis of traceability, something—is it a thing?—that pervades our lives in many different forms and for this reason also eludes our grasp.

What is traceability? As this book seeks to demonstrate, it encompasses the production of traces, tracking practices, and accounting. Taken literally, it means the "ability" to trace things and people on the basis of evidence. Yet it also signals something prior to this, namely the generation of the traces that enable tracing and tracking. Hence, at the outset, traceability has two faces—trace production and use. In addition to this inherent duality, traceability has many different connotations. It is something *valued* and imagined, for example in determining and accounting for food quality; it is visible and known via specific *processes* of tracing, for example in financial auditing; and it has an *infrastructural* basis by virtue of connecting multiple organizations and people, most obviously in the case of product supply chains. Yet, a unitary theory of these different aspects of traceability, what we might call its "variable ontology" as value, process, and infrastructure, is likely to fail. Rather, in this book I approach traceability and its manifestations cautiously and synthetically from a number of different but overlapping viewpoints and themes. And, insofar as traceability and accounting are intimately related to one another, this is also simultaneously and necessarily that most unlikely thing—a book of "accounting theory". To be more precise, it is a sustained attempt to develop a *traceological* theorization of accounting for which the various chapters provide building blocks.

Why does such a project, impossible or otherwise, really matter? The answer is, I hope, persuasive. In the "digital age", for want of a better term, the scale and scope of our capacity to trace and track food, people, and many other things, including viruses and carbon, continue to expand and intensify. This in turn has generated many issues and challenges, not least for privacy and the right to be untraceable, for the governance of artificial intelligence (AI) applications, for the ethics and security of food supply chains, and much else besides. Traceability in its various practice manifestations has become pervasive—society-wide—but also somehow systemically opaque and unaccountable. It can be thought of as a logic or, better, as a cluster of logics that operate in the shadows of organizational and personal life and which are consequential for collective forms of human sense-making and accounting. These logics of traceability must be dug out of their, often humble, contexts to understand their reach and power in shaping narratives of self-formation, both for humans and organizations. Stiegler (2016) refers to the systemic reach and significance of traceability as an "economy of traces", a motif that I borrow for the title of this work. It points to the substrate or infrastructure upon which new forms of capitalism and related social orders are being made possible and in which, as we shall see, conventional notions of traceability are mutating.

The idea of an economy of traces is broader than, and predates, developments in digital technologies for trace production. Traceability as a feature of human practices has a long history involving documents and records in paper form. Humans have always been engaged in collecting and processing traces for different traceability purposes, for example to understand the origins and quality of foodstuffs and wine; to map and secure territories; to predict the weather; and to catch prey. In all these respects, these practices of tracing are themselves dependent on the generation of traces of phenomena of interest. In general, the economy of traces in this infrastructural sense embodies and encodes cultural values about which traces matter and how they are to be organized and accounted for.

This is a book primarily about traceability and its implications for accounting, and only derivatively about digitization. This is a risky emphasis, and the reader must judge whether it succeeds. But many fine scholars in different fields are already fully embarked on analysing the history, nature, and effects of the digitalization of economy and society. Furthermore, between the time of starting this book in 2021 and its finalization in 2026, changes in digital technology, especially AI, have proceeded at an astonishing rate. It would have been impossible to stay close to such rapidly moving targets. The ambition here is more modest and less hostage to change, namely to reach for "digitally agnostic" theorizations of traceability that nevertheless take some account of the impact of advanced modes of digital automation on our ability to trace and to generate accounts. To execute this orientation, the book draws upon naturalistic analogies, such as "ruts in the road", to develop some of its arguments. Such analogies have the advantage of not being in the orbit of specialist languages and terminology, and they generate conceptual distance from the specifics of digital automation. Hence, the chapters of the book tend to zoom out from the detail of specific social materialities and digital devices—a move that may disappoint scholars of science and technology—in order to address the general organization of traceability. I will also argue that traces, while varied, underpin accounts in their broadest sense, accounts that scholars have shown to constitute persons and organizations, and thereby social orders. It follows that changes in the economy of traces, in the production and use of such traces, will change the accounts we live by, and many other things with that, including the nature of our empirical knowledge of the world.

The core thesis of this book is that the accounts we live by are undergoing a systemic shift in their nature, with consequences for humans and organizations. In what follows, I use the terms "accounts" and "accounting" interchangeably. This is intended to express the conviction that everyday account-giving and accounting in formal organizational settings are becoming fluid, cross over into each other, and increasingly share data infrastructures. Whereas personal diaries and work time sheets used to exist in entirely different and disconnected spheres, this is no longer the case in our digitized world. Hence, what we call accounts and accounting are intertwined and jointly constitute the "accounts we live by".

In sustaining this thesis, this book is also, at various junctures, an extended conversation with the work of Bruno Latour, drawing upon and differentiating itself from his extraordinarily rich thinking. In this respect, the analysis also takes me back to where I began as a philosophy student, first at Oxford and then Cambridge. Indeed, I have revisited my lecture notes on positivism for some of the material in Chapter 9. Those notes survive from the early 1980s, an age before Powerpoint slides and recorded lectures, when students had to learn the art of taking notes while listening. I hesitate to say this was a golden age, but it was a necessary skill at the time, and my notes from over forty years ago remain both useful and also, very surprisingly, legible. Readers who engage with this book will, I hope, tolerate its philosophical asides and reflections. I have never believed that there was a neat way to separate questions of ontology, about the nature of things, from questions about the nature of the knowledge practices that mobilize such things; they always implicate each other. But I admit that I may lean towards the former at the expense of engaging more fully with the sociomateriality of the latter. The analyses of traceability and accounting in the pages of this book are also grounded in broad sensibilities about the relational and connected nature of organization, governance, risk, self, and science.

As may be clear by now, this is a theoretically orientated book in the sense that it conducts its analysis primarily at the level of conceptual argument, interspersed by illustrative vignettes. Like previous endeavours of mine, it necessarily simplifies its subject matter in order to make issues of (presumed) interest stand out; it is broad rather than deep, horizontal in orientation rather than vertical, conceptual rather than materialist, a map rather than an archaeology. And it is also unfashionably propositional and *declarative* in its mode of argument. Inevitably detailed empirical work would introduce more complexity, nuance, and variation into such an analysis. Normally, I would make no apology for such an approach, but I am conscious, as a privileged academic, that I write these words during very troubled times for our world, when war, conflict, and environmental catastrophe seem to have no end in sight. Hence, it would be understandable to be accused of self-indulgence. Nevertheless, I offer this, albeit limited, defence: we humans are animals that may do awful things, but we also think and reflect to some extent, and this always contains at least some potential for change for the betterment of all. Theory and theorizing, no matter how abstruse, are extensions of this human and humanizing capacity, even when they appear to serve inhuman causes. Paolo Quattrone and Tammar Zilber have recently argued that we need to match our theoretical work to this world of disorder and crisis that confronts us, rather than presuppose implicit stabilizing forces. I confess that this book is more synthetic and ordering in its orientation than not, but I offer the modest and vulnerable proposition, which does not in any measure justify this or any other specific book, that theory and the reflective competences that inform it are especially important at this seemingly anti-theoretic time.

As I approach the end of my career, I now realize that I have been working on traceability in one form or another for decades. Several experiences brought this interest into sharper focus. Some years ago, my wife and I went to our favourite restaurant close to our home in London. On this occasion, outside the entrance to the restaurant on the pavement was a new noticeboard, which read: "*Skipper's catch – ask your server where your fish was landed and who by . . .*". I did ask the server and they did not know. But the chef did. As an ex-auditor, I also wanted to ask this chef how he knew where the fish came from, and whether he was confident that he could trust his sources. I wanted to ask him why he imagined that customers like me would be interested in knowing this, or indeed what they would do with the information. Might they say things like: "sorry, that fish has come from the wrong place"; or "that fish has travelled too far"; or "I don't trust that trawler crew"? I politely refrained from asking these questions, but the experience felt like a systemic shift, indicating something new but hard to characterize, something that placed auditing in a much larger frame of reference than financial accounting. What could make it possible for such a notice to appear one day outside that local restaurant? This book will suggest that the notice was a new kind of account in our lives, based on our enhanced ability for tracking many things, not only fish and trawlers.

Another push towards a more explicit focus on traceability arose from my experiences as a part-time independent director of three large public companies in the United Kingdom and the Republic of Ireland over a period of fifteen years. In addition to being on the main boards of those companies, I also served on their risk, audit, and valuation committees, often as the chairman. I consider myself to be enormously fortunate to have had these "coal face" experiences of corporate governance. Not only was I lucky enough to work with impressive people in each organization, but I was also able to observe, and probably contributed to, traceability in action. The UK financial services sector is regulated for the purpose of ensuring the financial resilience of firms and the financial system, and to protect retail customers who entrust their savings to others. I experienced the intensification of this regulation over many years, especially in the immediate aftermath of the 2008 financial crisis. It was very much an "epistemic intensification" in the sense that distant regulators wanted to know about more aspects of organizational operations in ever more granular detail, for example about the design and operation of risk management and internal control systems. From rules for "treating customers fairly" to "anti-money-laundering" and the "fitness and propriety" of senior management, the internal elaboration of controls increased the production and flow of traces between financial organizations and their regulators, with the ambition of providing "sufficiently reliable evidence" of good conduct, solvency, and compliance.

In thinking about these developments, this expansion of explicit and detailed rules provides evidence of what Max Weber called the "rationalization" of society and the bureaucratization of organizational life. It is also a further manifestation of an "audit society" effect in which organizations respond to external regulatory pressures by "making themselves auditable" via the elaboration of detailed control systems and performance indicators. This epistemic intensification of organizational control also intensified an invisible economy of traces to enable organizations and individuals to be traceable, auditable, and observable.

Traceability recently became the leading thematic interest in my work, with auditing being repositioned as one variant of it. Furthermore, advances in digital technologies broadly understood stimulated a new series of questions. Is the audit society now being supercharged in the digital age, or is something very different happening that requires a fresh perspective? How might traceability be at the centre of an emerging social order that has some continuities with the audit society but which also looks and feels very different from it, given, for example, the dramatic rise of self-tracking (which I discuss in Chapter 8)? While these questions motivated my original focus on traceability, I did not know when I embarked on this book, and Foucault would approve of my not knowing, that the concept of "tracking" would come to play such a pivotal role in its arguments and would emerge as the operating principle of a new economy of traces.

A prefatory word on books is needed. In academic management studies today and certainly in the field of academic accounting, the journal article has become the unit of career progression, and many readers will be familiar with the apparatus of journal ranking systems that have strengthened this emphasis. Whatever editors may say, and I have been one, journals tend to design-in intellectual conservatism in a number of ways, both explicit and implicit. Despite worthy quality and robustness ideals, they can be highly constraining outlets, which generate careerist orientations to research that are not conducive to intellectual risk-taking. Books are not so constrained like this. Furthermore, books can travel across intellectual specialisms and boundaries, even reaching policy circles, in a way that journal articles rarely do. Books can seed new sensibilities and agendas, almost independently of their quality and sometimes solely because of their titles! Time will tell whether this one has any impact in this regard but, given the aforementioned perilous state of the world as I write these prefatory words, the opportunity and freedom to write it remain a fragile privilege not to be taken for granted. I recently heard a story about a famous composer who was asked about the intended audience for his compositions. He replied that he did not compose for any audience or indeed for himself; he was simply trying to solve problems. I cannot pretend that my motives are as noble as this, but this book is an attempt to think through some of the implications of the economy of traces in which many of us live.

I conclude by thanking a number of people who have directly and indirectly supported and encouraged this project and have commented on earlier manifestations of it, thereby preventing the worst mistakes while leaving me with full responsibility for any lingering errors and omissions: Cristina Alaimo, Diane-Laure Arjaliès, Bruce Carruthers, Joep Cornelissen, Luciana D'Adderio, Quinn DuPont, Wendy Espeland, Mikkel Flyverbom, Marion Fourcade, Marian Gatzweiler, Tim Hannigan, Jannis Kallinikos, Finia Kuhlmann, Natalia Levina, Kari Lukka, Nadia Matringe, Afshin Mehrpouya, Andrea Mennicken, Yuval Millo, Eric Monteiro, Fabian Muniesa, Davide Nicolini, Tommaso Palermo, Neil Pollock, Ted Schatzki, Eija Vinnari, and Hendrik Vollmer. I add to this list many others who have greatly influenced my trajectory and from whom I have learned so much over many years of thinking about traceability. They include Chris Carter, Wai Fong Chua, David Cooper, Roger Friedland, Yves Gendron, Cynthia Hardy, Christopher Hood, Anthony Hopwood, Bruno Latour, Ken Lee, Martin Lodge, Mike Lounsbury, Donald MacKenzie, Steve Maguire, Anette Mikes, Peter Miller, Mary Morgan, Julia Morley, Brendan O'Dwyer, Brian Pentland, John Roberts, Keith Robson, Rita Samiolo, Crawford Spence, and Wim van der

Stede. This second list also encompasses my many Masters and PhD students over several decades. Though they do not know it, our engagements in class and in advisory meetings have always been a source of stimulation and reflection. I also thank many colleagues in the wider world of public and private organizations, with whom I have discussed some of my ideas and from whom I was able to learn. Most likely they will be surprised by this attribution, but I make it in the hope that it is a pleasant surprise: Richard Anderson, Sarah Bates, David Bellamy, Peter Bonisch, Iain Cornish, Andrew Croft, Ian Gascoigne, Cecil Hayes, Jonathan Hayward, Andrew Jones, David O'Regan, Maxim Parr, Amy Stirling, Bill Tonks, Mike Wilson, and Charles Woodd. In addition, I thank specifically James Cook and colleagues of Oxford University Press who took a chance on this risky project when others did not, and were patient enough to wait for it. I am confident that I will not be subjecting the Oxford editorial team to this again, but I thank this great Press for publishing my work over many years. My heart has always been with Oxford since my undergraduate days and, though the Press is a global organization with many centres, I continue to enjoy walking past its magnificent buildings in Walton Street.

Finally, I thank my wife Caroline from the bottom of my heart. She has stood by me in times of health adversity and has supported me during the many ups and downs of this writing process.

Michael Power
London, 2026

Contents

List of Figures and Tables

Figures

Tables

1
Traceability and Accounts

Overview

In October 2022 one of my sons ran the London marathon, thirty-two years after my own effort on the same course. In contrast to 1990, he was able to track his progress on a digital map of the London route via an app linked to his digital watch. This tracking application analysed his run in terms of "splits" and produced an overall summary of his "performance" beyond simply the time taken. The app also enabled him to monitor his heart rate. He became concerned at its level at the 32 kilometre stage and decided to slow down. In short, like many other runners that day, my son was "accounting" for himself in real time; he was able to self-monitor as I never could. Tracking his progress from a distance, using the same app, there was also a scare when his icon was stationary for a considerable length of time, only suddenly to jump to the finish. Had he "beamed" himself to the end? Perhaps that smart watch was smarter than I could ever imagine? But in fact the app connectivity had temporarily failed; the experience of tracking his progress in so-called real time was imperfect, with delays, lags, and correcting jumps. Clearly, much more is needed than a smart watch attached to a runner's body for successful tracking. An entire background apparatus must be in place, involving programmers, satellites, manufacturers, internet providers, and many more agencies, all distributed but also all connected and somehow interdependent. From this point of view, what becomes surprising is that the app worked at all—not that it misfired a few times, no doubt due to the volume of use that day.

Vignettes like this, which point to the entanglement of digital devices in our everyday lives, are increasingly familiar and well documented by scholars. This one has a number of ingredients worthy of note. First, there is the technology-enabled *traceification* of human action by which (some) bodily movements and states are captured and marked by a machine. Second, this traceification process enables the *tracking* of the runner both by himself and also by remote observers using the app, thereby increasing their observational reach. Third, traceification is also generative of a digital double or proxy of the runner, defined by various biometrics that provide evidence of "how he is doing". In other words, the generated traces of this app support *accounts* of his performance and bodily functions. The vignette is an example of what has been called the "culture of self-tracking" in which humans hold themselves to account and audit themselves (Lupton,

Economy of Traces. Michael Power, Oxford University Press. © Oxford University Press (2026).
DOI: 10.1093/9780197681527.003.0001

2016b). In the background, there is necessarily an infrastructure or platform that produces the app, provides the necessary *connectivity* for it to work, and which may itself co-opt the traces produce by the runner and datafy them for future commercial benefit.

Here then are most of the conceptual elements for the arguments in this book: traces, traceification, datafication, tracking, accounting, and connectivity. Of particular note, the vignette implies a tight relationship between the production of traces and their conversion into the performance data that make up accounts. The analysis of this relationship and its dynamics is a core focus for this book, and the ambition is to develop a *traceological theorization of accounting* that can be distinguished from an information perspective on decision-making, on the one hand, and from a sociology of quantification perspective on reduction and commensurability, on the other.

Remarkable things in our everyday lives, such as remotely tracking a relative doing a charity run, often become unremarkable to us. It is one of the tasks of social science, and philosophy, to recover that sense of the remarkable, and to problematize and to investigate the conditions of possibility for the production of the fabric of our everyday world. But such an analytic attitude is also methodologically daunting. In this book we endeavour to look through and beyond this specific and personal vignette to disclose aspects of the emerging form of life of which it is symptomatic. As we do so, we see that something bigger and more systematic is going on. It may seem at first glance that there is nothing to link this use of a smart watch during a marathon to, say, wine labelling, anti-money-laundering regulation, financial accounting, the legalization of cannabis, cryptocurrency trading, fingerprinting, credit scoring, and food-quality certification. Each of these practices and fields, and many more besides, has its own apparatuses of devices and knowledge production. Each has its own specialist followers and observers in industry and academic circles, with learned journals dedicated to the steady elaboration of a science of its practice. And each is mobilized, it seems, by different values and goals, focused on different objects. Indeed, we should not be surprised by this diversity; it simply reflects how our world is a complex portfolio of endeavours addressing distinct social and economic concerns and values.

Yet, these many diverse worlds of practice share a feature with each other, and with the smart watch example, which might seem unremarkable, but which points to a family resemblance worthy of further reflection. As we analyse in greater depth in this book, they each exhibit the ingredients already detected in the vignette, ingredients that combine to constitute practices of *traceability*. They are each involved with making specific things, processes, and people knowable, visible, and connected via the traces that they produce or that are produced of them, which they leave behind or which follow them, and which enable them to be tracked (i.e. to be observable and controllable).

By construction, traceability necessarily begins with traceification, with making things traceable by generating traces of them. Yet, traces are empirically heterogeneous. Some, like labels and tags, move with the objects and people to which they are attached, providing evidence of origins or quality, a process that may be more or less intensively regulated. Some, as in the marathon runner case, may be produced by sensors attached to human bodies, to enable the monitoring of blood pressure, distance run, calories eaten, emotional state, sleep quality, and much more. Some traces may take the form of routinely produced documentary inscriptions, records of processes and decisions, such as checklists and minutes. And some may be the results of scientific enquiry using laboratory instruments to identify, isolate, and even in some cases generate them under controlled conditions. In many of these instances, traces are produced, accumulate, and, with work, become organized as data to support statements of fact and meaningful aggregated accounts of personal and organizational performance.

Beyond this descriptive snapshot of both the extent and variability of the settings of traceability, why should we care about it? The thesis developed in this book is that we are experiencing a systemic shift in the nature of traceability and its components, a shift with profound consequences for human governance and oversight, for "the accounts we live by", for the nature of our experience and selfhood, and even for the conduct of the social sciences. To take one theme that is developed further in several chapters, digital transformations in all their variety are challenging the "audit society" model and its underlying hierarchical mode of governance based on the logic of the audit trail (Power, 1997, 2021a). These traditional oversight structures and their forms of accounting are being systematically transformed and, in a manner to be explained, "flattened" and "delayered". More generally, the purpose of this book is to understand the nature and potential consequences of this systemic transition from one economy of traces, based on the "documentality" of the audit trail, to another based on digital "traceification" and tracking. A traceological approach to accounting is developed that enables us to theorize this transition and its tensions.

To execute the theoretical task, it is necessary to be not only mindful of the power of digital technologies but also conceptually distant from them. Such an approach is risky, not least because it necessarily cuts across a formidable body of detailed work by scholars in information systems, surveillance studies, and the sociology of technology, to name only a few. We therefore begin this project in the next section with some general reflections on digitization and its implications for the organization of traceability in an economy of traces. Following these positional reflections, we provide general introductions to both traceability and accounting. We analyse the idea of traceability as it has become a value and purpose, what we call a *value-purpose*, for states, organizations, and individuals. Three broad value-purposes are proposed and elaborated—quality, security, and discovery—in order to provide further empirical texture to the landscape of practices. We then develop and justify a broad notion of accounting that is more than the production of information for decision-making and which is significant for the constitution of our individual, organizational, and collective lives, shaping experience, acts of organizing, and the very nature of what it is to "perform" (Lupton, 2016b, 2016c; Vormbusch, 2022). This broad conception draws upon, and seeks to recover, the continuities between everyday forms of "interactive" account-giving (Garfinkel, 1984a [1967]; Butler, 2005) and formal organizational accounting (Jeacle and Carter, 2023; Vollmer, 2019), continuities that have become more evident in the digital age. We use the terms "accounts" and "accounting" interchangeably to express these continuities and exchanges.

Finally, we introduce the individual chapters of the book and their respective thematic emphases, which will deepen these introductory remarks. The aspiration is to theorize traceability in a way that is "digitally neutral" but also mindful of, and engaged with, the implications of digital developments in a general sense. In this way, the analysis seeks to avoid being hooked by the "euphorias and paranoias of speed and change" (Haraway, quoted in Gane, 2006, p. 155) in order to understand how the economy of traces is shifting and what is at stake.

Economy of Traces

Scholars develop motifs and labels to dramatize new forms of social ordering. This is often how theorizing begins (Swedberg, 2014), and we are familiar with many of them: "algorithmic society" (Schuilenburg and Peeters, 2020); "granuläre Gesellschaft" (Kucklick, 2014); "embodied computing" (Pedersen and Iliadis, 2020); "surveillance society" (Lyon, 2001); "surveillance capitalism" (Zuboff, 2019); "risk society" (Beck, 1992); and "audit society" (Power, 1997), to name a few. The "economy of traces" is no less an organizing and theoretical motif of this kind. It is a critical notion originally coined by Stiegler (2016, p. 23) to characterize an increasingly pervasive and reductive automation that constitutes the enabling infrastructure for a new form of dehumanizing capitalism and assetization. In this book, we co-opt Stiegler's idea and use it to reference traceability, understood as a systemic, powerful, value-laden, but often hidden cultural logic of trace-production, organizing and accounting for ourselves both individually and collectively.

Within this economy of traces, personal tracking devices and wearables like watches with biosensors have not only become feeders for what Zuboff calls surveillance assets, but more generally, as we argue in Chapter 8, they also expand the realm of performing and performance. Even where such performances do not involve direct forms of monetary exchange or rewards, and even when gamified, they represent a form of "economization" in the sense of generating an orientation towards the metrics of performing. Going back to the vignette with which this chapter began, it is plausible to say that no human would have imagined using a watch in this way until it was possible and marketed to them. Yet it is also undoubtedly the case that cultures of self-monitoring and self-improvement have always existed. From the Socratic imperative to "know thyself", to ancient manuals of self-help, proper statehood, and commercial conduct, to the volumes that are easily found today in airport bookshops, preoccupations with self-monitoring existed before the explosion of biosensing wearables. In other words, successful digital technologies have been able to draw upon, supercharge, and economize pre-existing cultural dispositions to self-monitor. In this way, the economy of traces is both epistemic, as a form of knowing things and people, and political and moral in its implications.

Undeniably, these changes also represent business transformations amenable to economic analysis, for which platforms signify novel forms of economic organization. However, in the arguments that follow, we steer towards an infrastructural sense of the "economy of traces" as shorthand for the cultural organization of traceability. In effect, the motif of "economy of traces" references the sum of all forms of organized traceability practices and their enabling features of traceification, datafication, tracking, connecting, and accounting.

Concerns with traceability are long-standing and widespread, permeating many fields of practice, but they are also complex and variable. For example, practices of tracking may be animated by ideals of transparency and demands for evidence, but equally they can be objects of critique in the face of threats to privacy (Bernstein, 2012). The nature and extent of traceification also vary considerably according to the technological capacities that enable connectivity, tracing, and tracking (Leonardi and Treem, 2020; Flyverbom, 2021). And it is clear to any casual observer of our contemporary world that the expanded and expanding reach of automation, in the form of various digital technologies and devices, has supercharged and intensified possibilities for traceability, for generating new relations and objects and especially new forms of sociality (Pacchera et al., 2023). Digital traces enable practices of tracking that are now faster, less intermediated, and more granular in form, ranging widely from the use of barcodes, to GPS tracking, to blockchains, and now machine learning (Thylstrup, Archer, and Ravn, 2022). This expanded capability for trace production and hence for the tracking of things and people is not confined to the digital transformation of the routines and work processes of states and organizations. It has also become a prominent feature of private and personal activity, supported by a wide variety of social media platforms and devices that humans willingly attach to their bodies (Lupton, 2016a; Vormbusch, 2022). Indeed, many scholars and policymakers now agree that societies stand at the threshold of a new future, in which the digitally enabled automation of everything, including vast areas of human decision-making being displaced by machine-learning, has become not only possible but actual (Flyverbom, 2022; Zuboff, 2022).

These developments are known to be "disruptive" for traditional business models. They promise the disintermediation of many transaction services by placing control directly in the hands of consumers. They also challenge the very notion of an "organization" with well-defined boundaries and are argued to be generative and creative. It is not just a matter of "automation"; they are formative of newly visible objects, capabilities, and connectivities (Mennicken and Kornberger, 2021). Digital technologies also have profound ethical implications for how we think of, and account for, ourselves, for the nature of privacy and intimacy, and for understanding the place of humans in these newly constituted social and economic practices (Boellstorff, 2016; Velliz, 2023). To adapt an idiom from the philosopher Ian Hacking, it seems as if we are experiencing an "avalanche of traces" with far-reaching potential to redefine what it is to be human, what it is to "perform" across many diverse areas of life, and even what it is to be real (Andrejevic, 2013; Borgmann, 1999). Critical voices are concerned with how human physical actions are being captured as "clicks," stored and operated upon by machines and clustered into new objects and categories by powerful algorithms (Zuboff, 2019, 2022). Such algorithms, understood as codified instructions for processing traces of the human, are also at the heart of what scholars now called "datafication" (Alaimo and Kallinikos, 2024).

While many celebrate the great benefits and augmentative power of these developments, others fear for the future of human experience as we become "hooked" by, and on, data (Seaver, 2019), even to the point of becoming hybrids of digital data and human flesh (Gane, 2006:p. 2). Privacy, science, and democracy are argued to be at risk, and new kinds of discrimination are emerging from powerful apparatuses of surveillance fuelled by the expansion of artificial intelligence (AI) (Velliz, 2023). Furthermore, long-standing, juridically grounded forms of accountability and governance in many societies are being fundamentally reconstructed, and digitally enabled traceability in many areas is now big business as consumers and state apparatuses demand greater connectivity and efficiency in their quests for secure transacting free of risky intermediaries. There is also a desire to know more about the origins and reliability of things, especially food, and people. As this demand for traceability as evidentiary demonstrability, and the digital capability to address that demand, continue to co-evolve, critics like Stiegler (2016, p. 14) suggest that "we are witnessing the establishment of that complete and general automatization made possible by the industry of reticulated digital traces". He suggests that we now live in a pervasive non-documental "economy of traces" (pp. 22–27) whose formative logic we are only beginning to understand.

Digital transformations over at least three decades have undoubtedly accelerated and expanded the possibilities for practices of tracing and tracking. For example, advances in chip technology have enabled information processing to increase capacity, speed, and granularity. These functional attributes have come to be highly valued by organizations, and positive discourses of the augmentative power of digital technologies for individuals, businesses, and medical practice are widespread. However, as information systems scholars and historians of technology know well, what is loosely referred to as the "digital revolution" is not a single thing and certainly not a single kind of event. There are overlapping and temporal sequences with different emphases (Kolb et al., 2020).

From the invention of the internet and barcodes to blockchain, big data, and AI; from mainframes to personal computing and smart phones; from databases to Enterprise Resource Planning (ERP) systems and data warehouses, there is commonality. Indeed, all are based in some sense on the conversion of physical and material traces into mainly binary electronic pulses and then into combinable forms of notation (Kitchin, 2022; Alaimo and Kallinikos, 2024, ch. 3). There have also been profound underlying transformations in processing power, speed, and storage capacity underlying an ongoing transition from the digital automation of existing analog processes to forms of machine learning powered by meta-algorithms, which adapt to their experiences and produce new algorithms for data analysis and accounts production. Puranam (2025) conceptualizes digital algorithmic transformation as having three basic stages: digital representation (datafication); pooling (volume); and aggregation (valuable patterns for potential prediction). Indeed, these three stages are generic and apply to conventional accounting practices in which transactions are recognized and recorded, pooled by double-entry bookkeeping systems and aggregated into meaningful accounts.

Yet, beyond these commonalities there are also very different technologies and devices in play with different histories and maturities, different user communities, different applications and aspirations, and therefore different implications for the shape and scope of traceability potential and practice. Furthermore, the hegemony that critics often attribute to some, or even all, of these developments should be handled with caution. There is a danger of both over- and understating the dystopian risks identified by writers such as Zuboff (2019), Stiegler (2016), and many others. For example, Alaimo and Kallinikos (2024, p. 99) argue that we need to reach beyond macro-conceptual and negative framings of surveillance to understand its many forms and generative properties. Furthermore, despite societal demands for regulation and control, tracking and monitoring practices cannot easily be disentangled from the infrastructures in which they are embedded. This book aims at a theoretical analysis that is mindful of these complex and multifaceted developments and does not ignore them, but which is also, initially at least, agnostic about their newness and impact, even as we become "born digital", in order to avoid the dual extremes of celebration of the automated augmentation of human tracing capacity, on the one hand, and humanist blanket critique, on the other. Indeed, while the contemporary importance of digital technologies for trace production and expanding processes of datafication and tracking cannot be underestimated, and the rise of AI does seem to be a fundamental rupture, they are also long-standing features of calculative human practices (Lanzolla et al., 2020). Before we are intellectually swamped by the seeming digitization of everything, in which traces of nearly every conceivable human action can be created and processed, there remains a place for reflection on that which is continuous with earlier documentary practices. Here we aim at theorizing that is as "digitally neutral" as possible, while being nevertheless cognizant of the enormous impact of advances in digital technologies.

There are good theoretical reasons for attempting this digitally agnostic approach. The "digital" is itself a problematic category, for both historical and semiotic reasons (e.g. Haugeland, 1981). Scholars have shown that much more is at stake than just the rendering of information into computer-machine readable form, and there have been notable efforts to provide working taxonomies. According to Leonardi and Treem (2020, p. 1605), "digitization" refers to "the encoding of actions or representations of actions into a digital format (zeros and ones) that can be read, processed, transmitted and stored by computational technologies". "Digitalization" refers to "The ways in which social life is organized through and around digital technologies". "Datafication" refers to "The practice of taking an activity, behaviour, or process and turning it into meaningful data". Yet, as heuristically helpful as this and other taxonomies and their distinctions may be, they are often embroiled in each other and are interdependent: digitization preloads datafication, and processes of digitalization will influence practices of action-encoding or traceification. Unless otherwise necessary, we will tend to use the term "digitalization" to emphasize the embedded nature of digital technologies and the sense in which organizational work practices and technology co-evolve.

Another reason to avoid a fully digitally conversant entry point to the study of traceability is that the digital, understood more broadly than its computer-electronics setting, is a logic of (binary) distinctions and discrete units, and its opposite—the analogic—is more to be understood as process, continuity, and messiness. Both these orientations have been around a long time, and the encoding of actions in durable form—in what we call inscriptions—existed long before many of the developments discussed under the contemporary notion of digitization. Furthermore, the so-called "digital age" did not arrive suddenly, although there have been significant moments of change, not least the invention of the World Wide Web, the rise of home computer power, and the arrival of the smart phone. Alaimo and Kallinikos (2024, ch. 3) show how data emerged from recording technologies such as the punch card, whose material perforations progressively became autonomous semiotic tokens in a larger epistemic and economic system. Debates about the effects of automation on labour and the de-skilling problem also have a long history.

Galloway (2022, p. 228) argues that "digitality and analogicity are general modes of mediation; they are not facts about consumer electronics". Digitization should be understood more broadly as a process of making things discrete, and of finding notation to do that (Shannon, 1948), whereas analogicism is an orientation to synthetic qualities of liquidity and flow. From this larger point of view, it is somewhat ironic that the datafication phase of the digital revolution has occurred at a time when so many areas of organization studies, humanities, social sciences, and intellectual life in general, including the underlying theoretical orientation of this book, embrace forms of pragmatism, processualism, emergentism, relationality, liquidity, and heterogeneity—exactly the characteristics attributed to analog complexes. In this sense we also live now in a golden age of analog, according to Galloway, which is not to be read as "old" or "offline" but as a mode of mediation that aims at being expansive and non-reductive.

Daston's (2022) history of the rules we live by draws attention to another category—that of the "algorithm" which preoccupies contemporary discussion. Algorithms were also systems of rules that existed prior to any machine dreams of automation. The "thinning out" of rules in mathematical algorithms and their embodiment in machines for mechanical calculation became an early model of organizing as such. Taylorism and its variants are in this sense algorithmic models of organization, directed at eliminating the contextuality of the rules by which work is performed. Practices of quantification, including accounting, were always algorithmic and "digital" in this broader sense of being reductive, commensurating, and binary in their logic—we need only think of the debit and credit in double-entry bookkeeping. Hence, many algorithmic practices were always in effect pre-automated and "in waiting" for the computing capability to complete the automation of their binary mode of mediating.

The advantage of making the effort to step back from conventional notions of the digital and digitization is that it allows something else important to come into view, namely that traces can be *both* analog and digital in nature. Analogically they can be conceptualized as idiosyncratic signs and cues that support pragmatic and vernacular knowledges of weather, other people, the Will of God, and so on. Understood as discrete, homogenous, or commensurable units based on a duality of signifier and signified, traces can also be "digital" and are more closely associated with the idea of data. Traces in the coded form of binary electronic pulses are just a special case of the digital in its broader sense of discrete-ism and granularity, and algorithms are the operating codes that use them as input.

While we should not detain ourselves with the further elaboration and nuances of this analog-digital difference (which is itself an awkward dualism!), it points to a tension and potential conflict within the very notion of trace and traceification, which sits at the analog-digital threshold as a point of conversion. As we argue in Chapter 2, this also means that the distinction between trace and data is fluid and perspectival depending on how each is theorized, expansively or reductively. We also suggest that traceification and datafication processes bear a dialectical relation to one another; datafication begins with traceification, but data can in turn become traceified. In addition, the connectivities and relationalities that enable tracking, discussed further in Chapters 3 and 4, are not simply the technical pipework of the economy of traces—digital or analog—but also cultural reflections of what is and is not to be made observable via processes of traceification. While it is generally accepted that the "digital," commonly understood as technology, cannot be readily parsed from the social (Orlikowski and Scott, 2008), the digital and social are being continuously entwined in new ways to generate cultures of marking objects for tracking and accounting.

In summary, this book intends an approach to the analysis of traceability that neither ignores advances in digital technologies nor is hostage to their specific manifestations. Such an approach, if successful, can avoid the dangers of digital determinism, on the one hand, and cultural reductionism, on the other.[1] It also enables the navigation and expression of commonalities across the different value-purposes, traceifications, forms of tracking, and their accounts, despite seemingly very different practices, devices, and concerns—from financial regulation, to supply chain management, to self-tracking and many other settings. Scholars of information systems, computer science, and social scientists more generally have addressed issues about the nature and impact of digitalization for new markets and organizational forms, such as platforms. In particular, there is much debate about the gig economy and new forms of labour discipline and surveillance.[2] This book will touch on these debates at various junctures, but it is only and primarily concerned with their relevance for traceability as an implicit value or logic of marking, organizing, and accounting for ourselves, both individually and collectively.

[1] This is not to underestimate how the supply of hi-tech innovation can generate demand (Gordon, 2003)

[2] For example, the following is taken from a vendor promotional website, "Employee tracking software that tells you exactly how your employees use their time. Get powerful data for a more productive and efficient team". https://www.insightful.io/employee-monitoring (accessed 27 November 2024).

Traceability as Value and Purpose

The notion of "traceability" has two aspects. On the one hand, it embraces capabilities for the production of traces (trace-*ability*) as traceification, which enables objects, people, and processes to be observed and tracked through space and time. On the other hand, it connotes the evidentiary nature of traces and their connectedness (*trace*-ability) to phenomena of interest. The first sense is generative, the second is forensic, but they are interwoven and point to "a system that makes it possible, in real time and retroactively, to predict and record reliably the journey of an object from its origin to its destination" (Muirhead and Porter, 2019, p. 425). Beyond this general conceptualization, traceability as the production and use of traces is valued for different reasons, can be organized according to different value-purposes, takes many different practice forms, and has a long history, as long indeed as mankind and human communities have hunted animals and cultivated crops.

Traceability can be understood as an idea or aspiration, as an imaginary of control (e.g. Ortiz, 2022), and as something that is promised by politics, organizations, and systems of thought. It is proposed that individuals, organizations, and states seek to operationalize this imaginary of traceability according to three ideal-typical values, which are entangled with each other in practice but can be theorized as analytically distinct orientations towards *quality*, *security*, and *discovery*. This threefold model also suggests affinities between values and logics, and the manner in which they organize templates for practice and action (cf. Boltanski and Thevenot, 2006). Hence, our concept of "value-purpose" can be taken as more or less synonymous with that of "logic" in this sense.[3] And having initially articulated traceability in practice in terms of traceification, tracking, and accounting, we can also approach it from the "top down" as an idea, value, and aspiration that is mobilized for quality assurance, for security purposes, and in the discovery of new facts and bodies of knowledge. Let us consider each of these values-purposes or logics in turn.

Quality

Preoccupations with tracing for quality-assurance purposes have a long history within agricultural and related product markets. Buyers would often directly sample goods before committing to purchase, but knowing their origins was also important, hence the importance of labels, tags, and other certifying devices and

[3] Borrowing from Habermas (2015), we might think of value-purposes not only as logics but also as "traceability-constitutive interests".

traces created by producers. For example, the classification and labelling system for French wines emerged to regulate quality and to enable consumers to know where and when the wine in a specific bottle was produced, together with other features of its composition. In settings like this, a label or tag moves physically with the product as a trace of quality and enables a product to display its identity and origins. The production of such labels is often regulated, and there may be communities of experts and inspectors who engage in practices of tracing and auditing to ensure that the institutional "promise" of origin and identity indicated by a label is worthy of trust (Fourcade, 2012).

As sustainability-oriented change agendas have gained momentum, contemporary consumers want to know more not only about the functional quality and nature of products but also *how* they were made and by whom. The logic of quality is therefore elastic and has expanded in scope to include, for example, the traceability of environmental and ethical values in supply-chain practices. Importantly, advances in digital automation have transformed the capability for traceability, in the sense of trace production, in many areas. For example, GPS systems can now capture and record the exact point of harvest and trawler details in the setting of fishing (Lewis and Boyle, 2017). These traces are not the thing itself, or even a representation of it; they are rather the "digital double" of the specific catch and reference it. Digitally constructed traces of origins can also take a material form as a tag and become reattached to the real object (as bar codes have done since the 1970s), enabling the tracking of the object as it moves. The tagged fish carries with it its own mini-story of where it came from, as an "account" that is valued in the marketplace—provided, much like a wine label, that it can be trusted. In these settings, the traceability provided by tags is a promise but not a guarantee of quality, in part because the very idea of quality now includes the ethics of production and also because fraud is still possible and systems may fail. Hence, the evidentiary face of traceability in the form of inspection, auditing, and evaluation practices has emerged to test and demonstrate the trustworthiness of that promise on behalf of those who rely on it.

Beyond the setting of foodstuffs, traceability as the production and use of traces is important to manufacturing in general. Batch identifiers, product tagging, and barcodes (Kjellberg, Hagberg, and Cochoy 2019) are all critical tracing technologies that support transactional efficiency, enable management control, and are a source of assurance to the end consumer. For example, traceability for quality control is evident in the pharmaceutical industry, where companies must have a demonstrable capability to identify when and where drugs were produced so that instances of defective production can be tracked back to their origin. Relatedly, in their study of the formation of a market infrastructure for legalized cannabis, Pflueger et al. (2019) show how an accounting system designed by the regulator was important in defining the boundaries of the market and in enabling the tracking of cannabis from individual plant to consumer, for both quality and security reasons. Lezaun (2006) analyses similar systems for precise life-cycle control and traceability in the context of genetically modified (GM) foods. These examples suggest how the organized production and use of traces for quality assurance constitute an "infrastructure of traceability" (Power, 2019). They also suggest that the objects subject to traceability for quality are not always well defined and can be especially elusive when they are substances that undergo transformation and mixing in production chains. The promise of the quality of such production processes may only be redeemable by specialist analysis to *discover* the presence or non-presence of, say, a controversial chemical substance. Hence, values of quality and discovery overlap in many industrial settings.

Security

The second value-purpose or logic of traceability is that of security in its broadest sense. It concerns the production of knowledge oriented to the control and predictability of people and things, understood implicitly or explicitly as risks to be managed. States have been interested in knowing the characteristics of populations since the emergence of statistics (Hacking, 1990), so much so that state-building and technologies of population tracking and counting have often co-emerged, characterized famously by Foucault under his notion of bio-power (Foucault, 2008). For example, passport systems (Torpey, 2018) can be thought of in terms of traceability in our dual sense. On the one hand, they involve elaborate processes to control the production of passports as official traces of a person and proof of their identity as citizens. On the other hand, they involve equally developed practices of inspection and analysis of passports at national borders. Arrangements for tracking people may also vary greatly due to different cultural and value orientations, not least in relation to values of freedom and human rights. In the United Kingdom, internal identity cards have often been proposed but rejected; in the United States, the driving licence plays a de facto role in identity validation (Whitley and Hosein, 2008).

Security in its broadest sense may also include the health of a nation, which underpins economic performance. The onset of the pandemic in 2020 made this painfully evident as efforts to trace specific carriers of the virus in its early incubation stages could not control the spread, which eventually required the isolation of general populations and the restriction of movement. In anticipation of the easing of this lockdown, the United Kingdom initiated a system for "track and trace" by which individuals could be informed if they had contact with a carrier and were then obliged to isolate. Many countries invested in similar digital traceability practices, which had to be assembled in haste from many different elements. Political cultures of enforcement varied considerably, and there were failures and unintended consequences, but a COVID "passport" was eventually created to allow fully tested individuals to move more freely across borders. In short, in times of emergency and threats to security, the traceability of persons can become a pressing concern involving the rapid creation of technology solutions.

The manner in which traceability is organized according to values of security will vary according to political orders. We know that more centralized and totalitarian states invest heavily in technologies of granular population observation and control. For example, in the former East Germany (German Democratic Republic), the Stasi sought to know every detail of individuals' lives and created a population of internal spies to watch and create traces of them in files (Funder, 2002). Traceability as capacity for surveillance like this has undoubtedly been supercharged by the advent of digital technologies, including facial recognition software, which now enables all manner of individual behaviour and movement to be tracked and assembled into evaluative accounts, such as whether someone is a "good citizen" or not and deserving of a specific grade for social credit (Bach, 2020; Xu et al., 2023). Scholars have written extensively for many years about the newly intense forms of surveillance that digital technology now enables and which are common to predicting both consumer behaviour and also the seeming riskiness of citizens to the state and social order (e.g. Ericson and Haggerty, 2006). It is therefore evident that the organization of traceability according to security values, whether by states or corporations, is inherently political and often controversial, involving risks to values that many regard as fundamental, such as privacy and freedom of speech (Veliz, 2023; Zuboff, 2022). Furthermore, technology has itself created new opportunities for crime and insecurity (Van der Wahen and Pieters, 2015). Yet, it is also inherently difficult to isolate and regulate "bad" surveillance practices from the data infrastructures in which they are embedded.

Discovery

So far it has been proposed that traceability is valued for the generic purposes of assuring and controlling both quality and security. We might say that these value-purposes represent distinctive forms of knowing people, things and processes. Yet traceability, as the production of traces with evidentiary signification, also has a distinct value-purpose in the generation of the forms of explanatory and predictive knowledge that we associate with idea of "science". This points to a "logic of discovery" not in Popper's (1959) sense of a method for proper science, but as a shorthand for the general organization of science as investigative and device-saturated practice oriented to producing new—and testing old—facts about the world. Scientific practice as this work of potential discovery can be understood in part as seeking to establish causal connections in the form of associations between traces of phenomena, as potential signs of things in the world, associations that may confirm or disconfirm prevailing theories. Traceability oriented to discovery in this sense is not a matter of individual breakthroughs and achievements but is infrastructural and collective in nature. It involves systems and instruments that are organized for the production of *traces* of phenomena, and the specific tests and experiments that transform these traces into *data*, and which ultimately produce *facts* about nature (Rheinberger, 2011). A prominent example of such an infrastructure for discovery is the CERN particle accelerator and its high-energy physics communities (Knorr-Cetina, 1999) (see Chapter 9).

Traceability for discovery can also be explicitly *forensic* in character. Here, scientific practice is routinely enrolled for the quality and security purposes of tracking people, viruses, and chemicals, including carbon emissions. Indeed, forensic science as the analysis of "traces" has become a decisive resource for criminal investigations (Wiltshire, 2019; Servida and Casey, 2019). Its purpose is to discover and explain the "cause of death" and who is likely to have committed a crime. Discovery in such settings depends on the attribution of evidential strength, via Bayesian analysis or similar, to the trace(s) based on laboratory testing. Practice has evolved and so too have the traces of human behaviour and identity that it routinely examines, from fingerprints (Coles, 2001) to DNA (Aronson, 2007). Indeed, the latter has significantly extended the time horizon of discovery, thereby allowing "cold" cases to be reopened and solved.

Traceability as discovery is not restricted to scientific practice as conventionally understood. For example, "forensic accounting" (Williams, 2013) is a form of investigatory practice that draws on a range of traces as clues to a puzzle, usually about the "location" of financial assets that may have been deliberately hidden. In effect, forensic accounting uses existing documents as fragments to creatively reconstruct as far as possible a trail, an "audit trail", which enables the location of stolen assets to be discovered and known. The skill and professional judgement of the investigating forensic accountant is needed because such trails as connections are always incomplete, either by criminal intent or by neglect. Digitization has also spawned the data sciences with capabilities for traceification and datafication on a grand scale, enabling the discovery/generation of new patterns and relations, often with predictive power. Hence, to repeat, we should not associate the logic of discovery only with mainstream scientific activity. More generally, many professional and managerial practices, not least risk management (Chapter 7) have their own bodies of domain knowledge through which they engage in forms of exploration, experimentation, analysis, and tracing to discover things relevant to their practices. This is not formal science but borrows its general mode of rationality and evidentiary processes (March, 2006). Even organizational routines can be sources of innovation and discovery in this sense (Deken et al., 2016).

Traceability Hybrids

These three ideal-typical value-purposes or logics that mobilize traceability practices are rarely found in their pure form. They are always entangled with one another in empirical settings. Take, for example, the efforts of states to combat financial crime and money laundering. Regulation in this area focuses on the critical risk point of the individual-organization interface, namely the interaction and transactions between potential criminals and the banking system. States leverage the commercial interest of banks in "knowing your customer" for security purposes, and banks have built elaborate infrastructures to comply with financial crime regulation. Traceability in this setting involves "discovery" of the identity of a transactor and the source of their funds. Routinely, passports are used as proof of identity, but there are also specialist organizations, such as Experian and Kroll, that trace people and their activities. The case of AML (anti-money-laundering) regulation is therefore a hybrid—all three value-purposes are present but at different levels and in different ways. *Security* can be understood as the overarching value. The *quality* of AML systems at the organization level is the primary focus for board regulatory oversight. And organizations have been required to invest in statistical methods and other domain-specific forms of knowledge to *discover* and generate the "risk profiles" of customers, and thereby to understand ex ante causes or drivers of money laundering. Hence, when we set out to analyse traceability as organized practice in action, we always encounter a complex of these ideal-typical value-purposes. Figure 1.1 provides a topological representation of the overlap between the different value-purposes of traceability, their objects of concern, and some indicative methods.

We need to remain mindful that these purposes as value-orientations, both individually and in combination, are always aspirational. They may even be fantasies of observability and connectivity, which are themselves dependent on imperfect artefacts. On the one hand, technologies for traceification can generate new objects of interest and accounting, and new action-potentials, such as the notions of a "carbon footprint" (Kornberger et al., 2017; Mennicken and Kornberger, 2021) or "impact" (Power, 2015). On the other hand, they can fail in their operationalization for many different reasons: the stated purpose may exceed technical capability; there may be fraud and error at source where tags and labels are wrongly coded; and there is always the general nature of objects, such as people, things, and processes, to be more than, to *overflow*, their traces.

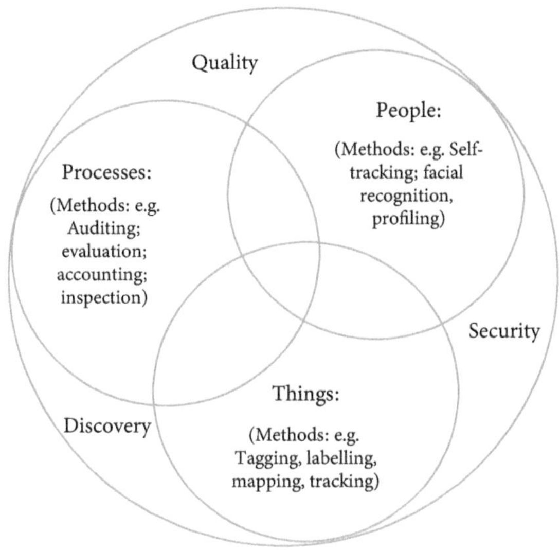

Figure 1.1 Traceability: value-purposes, objects, and methods.

Consequently, crises of traceability are normal and motivate new or intensified attention to value-purposes. The 2013 UK horsemeat scandal, in which consumers were misled about the composition of their food, led to widespread reform in foodstuff traceability and inspection (Elliot, 2014). Furthermore, people and things can be lost "without trace". Despite extensive investigative efforts to locate the final resting place of Malaysian Airlines MH370, and high-level assurances that it would be found, its whereabouts remain a mystery at the time of writing (to the general public at least). This event was especially shocking for a world in which digital technologies have increased expectations of perfect traceability and with it the belief that nothing can be lost. We accept that traces of ancient civilizations can disappear, but not a large modern aircraft subject to advanced tracking technologies by multiple aviation and military authorities.

Beyond these failures and scandals, it is also clear that traceability is not valued in the same way by all groups and individuals, especially regarding security, as already noted. Hence, there is an ongoing politics of *counter-traceability* involving conflict with other values, such as privacy and the "right to be forgotten". More generally, we must always locate the values of traceability in their cultural context as specific modes of institutionalized memorizing and tracing, which are often implicit and also involve modes of forgetting through trace erasure and non-production. These questions of value, about what we trace and why we preserve some traces and not others, are also being overwhelmed by advances in digital automation that operate behind the backs of individuals, effectively "extracting" their data without their consent (Zuboff, 2015, 2019). While we return to this theme in Chapter 8, it is interesting to note in passing that European legislation to protect privacy—General Data Protection Regulation (GDPR)—requires organizations to demonstrate their compliance with it, and therefore to make the practice of "making people untraceable" itself traceable. In other words, practices to manage and reduce the traceability of persons ironically increase the demand for traceability of the processes that demonstrate it.

In summary, we can think of traceability at an ideational level as a widely diffused aspiration organized around three general value-purposes or orientations, namely quality, security, and discovery. If we return to the example of the marathon runner wearing a smart watch, then his self-tracking can be said to be mobilized by interconnected values of quality (running performance), security (attention to key health factors), and discovery (analytics and data production). Furthermore, the example suggests how traceability has become big business, with new markets for personalized health knowledge and much else. Demands for governance and risk management (e.g. food-quality assurance and sustainability) have also emerged and have been supercharged by the promises of digital traceability (Muirhead and Porter, 2019; Thylstrup et al., 2022). Indeed, the sheer variety of tracing and tracking practice is intimidating for the analyst—threatening to be so broad and seemingly ubiquitous as to make the very category of traceability impossible to grasp and determine. Yet the proposal of these three ideal-typical value-purposes provides our first movement towards theorizing the organization of traceability. The second movement requires that we turn to accounting.

The Accounts We Live By

Accounting is conceptually and linguistically related to accountability as a value in many societies. Accountability can be achieved in many different ways (Donia, 2025), but in one basic form, the idea of accountability is a relational triad in which A has the capability and is somehow obligated or compelled to give an account B to, or on behalf of, someone else C. Such a formal relational structure encompasses enormous potential empirical and theoretical variety and breadth. How accountability as this relational triad manifests itself depends on cultural context and the precise referents for, and relative focus on, placeholders A, B, and C. Are we primarily interested in the duties of the "givers" of accounts and the AB dyad; or are we interested mainly in the receivers or so-called stakeholders and users of accounts defined by the dyad BC? Is the ABC structure fixed by legal or regulatory contract, or is it more a matter of interpersonal expectations? It is also often assumed that A and C are well defined entities and agents, and that the accountability problem is "simply" one of designing optimal forms of B to allow C to sufficiently observe and incentivize A. Yet, what if the accounting B has agentic, symbolic, and expressive properties of its own, even to the point of having the power to shape the identities and motivations of both A and C? Furthermore, what could "self-accounting" mean if A and C are the "same" embodied human being? At its most fundamental, A may stand for an "I" or self, which is shaped in the accounting encounter with an "other" C. The narration of self in the face of the other is a primordial form of accountability, in which A and C are reflectively co-formed but one that is shaped by prior norms and power (Butler, 2005, pp. 3–40). These and many other questions suggest that the relational space of account-giving is far broader than standard models of accountability and that methodological and normative choices must be made about the kinds of relations and the kinds of accounts that matter. Yet, one general claim can be made at this point: Bs are usually produced to make aspects of As observable and traceable for Cs. Yet, there is also always opacity, and traceability and transparency are always partial (Roberts, 2009). As Butler (2005, p. 43) puts it, "life might be understood as precisely that which exceeds any account we may try to give of it". Elsewhere in this book it is argued that we need to invert the traditional idea that accounting precedes auditing and tracking, an argument that forms a building block for a traceological theory of accounting. For now, we conceive of accountability and accounting very broadly (Vollmer, 2019), a breadth that is risky but is necessary to grasp both the meaning of the "accounts that we live by" and what is at stake. We consider three themes which underpin this breadth: account-abilities; worlds of accounts; and accounting agency.

Account-abilities

Levinas (1986) points to the uncanny nature of the encounter with the face of another as the primary source of human responsibility. In other words, the accountability structure ABC begins fundamentally with A's *recognition* of, and obligation towards, C (see also Butler, 2005, ch. 1). We might take this notion further in a more "phenomenological" direction by viewing the everyday accountings between individuals as the fundamental building blocks by which the social world is continuously sustained, reproduced, or changed (Berger and Luckman, 1966). The explicit production of accounts in the case of interpretations and explanations of individual behaviour is not normally required in everyday interaction, but the possibility of such production is tacit and underwrites all talking and interacting (Garfinkel, 1984a; Vollmer, 2019). Scott and

Lyman (1968) argue that accounts can be understood primarily and narrowly as forms of excuse and justification, which are produced by human agents when their behaviour somehow deviates from tacitly accepted norms. This influential conception of accounting as justification by exception builds on Garfinkel's famous "breach experiments" in which his students were instructed to violate norms in the home and with friends. Their puzzling behaviour triggered a mixture of reactions, including demands for "accounts," which revealed the unsaid norms governing expected interaction in specific situations. In short, an account must be given to justify non-conforming behaviour which disrupts tacit expectations, and A is deemed to have account-*ability* to do this and to provide an answer that C can accept.

Relatedly, but in a more general form, Habermas (1979) proposes that all talk is premised on a number of "validity claims" or presumptions that are assumed by others to hold, but which in principle can be "redeemed" or justified under challenge. In other words, the ability or competence for explicit accounting in Garfinkel's sense is generally inherent in, and a condition of, all human interaction and discourse. Indeed, Habermas wants to argue more strongly that such communicative accounting is a "transcendental" condition of the possibility of rational argument, conditions that point to ideal conditions of speech as a model of liberal democracy. While this notion of ideal speech is controversial, not least for its universalism (e.g. Hesse, 1995), it is nevertheless established by scholars since Garfinkel that human interaction is subject to continuous and more or less conscious monitoring or auditing of verbal and non-verbal cues. For example, such everyday monitoring determines whether it can be presumed that someone is being honest, or whether explicit accounts are needed to examine, justify, or challenge them. But, contra Habermas, the accounts we potentially live by and which inhere in communicative interaction should not be imagined as merely cognitive or free from distortion. As critical theorists like Butler (2005) remind us, accounts of and by selves are never cognitively innocent. The ABC accountability triads are themselves the products and expressions of institutionalized power structures and ideological forms, most importantly in the coding of the distinction between what gets made explicit and accounted for and what is silenced and without voice. Indeed, for theorists like Butler, traces become constitutively important to accounts in two senses. Not only are they the primary experiential matter—the verbal and bodily expressions to which we are constantly reacting and evaluating in the background—which make up continuous ongoing accounting as expectation-confirmation and sense-making. They are also the suppressed indications and signs of alternative accounts that could be given, but cannot find expression or must remain tacit (Vollmer, 2019). Critical accounting scholars have extended such arguments to the formal organizational level (Hines, 1988).

All accounting—of self and organization—is value-laden in the sense that it rests on choices and power relations, by design or otherwise, about what to make and not make explicit and "account-able", and therefore about the forms of accounting that count. From this general point of view, human everyday lives are necessarily permeated by account-abilities in the sense of capacities for narration of self through which relations to others are constituted. It may be argued that blurring the distinction between accounting and everyday sense-making like this is going too far. Nevertheless, studies of practice also demonstrate the deep continuities and exchanges between so-called everyday and organizational accounts as actors strive hard to generate "situated functionality" from arrays of activities and interactions (Ahrens and Chapman, 2007). These continuities and connections between the everyday and organizational are becoming even more evident under conditions of advanced digitization (Alaimo and Kallinikos, 2024, p. 101). In sum, the formal accountability triad ABC is in reality an accounting assemblage that blurs the boundaries of the personal and organizational by connecting "the production of accounts and accountabilities in everyday life with the more technical aspects of professional practice in a continuum" (Vollmer, 2019, p. 29).

A World of Accounts

The second way in which we must broaden our understanding of what counts as accounting is empirical, meaning simply that there is now a large and growing volume and variety of accounts that pervade both organizational and personal life (Vormbusch, 2022). In addition to the conventional forms of financial accounting, budgeting, costing, and cash-flow statements and their underlying books and records, there has been an explosion of metrics, both financial and non-financial, which seek to capture and measure a wide range of phenomenon, such as employee satisfaction, intellectual capital value, and other possible "drivers" of, and risks to, financial performance (Bukh et al., 2001). Indeed, studies of accounting grounded in information economics focus less on the conventional elements of financial accounting and more on the signalling properties of information and disclosure in general, thus also considerably broadening the horizon of what counts as accounting. As customer retention has become critical to many businesses, measures of retention risk have also been developed, and risk management more generally has moved towards the production of lead indicators as an accounting ideal (see Chapter 7). In addition, organizations now account and report on a large number of activities under the broad label of sustainability: measures of workforce diversity, carbon emissions data, and much else have become commonplace, although problems of reliability and comparability are also evident (Kotsantonis and Serafeim, 2019). These relatively new accountings are often hybrids of the numerical, narrational, and visual, organized into "dashboards" that connect different sub-accounts and enable the tracking of performance (Pollock and D'Adderio, 2012; Quattrone, 2017; Ronzani and Gatzweiler, 2022). Indeed, while accounts have always had visual properties, visualization has become a form of accounting in and of itself (Quattrone et al., 2021).

Many other practices, which exist beyond formal organizational boundaries, also produce what must count as "accounts", such as audit reports, rankings, compliance certificates, credit ratings, social media ratings, social credit scores, risk maps, and much more, including even the humble list (Gawande, 2010; Crvelin and Lohlein, 2022). In addition, employees are also known to keep their own idiosyncratic and local vernacular accounts (Kilfoyle et al., 2013), including "black books" and other devices, which supplement or replace formal systems. And, as the example of the smart watch with which we began this chapter shows, technologies and sensing devices of many kinds mediate and enable possibilities for accounts of personal bodily "performance"—athletic, health, and emotional. With such accountings we move beyond a purely justificational or evidentiary conception of accounting and accountability. Rather, the accounts produced by new capabilities of tracking are implicated in the creation of novel objects of concern and new account-*abilities* at a high level of granularity for individuals and organizations. They are generative of new worlds of practice and experience (Kornberger et al., 2017). Whether a new kind of self is constituted by such tracking-based accounts is a question we address in Chapter 8, but the digital transformation of formal organizational accounting is undoubtedly blurring traditional boundaries and temporalities (Bhimani, 2015; Bhimani and Bromwich, 2009; Knudsen, 2020), as well as shaping the production of accounts to suit the application of coding (Rowbotham et al., 2021). One further conspicuous effect of these transformations is the crossover between work and play, which is evident in the emergent gamification aspects of performance management and accounting.

Despite all these arguments the differences between "everyday" account-abilities and highly institutionalized "accountings" may still seem obvious and great. They certainly involve very diverse bodies of knowledge, expertise, expectations, and settings. So it might seem that the very concept of "accounting" is being stretched to the breaking point and is in danger of becoming meaningless. Yet, as we shall see in Chapter 8, this expansion of accounting is not an analytical contrivance. It corresponds to something real to be explained theoretically and empirically. Devices are expanding their reach to make the self and its "everyday" nature in Garfinkel's sense newly visible and calculable (Fauré et al., 2010). Programmed mechanisms of feedback multiply, which are more than simply sense-making and which challenge the supposed interiority of sensed experience (Vormbusch, 2022). Hence, the "quantified self" (Lupton, 2016c) represents a digitized and mediated intensification of Garfinkel's notion of everyday accounting, reducing the supposed difference between everyday and institutional accounting as the behavioural reach of quantification is extended (Thaler, 2016). Indeed, traditionally conceived differences between institutional and personal worlds are becoming harder to sustain (Vollmer, 2019). Boundaries are frequently crossed in both directions and continuously remake each other via the fluidity of data in which organizations and personhood are becoming more distributed and decentred (Alaimo and Kallinikos, 2024). Limiting what counts as accounting to institutionalized and specialized practices, say for insurance companies, would arbitrarily restrict our analysis of traceability and accounts production.

Latour (2005) also provides support for this expansive notion of accounting. He argues that the very agency of things and people can only be grasped and accounted for to the extent that they leave observable traces that can be tracked and assembled into accounts (2005, p. 53). These traces in his sense are not only "out there" as products or imprints of both human and non-human agents, but can also be produced explicitly by the analyst-sociologist or critical observer who must "traceify" objects and track their connections as an activity of accounts production. In this respect, there are methodological affinities between Latour's thinking and studies that attend closely to the traces of actions in order to map and analyse the grammar of organizational routines (Pentland and Rueter, 1994). A good social scientific account for Latour is one that tracks a network of connections of interest, and which demonstrates the forms of connectedness that are productive of our singular and perhaps mythical conceptions of agency. This analytic work involves the effortful re-presentation and mapping of the traces left behind by these various agencies. The result is what he calls "risky accounts" which can "easily fail" and often do (2005, p. 132). Importantly, for Latour, there is no difference in principle between this accounting work as it is done by both analytic and non-analytic actors, both of whom must become "attentive to the material traceability of immutable mobiles" (2005, p. 226). Indeed, he suggests that traceability in this sense of network construction underpins all accounts production as the connecting of traces created by people and things.

If we dare to follow both Latour and Garfinkel, accounting emerges as an important general model of knowledge production and experience. It is a continuous thread that connects and mediates worlds of everyday interaction and specialist analytical practices, like the natural sciences or insurance. Using a predigital vocabulary, Latour argues that we (meaning anyone claiming to do the sciences of the social) have to put these "humble paper tools in the foreground"

(2005, p. 230) and attend to the circulation and connectedness of traceable documents in all their varied forms. Indeed, for him, this connectedness as traceability, and the accounts we generate from it, is the very source of what we mean by "society".

Latour (1986, 2005) is not especially precise about the ontological nature of traces, although he inspires us to take them seriously as features of fact-building. He tends to equate them with documents and inscriptions and sometimes things. Being concerned primarily with the deployment of durable traces to produce "hard" facts in agonistic and competitive scientific settings, he is also relatively silent about the variety of institutional forms of traceability and the specific circuits of connectivity, which enable tracking and accounting. He is primarily interested in the active construction and mobilization of the connections that underpin science, law, and other projects and their accounts, rather than the preoccupation in this book with how traceability in general is organized and may be changing. However, his level of analysis helps to cement the traceification-accounting relationship and reminds us that if the traces, and the processes by which they are traceified and datafied, shift systemically, then this will have consequences for the accounts that we produce and live by, all the way from the everyday to the institutional and back again.

Agentic Accounts

The third theme, which builds on the observed variety described in the previous sub-sections, concerns the many effects and roles that accounts may have, regardless of their formally stated purposes. In this respect, it can be proposed that accounts as the Bs of the ABC accountability relation are socio-material artefacts that may have their own agency and contingent conditions of operation. For example, it has been established that accounts may have many different roles and effects, which drive their technical elaboration and variety. In their seminal paper, Burchell et al. (1980) draw attention to the role of accounts beyond the mainstream conception of information for decision-making, a conception that, in the case of financial accounting, was "invented" as part of the post-war rise of decision sciences (Young, 2006). It is argued that accounts can be used as "ammunition" in adversarial settings (e.g. contested takeovers) and can provide ex post forms of rationalization and justification (much like the "excuses" of Scott and Lyman [1968]). As we discuss further in this book, accounts can be generative of their own facticity and seeming objectivity, and studies have also demonstrated their expressive and affective aspects (Chenhall et al., 2017), including their role as vehicles for supererogation (Horvath, 2023). Hence, accounts are not simply channels of information for well-defined decision points but, in specific contexts, produce or reduce comfort, and can alleviate or amplify fear and anxiety (Guénin-Paracini et al., 2014; Vollmer, 2019). Accounts are known to be flawed by practitioners who nevertheless use them as resources interactively to generate control activities (Ahrens and Chapman, 2007).

Quattrone (2015), like Garfinkel, argues for a *maeutic* and processual conception of accounts as forms of individual and collective sense-making that are not static, and in which reality is a continuously unfolding referent of practice where the tacit becomes explicit. Furthermore, accounts are necessarily and inherently projective and can be thought of as technologies and devices that stand in a relation of temporal co-formation with humans, meaning that the many different accounts that we live by are not simply modes of excuse, justification, and legitimation to be tested and proven by audits. They are themselves a constitutive part of the many and changing ways in which we narrate who we are and might be, collectively and individually (Brown, 2009). Indeed, even accounts in explicitly calculative form are generative narrations that bring together and organize traces and purposes and which project future possibilities (Stiegler, 1998; Matringe and Power, 2024). Hence, we must always be mindful of the dual temporality of all accounts, which is inherent in their traceification, of marking what has happened and projecting what will or should happen (see also Chapter 7). This duality is not just a new version of the age-old tension between backward-looking stewardship and forward-looking decision relevance. It is a more phenomenological point about accounts and accountability that "pull" the human user towards an open future in the very act of marking what has been (Chua et al., 2024). This dual temporality of accounts, which operates between their historical residues and imagined futures, is more than just a proposition about the changing nature of accounting forms; it requires us to position accounting within a process of on-going design, which seeks realization and operability, and for which continuous repair is normal (Bottausci et al., 2024).

In effect, accounts, in all their variety, should not be understood narrowly as passive conduits or intermediaries for information; they can be agentic mediators in their own right, and in this sense the accountability triad of ABC is a socio-material assemblage consisting of three agent-placeholders, two human (so far, but this is changing) and one non-human: giver, receiver, and the accounts themselves, which enable aspects of the giver's actions to be "tracked" by the receiver. We should also be mindful of the institutionalized mythologies and fictions that pervade this triad, not least the idea of the "user". And we should be wary of overstating the agency of accounts; they are always, even in the most automated settings, embedded in human practices. It is also well known that: organizations produce more information than they use (the ABC triad is full of surplus and overflow); accounts are often produced for symbolic reasons (March, 1987); and even flesh-and-blood users are somehow "made up" by the accounts through which they engage in organizational life. These messier agentic properties of accounts are not always evident from their official rationales.

In summary, we have considered three themes which suggest that when we think of the different kinds of accounts that organize our lives and behaviour, as individuals and organizations, then we must not prematurely circumscribe what counts as accounting and must a priori take a broad view of accounts as stories, often told with and through numbers. The accounts we live by can be broadly defined as the diverse forms of narration, numeric representation, and summation that organize and mediate human and organizational relations. So we should not allow only professional accountants to define and bound what is, and is not, the apparent nature and limits of accounting. The formal, specific, collective forms of accounting that make up the pedagogy of accounting students as aspiring practitioners are themselves specialist abstractions from, and extensions of, the primary interactive settings that interested Garfinkel and his followers. The history of accounting demonstrates this. For example, in feudal Britain, stewards entrusted with the management of the affairs of a manor were required to present in person accounts indicating their "charges and discharges"; and early modern merchants in northern Italy used double-entry bookkeeping to record and control transacting and indebtedness. In both these historical contexts, accounting was not understood abstractly but was deeply embedded in social relations in which personal credibility and reputation were always at stake and where justification might be required (Matringe and Power, 2024). Today, highly institutionalized and rationalized practices of accounting seem to have a more self-referential and dis-embedded life of their own within formal organizations and markets (Vollmer, 2007). This is no doubt a product of the professional mobilization of accounting practitioners and their institutionalized power to define knowledge. But accounting numbers also do not speak for themselves, and an important focus in the project of critical accounting has been to reveal and deconstruct this seeming autonomy, to expose the embedded nature of accounting practices and the interests that mobilize them, and to "bring society back in". This critical agenda extends to the production of alternative or "counter accounts" that reconnect the everyday and its values to organizations more explicitly. The sustainability accounting agenda that has taken off in the 2020s (although elements of it reach back decades) represents both the expansion and potential normalization of this critical agenda, although, at the time of writing, these efforts are still characterized by considerable fluidity, experimentation, and political contestation.

To conclude: the notion of the "accounts we live by" has been introduced as a provoking category. It is intentionally jarring and dissonant in order to challenge conventional ways of thinking by practitioners and scholars about the technical boundaries of accounting. It is also implicitly expressive of the constitutive power of accounts for human experience. In this sense, accounts can be understood most generally as products of the restless dialectic between life and form that Simmel (1971 [1918]) articulated, a dialectic in which form continuously dominates but cannot escape its grounding in life. In later chapters of this book, it is argued that the accounts we live by are undergoing a systematic shift, a shift that is symptomatic of changes in this life/form duality itself.

Chapter Summaries

Scholars have studied the co-constitution of accounting, organizing, and society for at least four decades and have shown how accounting systems are contingently influenced by organizational and institutional factors (Chapman et al., 2009; Miller and Power, 2013). They have shown how accounting technologies and practices have agentic properties of their own, are carriers of values, and shape the attention and behaviour of organizational actors, even to the point of generating new organizational realities. There has also been increased attention to the raw material from which such accounts are fabricated, including the inscriptions and material technologies, and the transactional systems and rules, which underpin accounts production. Yet the traces and data on which accounts are grounded, and which have an institutional life and significance of their own, deserve more theoretical and empirical visibility in their own right (Alaimo and Kallinikos, 2024). This book is an invitation to see how the changing production of traces and the accounts we live by are intertwined in the organization of traceability. The scope of the argument is broader than the formal accounts produced by organizations for capital markets or for internal-control purposes, and includes the many narratives that we produce of ourselves and others as we navigate and mediate between personal, social, and organizational life. This breadth is not simply a methodological contrivance. It reflects the fact that there are increasing exchanges between the personal and organizational as digital transformations reconfigure and re-proximate these relations.

Each of the chapters that follows discusses the organization of traceability and its components from a different thematic angle. They include a number of vignettes for illustrative purposes, which are drawn mainly from the author's experience and do not reflect systematic fieldwork. In addition, each chapter concludes with a series of summative propositions that capture the essence of what has been said and are provided to aid reader navigation. In broad terms, Chapters 2–5 build key concepts and Chapters 6–10 apply them to contexts. However, the unifying aspiration is that all these chapters in aggregate provide a synthetic grasp of traceability from different entry points. They can also be understood as building blocks for theorizing the traceological basis of accounting and how it is changing in the "new" economy of traces in the digital age.

Chapter 2 deepens our introductory remarks on traces, traceification, and tracking. In doing so, it unpacks the relation between traceification and datafication, and develops the distinction between tracking-led accounts and accounts-led tracking, which is at the centre of the book's thesis regarding a shift in the accounts we live by. Drawing on the analysis of traceability and accounts in Chapter 1, the idea of the "traceability complex" is advanced in which value-purposes, traceification, datafication, tracking, and accounts are interconnected.[4] The idea of a traceability complex provides a working template for a traceological approach to accounting and governance.

Chapter 3 revisits critical studies in accounting to suggest that, despite the Latourian-inspired "inscriptivist" turn in accounting theory, a primary focus on quantification and its effects has tended to understate the constitutive role of traces and audit trails. We invert the traditional conception that accounting comes before traceability and auditing, thereby placing the audit trail, as idea and practice, at the centre of our analysis. Furthermore, a core pragmatist proposition in this traceological approach to accounts production is that *tracking precedes representation*. The chapter also develops the notion of "primary traceification" as a boundary condition of the audit trail that is value-laden in the sense of making some things visible and accountable and not others. Chapter 4 provides further development of the audit trail concept, emphasizing its role as mode of connectivity in general, which must be generated to make tracking and accounting possible. It is argued that infrastructures of connectedness and practices of connecting co-develop. The argument then turns to variations in the nature of audit trail connectedness under conditions of digitalization. The thesis is that audit trails become less deep and less dense, and this is associated with the rise of tracking-led accounts. The chapter concludes by articulating the paradox of audit trail connectivity: as digital connectivity increases, the audit trail as a basis for human oversight decreases and may disappear entirely.

Chapter 5 approaches traceability as a core feature of *organizing and governing*. It builds on prior studies to argue that traceification and tracking are

[4] It has been pointed out to me that the term "traceability complex" might refer to a psychological form of complex, i.e. a condition of fearing or even being obsessed with being traced or engaging in tracing activity. Although this is not the intended theoretical meaning of the concept in this book, it is not entirely without salience. For example, as we see in Chapter 8, widespread enthusiasm for self-tracking could be interpreted as a "traceability complex" in this sense. Furthermore, to the extent that psychological concepts can be extended to the societal level, the economy of traces potentially reflects a collective "complex" about traceability. For these reasons, while the notion of complex will be used very differently, this ambiguity is also useful to retain.

constitutive of the entities we designate as organizations. Borrowing from theories of documentality and scripting, it is argued that organizations are constituted by scripts that may be more or less explicit and which provide a point of orientation for communication, both formal and informal. It is also proposed that the stability of organizationality over time and space requires some minimal degree of self-observation or oversight, often enabled by accounting systems. The chapter develops the distinction between tracking and "oversight", arguing that they are always combined but may vary in mix. Oversight is conceptualized as layered, drawing on metaphors-in-use of "lines of defence" and "supply chains". Oversight practices are generally enabled by audit trail modes of connectivity and hence systemic changes in the latter will have consequences for the former and the governance supply chain. Chapter 6 builds directly on Chapter 5 and uses the traceability complex template to compare several governance and regulation settings. It is argued that under conditions of digitalization, conventional notions of governance are being de-layered and platformized. The "traceability lost" thesis is developed by an analysis of the debate about the audit and governance of algorithms. It is argued that our capacity for trace-generation at scale is overwhelming the human evidentiary basis of traceability.

Chapter 7 draws on Stiegler and others to establish the ontological relations between traces and temporality. It builds on this argument to develop the idea that anything can be coded to be a trace of the future, which can in principle be tracked and accounted for. It also revisits Hilgartner's theory of risk-object formation to show how the temporal depth of such accounting is critical and controversial, and influences credible risk-indicator design. In general, the idea and practice of risk management is positioned as a distinctive general form of traceability complex that embodies contrasting temporal orientations to past, present, and future. Digital forms of traceability can also be framed as risks—in aiming at the elimination of uncertainty and at predictability, they potentially elevate a continuous algorithmically produced present over human projective capacities. Chapter 8 turns its gaze towards the humans who are entangled in different traceability complexes. Building on relational theories of the self, the chapter first revisits studies of the formative role of quantification and accounts, arguing that in digitized self-tracking, this takes an extreme form, even to the extent of such tracking becoming a valued end it itself. Three critical vectors of self-formation are considered: profile construction and curation; the self as feedback machine; self-tracking and data-doubles. In each case, the traceification of self involves exchanges across the boundaries of organizational and private life, which blur and deconstruct those boundaries. And with this blurring, the very notion of performance has expanded its scope and reach. In sum, the chapter proposes that traceability complexes are increasingly populated by trace-enabled humans within thin, digitally mediated relationalities, a transformation process that can be theorized as cyborgization.

Chapter 9 considers the implications of traceability as a distinctive social epistemology and revisits the value-purpose of discovery. The chapter discusses and distinguishes between traceability as practice and as method within relational theorizing of science. However, studies of big science also suggest a convergence between these two senses of traceability as data and knowledge production are increasingly platformized. Furthermore, a form of digital positivism is increasingly evident in both natural and social science in which digital data are more than a new resource but also define the nature of the investigatable empirical domain and thereby influence research agendas. To illustrate this strong thesis, it is argued that developments in accounting research represent a general form of this digital positivism—"accountics"—which is reshaping our conception of the empirical world and generating a convergence between the social sciences and managerial control. The chapter concludes by proposing the idea of a "critical traceology" focused on the mechanisms by which this digital positivism is expanding. Finally, Chapter 10 pulls these different arguments together to consolidate a traceological theory of accounting and to discuss how the digital economy of traces is transforming or intensifying audit society and expanding the range of human activities that can be thought of as "performing". If the audit society was essentially an oversight explosion, what we see now, sometimes designated as "surveillance capitalism", can be said to be a tracking explosion. The latter is changing the mix within organized forms of traceability from oversight to tracking.

Other than building a more traceologically sensitive theory of accounting, why does it matter to establish traceability as an object of analysis like this (cf. Muirhead and Porter, 2019; Power, 2019)? There are two main reasons. First, traceability complexes, understood as bundles of practices, are implicated in generating new markets for governance (Hinings et al., 2017), new forms of distributed agency in supply chains (Enfield, 2017; Bernstein, 2017; Kockelman, 2017), and new capabilities for surveillance by states and organizations (Zuboff, 2019). They also expand definitions of "performance" that span the organizational and the personal, and which, as we argue in Chapter 8, elevate "feedback" as a mode of evaluation. Traceability complexes are therefore material realizations of variable social demands to fix, memorize, track, and account for our individual and collective activities. They are sites of an emerging politics of traceability involving struggles over purposes, over the capture and extraction of digital data, over the ethics of tracking as observation, and over the manner in which the organization of traceability itself can be somehow governed, not least when it is saturated by algorithmic processes.

Second, as noted already, traceability is profoundly epistemic. This architecture of value-purposes, traces, tracking, and accounts is a way of knowing people, processes, and things, and of making them observable and thereby connected, both to others and to themselves. Philosophers through the ages have been preoccupied with seeing and observing as primordial forms of knowledge that underpin science and much else. As pragmatists, like Rorty (1980), have argued, this claim to insight about the foundations of knowledge has given philosophy its professional identity as epistemology (an identity which he challenges). In this book we argue that it is practices of tracking, and their documentary and digital form, which utilize traceification and which make certain styles of observation and connection, and therefore knowing, possible (Latour, 1986). They do so not with a transcendental foundation but as a form of pragmatist rootedness in the world of material trace potential. Humans tracked prey long before they tracked marathon runners on apps.

The epistemology of tracking is necessarily permeated by interests that make some aspects of the world observable but not others. As we go deeper into the epistemic character of tracking, and how it conditions and is conditioned by observation capacity, the practice landscape becomes more differentiated. On the one hand, it can be organized to be evidentiary, forensic, and justificatory, underpinning hierarchical forms of regulation and governance. This tends to be productive of accounting-led forms of tracking. On the other hand, it must also be understood as creating often surprising, novel realities and new relations between people and things, including new topologies of organizationality and ways of steering and controlling societies (Kornberger et al., 2017). Whether we like the social orders generated by tracking or not, we cannot but reflect on their trajectory and their implications for the accounts that we live by.

In this book, we theorize these politico-epistemic stakes of traceability and their organization in terms of a fundamental tension between two different ways of configuring the relations between value-purposes, traces, tracking, and accounting. These different ways are ideal-typical, and in reality they are blended, but they define contrasting modes of organizing traceability in terms of whether they are oversight or tracking-orientated. These oppositions are stated simplistically, but this is no mere play on words. They define the very axis on which societies may be turning in the digital age and lie at the heart of a postulated transition between the motifs of audit society and surveillance capitalism. Humans have always lived in an "economy of traces" of some kind. However, today the accounting potential embedded in the traces that we datafy and the data we traceify and our ability to track and narrate our own lives and possibilities, and those of others, are greatly expanding and changing. If the "accounts we live by" refers to the role of accounting in generating the facticity of that which is valued by humans, then nothing less may be at stake in the analysis of traceability than the nature of human experience and purpose itself.

Chapter 1 Summative Propositions

The following propositions provide four working definitions of key concepts that are used throughout the book and two key claims that are developed in later chapters:

1. **Traceability is a capacity both to generate traces and to use such generated traces for evidentiary purposes.**
2. **Traceification is the process by which traces are generated for specific practical purposes where traceability is an organizing interest.**
3. **Traceability is mobilized by one or more of three general value-purposes or logics: quality, security, and discovery.**
4. **The "accounts we live by" are broadly understood as the diverse forms of narration, numeric representation, and summation that organize and mediate human and organizational relations.**
5. **Tracking precedes representation.**
6. **For all their evident variety, the accounts we live by are undergoing a systematic shift in the digital age.**

2
Traces, Traceification, and Tracking

Overview

In this chapter, we build on the introductory discussion of traceability and accounts to develop a more processual view of the dynamics of traceability. Specifically, we conceptualize these dynamics in terms of a process architecture which connects the value-purposes of traceability to accounts via the mechanisms of trace production and datafication, and the tracking practices that they enable. While traces have been mentioned in the introductory chapter, we discuss them here in their widest possible conceptual and philosophical senses and use this as a point of departure to develop the notion of *traceification*. This concept of traceification draws upon the Peircean understanding of traces as constructed signs (i.e. as "traces of" something of interest for, and relative to, a practice which utilizes those traces). The chapter then identifies an important duality in both the notions of trace and traceification. One the one hand, trace production is a *generative* process, creating marks which stand for an object that may be present or absent to varying degrees. On the other hand, traceification is also *evidentiary* in nature, since it generates not just an object of interest but also a potential for observing and connecting it to other objects at a distance in space and time. This generative-evidentiary duality, which in Chapter 1 was argued to be at the heart of the idea of traceability, matters greatly in the digital age since these two faces of traceification are becoming increasingly disconnected from each other. The nature and effects of this fragmenting duality will come into view repeatedly throughout the book.

The chapter then considers the similarities and differences between traceification and datafication, a concept which has become familiar to information systems scholars. It is proposed that traceification and datafication are intertwined material and semantic processes in which the latter co-opts the former and aims at eliminating its originating relationality and indexicality. While traces are always in some sense "traces of", data are signs that deny their origin and affirm their self-sufficiency. This is not such a dry point to make and matters to the accounts we live by; data are always implicated in processes by which they are disconnected from the very things they represent, even to the point of denying a world beyond itself. This is generally understood as "positivism"

Economy of Traces. Michael Power, Oxford University Press. © Oxford University Press (2026).
DOI: 10.1093/9780197681527.003.0002

and is especially radical and post-representational in digital form, as we argue in Chapter 9.

From this theorization of traceification, the chapter considers the practice-forms that it enables, namely tracking understood as a form of first-order observation of an object, usually mediated by technologies. It is argued that while tracking is an observational basis for action, it also necessary involves the production of accounts as manifestations of minimal oversight of, and accountability for, its operations. This conceptualization of tracking supports the development of an important distinction for the arguments that follow, namely between *tracking-led accounts* and *accounts-led tracking*. The thesis of the book is that digital transformation, and especially intense datafication, has led to the relative expansion of the former, with consequences for the portfolio of accounts we live by.

Finally, we propose a dynamic model linking traceification and tracking to the traceability purposes and accounts discussed in Chapter 1. This is the *traceability complex*, which, being neither empirically descriptive nor purely theoretical, provides a heuristic or template for the articulation of the different perspectives on, and problematics of, traceability that follow in later chapters, namely governance, risk, selfhood, and science. The traceability complex also provides the conceptual architecture for a traceological theory of accounting, which will be further elaborated in later chapters.

Why Traces Matter

The idea of the trace has a complex intellectual and practical history. Traces have materiality in that they can be seen, experienced, sensed, and encountered. Yet, they can also be thought about in different ways. They are understood in many fields of enquiry as fragments, clues, hints, puzzles, residues, and surprises that are perceived as relevant to the interests of specific epistemic communities and to the organization of their knowledge practices. Traces as marginal residues are often unintended but can become evidentiary and "inadvertently telling or unintentionally insightful" (Comunello et al., 2024, p. 625). Furthermore, this evidentiary status is relative to the perspective of the analyst rather than the nominal producer of the trace (Communello et al., 2022). They are symptoms and indicators rather than statements of fact, and they invite further probing and investigation. Indeed, traces are referenced implicitly and explicitly in many academic disciplines—in history, archaeology, forensic science, law, psychology, psychoanalysis, and sociology, to name only a few. Ancient manuscripts or correspondence are both material documents and also traces in the general sense of being artefacts that happen to endure. Yet they may become regarded as traces in a more specific way as scholars use them as evidential resources to, say, rethink existing historical accounts and theories. From this point of view, archives are repositories of trace-potential. Material residues, such as food particles on prehistoric implements, can also be traceified in this practice-relative sense, thereby enabling inferences to be made about ancient eating habits and health (Fullagar and Matheson, 2014). Traces are metaphorically and sometimes literally "research crumbs" (Pitti, 2024). Yet, they are more than accidental vestiges and can become evidentiary resources. In this sense, they can also encode profound epistemological and ethical features, as we now discuss.

Traces as Signs

The philosopher David Hume famously distinguished between "impressions", understood as the result of immediate and direct experiential contact with the world, and "ideas" as the "less vivid" residues or traces of those impressions, which can be remembered and organized into more or less complex forms (Hume, 1955 [1748], Section II). This dualism of impressions/ideas has been extensively criticized, and yet his project of grounding knowledge, and therefore science, in perceptual experience defined a radical and influential form of empirical sensibility (Buchdahl, 1969, pp. 349–357). Traces of experience were to be understood as the primary matter of knowledge. While Hume's architecture of the mind was crude by today's standards, the causality he attributes to the things he calls impressions as "data" in its literal sense (i.e. as that which is *given* in experience) is broadly consistent with neurological science. The latter focuses on the operations of the brain and how the external world produces stimuli, which are processed to provide the dimensionality, temporality, colour, shape, and many other qualities of our sensed external world—impressions in Hume's sense. The difficulty is that we must account for how we move from these primitive "raw" traces of the world to the organized nature of our experience consisting of well-formed discrete objects in space and time, not to mention the great puzzle of consciousness itself. These traces also seem to be the conditions of possibility for memory and hence of the kind of human life that we take for granted. They are somehow organized by the brain to create our experience of exteriority and are causally connected to a world that forces itself upon us and in which we find ourselves.

Hume's radical empiricist programme generated as many problems as it solved, one of which was how to account for our cognitive and linguistic ability to identify particular, singular features of experience and situate them within general categories. This is known as the problem of "indexicality," which preoccupied later philosophers, including Peirce and Wittgenstein (1976, para.

34–38). They regarded it as a much neglected, but primary, cognitive ability that humans possess and which enables us to identify specific features of the world. This ability is evident, as Wittgenstein understood and demonstrated, in our largely successful use of linguistic expressions where reference changes with context, such as "here", "now", and so forth. For both Peirce and Wittgenstein, this *indexical* ability, an ability to indicate and refer to particulars, is fundamental to how we navigate the relational situatedness in which we find ourselves. Furthermore, Peirce regarded traces as a subclass of these indices in general, as a particular kind of indexical sign. As one commentator on Peirce puts it: ". . . every individual trace which we may find is a material item that stands for whatever it signifies indexically and for those sharing the search interest for this object" (Pape, 2008, p. 9). The signification function of a trace, understood as a trace of a specific thing, establishes for Peirce a connection between an object in the world and a person with an interest in it, an interest that is grounded in a practice. Borgmann (1999) provides a similar conceptualization of information as a cognitive relation between persons and things mediated by signs.[1]

To summarize: following Peirce, a trace is only a trace if it can be embedded in a network of interested parties committed to searching for lawlike regularities as they move abductively between specific traces and their general meaning. Yet there is also more to traces than their foundational role in epistemology. As practice-relative constructs, they are also imbued with the purpose of the practices of trace usage that they enable, and are therefore bearers (and suppressors) of values.

Traces and Value

Derrida and Levinas provide a reading of the trace which, at first glance, stands in stark contrast to that of Peirce. Theirs is a more ontological and existential analysis and, in Levinas's case, points more to values and ethics than to knowledge-building. For Derrida (1982), traces are pure singularity as marks. They are variously understood as remains, supplements, and difference, which are sources of anxiety and which disturb dreams of universality, of completeness, and of law itself. And yet, as Derrida implies, such traces are the very conditions of possibility for the projects of law and science, which are both impossible yet necessarily sought. He seems to be telling us that traceability as connection

[1] Peirce also argues that meaningful signs are to be distinguished from meaningless sub-semiotic marks, although this is much debated, not least within the philosophy of art. For example, Elkins (1995) challenges Peirce's view by arguing that a brushstroke, part of an aggregate which is a painting's meaning as a whole, can nevertheless be semiotically significant. More generally, an object qua trace cannot be grasped essentialistically using dualisms such as "semiotic/non-semiotic", "sign/mark" or "matter/meaning".

and integration via traceification is impossible and will always fail, but is also something that humans must constantly strive for. To deconstruct in his sense is to live with, recognize, and ironize, the incoherence, disconnectedness, and anti-totality of traces as horizons of experience and of all projects of ordering, including our notion of traceability and the very possibility of tracking.

Rorty identifies affinities between Derrida's thought and Peircean pragmatism (Rorty, 1995). However, unlike Peirce, Derrida conceptualizes traces as unconscious irritants that resist being brought into the open as coherent, self-standing objects and subsumed under laws of nature or institutional orders (Kellogg, 2009). Traces of experience, especially traumatic experience, become suppressed and must be recovered through an analytic process. In the classical version of this, dreams for Freud (1900) are the mechanism for processing traces of the distorted and suppressed remnants of experience. The terms of these debates notably contrast strongly with contemporary discussions about "digital traces," which generate an "overlit" world (Flyverbom, 2015, 2022) in which nothing is hidden and in which we become our "data selves" (see Chapter 5). Traces here are conceptualized as the limits and boundaries of experience, as the uncanny or even as the suppressed, which must be recovered. In this sense, they are far from being coextensive with data as signs that point mainly to themselves. Data imply a very different relation to the trace and to the Derridean problematic of *différance*. Data are traces that become signs without any nostalgia for lost contact with the world; *différance* as absence is normalized and co-opted as mere difference in a world where the empirical is not uncanny but is coextensive with data and where there is no puzzle of indexicality (see Chapter 9). Indeed, as this chapter argues, data can also be imagined as the outcome of conversion of the trace, of a process of homogenization and distantiation from the indexical qualities of the trace to become a signifier in and for itself.[2] Where traces as signs retain some sense of mediating persons and things, digitized data remake both, while relating them to each other.

Levinas's (1986) thinking on traces moves in the same broad direction of travel as Derrida and against its datafication. However, for him, the significance of the trace is primarily ethical; it is the product of encounters that enable us to be touched by "the other" (Steiner, 1989, p. 147) and it is the source of an ethical accountability in which the self is at risk (Levin, 1998; Roberts, 2009). The trace thereby has a profoundly moral and near mystical quality. The ultimate human trace is the "face" of another, which, in the abstract, does not belong to what Levinas calls the visible world of "disclosure". It is rather a trace of something "absolutely absent" and bygone, which is encountered as something disconcerting and which "overwhelms egoism". Levinas juxtaposes this notion of trace to

[2] I am grateful to Jannis Kallinikos for helping to clarify these reflections.

mere signs that are, in a Peircean sense, part of the empirically disclosed world. He states that "a trace is a presence of that which properly speaking has never been there, or what is always past" (1986, p. 358). Yet this pure exteriority of another, as a face that we encounter, is for Levinas a source of responsibility to that other. The epiphany of the encounter with another creates a relationship of responsibility to the completely ungraspable.

At one point in his essay on traces, Levinas admits of another sense of them as signs and clues *within the world* in all its variety. In a strikingly concrete moment, he writes: "When in transactions one 'pays by check' so that there will be a trace of the payment, the trace is inscribed in the very order of the world. But a trace in the strict sense disturbed the order of the world." Here he also makes a point that will be salient for later analysis in Chapter 7, namely that "in addition to what the sign signifies, it is the past of him who delivered the sign" (1986, p. 357). In this respect, traces are temporal in that they signify the irrecoverable past of the objects and people who created them, even when they point to the future. Yet, we might also say that such traces, which are inscribed in the world, are closer to being data. They are institutional, evidentiary, and "time-stamped". They are not mysterious.

Levinas's remarks about traces must be understood in relation to his theological mysticism. The ultimate trace is existence itself, the pure externality by which we experience the world. For both Derrida and Levinas, traces are fundamentally ambiguous primary matter at the horizon of human experience. They point, as Steiner (1989) argues, to something that can never be fully grasped but which is insistently present. While there is definitely an implicit theory of signification in Levinas's thought, it differs from that of Peirce. For Peirce, the pointingness or referentiality of traces constitutes our varied sensory worlds of the everyday and may creatively enter scientific practice. For Levinas, traces are clues that always point to that which is necessarily and purely absent, namely God. Traces are at best liminal objects of experience which somehow "reside at the intersection of the seen and the unseen . . . the coming into being of the social" (Napolitano, 2015, p. 4).

These general conceptualizations of traces as sources of value provide background analogical support for more concrete, critical analyses that deal with the fortunes of minority groups and individuals within prevailing structures of power. The focus here is on traces not only as absence and as products of suppression but also as sources of possible voice, via new forms of tracking and counter-accounting. For example, the "sociology of the trace" (Gomez-Barris and Gray, 2010) represents a collective project to speak for those who lack or cannot give an account of their lives. Such ethically motivated traceologies are frequently visible in literature. For example, Gray's famous poem "Elegy Written in a Country Churchyard" is a melancholic homage to those who have lived, worked, and died and who leave no trace, who are traceless in history. Authors, such as 2014 Nobel Prize–winner Patrick Modiano, also focus on tracing such forgotten lives. His preoccupation is with the Jewish Parisians who were deported to concentration camps in the Second World War. Like many others, his work reminds us how our lives are essentially fragmentary, and how we assemble and reassemble these fragments and traces in the restless search for meaning, identity, and completeness. He aims at building new "accounts to live by", accounts that are tantamount to histories of self, organization, and social order. Memory and identity in Mondeau's work are nothing but the accumulated strata of traces, and much is lost in the flux of time. It is the job of the novelist, psychoanalyst, and archaeologist—like a forensic auditor or investigating detective, perhaps—to *discover* and recover what has been buried, marginalized, displaced, or suppressed and to make our lives newly traceable and accountable. By narrating such traces and making them visible, it is possible to track, and give an account of, lives and events that might otherwise be forgotten (Scribano, 2023). Traces in this sense can be understood as "cultural survivals of idiosyncratic encounters"; they are residues that could not become official histories (de Certeau, 1988, ch. 5) and for which the analyst must become a witness.

Traces are not only to be understood as ethically and politically charged forms of visibility for those who are forgotten, invisible, and dispossessed. The very notion of the empirical and what we mean and take for granted as a world is also at stake (see also Chapter 9). New and surprising articulations of traces may generate new views of the world and possibilities for action. The production of accounts on behalf of those who are traceless, voiceless, and powerless—not least by encoded biases in algorithmic systems—is therefore also a project of redefining and reconstructing our notion of the empirical. The task of a critically oriented traceology is somehow to make visible that which has been systematically hidden, to recover an ethics of the trace that is deeply implicated in our humanity, in the nature of our individual and collective experience, and in how we account for, and give voice to, ourselves and others (Butler, 2005). Hence these politics, sociologies, and poetics of tracelessness constitute a potential for *counter-accounting*, seeking to recover traces and making lives and experiences traceable and accountable, when they might otherwise remain invisible (Vinnari and Laine, 2017).

From these reflections, it seems that traces occupy shadowy spaces in-between things and people. They can be public goods in the service of democracy and freedom, or part of invasive infrastructures of observation of the personal. They can be not only the foundation of empirical knowledge and inference but also morally infused signs of that which is forgotten, hidden, and suppressed. Notwithstanding this breadth, which may seem too great to be analytically useful, the fundamental puzzle of traces is how they mediate dead matter and representation, thereby generating meaning. To grasp this puzzle, we must shift our attention from traces as things to the processes of traceification that produce them from phenomena.

Traceification

Following Peirce's lead, we can propose that what counts specifically as a trace is relative to an epistemic or regulatory purpose. Traces may have artefactual and material dimensions, but this is not what makes them traces. All manner of things can be encoded as, and be given, trace-status: numbers, bodily residues and marks like thumb- and footprints, signatures, documents. They have material durability. but their meaning as traces that mark the boundaries of empirical phenomena of interest is practice-relative. Hence, as trivial as it may sound, traces are always products of a *traceification* process by which they are endowed with signification (i.e. become signs). Thus, traceification as a process can be understood as collective "semiotic work" in that material inscriptions are invested with meaning as "traces of" events and things, and can be systematically assembled in books, records, and documents, ranging from encyclopaedias to personal diaries to accounting ledgers to operational protocols (Ferraris, 2012). For example, unlike the traces that accidentally acquire significance as evidence (Communello et al. 2024), ticks, signatures, and other marks *intentionally* traceify actions relevant to the institutional purpose of their production, constituting them as evidence of, for example, compliance with safety legislation. In such practice settings, traceification makes safety-relevant actions observable, trackable, and matters of potential accounting.

In general, we propose that to designate a material thing, including an inscription, as a trace is to emplace it materially and semiotically as a feature of a practice with some form of traceability as its purpose. The trace does not subsist in and of itself qua trace; it is the practice that endows the thing—human behaviour, text, mark, and so forth—with this status, which traceifies it, and which gives it a role in enabling the tracking of a thing or action. For example, in the case of old-style computer "punchcards", the hole in the card is both a material trace and a representation of data (Alaimo and Kallinikos, 2024, ch. 3). Whether something has the status of a trace is therefore a product of *attributional semiotic work* within a traceability-oriented practice. This conception of the trace also means that it is an empirical, rather than a purely conceptual, question as to when things can be regarded as traces and when not. In short, any material thing or event can be traceified (i.e. can be made to count as trace, or leave a trace), but not everything does; it all depends on the broader practice context in which traces are constituted as objects for specific purposes. Such a practice-relative conception of traces necessarily shifts our theoretical attention from the quasi-philosophical discussion of what traces are as things, to a more processual focus on how they are generated and the consequences of such traceification.

Traceification and Datafication

At this point, it is necessary to clarify the relation between traces and "data", not least because of the widespread tendency to use the terms interchangeably.[3] This clarification necessarily involves reflecting on the relation between traceification as described earlier and the increasingly prominent notion of *datafication* as the "translation of the diversity of cultural codes and conventions . . . into the language of machines" (Alaimo and Kallinikos, 2024, p. 57). The first way of thinking about their relation is to see traceification as a primary process which comes "before" and enables datafication. Drawing on Simmel's (1971, pp. 351–352) elusive notion of the interdependence between life-process and form, we can think of traceification as marking the fundamental point of contact or encounter with material life-processes, and which produces from that encounter the traces that are the primary material available for datafication. On this first view, datafication can be understood as the semiotic, technical, and institutional work of further constructing the trace into the durable and mobile form of data, supporting further levels of articulation and aggregation as facts that can travel (Latour, 1986; Howlett and Morgan, 2010). This conversion process is also akin to Latour's (1999) notion of "circulating reference" as a process of abstraction by which three-dimensional objects become two-dimensional representations in increasingly standard notational form. Here traceification precedes datafication in the chain of abstraction and they operate in a kind of partnership; data are constituted from something that they are not (i.e. a trace of . . . something) (Gitelman, 2013; Rosenberg, 2013; van Dijck, 2014; Alaimo and Kallinikos, 2022; 2024).

As analytically attractive and logical as this first version of the relation between traceification and datafication may be, it is harder to sustain empirically, especially under conditions of intensifying digital automation. More aspects of the world, life, and behaviour are traceified at high speed by machines and processed according to rules—algorithms (see Chapter 4)—and are formed into further categorical "data objects" on the way to becoming part of "datasets" as we commonly understand them (Kitchen, 2022; Alaimo and Kallinikos, 2024). It seems as if traceificaton must be understood as a more intimate aspect of datafication

[3] Communello et al. (2022, p. 6) refer to "personal digital data" and Communello et al., (2024, p. 627) talk of "trace-like data".

and its devices. Traces are not so much experiential encounters as already precooked data-in-waiting by devices that homogenize in the form of electronic pulses generated by human bodies, making them ready for further organization into data on the way to becoming facts. Yet, even in such highly automated settings, we can hold on to the idea that traceification as the production of traces is a boundary condition of datafication. And even if this boundary is very difficult to observe empirically, we know that there is at least a stimulus of some kind outside of the machine but which the machine has been designed to organize and translate, thereby leading to datafication.

This transformation and conversion from the trace to data are hardly visible processes of distantiation and homogenization in which the Derridean problem of absent reference is erased. This transformation is more radical and pronounced under digital conditions of "pulverizing" the world for processing. In this sense, digital forms of datafication loosen the links between data and specific forms of domain knowledge, and between traces, things, and people. But as data acquire organizing power to shape perception, we must nevertheless also avoid clinging to traces as somehow exterior to all this and "raw"—whether digital or otherwise—since, as already noted, they are themselves attributional constructions of interested, value-laden, and device-dependent practices oriented to the harvesting of "life" for the production of "form". In this respect, the trace is never the epistemologically innocent partner of data; capacities and possibilities for such encounters with, and openness to, traces are always organized and cultural in nature even, and especially, when we think we have unmediated experience of them. Digital footprints, like footprints in the sand, are invitations to enquire and explore.

To summarize: traces as puzzles, clues, and anomalies do not exist in and of themselves but only in different settings for knowledge production, including ethically informed knowledge. And put very simply as a linguistic matter: if datafication is a process, then it must logically be a process that operates on something that is *not* itself (i.e. the trace). Yet, these reflections on the temporal and processual priority of traceification over dataification threaten to take us into deep philosophical water and raise acute issues of observability. This potentially endows the idea of the trace with more metaphysical status than the present argument needs.

The Duality of Traceification

So far we have positioned traceification as a discrete primary conversion process at the frontier of knowledge and experience. This generative meaning of traceification accords with the idea of traceability introduced in Chapter 1, as the ability to create stable traces of things and to enable them to be tracked and observed.

Traceification in this sense is ontologically significant in that it is the work of constituting and maintaining the basic objects of traceability practices. However, there is also a second nuance of traceification, which emphasizes the *evidential* role of traces discussed in the previous section. Here, it is not that traces are converted into data, but that data are converted into traces, which are invested with evidential meaning. This second generative nuance of traceification still involves the "semiotic work" of conversion, but instead of operating at the mystery-laden limits of experience to generate primary objects of interest, it acts on existing data and effectively converts them into "traces of" a performance of relevance to quality, security, or discovery as value-purposes of traceability practices. Traceification as the attributional construction of evidentiary material in this sense also makes remote tracking and observation possible.

This evidentiary nuance of traceification can also be understood as a form of explicitization (Strathern, 1995) and has affinities with the idea of "making things auditable" (Power, 1996). For example, the policy need to observe and demonstrate the "impact" of academic research involved initially the co-optation, organization, and re-coding of different data sources as "traces of . . ." (i.e. evidence of) impact (Power, 2015). Napolitano (2015) argues similarly that not all ethnographic data/details become anthropologically significant traces. There is rather a careful selection of evidential "trace-hood" within anthropology. What counts as a trace of something significant and worthy of tracking is therefore a matter of construction, of traceification, such that "apparently uneventful data [can become] meaningful traces" (Napolitano, 2015, p. 51). In general, we can say that in an extensively datafied world, not all data are significant for traceability purposes. Where there is need or purpose in the sense outlined in Chapter 1, which explicitly requires traceability as demonstration, proof, assurance, evidence, and oversight, then data must be traceified to be a relevant evidentiary trace for a practice. However, we must always bear in mind that notions of evidence and its sufficiency are prone to change, and this may leave existing modes of traceification stranded as new conceptions of evidence come into being.

These two nuances, or faces, of traceification are its generative and evidentiary modes. They always exist not only in combination but also in tension in relation to datafication processes. Traces are generative of data and can become datafied, while data are often traceified in the sense of being made into evidential traces. Figure 2.1 visualizes these mutual dynamics of traceification and datafication.

These dynamics matter because they correspond to two different ideal-typical problematics of societal ordering. To anticipate later arguments in this book, it is proposed that the audit society phenomenon was the politically motivated and institutionalized elevation of traceification in the *evidential* sense, namely the reconstitution of performance data into "evidence" of auditable performance, a drive that in turn intensified the elaboration of that data. This is to be contrasted

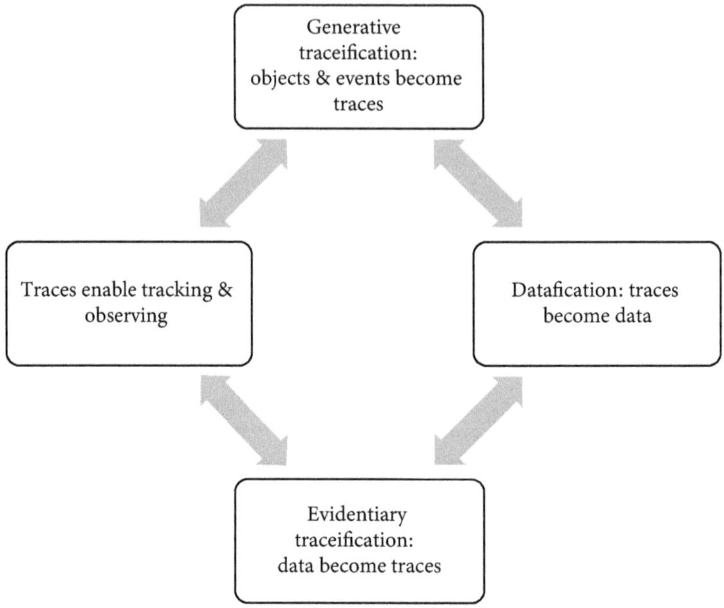

Figure 2.1 The duality of traceification and datafication.

with traceification in the *generative* sense, which has intensified under conditions of digital datafication and is arguably a prominent feature of so-called surveillance capitalism (Zuboff, 2019). These two nuances of traceification, and hence of traceability, are significant in enabling and expanding the tracking of things, people, and processes. They encode and emphasize different temporal orientations—backward- and forward-looking, respectively. And they constitute two ideal-typical modes of accounting which coexist in a similar tension and dialectic, which we discuss further in this chapter.

To conclude, we can define traceification for the purposes of the arguments that follow as: *the process by which traces are generated for specific practical use where traceability is an organizing purpose.* One such use of traces has already been mentioned, namely tracking, which we now consider, bearing in mind that the objects and events that we want to track and observe, and our capacity for marking them, will shape the nature and scope of the traceification process.

Tracking

The category of "tracking" has been mentioned frequently already in this book and the intention is to use it broadly to characterize a basic mode of trace and data utilization. It is useful to recall that tracking has commonsensical and vernacular nuances. We associate it, for example, with hunters tracking prey and looking for signs (traces) to follow. Or we might track the changing position of the sun in the sky using a sundial to tell the time. And footprints in the sand, which are temporary traces, can nevertheless enable tracking. When we reflect further, our contemporary world is rich in practices that involve the "tracking" of things, people, and processes across space and time. Digital technologies have also greatly increased possibilities for tracking by extending the observational reach of humans, and we consider specifically practices of self-tracking, with which we began this book, in Chapter 8. But what can be said of tracking in general? We provide a working definition as follows:

> *Tracking is a trace-enabled practice by which an observer is connected to, and can act upon, as well as account for, an object of interest. Tracking practices will vary in terms of their "observational reach" and evidentiary connectivity across space and time.*

This broad definition of tracking frames it in terms of the connectivity that enables the observation and surveillance of things, people, and processes. The movement of things like foodstuffs may be tracked via labels, which also provide an "account" of their origins and quality; the movement of people may be tracked using different possible devices to determine if their behaviour poses security or health risks. In contrast to the tracking of well-formed, determinate objects, the idea of *tracing* is more suggestive of settings where traceability as the discovery of an elusive, less well-formed object of concern is at stake. For example, water managers are interested in detecting the presence of harmful chemicals, or accident investigators will seek to discover the cause by tracing possible antecedents and risk factors (see also Chapter 7). Tracing in this sense has more to do with the postulated logic of discovery and its related forensic practices. It is not just a linguistic accident that the COVID virus needed to be "traced" while its human carriers needed to be "tracked". However, we should not overstate this difference between tracking and tracing. Tracking itself always, at least partially, constructs its object; animals are made up as "prey" to be "tracked down"; footprints can suggest enemies are near; worker performance can be made visible via indicators. In this book, we use the notion of tracking unless there is an explicit reason to refer to tracing.

A focus on tracking as simultaneously observation and evidentiary connection provides a more critical perspective on studies of quantification and accounting, which have been preoccupied with "what numbers represent", with their cultural authority and with calculative practices. The concept of tracking also invites the further development of "inscriptivist" accounting scholarship, which draws on the work of Latour and emphasizes both the durability and mobility of numbers as inscriptions, and how they enable or disable connectivity (see Chapter 3).

At the same time, we should also not overestimate the power and coherence of tracking practices so-defined. As already noted in Chapter 1, tracking can be a failing practice in many different ways—people and things can be lost, the wrong things can be tracked, and the real (as opposed to desired) capacity for observation may be partial or weak. Moreover, in the background, there are always concerns and debates about the ethics of tracking, especially with new digital capabilities to track people and their behaviour in fine-grained ways. Tracking is in this sense not neutral but is both value-laden and also generative of the "tracks" that enable it (see Chapter 4).

Finally, tracking is not just important *to* accounting. It also a basic form *of* accounting practice itself. For example, if I track and catch an animal, then I might tell someone about it. In this case, tracking and accounting are related but conceptually and empirically different activities. However, for more inscription-based tracking practices, such as where a teacher takes a class register to know who is present, the tracking of the children and accounting for their presence are very closely related, if not the same. Indeed, the accounting in this case is actually the doing of tracking. This is an example of what we call "tracking-led accounting," and it is to be distinguished from "accounts-led tracking".

Tracking-Accounting Hybrids

In Chapter 1 a broad view of what counts as an account was proposed. There are a number of ways to structure and conceptualize this breadth. One possibility is to use the available and highly institutionalized taxonomies that already do this. For example, it has become mainstream to make a distinction between accounting for managerial (internal) and financial reporting (external) purposes. Much of the pedagogy of accounting is organized around some version of this distinction, although there are cross-national variations, such as the enterprise focus of *Betrebswirtschaftslehre* (Napier, 1996a; von Colbe, 1996). Another distinction that has come to the fore in recent decades is that between financial and non-financial forms of accounting, with the latter including both narratives and non-monetary metrics. Devices such as "balanced scorecards" have sought to accommodate and combine these different accountings (Qu and Cooper, 2011). Underlying these developments in practice, there are broader debates about the nature and effects of quantification in general and accounting in particular. Here the commensurating urge to reduce phenomena to quanta is contrasted with values and practices that are regarded as incommensurable (Espeland and Stevens, 1998; Mennicken and Espeland, 2019). Many, but not all, forms of accounting understood as "calculative practices" (Miller, 1992) find themselves on the "commensurating", reductive, and digital side of this distinction. Furthermore, that we speak more easily of accounting "data" rather than traces suggests the distantiating and abstracting capacity of accounts to absorb the situationally specific in general schemas of representation; datafication and formal accounting are similarly reductive in their logics.

These and other ways of mapping the broad territory of accounting practices and their devices have led to rich analyses of the craft and have expanded our understandings of its social significance—understandings that have travelled to, and have influenced, other social sciences. Yet, for the purposes of theorizing what is at stake for the accounts we live by, another taxonomy is proposed, based on the concept of "tracking" rather than those of quantification and calculation. Accounting numbers have of course been very important to the capacity to somehow mark, inscribe, and track transactional events. Indeed, it can plausibly be argued that the historic cost method of accounting was favoured primarily because it enabled the tracking of business items, rather than their economic measurement or valuation. From this point of view, double-entry bookkeeping can also be understood as an elaborate tracking system onto which summative accounts of performance and profitability were later superimposed. Accordingly, the thesis, to be developed further in Chapter 3, is that *tracking is the analytical and historically primitive foundation of accounts production.* The concept of tracking draws our attention to the material foundations of the calculative and information conceptions of accounting in the production of traces in durable form. And with a tracking-based focus on accounting, we can suggest two ideal-typical modes of tracking-accounting hybridity, namely "accounts-led" and "tracking-led".

Accounts-Led Tracking

Accounts-led tracking implies that it is the production of accounts, mobilized by the need for accountability and oversight for one or more traceability value-purposes (Chapter 1), that influences the nature of traceification and tracking. Financial accounting is a paradigm case of accounts-led tracking in this sense. Organizations are accountable to various suppliers of finance and must periodically account to them. Relevant economic transactions do not exist and cannot be seen without being traceified and datafied, enabling them to be tracked and aggregated into summative accounts of performance. Furthermore, this general "top-down" configuration of the accounting-trace-tracking relation is at the heart of many designs for oversight and regulation (see Chapters 5 and 6). Hence, accountability for a performance object of interest, such as academic research, can be traceified in the form of academic citations, which can be "composed" or aggregated by a legitimate evaluator/accountant into summative accounts in qualitative and narrational form.

Even for highly institutionalized accounting forms, the need to convince audiences to accept new accounts can arise, as debates about brand accounting and fair value indicate (Power, 1992; 2010). It follows that for alternative and counter-accounts, new forms of traceification are required to generate the observability and tracking of new objects of concern, accountability, and performance, such as gender diversity. Whether such accounts can convince on a sufficient scale is a contingent matter. The general point is that for accounts-led tracking, it is accountability for fulfilling an explicit value-purpose—quality, security, or discovery—that mobilizes traceification and shapes tracking practice. This stylized model of accounts production is hierarchical and compositional; tracking is a means to an accounting end.

Tracking-Led Accounts

Tracking-led accounts are, unsurprisingly perhaps, the inverse of accounts-led tracking. They reflect how it is the practice of tracking things and people, including self-tracking, which is the primary driver of both accounts production and traceification. In general, tracking-led accounts are less hierarchical and more plural, often with weak to non-existent audit trails (see Chapter 4; Kornberger et al., 2017). These characteristics have given rise to extensive debates about the effective oversight and accountability of tracking practices in the digital age, to be considered further in later chapters of this book (Rahman et al., 2024). Tracking-led accounts tend to have a strong orientation to the surveillance of things and people for a range of security-like and control purposes, but they are also visible in the recent wave of digitally enabled self-observation practices. A priori we can say that tracking-led accounts emphasize *first-order* observability, whereas accounts-led tracking emphasizes *second-order* observability and *oversight* of first-order observing.

Tracking-led accounts can be enabled by a wide range of observational devices, about some of which there are significant ethical debates (Veliz, 2021). Thus, CCTV, GPS, bar code tags, and a plethora of sensors generate the traces that enable practices for tracking food, people, ships, and much else. The "accounts" that these tracking practices produce are unlike the financial reporting model; they consist of highly varied metrical and narrative summations and constructions, which process these traces for tracking purposes. Tracking-led accounts are characterized by a tight fit, if not identity, between the tracking and accounting in the form of primary indicators of an object. For example, control devices like dashboards and scorecards are common ways of both tracking and accounting, bringing together a variety of performance metrics. Tracking-led accounts might include visual "maps" of citizen movements, workplace attendance scores, social credit scorecards (black and red lists), risk-profile reports, dashboard summaries of operating performance, evaluations of logistical performances, not to mention a host of private self-tracking reports, enabled by smart phones and wearables, on aspects of personal health and sociality.

Tracking-led accounts also encompass "profiling", a practice that has its history in the criminological sciences (e.g. profile factors associated with likelihood to offend), insurance services (e.g. risk profiling of smokers, young male drivers), employment screening practices, and many other fields, including medicine. While profiles may appear specific and individuated, they are also products of classification practices that construct objects for tracking. Indeed, a distinctive from of tracking-led accounting involves the traceification of behaviour by digital devices and the datafication of these traces to enable the building of classifications based on statistical associations (Alaimo and Kallinikos, 2020). It may be argued that such profiles and patterns are not themselves "accounting", and that this is stretching the meaning of accounts too far. But the thesis of this book is that digital datafication, as a distinct form and manifestation of traceification, is changing accounting. So there can be no doubt that such profiles are a kind of aggregate "account of the self"; they are outcomes of algorithmic "calculative practices" in the service of tracking as observation. And profiles, as tracking–led accounts of the self and the patterns they reveal, have also come to be regarded as economic assets—"surveillance assets", according to Zuboff (2022)—in their own right with a promise of commercially valuable predictive power. Many examples of tracking-led accounts are therefore surveillance- and control-based, and there has been much critical analysis about the non-consensual nature of the digital trace extraction upon which they are often based. We address some of these issues further in Chapter 8, not least the manner in which profiles as accounts can become a kind of "data double" that is generative for humans.

It must be emphasized that this proposed duality of accounting-led tracking and tracking-led accounting is an *ideal typical* formulation and is introduced to suggest a tension in how we account for self, organization and society. Empirically the world of accounts described in Chapter 1 does not divide itself up neatly in this way, and it is not proposed that one mode of accounts production is ethically superior to another. In fact, specific instances of accounting practice will always be combinations of both top-down accounts-led tracking, which emphasizes possibilities for oversight and broad accountability, and bottom-up tracking-led accounts, which emphasize possibilities for surveillance and more restricted forms of accountability. Hence, the theoretical issue is not a choice between one or the other but rather to understand how accounting practices can be analysed as configurations and combinations of these ideal types, what we shall call the "tracking-oversight" mix.[4] What is at stake for the accounts we live by is that a digital datafication "undertow" (Orlikowski and Scott, 2023) is shifting this mix systemically towards a more tracking-led accounting emphasis with potential consequences for human oversight capacity (see Chapter 6). At the not entirely imaginary extreme, tracking-led accounts can arise from machine-learning-based tracking that has no specific purpose other than to explore and to collect and process traces into higher-order patterns. On this view, accounts, if they exist at all, are reduced to contingent epiphenomena of tracking, which becomes its own purpose. In effect, and in contrast to accounts-led tracking, tracking-led accounts are premised on tracking as an end in itself.

Table 2.1 provides a stylized summary representation of how the distinction between accounts-led tracking and tracking-led accounts relates to the three value-purposes of traceability outlined in Chapter 1.

In each of six cells of Table 2.1, there is an example of an "account" that reflects a dominant traceability purpose and an accounts-led or tracking-led emphasis. It is proposed that under conditions of digital datafication, the right-hand column

Table 2.1 Traceability Value-Purposes and Ideal-Typical Accounts

		The accounts we live by	
		Accounts-led tracking: Emphasis on second-order observation (OVERSIGHT)	Tracking-led accounts: Emphasis on first-order observation (TRACKING)
Value-purposes of traceability	Quality	e.g. annual financial audit reports; annual safety certifications; university research rankings	e.g. wine labels; drug batch controls; foodstuff bar codes
	Security	e.g. quarterly AML reports to regulators; environmental risk reports by NGOs	e.g. air traffic separation live reporting; facial recognition software; KYC risk profiles
	Discovery	e.g. peer evaluation of scientific work; periodic research impact assessments; verdicts in criminal court cases	e.g. dashboards for self-monitoring of health; platform-enabled customer ratings; entries on whistleblowing social media sites

Abbreviations: AML = anti-money-laundering; NGO = nongovernmental organization; KYC = know your customer.

[4] Oversight is a form of surveillance and vice versa. Hence we need a more complex, nuanced and less negative notion of surveillance in which it can be both generative and controlling (Alaimo and Kallinikos, 2024, ch. 5). Yet, despite their overlapping nature, we reserve the idea of oversight for the possibility of human-centric forms of accountability.

of this table is growing in significance, representing a broad shift in the mix from an oversight to a tracking emphasis. Within this shift, accounts-led tracking and its associated styles of public governance are being progressively displaced and weakened.

Finally, it is necessary to note that accounts are temporally structured; they are always accounts produced "in time" in two ways, one of which has become highly consequential for human beings. First, formal accounting practices in which traces are aggregated into reports often have stable temporal *rhythms* of production (e.g. quarterly reports, annual budgets, daily operational reviews, and real-time monitoring). Studies have addressed how this temporal structuring disciplines different workplaces and controls labour via time management. Second, accounting practices are forms of collective and individual memorizing and projection; this is the temporal duality mentioned in Chapter 1. Accounts also embody and institutionalize a mix of temporal *horizons* that shape how humans, organizations, and societies project both forward and backwards in time (Quattrone, 2015; Matringe and Power, 2024; Chua et al., 2024). For example, the pull of long backward temporal horizons corresponds to notions of tradition and its influence, which will impact the projective, imaginative, and expressive aspects of accounts. Yet temporal duality also raises a broader question of the extent to which accounting time horizons influence, and are influenced by, traceability capacity. Given the existential urgency of climate change, in what sense can we trace and account for the future in a way that institutionalizes longer temporal horizons for decision-making? These questions will be addressed in more depth in Chapter 7, but for now it is important to note that the accounts we live by also reflect the temporalities that we live by. Tracking-led accounts in Table 2.1 correspond to not only an increase in both granularity and frequency of accounts production, but also a potential shortening of temporal depth (Reinicke and Lawrence, 2023).

To conclude: in this section, we have developed the notion of tracking and have advanced two ideal-typical versions of the traceability-accounts nexus. The empirical operationalization of traceability value-purposes discussed in Chapter 1 will vary empirically in terms of how they blend these two modes of traceification and accounts production, and whether tracking practice leads as an end itself or is led as a means. Accounting, as we shall see in Chapter 3, is understood by many scholars as making organizations and individuals observable and visible and has therefore always been partly a form of surveillance. Indeed, Foucault's panopticon has been a powerful metaphor for how accounting not only disciplines through making its subjects feel as if they are seen, but also is generative of selfhood and enabling of new capacities (Miller and O'Leary, 1987). Hence, we need to adopt a nuanced conceptualization of surveillance that is sensitive to both its generative and disciplinary features. All accounts are hybrids of tracking and oversight, which combine these nuances of surveillance. The thesis of a shift in the accounts we live by is about how technology is changing the composition of this accounting hybridity. This is ultimately an empirical question for which this book provides a number of pointers.

Organizing Traceability

In Chapter 1, we considered the value-orientations or purposes of traceability and identified three broad categories. We also argued for a more expansive view of accounting and the accounts we live by. In this chapter, we have probed the traceability-accounting nexus in more depth by addressing the nature of traces as compared with data, adopting a processual approach in which traces are outcomes of traceification. We then focused on the notion of tracking as a practice that is enabled by traceification to "mark" its objects of interest, constituting them and endowing them with evidentiary status. Finally, we argued for a model of accounts as an inherent hybrid of two ideal types—accounts-led tracking and tracking-led accounts. These four elements—value-purposes, traceification, tracking, and accounts—and the practice bundles that operationalize and *connect* them to each other, underpin the collective organization of traceability.

This organization of traceability can be understood in terms of a dynamic duality of "platform" and "application". In other words, conceptually we can distinguish between a system that materializes traceability *potential* and the practices of trace production, tracking, and accounts that *actualize* traceability according to one or more of the three value-purposes or logics. We discuss this dynamic duality of platform and application further in Chapter 4, but we are agnostic about any supposed rational or functional design of the organization of traceability. Historical analysis may reveal explicit and intended design in some cases, but many of the practice elements of traceification, tracking, and accounting have emerged incrementally and often as responses to events. In this sense, organized traceability is more like a "complex", defined by the *Oxford English Dictionary* as "made of many different things or parts that are connected; difficult to understand" (OED, accessed 29 December 2025). This concept of complex certainly applies to that of "infrastructure" (Power, 2019; see also Chapter 4) and is preferred here for its affinities with Foucault's notion of *dispositif*, which references the heterogeneity of the elements—ideas, laws, technologies, devices, and inscriptions—that get connected to each other (see Miller and Power, 2013, pp. 586–587 and endnote 3).[5]

[5] The four elements of Miller and Power's (2013) "accounting complex" loosely correspond to themes to be discussed in this book. Territorializing relates to purposes and boundaries; mediating relates to the theme of connectivity (Chapter 4); subjectivizing relates to the theme of selves and performance (Chapter 8); and adjudication relates to the theme of governance (Chapters 5 and 6).

Viewed as a complex, specific purposes of traceability and their sites of articulation may be more or less coherent, more or less intended or emergent, and more or less contested and political. Furthermore, the practices of traceification that define, collect, and utilize relevant traces for tracking according to purposes can also be diverse. In turn, these practices must usually demonstrate their conformity to, and fulfilment of, the purposes and accountabilities that animated them by producing accounts that have their own life and are expertise-based. For these reasons, the coherence, durability, and directionality of the connectivities between elements of traceability as a "complex" should not be assumed.

This notion of a traceability complex of linked but heterogeneous work processes generates a number of questions, which this book addresses at the conceptual level:

1. *Value-purposes*: Why trace? What is the concern (quality, security, discovery)? What risks and accountabilities motivate traceability? What institutional structures enable it? What is their primary focal object: people, processes, or things? Is traceability becoming its own purpose?
2. *Traceification/Datafication*: How and why are specific traces produced and endowed with meaning for practices? How are traces converted into data? How do data, objects, and inscriptions come to count as traces?
3. *Tracking*: What forms of tracking *practice* are afforded and enabled by varieties of traceification? What kinds of first-order observation are made possible, and with what reach?
4. *Accounts*: What forms of accounting are produced based on tracking? How are accounts-led tracking and tracking-led accounts combined? What are the consequences of a shift in emphasis towards tracking-led accounts?

The schema in Figure 2.2 explicitly represents the traceability complex as four practice clusters related by their mutual co-formation and dependence. Such a model of a "complex" threatens to contradict itself with functionalist abstraction and over-rationalization, but it has the merit of making possible the visualization, mapping, and comparison of different traceability arrangements (see Chapter 6). To repeat: empirically the elements of the traceability complex can be more or less tightly or loosely integrated, depending on their institutional and organizational contexts. Thus, *value-purposes* may have their own politics of formation and can embody many different kinds of accountability; *traceification-enabled tracking* may be more or less developed as a form of observation; and *accounts* can be ad hoc and random epiphenomena of other practices. Furthermore, there is considerable co-production of these elements; we know that accounting practices can generate a search for the purposes in whose name they are conducted. Equally, accounting purposes can drive the

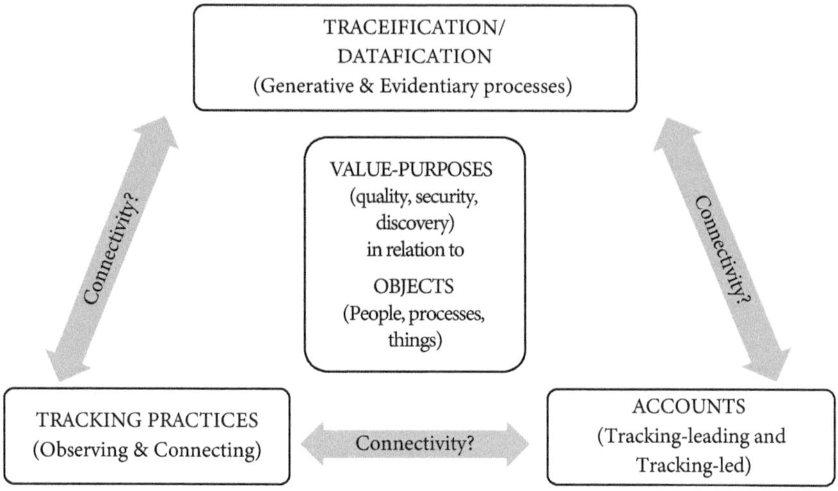

Figure 2.2 The traceability complex model.

production of traces. The precise nature of these co-formative dynamics depends on the setting and its historical organization of traceability.

In terms of the empirical analysis of traceability complexes, existing laws, regulations, and the accounts embodying purposes are likely to be their most publicly observable features. Practices of traceification are more difficult to access, and tracking practices will often and increasingly be embedded in, and features of, broader information and control infrastructures, making them harder to identify discretely. They need to be "dug out" to enable the analysis of how they generate modes of observability that are sufficient for specific practice communities. Yet, notwithstanding these barriers to empirical analysis, we can think of each of the four practice-clusters as existing in multidirectional dynamic relations with each other, and in a continuous process of development, not least due to continuing technological changes and new capabilities for tracking.

The example of geographically dispersed food supply chains brings out some of the potential dynamics of the traceability complex idea. In this setting, notions of purpose have expanded well beyond food quality and logistical efficiency, to encompass a wide range of sustainability and human rights concerns; locational traces are produced by digital technologies such as GPS, enabling precise tracking of point of harvest; and digital tags also enable the tracking of foodstuffs on their journey to customers. In turn, these developments have generated greater commitment by suppliers and intermediaries to invest in the improved connectivity and the interoperability of their systems; and accounts of food quality and sustainability can be given in the form of labels and certifications that are intended to enhance product and producer reputation, and which themselves can in principle be audited or verified. As this traceability complex and its associated expectations coalesce, defective traceability has become a new operational and reputational risk for supply-chain participants. This supply-chain setting also shows how there are no a priori assumptions to be made about the jurisdictional and operating boundaries of the traceability complex; it is spatially and temporally fluid, for which Figure 2.2 provides a very simple preliminary analytic structure.

To conclude, following Bowker et al. (2019, p. 8), we can think of traceability complexes as linked bundles of practices—aspirational, material, and processual—which, in some settings, as we discuss in Chapter 8, are generating new forms of self-tracking and sociality. In addition, it must be emphasized that what we may call from time to time in this book a "trace" has no meaning or ontology outside of its generated role in traceability complexes. And, notwithstanding the conceptualization that supports Figure 2.2, it is just a working template, and the empirical organization of traceability will not be as coherent as this. Traceability in action is more of a bricolage in which fragmented *centres of traceability*—operational departments, board committees, regulatory agencies, suppliers, and so forth—get linked together and mobilized across geographic and organizational spaces.[6] However, the traceability complex model is also important as a first step in building a *traceological theorization of accounting*, to be elaborated further in later chapters. Rather than emphasising power of quantification and/or the role of accounts in decision-making, such a theory focuses on practices of traceification, tracking, and accounting and how they are linked together in audit trails. Indeed, as we will see in the next chapter, the traceability complex and its connectivity can be understood as a form of audit trail.

Conclusions

This chapter began with a philosophical excursus into the notion of the trace as a concept with a rich and varied history, and which is always in relation to, but distinct from, the idea of data. This discussion alighted on a more processual treatment of traces, encapsulated in the idea of traceification as a practice that is both generative of objects for datafication and also of evidentiary connectedness between objects. We then considered tracking as a traceification-enabled practice, and revisited the relations between tracking and accounting to develop two ideal-types: accounts-led tracking and tracking-led accounts. While these

[6] For example, Bach (2020) shows how the Chinese social credit experiment is a network of legacy systems, built on ideas of financial credit that become extended to the tracking of moral credit.

two ideal types are always found in combination, the thesis of this book is that the mix is shifting towards the latter under conditions of advanced digitization and datafication. Finally, the argument builds cumulatively on Chapter 1 to develop the model of a "traceability complex", understood in terms of the dynamic relations of mutual formation and connectedness between value-purposes, traceification/datafication, tracking, and accounting. In effect, the traceability complex as an analytic device provides both a template for empirical analysis and the skeleton for a traceological theorization of accounting, which subsequent chapters will develop.

Chapter 2 Summative Propositions

The following propositions articulate the linkages between key concepts and introduce the distinction between accounts-led tracking and tracking-led accounts:

1. **A trace is any object, inscription, document, process, thing, electrical pulse, datum that is generated, constructed, and attributed as a "trace of" and signifier of something of interest relative to a practice.**
2. **Traceification is the process by which traces are generated for specific practical purposes under proposition 1.**
3. **Datafication is the semiotic, technical, and institutional work of converting traces into durable, mobile, and commensurable forms supporting further levels of articulation and fact-building.**
4. **Tracking is a trace-enabled practice by which an observer is connected to, and can act upon, as well as account for, an object of interest. Tracking practices will vary in terms of their "observational reach" and connectivity across space and time.**
5. **Tracking-led accounts emphasize the first-order observation of things and people.**
6. **Accounts-led tracking emphasizes the second-order observation of first-order tracking for a range of oversight and governance purposes.**
7. **The accounting mix is shifting systematically to emphasize tracking-led accounts with a corresponding weakening of accounts-led tracking and associated forms of oversight.**
8. **A traceability complex is the organization of traceability in which value-purposes, practices of traceification, datafication, tracking, and accounting are connected.**

3
Toward a Traceological Theory of Accounting

Overview

Sometime in late 1983 I joined the firm of Deloitte Haskins & Sells in London as a trainee accountant and auditor. My induction included a three-week introductory course in bookkeeping. Having studied philosophy for the previous seven years, this technical training was new and challenging. I could not see it at the time but, in retrospect, that introductory course was not merely the learning of an important technical skill for the preparation and analysis of financial accounts. It was also a process of socialization into the worldview of accounting and auditing. This worldview is a normative order or rationality based on the elegance, balance, and precision of double-entry bookkeeping. The introductory course also dealt with fundamental and consequential assumptions about the conditions of possibility for accounting: the need for well-defined accounting entities with clear boundaries; presumptions about the future orderly continuation of the entity in terms of "going concern"; and the need to quantify the representation of economic performance in financial statements (entfication, temporality, and quantification).

In 1983 I was so immersed in learning the art of accounts preparations, its rules and regulations, that I could not see the broader normative power that is plain to scholars of accounting, namely that some version of these humble techniques underpins every formal organization and is bound up with their very "organizationality". Yet, there was also something else in that introduction to bookkeeping, something seemingly so mundane and foundational that it has not been the object of critical reflection. It was the "audit trail".

It is reasonable to assume that one can only account for things, people, and processes if there is already some underlying connective infrastructure that facilitates their observation and enables them to be tracked by different interested agencies. For example, financial accounting and auditing practices for tracking and recording the performance of an organization are dependent on some underlying system, track, or chain that connects and combines the many parts into a whole. In this chapter, we address and analyse a distinctive mode of this connectivity, namely the "audit trail". It is a notion that originates in, and is strongly associated with, financial accounting practice, as the opening vignette

Economy of Traces. Michael Power, Oxford University Press. © Oxford University Press (2026).
DOI: 10.1093/9780197681527.003.0003

of this chapter suggests, but which is also an organizing logic with wider significance and reach (Power, 2021a). For this reason, audit trails as modes of connectivity are worthy of further analysis, especially because they are undergoing fundamental change in the digital age, with implications for the accounts we live by. Furthermore, in what follows, these underlying connective and combinatorial features of audit trails are the basis for a traceological theory of accounting practice.

We approach this traceological agenda by revisiting key themes in critical accounting studies in order to comprehend the institutional and cultural power of accounting. First, we review how this power is grounded in the abstractive and quantificational qualities of accounting, qualities that in phenomenological terms can be said to generate the *facticity* of accounting numbers. More specifically, we consider the manner in which accounting plays a key role in the so-called "economization" of organizations. In this respect, accounting does more than generate partial representations of organizations that acquire facticity; it also performs and constitutes them as entities oriented to economic values. Second, the analysis of economization provides the pretext for a consideration of the relationship between accounting and values. This accounting-value nexus is increasingly visible in the expansion of efforts and experiments to generate forms of accounting constituted by a variety of different values and concerns. In these emerging settings, the very nature and quality of the connectivity between data relevant to these values and the accounts they compose are major issues.

As important and compelling as these critical accounting studies are, they do not fully theorize the mechanisms by which the power and facticity of accounting are produced and maintained by audit trail structures, an issue especially important for the many attempts to generate new value-based accounts. What may be broadly described as "inscriptivist" theories of accounting, drawing on the insights of Latour and many others, provide more in the way of such micro-structures and point towards the formative significance of practices of trace production, emphasizing the power of tracking over that of quantification as such. The discussion of these inscriptivist studies, in which accounting is conceptualized as writing and script, are strongly suggestive of an explicitly *traceological* theorization of accounting in which the audit trail is central, and which inverts conventional ways of thinking about the traceability-accounting relationship.

Broadly speaking, audit trails are arrangements and transformations of connected traces. While Chapter 4 discusses the nature of this connectivity, here the focus is on the traces that ground the audit trail. In Chapter 2 it was argued that there can be no tracing/tracking without the "marking" or primary traceification of an object to be traced/tracked and made observable. These traces are the building blocks of specific traceability and accounting practices. They are the marks, tags, and inscriptions that enable the tracking of objects and events that cannot otherwise be observed and followed directly. Primary traceification selectively *constitutes* these trackable objects by materializing essentially transient events and activities, and by providing them with an inscriptive or documentary reality and stability. It is proposed that such primary traces can be mechanisms by which organizations become deeply economized, but they also have a potential to embed and generate the facticity of other values.

The Power of Accounting

In Chapter 1, we situated accounting within a well-established relational model of accounting and accountability, "ABC," in which A provides an account B to C. Accountability here has two faces, being both account-*ability* as the capability of an A to produce an appropriate account for C and *account*-ability as the institutional and expectational requirement for A to do so. Accountability relations in this sense may define multi-organizational relations or may be deeply embedded in organizations (Roberts and Scapens, 1985). Beyond its simple formality, the ABC triad may be specified by a rich variety of relations and accounting forms, from the conditions of everyday interaction to formal contractual arrangements to the naked exercise of power. In Chapter 1 we also noted how the accounts B that connect As and Cs may be agentic in their own right as mediators of values and as features of powerful "acts of organizing" (Latour, 2013). In addition, Chapter 1 suggested how accounting encompasses many different ways of narrating the performance of individuals, organizations, and states. Reflecting this breadth, Chapman, Cooper, and Miller (2009) define it as:

> all those spatially and historically varying *calculative* practices—ranging from budgeting to fair value accounting—that allow accountants and others to *describe and act* on entities, processes and persons. (p. 1, emphases added)

Accounting so defined includes published income statements and balance sheets, numeric and narrative disclosures, budgets, plans and costing estimates, rankings, ratings, solvency ratios, sustainability metrics, performance indicators, risk registers, costing-analysis, balanced scorecards, diversity scores, "value at risk" (VAR) measures, questionnaires, and even lists (Gawande, 2010; Crvelin and Lohlein, 2022). As noted in Chapter 1, the scope of accounting seems to have no limit, as new objects of concern like "student satisfaction", "patient experience", and "research impact" come to be defined and refined via emerging attempts to account for them (e.g. Pflueger, 2016). These many different accountings vary greatly in their degree of institutional stability and standardization, in their public visibility, in their intended audiences, and in the underlying data and forms of traceification from which they are produced. Yet they constitute a broad and growing family of calculative practices and metrics, which define and quantify, in both financial and non-financial terms, ever more diverse aspects of human and organizational activity and frame it as accountable performance. We suggested that there may be no a priori limit to the range of things that can count as accounting and which are part of organizing individual and collective life. Accounting at the organizational level may appear different in kind because of its greater elaboration, technical rationalization, and expertise demands, but it nevertheless shares something in common with a personal diary in which someone records daily expenditure. Furthermore, social media and platforms have undoubtedly become significant producers of accounts of many different kinds as users are enrolled in their operations. Notwithstanding this breadth and variety, the power of accounting to gain attention and shape experience and action also has something to do with its abstractive qualities, which we now consider.

Abstraction

One of the theoretical puzzles of accounting in its various calculative forms is that it is a practice whose "practicality" or efficacy is based on reduction and abstraction from the specific features of a setting. For example, financial accounting has become powerful precisely because it abstracts from organizational specificities and imposes its own typologies for quantifying and representing organizational and individual performance. Accounting is in large part a process of conceptualizing organizations and individuals in such a way as to make their performance commensurable and comparable across time and space. The effect of these reductions, both in terms of general classifications and of quantifying performance, is to constitute accounting, somewhat paradoxically, as a profoundly "theoretical practice" (Espeland and Stevens, 1998; Astley and Zammuto, 1992, p. 455; Strang and Meyer, 1993), meaning that it is a practice whose practical efficacy and normative diffusion depend on abstraction from the specific features of a person or organization.

This abstractive character of accounting is a necessary, but not usually sufficient, condition of its power to shape organizations. Indeed, many critical or "counter-accountings" seek to bring the abstracted-from features and values back into partial performance representations, and to re-embed accounting in its context. Hence there is an underlying tension and dialectic in all accounting practice, between an orientation to values of comparability and of individuality, between the imagination of standardized universality and an often resistant and vernacular locality (Kilfoyle et al., 2013), and between the abstract and concrete. These tensions give rise to considerable variation in abstraction and to a continuous interplay between extremes, producing and reproducing accounting hybridization and multiplication in waves of action and reaction in accounting innovation, not least at the margins of accepted practice (Miller, 1998). For example, accounting devices like the balanced scorecard are themselves hybrid accounting forms that seek to overcome the hegemony and singularity of economic reductionism and yet often end up reproducing it via the de facto dominance of financial metrics. Similarly, hybrid accounting forms are visible in the development of indicators for ESG (environment, social, and governance), which often begin life in organizationally specific forms with weak data quality, thereby disabling comparativity across space and time (Kotsantonis and Serafeim, 2019). In addition, there is much debate about the use of GAAP (generally accepted accounting principles; standardized) and non-GAAP (non-standardized) measures in financial reporting as organizations seek to communicate their distinctiveness to the market as well as their similarity to comparator peers (Black et al., 2021). In short, while accounting is a "theorizing" and "abstracting" practice, it is also always changing and adjusting to overflows and counter-values which problematize that same abstraction.

For Latour (1986, 2013), abstraction has a particular meaning in the context of moving from three-dimensional objects to their representation in two-dimensional documents and even digitization. Abstraction on this view is not a singular conceptual quality but an empirically observable process at the heart of knowledge production. As a process, it involves work to generate "light" and durable inscriptions and traces, which become connected in data production, and which lead to "scaling-up" in the sense of generating representations that seem to be a view "from nowhere" and simply how the world is. As we shall see in this chapter and in Chapter 4, this work of abstraction is a feature of the audit trail and its modes of traceification. The process of turning things into numbers—*quantification*—is an especially important and powerful form of abstraction at the heart of many accounting practices, and is the source of a rich body of critical work on its effects.

Quantification and Facticity

The way the world appears to us as a world that has exteriority and temporality has greatly puzzled many philosophers, such as Husserl (1970), Heidegger (2013), and Merleau-Ponty (1968). This puzzlement has motivated their enquiries into the fundamental structure of experience, enquiries known under the broad label of *phenomenology* (see also Chapter 7). The experience of the "givenness" of the world, or what can be called its "facticity", reflects our existential condition; we are just thrown into life and must learn to navigate it. To varying degrees, phenomenology and the pragmatism of Peirce and others, discussed in Chapter 2, share an underlying perspective that was formalized earlier by the philosopher Kant, namely that we human subjects inject a great deal of structure into what counts as experience. In other words, the exteriority and temporality of the so-called objective world is self-produced in some general sense (Friedland, 2017).

These basic phenomenological insights and analyses largely operate at the level of experience in general. Yet they have influenced more specific investigations of organizational reality and practices of representing that reality, like accounting (Holt and Sandberg, 2011; Chua et al., 2024). By taking a more "social turn" in the phenomenological programme, the philosophical puzzle becomes empirical in nature, namely, how do specific representations of the world acquire and maintain their facticity, or not, for human agents in their ongoing sense-making and world building? How and why do we live by some of these accounts and not others? This is not a question to be answered by philosophical reflection alone but also by careful attention to the manner in which the exteriority of the world and the facticity of our representations of it are produced in, ground, and sustain practices. Berger and Luckman (1966, p. 49) follow this underlying approach by arguing that "objectivation" (i.e. the experience of objectivity) is produced by social actors. And as Garfinkel (1984a [1967], p. 33) puts it: "every feature of an activity's sense, *facticity*, objectivity, accountability, communality is to be treated as a contingent accomplishment of socially organized common practices" (p. 33, emphasis added).

This notion of facticity should not be confused with truth. "Fake news" (Allcott and Gentzkow, 2017), "false" numbers (Lampland, 2010), "bad" measures (Dambrin and Robson, 2011), and "selective disclosures" (Marquis et al., 2016) can all acquire facticity in that they can be taken to refer, albeit imperfectly, to how the world is. Facticity in this sense is the outcome of a distinctive kind of sense-making that exteriorizes and naturalizes values and representations, as Berger and Luckmann show. The issue for both phenomenological analysis and its sociological variants is to understand how specific forms of facticity are formed (or not) and maintained (Berger and Luckmann, 1966, p. 78) and how they become widely taken for granted by some social actors but not by others.

It is likely that the experienced facticity of quantification may vary across individuals and groups. Accountants may be able to "look" through numbers to grasp how they are assumption-laden and arbitrary, but non-specialists may see them as simply showing economic "facts". Quantification is often regarded as the most important and even paradigmatic source of facticity, but this is closely related to the cultural position of numbers in the sciences and their role in the production of our knowledge of the objective world (Drori and Meyer, 2006). Accounting numbers can generate a distinctive "administrative objectivity", and this is as much an institutional, rather than a phenomenological, feature of their quantified form (Porter, 1996; Douglas, 1986). Hence, facticity can be a variable and uneven feature of specific accounting practices; they are not a mirror of reality but are rather mechanisms by which humans live, encounter, and further construct fluid and evolving realities (Quattrone, 2015). Not all forms of accounting quantification are equally generative of facticity. For institutional and cultural reasons, some become more powerful and agentic than others, in particular those that express and reproduce economic values.

Accounting and Economization

Human actors, at least for some of the roles they inhabit, see themselves through the lens of accounting representations of their performance (Chapman, Cooper, and Miller, 2009; Dent, 1991; Mazmanian and Beckman, 2018). At its most basic, accounting has cognitive effects: it generates the visibility of a field of practical concern and is attention-directing. It has also been argued that accounting disciplines and "subjectivizes" human actors in that it provides not just an orientation but also self-identification and self-definition in terms of the accounted-for performance (see Chapter 8). The strongest claimed effect is where the accounting somehow shapes and formats the very context of its operations. In other words, accounting representations are "performative" of the very practice reality to which they refer, and there is strong and tight recursive feedback relation between the two (Callon, 1998; Mackenzie, Muniesa, and Siu, 2007). Specifically, studies demonstrate how accounting is implicated in performing and constituting organizations as economic entities by encoding and projecting powerful representations of performance, representations that abstract from idiosyncratic and contextual specificities, including values, such as the gender, race, or well-being of employees. This is *economization* (Miller and Power, 2013).

Accounting is a source of economization in the specific sense that it has the potential to transform conceptions of organizations and persons into, and intensify them as, individuated, standardized entities that are more or less oriented to prioritize economic performance (Espeland and Hirsch, 1990; Mennicken and Espeland, 2019). Yet, this process of economization is far from being one-directional. It is not simply that accounting more or less "implements" economic ideas. It has been shown that economic theories also draw heavily on accounting concepts (Klamer and McCloskey, 1992) and that accounting and economics have emerged as mutually legitimizing bodies of knowledge (Hopwood, 1992;

Vollmer, Mennicken, and Preda, 2009). Indeed, one of the reasons that there may be difficulty in accepting the broad view of accounting proposed in Chapter 1 is because of this specific conceptual affinity between accounting and the economics of information, which is reproduced in textbook pedagogy and research (see Chapter 9).

Today we take for granted and "naturalize" the fact that the economy can be imagined and modelled as an accounting system (Morgan, 2012). Yet, as Callon and Latour have shown, the economy and the markets that compose it have had to be carved out, dis-embedded, and formatted (by accounting) as discrete domains of action and modes of existence; "If *economies* are the outcome of *economics*, as Michel Callon has argued, the humble paper tools allowing coordination are at once placed in the foreground" (Latour, 2005, pp. 229–230; italics in original). Economic theory itself therefore plays an important role in this carving-out process, at least indirectly. It has also been shown that the performativity of economic ideas requires many "felicitous" material conditions (Marti and Gond, 2018), and accounting practices embody this material enabling potential. Indeed, in drawing on economic notions of cost and efficiency, they also operationalize them as sources of further economic theorizing. For example, cost of patient care was a "conceptual idea promoted by health economists but, without accounting, it could not become operational as an 'organizational fact'" (Hopwood, 1992, p. 141). In short, accounting can be analysed as a vehicle for economization and as a distinctive and powerful form of organizational facticity insofar as it operationalizes and mediates economic ideas, enabling them under certain conditions to be jointly constitutive of both economies and the organizations that make them up. Overall, the role of accounting in the economization of organizations suggests more generally that representations and metrics are not only, if at all, oriented functionally towards "better" decision-making. Rather, accounting is a more or less explicit carrier and mediator of values, such as precision and rationality (Carruthers and Espeland, 1991), as well as assumptions concerning the boundedness of organizations from their environments (Hines, 1988).

The different nuances of economization and performativity are much debated by accounting and organization theorists, not least because accounting practices also require many other agencies and conditions (their own "felicity conditions") to bring about organizational change. And given that such conditions also have their own conditions of formation, this seems tantamount to reducing performativity to the trivial idea that processes of change are essentially relational and depend on many things (D'Adderio et al., 2019; Garud and Gehman, 2019). Yet, we have to remember that performativity-based theorizations of accounting became attractive to scholars as part of a general reaction against unidirectional models of the relation between accounting information and human behaviour.[1] Indeed, it is now well known that human actors use accounting information not only reactively to make informed decisions but also to rationalize and defend decisions (Burchell et al., 1980). Furthermore, the very idea of a "decision" is something that emerges from, and is performed, by accounting in its recursive relationship with behaviour (cf. March, 1987; Chia, 1994). Studies also draw attention to the endemically changing and "failing" nature of accounts, such that they need constant attention and repair if they are not to come to an end (Palermo et al., 2022). Even forms of accounting recognized to be false and imperfect may become accepted at specific times and places, and what was once regarded as nonsense or too subjective can come to be institutionalized and normalized (Miller, 1991; Power, 1992). We should also not think of accounting practices and their performative and facticity-generating potential in singular terms but rather as hybrid clusters of related activities, which may be gathered and jointly represented in "balanced scorecards" and "dashboards" and which may allow for selectivity and switching.

In summary, we have considered three much-discussed features of accounting practices that underpin their power and reach into our personal and organizational lives: they are abstracting, quantifying, and economizing. The processual emphasis of this formulation is important—they are each dynamic and often conflictual processes that define the arc of a politics of accounting in which different values compete for representation and attention. Yet the many studies that address these processes tend to overlook their traceological foundations. The very act of *traceification*, as defined in Chapter 2, is inherently abstractive and reductive. Quantifying is as much a technology for *tracking* as it is for measurement and valuation. Economizing is also hard-wired into the audit trails that connect data to valued performance representations. And, to come full circle, the accounting facticity of the economic begins with traceification. Before we develop these traceological features in more detail and argue for their theoretical merit, the economizing tendencies of accounting practices necessitate a step back to consider the broader question of accounting and values.

Accounts and Values

Many critical studies tend to argue that accounting and its abstractions are value-deforming, not least because non-economic values can become sidelined. Accounting is held responsible for the one-dimensional economization

[1] The "behavioural turn" in accounting research was itself significant as a critical challenge to presumptions about the relation between accounting and decision-making. See Hopwood and Miller (1994); March (1987); Miller and Power (2013).

of organizational life (Townley, 1997; McGivern and Ferlie, 2007) in which the "language of indicators takes over the language of service" (Strathern, 2000b, p. 314). Accounting and quantification are said to threaten and distort human identities, dilute many values in the name of commensurability, and lead to goal-displacement and gaming in organizations (Hood, 1995; Bevan and Hood, 2006). The transparency of performance that accounting delivers is also paradoxical in its effects when intrinsic value-based motivations are crowded out by control and monitoring practices in organizations (Frey and Jegen, 2001; Falk and Kosfeld, 2006; Bernstein, 2012). In reaction to this economization and one-dimensionality, there are widespread attempts to "bring values back in".

The questions of what value is and where it comes from have long preoccupied many philosophers. Some have adopted what we might call a top-down, transcendental, and theological account of the sources of "fundamental" values as rules for living. Others are more pragmatic and bottom-up in orientation, seeing values as the outcome of self-generated human projects in which certain things come to be regarded as essential for human flourishing (Parfit, 1984; Joseph, 2015). And into this mix must be added the thorny and intractable problem of whether values are objective—whatever that means—or subjective—whatever that means. Joas's (2001) historical-philosophical analysis of value suggests, similarly to Levinas as discussed in Chapter 2, that values and value commitments commonly arise in "experiences of self-formation and self-transcendence". We can take this to mean, perhaps controversially, that value commitments are grounded in emergent processes of mutual recognition, not metaphysics.[2] These processes may have a transcendental or theological meaning for human actors, but they only become manifest and real in practices that enact and repeat forms of reciprocity, connection, and orientation to others.

The details of this dual "self-formative" and "other-oriented" process of value accretion have been elaborated in many different ways by different thinkers. But there seems to be wide agreement that there was not first a self, which then becomes social (see also Chapter 8). And, notwithstanding variations in metaphysics and theology, there also seems to be a shared secular and practical core in which value formation is understood as a socio-material process of accumulation arising from repeated and shared actions in conjunction with technologies, like accounting (Bergen and Verbeek, 2021). Such actions may be codified in frameworks, rituals, and systems over time, such as codes of ethics and even formal laws. Indeed, this more processual conception of the generation of values grounded in sociality suggests that the famous analytical distinction between "fact" and "value" is itself something that has emerged from a specific

[2] Nietzsche's ethics is counter-Christian. He refers to this emergent reciprocity as a "low" value generated by the "herd".

cultural milieu and has become axiomatic for Western rationality, notwithstanding many critiques of its coherence. By adopting a more processual and material approach to value, we can recover a sense of the co-formation of fact and value as humans navigate the world, constitute themselves collectively within socio-material assemblages, and make values real and actionable via a multiplicity of connected inscriptions, including accounts.

From this general viewpoint, values are not external inputs into practice routines, although they may be experienced as such. Indeed, since Durkheim's analysis of "social facts", we know that facts and value are intertwined, despite the history of the so-called is-ought problem that Hume had set in motion (see Hudson, 1969). Social worlds as experienced are permeated by norms, conventions, and value commitments that sometimes coalesce and stabilize as action-orienting social facts embodied and embedded in technologies. These norms have been variously analysed as "logics" (Friedland and Alford, 1991) and "orders of worth" (Boltanski and Thevenot, 2006), which point to fact/value complexes that orient practices, are experienced as external, and are cognitively compelling. This is what can be called—to come back to phenomenological language—the *facticity* of value.

As with the earlier discussion of accounting facticity, the facticity of value can be understood as the manner in which it is experienced as a feature of the natural order of things, even to the extent of being embedded in operational routines and institutions. Indeed, following Garfinkel, we have seen how values as commonsensical account-abilities are woven into the fabric of everyday interaction. Yet, at the same time, such embedded facticity—their traceification—is also paradoxically a source of risk to values. Long before the post-phenomenological turn in values (Verbeek, 2011), Selznick argued that values and technical operational practices, like accounting, are formatively intertwined (Besharov and Khurana, 2015). He also suggested that values require *completing* by being expressed and operationalized by technical routines (Selznick, 1957; 1996, p. 273). Similarly, Friedland (2017) argues that values are unable to manifest themselves outside of material and documentary practices. Producing the documentary facticity of values in this way is always a contingent process—values can be transformed by their traceified material realizations. For example, it has been shown that diversity values embodied in law become "managerialized" by organizations in policies and practices, an implementation process that is paradoxically value-dilutive (Edelman et al., 2001; Edelman, 2016). Hence, the produced facticity of values is, as Selznick suggests, a risky outcome of a dialectic between their ideal and operational manifestations. Yet, this riskiness is also a condition of possibility for their actionability and traction (Bernstein, 2017; Wijen, 2014, 2015; Kraatz and Block, 2008; Kraatz et al., 2010, p. 1522; Kraatz and Flores, 2015).

Values are necessarily "at risk", and this is arguably a feature of the human condition. For example, a specific value like diversity may be operationalized in a corporate policy as noted, but it is also derived from what could be regarded as more fundamental values or "goods", such as fairness, respect, and equality, which have themselves emerged as principles from practices of mutual recognition and reciprocity (Joas, 2001). Thus, specific values as operationalizations of more fundamental but less precise and explicit ones necessarily put the latter "at risk". Not only can these fundamental values fail to acquire the necessary facticity to orient action, but they can become compromised as they are operationalized. From this point of view, values are not simply "given" as ends worth pursuing in themselves, although they may come to be experienced in that way, and are often supported by transcendental accounts of their origins. Rather, they are continuously and contingently *formed* as ends that may acquire facticity within technical human practices and even stabilize in institutions, such as the church and law (Haack and Schoeneborn, 2015; Wijen, 2015). This is not to deny or belittle any transcendental warrant for fundamental value precepts but is rather to adopt a more socio-material lens on their genesis and maintenance and on the specific role of accounting in generating value facticity.

Accounting, Traceification, and Value

In the mid-1970s in the United Kingdom, there were attempts to institutionalize the practice of "value added accounting", which sought to represent explicitly how economic value was the outcome of cooperative effort between labour and capital. It was a short-lived experiment in corporate disclosure, and the case demonstrates that accounting change which seeks to promote new values is as precarious as Selznick suggests. Not only did this initiative require societal support and cultural consensus, which evaporated after the election of the Thatcher government in 1979 (Burchell et al., 1985), but we can propose that it also failed due to its lack of strong socio-material grounding. We might put it like this: while there was "surface" accounting recognition of the value and critical role of labour in corporate success, this never became systematically integrated into an infrastructure or platform for trace and data production that could institutionalize and reproduce the facticity of the values it sought to represent. It was easily swept away.

Over the years, there have been many more such experiments to design forms of accounting that express and promote non-economic values and value pluralism. As I write these words, we are in the middle of a new phase of this experimentation with corporate social reporting under the umbrella notion of ESG (environment, social, and governance) metrics and ratings and sustainability reporting. The idea of organizational "performance" is becoming infused with different values, but there remains controversy and debate about how and whether the conventional accountability relations of ABC (see earlier in this chapter) must change their placeholders. If As are corporations, are the Cs their shareholders or other stakeholders, or "biodiverse nature" or future generations? And what is the relation between new value-based accounts and the behaviour of corporations? Do As, as the producers of these new accounts, truly "live by them", or is the accounting some version of "washing"—green or white? Notwithstanding these debates, in which many scholars are deeply engaged, Bs in the form of accounting metrics are constantly evolving, due in part to an increase in traceification and datafication capacities—augmented by advances in digitization—which in turn increase the ambition to define, measure, and report on new objects directly or by proxy. For example, staff happiness and well-being, rather than "satisfaction", have become newly traceified objects for tracking and accounting for many organizations, captured in questionnaires and survey instruments. Indeed, values that might seem inherently narrational and qualitative in form—such as "decency" in the treatment of prisoners—can now be expressed as performance indicators in quantitative form (Guter-Sandu and Mennicken, 2022). Furthermore, *impacts* on communities, environment, and society at large, which might in the past have seemed causally remote from organizational activities, are being quantified and counted as never before, not least in academic life itself (Power, 2015). These and other initiatives are driving the expanded supply of accounts and metrics based on new primary traceifications, noted both in Chapter 1 and earlier in this chapter, a supply that cuts across so-called "civil society" and economy (Horvath, 2023). It is therefore no surprise that controversy and debate have punctuated these developments beyond the fundamentals of accountability: an explosion of indicators has challenged traditional accounting values of reliability, relevance, and materiality; there continues to be competition for authority to set standards in this space and thereby become the single voice of accounting integration (e.g. Busco et al., 2020); and notwithstanding the expansion of capability to track compliance with values, critics remain concerned with the excessive tracking of labour.

All of the many initiatives very briefly described in the preceding represent, at least on the surface, efforts to produce new value-based accounts to motivate and reflect new ways of living collectively and sustainably. The scholarship on these matters is large and growing, with justification given the urgency of the climate issues that we face. Yet despite extensive work by scholars, regulators, and many others, relatively little attention has been given to how such new and alternative accounts can be value-formative and accretive in their power. As Burchell et al.'s (1985) study suggests, new accounts and metrics are often long on purpose and aspiration, but are detached from the technical infrastructures that would give them organizational and institutional stability (Power, 2015). For example, ESG indicators are often ill-defined and plural; data quality is weak or ambivalent; and the very notion of accounting materiality is also unclear—material to whom, shareholders or the planet? In short, the emergent values that mobilize investment in various new metrics and indicators lack a basis for firmly grounding and accumulating their "facticity", despite general arguments about the power of numbers. For this facticity of value to emerge, both techno-phenomenologically and institutionally, it is proposed that the connectivity through which value-conformity can be tracked must be constructed, accounted for, and made auditable. In other words, audit trails and traceification matter to the power and facticity of accounts and the values they embed.

Before we consider the audit trail directly and in more depth, we need to consider a body of scholarship that brings us closer to our proposed traceological perspective on accounting. We call this body of work the "inscriptivist school"; it consists of scholars who emphasize and theorize accounting both as a form of writing and as a source of social organization (Goody, 1986).

Accounting as Writing

It is widely accepted that the earliest forms of human writing were accounting documents (Ezzamel 2012; Robinson, 2009, ch. 1). Indeed, ancient accounting artefacts are traces of interest for archaeologists and anthropologists; they are remnants of the recording practices of the communities that created them. These artefacts are therefore themselves "traces of tracing practices" (i.e. they point to what may be paradoxically describable as a "simple traceability complex"; see Chapter 2) supporting the earliest forms of trade and exchange. Ezzamel and Hoskin (2002) build on this history to argue that accounting is somehow prior, logically and historically, to both writing and money. This is an interesting and important argument because we are tempted to think of the relationship between accounting and money the other way round, namely that accounting is a derived practice, which follows and reflects monetary-based exchange. Yet Ezzamel and Hoskin demonstrate the primordiality of material accounting tokens in the form of clay tablets. The practical use of these tokens must have been based on local agreements that a material thing, such as mark on a tablet, can stand for (i.e. be a primary trace of, and refer to) another thing, which could be an absent commodity that needs to be returned. The token in this setting is therefore indexical in Peirce's sense discussed in Chapter 2. It is an early notational mechanism for marking reference to a specific thing in a world dominated primarily by agriculture. It might or might not represent that thing in any pictographic or iconic sense; it is a system of tracking that is enabled by basic notational registration.

The token has material form as a technology that supplements memory and operationalizes an agreement. And insofar as it encodes such obligations, it is also a moral institution (Verbeek, 2011).

The clay tablet, or rather the mark on it, is traceified and made meaningful to enable the tracking of goods and obligations in the sense of generating "observational reach" across space and time. From a contemporary perspective, we can observe that these explicitly created traces—primary traces, as we discuss further later in the chapter—do not have a valuation purpose; they are purely denotational or referential in nature. Their purpose, we must presume, was a form of accounting hygiene or stewardship as traceability, which supported the reciprocal exchange of commodities.

Ezzamel and Hoskin go further to argue that these material tokens predate, and are the foundations or beginnings of, writing itself as a system of syntactically related signs. In addition, the progressive attribution of value to commodities necessarily begins with these simple designations or marks that function as "traces of. . . ." They call this emergent function of tokens "money of account". In other words, this early tokenized form of accounting is generative of a kind of non-coinage-based money. Money at this early time was not yet independent of these material accounting objects. It could not yet circulate freely in the sense we understand today; this money of account was situationally embedded in the specific exchange.[3] Value is not yet an abstract property of commodities but is an epiphenomenon of bilateral exchange. These indexical forms of accounting-money grounded in material tokens began to change as economic relations moved beyond bilateral transactions and became more complex. Multilateral exchange created functional pressure for a more portable form of money—like coinage—which could circulate in relatively durable form. This emergence of coinage involved the "writing" of standardized value onto metal and, with this innovation, value reciprocity in trade begins to change, to become less situated and more abstract in the sense of mobile and calculable, albeit still tied to the material artefact of a metal coin. In very broad and simplified terms, the concrete indexicality of money is gradually *dis-embedded* from specific exchange settings and acquires, after many centuries of state development, a new institutional referentiality in terms of redeemability in gold, held in the vaults of central banks. It is not long before even this myth of *in specie* backing gives way and money becomes a self-referential belief system.

For Ezzamel and Hoskin, this early history—highly stylized in the preceding summary—shows how accounting begins with mutual needs to track things and related obligations. Hence, we propose that the traceological nature of

[3] Ironically, it is a form of ancient "accounting money" that is presently descriptive of cryptocurrencies. See Caliskan (2020, 2023).

accounting practice necessarily *preceded* its more quantified and calculative forms by many centuries. Tracking, and the relationalities it supports, can be said to be the fundamental form of accounting enabled by the creation of "primary traces". The latter are material tokens with durability, enabling observational reach, albeit initially limited, across space and time. Such traces provided what we shall call "sufficient observability" for each interested party and could be said to constitute a primitive form of economization of their relations.

These early accounting and memorializing practices precede both writing and money, which can be positioned as a "secondary" effect of this primordial accounting and its use of material objects as signs. With the progressive institutionalization of autonomous circulating money noted earlier, the original primacy of accounting is superseded and becomes itself a secondary effect, namely the derived technology of "representing" and shaping the already-constituted-economic-objects as assets/liabilities, which we recognize today. This development is not unusual in itself; practices often generate "supplements" that go on to acquire their own autonomous logic of reproduction. However, Ezzamel and Hoskin's analysis points to something of contemporary, as well historical, interest, namely the significance of marks or inscriptions on the clay slabs as intentionally created primary traces. These traces in effect connect accounting practices to a material world of exchange and reciprocity. They generate a shared and taken-for-granted referentiality that supports the practice of exchange and provides prosthetics for human memory, thereby increasing observational reach across time and space and enabling the tracking of obligations.

While the clay tablets described by Ezzamel and Hoskin were in principle portable, it is likely that they were also cumbersome for humans to transport over long distances. Jumping forward several millennia, critical accounting scholars have explored how the power of accounting consists in its ability to do exactly this: to connect and "act at a distance" across organizations and markets as well as geographies (Robson, 1992; Corvellec, Zapata, and Campos, 2018). These analyses of accounting draw on the work of Latour (1986) and Callon (1984), which emphasizes the significance of *inscriptions/marks* and their mobility for the production of all forms of "modern" knowledge (Robson and Bottausci, 2018). Crucially, this mobility consists partly in their ability to flatten bulky three-dimensional realities into two-dimensional documents (Latour, 1999). Scholars argue that this inscriptive character of accounting also generates the possibility of connectivities in the form of networks that can link ideas and values to actors—human and non-human—in different locations (Burchell et al., 1985; Latour, 1986, pp. 31–32; Miller and Power, 2013). This is mediation and connectivity of a distinctive kind, born of the visibility and observability that durable and "light" accounting inscriptions create as they are transmitted across space and time, and become "contextless". Accounting inscriptions are central to organizing and organizationality (see Chapter 5) because they connect different and often spatially remote "centres of calculation" and, as they do so, they acquire and reproduce networks of support—allies—who reinforce their facticity for specific practice audiences (Qu and Cooper, 2011). For Latour (2013), this myriad of accounting inscriptions that pervades and constitutes organizations is not generated by something called "capitalism". Rather, the latter is nothing more than shorthand for the distinctive accumulative power of the former.

For inscriptivist accounting scholars, it is the abstractive and mobilizing role of quantification, rather than the issue of accurate measurement, which occupies their empirical and theoretical attention. The inscriptivist view focuses on this organizing and connecting power of accounting reductions and not primarily on their truth or the accuracy of their measurement of phenomena (Busco and Quattrone, 2018; Jordan, Mitterhofer, and Jørgensen, 2018). As argued earlier in this chapter, quantification is clearly an important form of abstraction that gives accounting—as well as the sciences—its astounding "observational reach" and "auratic" power (Napolitano, 2015). This reach and power are not only a function of quantification but are also evident in the visual properties of accounting inscriptions (Busco and Quattrone, 2015; Mouritsen, Larsen, and Bukh, 2001; Pollock and D'Adderio, 2012). From this point of view, even the traditional balance sheet is primarily a series of visually organized numeric inscriptions that enables the scaled-up representation of an entire organization as a structured arrangement of its assets and liabilities. In other words, accounting combines numbers, narratives, and visuals. Furthermore, accounting is not only a practice that makes organizations visible and legible in specific ways (Hines, 1988) but through its varied inscriptions is also generative of organizationality as such. From an inscriptivist point of view, we can no longer sharply distinguish organizations from the many accounts that make them up (see Chapter 5 for a more developed version of this argument).

That accounting inscriptions are the outcome of inscribing or writing/drawing practices is not as trivial as it sounds. The marking of the clay tablet is an accounting action that generates a primary connectivity and enables an absent event of exchange to endure. Quattrone's (2015) historical analysis of the Jesuits demonstrates that their accounting books and inscriptions cannot be evaluated as imperfect representations or measurements of an independent economic reality. Rather, they must be seen as products of a continuous process of engagement with the world, of a never-ending and unfolding enquiry into reality. In the terms discussed in Chapter 2, this conception has some affinities with Levinas's mysticism in that accounting inscriptions—primary traces especially—point to a reality that can never be fully grasped and is radically absent. It remains beyond reach yet invites exploration and can be encountered via what Quattrone calls the "maeutic method", directed at bringing issues to consciousness. Busco and Quattrone (2015) analyse contemporary accounting devices like the balanced scorecard in these terms and argue more generally and prescriptively for this maeutic conception of accounting, which is both method and process ontology. Just as Levinas imbues traces with metaphysical and ethical status, so too do Quattrone and colleagues imbue accounting and books of account with the theologically grounded mystery of the Jesuits. While this may seem very different to the clay tablets discussed earlier, in both cases a material object (book, tablet) and the inscriptions on and/or within it are made via semiotic work to refer to something empirically or metaphysically absent. This, as is discussed in Chapter 7, is an absence that is also inherent in the temporality of plans and projects, whereby an imagined but necessarily absent future is realized as an object in the present by plans and accounting devices (Chua et al., 2024).

Notwithstanding these many compelling analyses of the inscriptive character and power of accounting numbers, relatively little work exists on the inscribing process and its traceological features. A possible reason for this is the critical-theoretical preoccupation with the organizing power of quantification as a dominant mode of inscription, and therefore with calculation as the hallmark of the accounting craft. This is understandable. The additivity, mobility, and cultural standing of numbers provide all manner of accounting practices with reach and influence. Yet, as rich as this path of analysis has proved to be, it has, despite the emphasis on inscriptions, tended to understate the significance of tracking and traceability as the basic mode of what we have earlier referred to as the ability to produce accounts, or "account-ability".

The making of a mark on a clay tablet undoubtedly required prior agreement that the tablet would be a record of some kind, stemming from a functional need for exchange. In addition, as simple as it might seem, a way of making the mark in the clay would also be needed. And it is likely that a common understanding of the mark could only be generated by physical actions, such as pointing, to generate the semantic connection between the mark and the object. These are monumental cultural achievements and amount to nothing less than the creation of a practice with durable (i.e. proto-institutional) features supporting future potential repetition and elaboration. But it is not just accounting as we think of it today that begins here and is written into existence. Rather, the "accounting" as the semantically meaningful mark is just a means of generating the traceability of something absent. With these primordial traces and the spatio-temporal tracking of things and obligations that they enabled, new human relationships, temporalities, socio-material connectivities, possibilities for exchange, and trust (and fraud!) are all co-created. The clay tablet and its inscriptions are thereby the material components of a primitive *traceability complex* (Chapter 2). Their purpose is to support trade by marking obligations or assets and to enable them to be tracked (i.e. observed) across space and time. Here the observational reach and connectivity generated by the marks on the clay tablets are simple and limited in space and time. They are not "modern" in Latour's sense, yet they represent a profound but largely invisible institutional achievement that has evolved into the advanced forms of traceability practice we see today. And if we accept that traceability in general is indeed the original end for which accounting is the means, then any *traceological theory of accounting* must begin by effectively inverting the traditional conceptual priority given to accounting over auditing (i.e. the view that "without accounts there is nothing to audit!"). To complete this inversion, we must afford a central theoretical role to the audit trail as a widespread and distinctive mode of connectivity.

Audit Trails and Traceability

The "invention" of the double-entry bookkeeping system was often attributed to Luca Pacioli, whereas there is now widespread agreement that his *De Arithmetica* was more of a consolidation of pre-existing practices. Goethe famously described double-entry bookkeeping as one of the "finest inventions of human mind" (Jackson, 1994, p. 409) and it has been powerfully argued that such techniques of bookkeeping are a form of procedural logic that is in essence maeutic and revelatory in the sense discussed earlier in this chapter. The audit trail can be positioned as the enabling platform for double-entry bookkeeping, understood as the process by which individual transactions can be represented, connected, controlled, and aggregated for reporting in financial statements. While this process of producing accounts from underlying transactions and events has become progressively automated, the principle of the audit trail remains the same as a two-way trail or track for composing and, when necessary, decomposing accounts from/to their underlying components (cf. Latour, 1986). Such an audit trail has been defined as:

> the documented flow of a transaction. It is used to investigate how a *source document* was *translated* into an *account entry*, and from there was inserted into the *financial statements* of an entity. The audit trail can be used in reverse, to track backwards from a financial statement line item to the originating source document. A well-run accounting system should have a clear audit trail for all transactions. An audit trail is used by both external and internal auditors to *trace* transactions through an accounting system, as well as by the accounting staff to *track* down errors and the causes of variances in the financial statements. (Accounting Tools, 2018, emphases added)

Defined thus, the audit trail can be understood as a functional feature of a well-run accounting system, whose orderliness also provides the evidential support for the financial audit of that system and its outputs. Accounts and audits are therefore symbiotic. The definition points to a process for producing accounts of performance involving the aggregation of accounting data, mainly numeric, contained in primary transaction documents, such as invoices. Audit trails in this sense are mundane and technically specific. Yet they are also a form of platform-like infrastructure that is invisible when it works and which we only notice when it is not there or fails in some way, such as in cases of fraud and error.

While the preceding definition appears narrowly to do with the practices of financial accounting and auditing, it also references a process of more general significance for thinking about connectivity and traceability. The audit trail is the material basis by which source data enter into accounts, and which enables the tracking of transactions, events, and other objects of interest. The trail is a distinctive mode of connectivity that "begins" with the marking or recording of events for accounting purposes. These events are often manifestly "economic" in nature. For example, pre-digital accounting pedagogy tells us that, in the very simple case of sales, such events, understood as transactions, acquire documentary reality in primary documents, such as invoices. These details should be simultaneously recorded in the primary books of the account system, such as a so-called "day book", and periodically the totals in these primary day books are "posted" to ledgers in the double-entry system. They are then subject to further aggregation and adjustment, to produce the figure for sales for the year that will appear in the annual accounts. Ignoring fraud, error, and other adjustments for the moment, that final figure is in principle a numerical aggregate or combination of all the individual economic transactions of the organization for a specified time period. In principle, the trail enables this sales figure to be decomposed into its individual constituents, reaching back to the original sales transactions documents; the trail is a connected system of artefacts with evidentiary status that constitutes what it is for total sales to be traceable and auditable. In principle, this is as true for manual as it is for automated accounting systems.

In this simple digitally neutral and stylized example, the sales invoice or its equivalent is traceified in that it becomes the "primary trace" of the sales transaction relative to accounting practice. However, exactly where an audit trail begins and ends is not always clear-cut. There are other possible candidates for primary traces, such as inscriptions in order books and despatch records. And for integrated and automated accounting systems, these different items of transactional evidence are likely to have a single common source, rather than being discrete entries in separate physical books and records. Furthermore, the primary traces (from the accounting rather than the anthropological perspective) are the numbers for sales (and tax) that appear on documents; numbers are the monetary "traces of" transacting activities that become relevant data for the purpose of the accounting system. Regardless of how we define the boundaries of an accounting system, and hence where an audit trail begins and ends, these primary traces of transactional activity point to something essentially absent and past. Goods sold still exist in the world in some sense, even if they have moved in space and time, but what we call the "sale" is essentially documentary and juridical in nature, and it is documents and their inscriptions that determine if and when a sale is completed and "realized" for the purposes of accounting. There may be cash received in the bank, or the accounting system will record a debtor until payment is made, but the sale only exists as a specific arrangement of traces, which then become datafied in analog or digital form for a specific practice community, namely accountants. In the event of problems and disputes, such traces also acquire the status of data for lawyers, but the essential point is that there is not just a sale that is recorded. Recording and selling are part of the same organizational process. The record or inscription is a mini-account that constitutes the transfer of goods as a "sale" in law, and which makes a complex event, which is absent both legally and economically, present and durable.

Traceability and Accounts: An Inversion

The audit trail model, as outlined so far in this chapter, embodies a bias. It is a bias that reflects the contemporary priority given to accounting over auditing and monitoring. The traditional idea of an audit trail consists of a data structure, accounts, and oversight in the form of auditing, with the latter being derived from accounting and accountability. This conception of the accounting/audit relationship is understandable; auditing seems only possible if there are accounts to audit, and today the production of financial accounts has a highly developed and autonomous institutional infrastructure of rules and regulations. But if we go back to the model of the clay tablets, this implicit bias in thinking about audit trails must be turned on its head. We need to begin with auditability and implied traceability as the deeper purpose for which the accounts and their underlying data are the means. This inverted view, which is close, but not equivalent, to what is called a "stewardship" conception of accounting, places traceability, and evidentiary processes enabled and initiated by traces, in the foreground. From this perspective, the audit trail is a mode of connectivity that makes a form of traceability possible; accounts are the means to this end. Furthermore, it is the primary traces of the accounting system—the marks in the clay tablets—which ultimately ground this goal of traceability as an ability to "track-back", to evaluate and to verify.

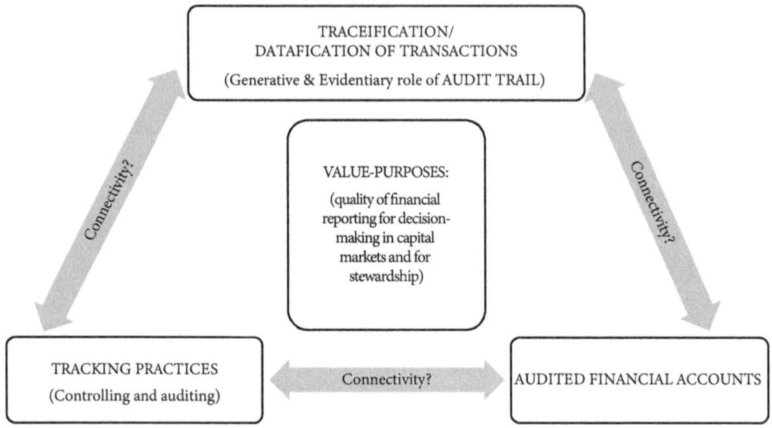

Figure 3.1 Financial accounting as a traceability complex.

This inversion of the contemporary accounting-auditing relationship is core to the traceological view of accounting being advanced in this book. It is a perspective that contrasts with prevailing conceptions of accounting as information for decision-making and/or calculative practice. These familiar conceptions are not invalidated but are in some sense "layered" onto their traceological foundations. The propositional provocation of this inversion is this: "no traceability, no accounting". The inversion also invites an adaptation and application of Figure 2.2 to financial accounting (see Figure 3.1) as a specific mode of *traceability complex* in which the audit trail is a platform that connects in both directions—generatively from transactions to accounts, and evidentially from accounts back to transactions.

Beyond financial accounting practice, a non-accounting example can help to cement this inversion argument and position the audit trail as general mode of traceability-enabling connectivity. Writing against prevailing critiques of the mechanical and "tick-box" nature of checklists (e.g. Boyle, 2020), Gawande (2010) analyses their power and benefits in medical procedures and other fields, where safety is of paramount importance and cannot be left to imperfect human memory. It is a compelling case for the use of checklists as accounting prosthetics; such lists ensure that all relevant features of a situation have been considered. Furthermore, checklists often grow "from below" (like the clay tablets discussed earlier) as forms of "account-ability" in which practitioners refine, codify, and account for what they do (Dourish, 2001; Suchman, 1995; Crvelin and Lohlein, 2022). If we take the example of take-off protocols for airline pilots, they complete such checklists—usually in pairs—by "ticking" a relevant cell when a control action has been performed (e.g. to ensure the wing flaps are working) (see Gawande, 2010, ch. 6). Such checklists have become highly regulated and are required to demonstrate that operational processes are working; they are primarily there to make sure it is safe to fly, which is their accounting purpose.[4] The "tick" on the checklist is not the "control action" itself; it is the making of an entry on paper or digitally, which is quite different from actually testing the flaps. Importantly, the tick as a mark is also an institutionally accepted primary trace of the control action; it is its referent, and a durable account of performance, which can easily circulate (Latour, 1999).

We know there can be fraud and false entries, so such ticks/checks as primary traces are not always perfect or faithful marks of what they claim to be. But we hope that this is never the case for pilots, who are highly motivated both to complete checklists honestly and also to improve them. The action to test the wing flaps happens, and is an event which is gone forever in the effluxion of time. The pilots may remember doing it; someone on the ground may have seen the flaps being tested and will remember this. But one of the key traces that matters (assuming the flight recorder is also switched on prior to take-off) is the tick in the checklist. The checklist is the script; the tick is an inscription that activates the script. It is a form of notation, and its function is to be a primary durable trace of an event that is necessarily past and absent. Here, the checklist is *both* tracking and accounting. It enables the pilots to "self-track" their safety performance and to observe whether their actions are complete; it thereby increases their observational reach and connects and compresses a series of very different actions and events into one single accounting document that is easily read and transported.

The tick in the take-off protocol is a *primary trace* of the action of testing the flaps for the pilot herself, but it is not only a local prosthetic for pilot memory, allowing her to track checklist completion as a "first-order" form of observation. The tick as trace also becomes datafied and is combined in the production of accounts of safety performance for the airline organization. The checklist and all its ticks are connected, pooled in an audit trail in which traces of control actions are collected and stored by the safety department as organizational accounting records. In the event of problems or events requiring investigation (see Chapter 7), the individual checklists can be retrieved and examined. They are therefore documents that have an organizational trajectory and forensic potential, and are not just for the use by the individual pilot. The checklists are traceified (Chapter 2) as *evidence* to support second-order observation or "oversight" by regulatory agents of the first-order pilot observations. The checklist generates traceability as the basis for the accountability of both pilots and airlines for safety. Remote third parties, such as regulators, can track back to

[4] See https://en.wikipedia.org/wiki/Preflight_checklist (accessed 28 August 2024).

individual checklists in order to evaluate the practice of the pre-flight safety protocols. The tick in the checklist is therefore a primary trace of an action that can also make that action auditable by distant others, as well as by the pilots themselves. It can do this because the checklist reduces complex actions in space and time to two-dimensional representations, making them easily mobile and connectable to other reporting forms all the way along a trail to regulators (Latour, 1986). Hence, the audit trail enables this possibility of connection as the "transportation" of traces from pilots in the field to "centres of traceability", which use the checklists in aggregate to "track back" and to check the checking practices.

The difference in principle between the pre-flight checklist and the clay tablet is not so great, despite being separated by millennia. But their respective traceability complexes are very different in scale and complexity. Unlike the clay tablets, individual checklists can be subjected to further abstraction and may be assembled into aggregate organizational accounts of safety. Hence, in this checklist example we can begin to see the "audit trail" and its connectivity not only in narrow financial accounting and auditing terms but as a general model of how inscriptions can move and "scale-up" (Latour, 1986). We can also begin to see the shape of a general traceological theory of accounting in which trace-enabled tracking is the foundation of accounts production at different scales. Primary traceification as a process sits at the very centre of this theory.

Primary Traceification

In Chapter 2, the notion of traceification was introduced in part to emphasize that there are can be no "raw" traces as such. Even in the case of a mark on a clay tablet, it is a form of materiality that is semiotically encoded as a "trace of" something that matters relative to an emergent community defined by shared practical interests. Hence, traceification was defined as: *the process by which traces are generated for specific practical purposes where traceability is an organizing interest.* It is a technological act of generating traces that inscribe and memorize events, thereby providing the basic material of audit trails. On this view, traces have a micro-institutional character. Inscriptivist theories of accounting, as discussed in the previous section, draw our attention to these micro-components, but they do not explicitly focus on their origination as "traces" (often arising from bodily interactions with technology) or their role in building connectivity. And while there can be many kinds of inscriptions that can be traceified and thereby play a role in the combinatory and connective stages of an audit trail, including tables and illustrations, what we call "primary" traces have a distinctive status as *those inscriptions that are produced at, and define, the boundaries of an accounting system in its broadest sense.* At this threshold, semiotic and technical work takes place to define and traceify the primary traces that compose the content of accounts. This is where economization begins.

Returning to the case of a sale, discussed earlier in this chapter, goods may change hands physically or a service may be performed. This event is subject to economic traceification in the form of an inscription or trace, which constitutes the "outer edge" of a financial accounting audit trail and the boundary between the accounting system and its event environment. While events may have unique spatio-temporal properties, primary traceification abstracts from these properties to mark and record them in standardized form and notation, such as monetary quantification or as a tick on a checklist. These generated traces constitute and register the economic and legal reality of the transactional event, providing it with more durable form than the event itself. At the same time, a primary trace is arbitrary and selective; a great deal of transactional reality may be left out and is not marked, such as the relationship between buyer and seller, or the impact of the transaction on the natural environment. Primary traceification references some valued features of a situation or activity deemed relevant to an interest or performance, but not others. It follows that the production of primary traces is a value-laden process of marking reality in a specific way for specific practical purposes. It is a process that marks and constitutes an infrastructural feature of the economy.

In the case of the mark on the clay tablet, a seemingly primitive act of traceification is nevertheless a huge technical and cultural achievement, effectively materializing accountability relations between two parties. However, as Alaimo and Kallinikos (2024) show, it takes more for this mark as a form of notation to become systematically organized as "data". For example, if the pre-flight checklist were purely a private aide-memoire for the pilot, like a shopping list perhaps, and was disposed of shortly after completion, there would be temporary traceification but no datafication in the sense of a systematic ordering of the domain knowledge relevant to aircraft safety. There would also, obviously, be no audit trail, and the primary trace would be fleeting and lost forever. The pilot would not be able to demonstrate to others that she had performed the safety checks; in such a case, the trace of an action is purely local and operational and is exhausted or disposed of once produced. This would be akin to a form of temporary and disposable accounting (cf. Palermo et al., 2022). Hence, we can postulate that the trace only becomes data, is datafied, as it is drawn into and becomes the durable taken-for-granted input for this specific and systemic regulatory practice of knowing and ensuring safety and security. Once it is secured and articulated as "safety data", it can be subject to further traceification as evidentiary material for auditing, evaluation, and investigatory and oversight purposes (see Chapter 2). This example suggests how the audit trail is the sum of processes that create and connect phases of abstraction and accounting, placing them in an evidentiary and forensic relation to each other. Hence, we can propose that an audit trail is a distinctive form of relational infrastructure for accounting purposes, which may be more or less developed and elaborate.

The value-laden nature of traceification and the audit trail mean that they are not just hostage to audit society pathologies, as discussed earlier, but have the potential to "crowd in" values of different kinds, albeit subject to the risks of distortion that Selznick outlines. This suggests that we should be agnostic about the value-bearing potential of accounts, even under conditions of intense economization. If we consider organized practices of traceability in all their variety (see Chapter 6), there can be multiple "accounts" of organizational performance, which are mobilized by values as diverse as food quality, child safety, biodiversity, anti-slavery, and many others. These values can be operationalized and reproduced by anchoring them in traces of actions (e.g. checklists) that "materialize" those values and enable conformity with them to be tracked. Traces of these specific values and their datafication in lists, indicators, and metrics make it possible in principle to ground new accountings for value and cumulatively generate their facticity. This would be a mutually accretive process in which both the audit trail as infrastructure and the facticity of the values it supports are co-produced (see Chapter 4 for more on this co-production).

Primary traceification, as discussed in the preceding, is never innocent and neutral, but produces marks that encode the specific value-purposes of quality, security, and discovery. The traceological significance of primary traces lies not in their form—as numbers, marks, or words—but in their potential to enable the audit trail as connectivity that underpins the production of accounts. They are the value-infused raw material of accounts, which can travel and become further assembled and combined in ever larger-scale accounting narratives. Their repeated production is an engine for generating the facticity of these values, which may be more or less strong, and more or less accepted as referring to an exterior world (Douglas, 1986). In other words, the facticities of different value-oriented accounts vary in their "pull" or "compelling and coercive power" (Durkheim, 1982, p. 51; Power, 2021a). At their strongest, accounts appear as factual representations of valued organizational and individual performance, and the process by which their facticity accretes is largely invisible. This action-orienting pull or allure of accounting numbers, ratios, and rankings has been extensively documented (Kurunmäki and Miller, 2013; Espeland and Sauder, 2007, 2016; Esposito and Stark, 2019), but the role of primary traces within audit trails as the endogenous mechanisms for constructing this pull is also fundamental to the observed power of accounts.

It is possible in principle to observe primary traces "in the making" when new accounting systems for tracking and recording performance are being generated, and when the question of what counts as a relevant primary trace, and hence data, is still open (see Chapter 8; Power, 2015). In cases like this, where there is uncertainty about the relevant primary trace to be created, and hence about how to account for a performance of some kind—ESG or sustainability accounting would be examples—it may be possible to discern competing traceification processes as different ways of marking a relevant practice reality. Such competition often ends with a pragmatic settlement about which primary traces can best be combined and accumulated and operated upon within acceptable time frames and economic cost in further calculations and analytical operations.

As already noted in Chapter 1, the value-purposes of quality, security, and discovery mobilize traceability complexes. We might also think of traceability itself as an overarching meta-value or logic, which is valued as a procedural means to realize other substantive values. Yet, this way of thinking positions values too much as "external" inputs to traceability complexes and drivers of accounts. Rather, it is proposed that through technology-embedded primary traceification as the motor of the audit trail, vaguely formulated purposes and interests can become cumulatively, if unevenly, endowed with varying degrees of "facticity" and organizing power (Thornton et al., 2012, p. 85; Power, 2021a). Having said this, we also should not assume that accounts are simply effects; this would take the inversion model too far. Rather, scholarship shows how accounts can be agentic in the sense of recursively shaping the forms of traceification and datafication that underpin them, thereby driving the content and scope of audit trails. Beginning a change process by experimenting with new accounts like "value-added" is not therefore necessarily a poor strategy. The facticity of value can emerge from any of the components of the traceability complex: traceification/datafication, tracking, connectivity, accounts, and value-purposes must be understood as mutually co-formative. And notwithstanding the relative institutional stability of many traceability complexes, change and instability can also originate in any of these stylized constituent elements. Thus, even nascent forms of value accounting, which are weak in the sense of being poorly grounded in audit trail modes of connectivity, can be catalysts for traceability complex-building and repair, and can be value-performative over time.

Experiments with new accountings may well begin life as so-called "greenwashing", which we can understand as being cynically decoupled from the wider functioning of an organization. Yet, as critical social theory reminds us, even distorted, imperfect, and cynical forms of value communication contain the promise or hope of change (Horkheimer and Adorno, 1972). A traceologically oriented theorization of accounting enables a reframing of the greenwashing problematic in terms of the need to generate audit trail connectedness and "green value" facticity. The performativity of new green or social accountings at the organizational level may be weak initially but may strengthen as audit trails form. Selznick reminds us that values don't perform themselves; they require material enabling conditions, which partly explains why economic values embedded in traditional forms of accounting have acquired such powerful organizational facticity in a way that other values, such as environment protection, have not unless mediated by punitive financial liability (Marti and Gond, 2018). The prescriptive thesis being advanced is that the accounts and the values that we wish to live by must be traceified on something like an audit trail platform.

Conclusions

In the opening two chapters we introduced the notion of traceability as an idea and value that are mobilized in practice by: the articulation of value-purposes (quality, security, and discovery); the production of the traces (traceification and datafication) that enable tracking and oversight; and the production of accounts. The relationships between these elements—loosely conceptualized as a "traceability complex"—should not be taken to be linear, sequential, temporally continuous, or even fully coherent. Purposes may emerge and take shape as traces and accounts are produced. Accounts as vehicles to represent purposes may influence the nature of the traces that are collected and used for tracking. And the selective value-laden production of traces may determine the nature of the tracking and accounting that is possible. Hence, the traceability complex as a conceptual model of value-purposes, traces, tracking, and accounts will manifest itself empirically in many different ways with different dynamics of connection between its constituent practice elements. One manifestation of these connecting dynamics is the audit trail.

In this chapter, we selectively reviewed critical accounting scholarship to argue that the significance of the audit trail has been largely neglected, not least in relation to the abstractive and economizing effects of accounting. Building on inscriptivist theories of accounting, it is proposed that the marking of objects for tracking is a more primordial aspect of accounting than quantification. These reflections lead the argument to a consideration of the audit trail as a form of accounting infrastructure in which traces are created, combined, and constructed as evidence of performance. The chapter also generalizes the audit trail model by inverting the presumed and implicit relation between accounting and traceability. Primary traces, defined as inscriptions that are created at, and constitute, the boundaries between accounting systems and their event environments, are foundational components of audit trails. They may be difficult to observe, but they matter to the extent that they encode values and are foundational for the accounts we live by. Having established both the potential general salience of the audit trail as an infrastructure of traceability and accounts production, and the role of primary traceification within it, we next need to address the nature of its connectivity and variation.

Chapter 3 Summative Propositions

The following propositions position a traceological theory of accounting in relation to prior scholarship and define audit trails and their components:

1. **Accounting theory has tended to emphasize the calculative and quantitative features of accounts over their role in tracking.**
2. **The "inscriptivist" turn in accounting theory provides the point of departure for a traceological theory of accounting that focuses on the dynamics of audit trails.**
3. **A traceological theory of accounting is characterized by an inversion of the assumed priority of accounting over auditing; accounts are a means to realize traceability and enable tracking.**
4. **Audit trails are specific modes of two-way connectivity involving the primary traceification of objects of interest for tracking and accounting.**
5. **Primary traces are inscriptions and marks that are produced at, and define, the boundaries of an accounting system in its broadest sense.**
6. **Values can acquire social and organizational facticity as they are continuously produced by the dynamics of traceification, tracking, and accounting.**

4
Audit Trails and the Paradox of Connectivity

Overview

Chapter 2 identified traceification as a core generative process of accounting, and Chapter 3 developed the idea of the audit trail, emphasizing the significance of *primary* trace production. In this chapter, we build on these analyses to develop a dynamic model of the audit trail that draws upon the metaphor of "ruts in the road". The general form of this argument is that audit trails, as infrastructures that connect and pool traces, emerge cumulatively from practices of tracking and their accounts. While it was implied in Chapter 3 that tracks, trails, and forms of connectivity are the preconditions for successful tracing, tracking, and therefore accounting, we now go further to propose in an ideal-typical fashion that all these elements can be theorized as mutually constitutive. They define the dynamics of traceability complexes through which the facticity of general values of quality, security, and discovery are accretively produced in specific settings.

Empirically, this value-constituting process is likely to be uneven, and much will depend on the specific nature and dynamics of the agencies that become connected in audit trails, the connecting work they actually do, and the strength of any path dependency linking them. This chapter theorizes the contingent variation in the configuration of audit trails, in terms of their "depth", "density", and "temporality". The substantive proposition is that under general conditions of digitalization, especially the rise of algorithm-driven automation, audit trails, if they exist at all, are becoming less deep in their connectivity despite the observational reach that they facilitate, less dense in terms of the numbers of agencies or "centres of tracking" that they connect, and closer to real time in their temporal rhythms. While these shifts in audit trail structure correspond to an intensification of efficiency in traceability as remote observation, they also have implications for the nature of the accounts we live by, in particular for the institutional capacity for human-based governance and oversight. Drawing on blockchains and machine learning as indicative illustrations, the chapter concludes by highlighting the paradoxical of nature algorithmic connectivity. Human capacity for understanding and oversight is either rendered irrelevant (blockchain—"code is king") or impossible (machine learning—"opacity").

Economy of Traces. Michael Power, Oxford University Press. © Oxford University Press (2026).
DOI: 10.1093/9780197681527.003.0004

The paradox is that as we become more algorithmically connected, audit trails as a basis for human accountabilities become more disconnected and fragmented. Indeed, the impacts of digital technologies on societies and individuals are exemplified by the fortunes of the audit trail as a mode of connectivity undergoing mutation in the new economy of traces.

What Is Connectivity?

It is often said casually that we now live in a highly connected world, meaning all manner of digital media that enable communication across vast geographic distances. There has undoubtedly been a "surge in technical connectivity" (Kolb et al., 2008), which implicates the possibility of being at work anywhere in the world and "always on" (Wacjman and Rose, 2011). Yet, we have also come to recognize the ironies and paradoxes of these developments, for example in the experience of being in a café full of individuals who are talking via headphones to someone else somewhere else. They are connected via communication media to distant others, in turn enabled by GPS connections, but not to each other. They are "anywhere" (Goodhart, 2017) and are profoundly disconnected from their neighbours at other tables. This is a salient example of what scholars call the "duality of connectivity" in which all connecting work is also necessarily a source of disconnection, not least in the contemporary digital age (Hafermalz and Riemer, 2020; Nurmi and Hinds, 2020). The idea is that connectedness and connecting are never absolute but are always partial, selective, and perceived "relations" around which human practices are organized (Strathern, 2005). Normatively it is also often argued that we have too much connectivity, that we fetishize connectivity (Pedersen, 2014), and that we need disconnectivity for human flourishing, suggesting an optimal balance for work tasks that can now be done anywhere at any time. As the constant connectivity of work is possible, complex trade-offs are emerging between freedom and control, sanctuary and surveillance, and privacy and transparency (Bernstein, 2017; Kolb et al., 2012; Kolb et al., 2020).

Connectivity has been defined generally as "the mechanisms, processes, systems and relationships that link individuals and collectives (e.g. groups, organizations, cultures, societies) by facilitating material, informational and/or social exchange" (Kolb, 2008, p. 128). This broad socio-technical definition is somewhat circular, but it encompasses many dimensions and ways of thinking about connectivity—spatial, temporal, technical, geophysical, collective, and organizational. And while debates about connectivity (and traceability) are associated with the advent of digital technologies and personalized devices, such as smart phones, studies in the history and sociology of technology remind us that forms of transport, from horses to railways and aircraft, have also generated connectivities with profound effects on human societies and expectations.

Beyond geographic modes of connection, a family can be said to be connected, at least genetically, even when its members are geographically dispersed. Furthermore, connections as "relations of relations" in the sense of kinship structures have come to shape the observational focus of the anthropological sciences (Strathern, 1995). Even individuals with similar backgrounds—school, university, profession, and so on—can also be said to be connected although they never meet, as revealed in the techniques of network analysis (Kolb, 2012). More radical still, connectivity is also built into language in the form of categories and classifications and the relations of similarity that they embed (Hacking, 2002). While people may become connected by consciously inhabiting and embracing the shared classifications that make them up, digital technologies are also generating classifications and social groupings that, being statistical artefacts, are not always readily comprehendable by their connected human members. We can now be members of a group and thereby connected to other members in ways we do not understand or control (Farrell and Fourcade, 2023).

Like accountability, connectivity is necessarily and obviously relational in nature. Thus, A can be connected to/related to C by something else B, such as accounting, which mediates their relation as connection. There are many ways to fill out these placeholders A, B, and C, and therefore many ways to define relations and (dis)connectivity in empirically specific terms. And we should not imagine that the things that act as the Bs—the material and social connectors such as accounting devices—in this simple framework necessarily leave A and C intact as they were before they became connected. Digital technologies of various kinds play an increasingly prominent and constitutive role in this triad, not least algorithms in placeholder B position that are being intensely studied for how they are generative of new relationalities (Kornberger et al., 2017). People, processes, and things can therefore be changed when they are brought into new relations with each other, when they are connected by new connectors. Latour (2005) captures this idea in his much cited distinction between a mediator with agentic capacity to change things as it mediates, as compared with an intermediary that does not. And within his pragmatist-anthropological vision of knowledge production, connectivity is not a thing but the outcome of acts of connecting, a myriad of small inscription-rich operations of back-and-forth mediations in chains of translation and abstraction. This is a process he describes as "circulating reference" (Latour, 1999, ch. 2) through which we can model the audit trail as a knowledge production pathway (see also Chapter 9).

The systematic analysis of connectivity presents several theoretical and empirical challenges. First, connectivity as relationality may be pervasive (Kolb et al., 2012), but, as Simmel (1909) notes, we can only know it and observe it via a focus on the things that get connected and events of connection (Angwin and Vaara, 2005). Second, this observational challenge creates an analytical bias towards familiar material connectors—the electricity wires, pipes, railway tracks, roads, broadband cables, and similar technologies—which can be studied in their own right and which are also powerful metaphors for connectivity in general (Kolb, 2008). Third, it can be difficult to shift the theoretical optic from the noun forms of "relation" and "connection" and their ontological presumptions to a more processual focus on what we might call "acts of connecting". And there are two reasons for this particular difficulty. If such acts of connecting are successful and stable, then one is left with connection as the only observable outcome. It is hard to catch connection in the making. Furthermore, on closer inspection, acts of connecting may themselves be manifold outcomes of prior "technical" connections that generate further acts of "social" connecting. We need only think of digital algorithms as rules for connecting that are themselves the outcome of a myriad of agencies linked together. Indeed, if there is, as Latour (2013) argues, nothing to what we call "society" and "organization" but connections, the very idea of connectivity begins to slip from our grasp.

Various approaches have sought to make connectivity more theoretically and empirically manageable, and less prone to technological bias, often by reducing it to formal nodal points and density functions in network analyses. These studies abstract from physical human interaction and focus on a limited range of attributes as proxies for connectivity (e.g. neighbourhood proximity, shared educational background, or overlapping board memberships). Yet while these maps are able to reveal compelling and often surprising structural features of networks, and therefore illuminate the texture of the connections that characterize fields of practice, they do so by necessarily restricting the operational meaning of connectivity, which ends up being primarily describable in statistical terms, even to the point of being unrecognizable to the human "members" of the network.

Latour also adopts a network approach to connectivity but it is radically empiricist in its orientation, seeking to reveal the many different "agencies" as he calls them—human and non-human—that constitute so-called "nodes" and which accomplish connectivity. Hence his focus is on connectors, not least among which are the traces, inscriptions, documents, and forms that allow "something else to be *transported* from one site to another" (2005, p. 223, emphasis added) and whose very formalism underpins this connecting capability. For Latour, formalizers and standardizers, such as accountants and statisticians, are agencies that enable the expansion of facts and theories to other settings, reworking those settings and contexts in the process (2005, p. 232). He thereby understands traceability very broadly and ontologically as the basis for constituting or assembling what we mean by knowledge via these formal agencies—the "number crunchers and their humble tools"—which are able to expand the universality of their formalism and which occupy nodes that he calls "centres of calculation". Hence, traceability and connectivity (and circulation) are often interchangeable in Latour's thinking as mechanisms by which the micro and macro, the local and the universal, are somehow fabricated from a myriad of, in principle empirically observable, inscriptive devices and their outputs.

As noted in Chapter 1, our focus on traceability in this book is more restricted in scope than Latour's and engages a different problematic. He is critically targeting a certain way of doing sociology ("social studies of X"), whereas our focus is more on the manner in which *traceability practices* are organized and on the implications of tracking for accounting. Yet, we draw considerably from the direction of Latour's thinking, not least because he places emphasis on the connecting and mediating role of practices like accounting. In addition, his model of knowledge generation is traceological in form and has many affinities with the notion of an audit trail discussed in Chapter 3, enabling us to theorize it as a cycle of acts of connecting by agencies that generate connective infrastructure.

Connectivity as Infrastructure

In the previous chapter the audit trail was positioned as a mode of connectivity with infrastructural significance for accounts production. It is helpful to consider briefly the notion of infrastructure, not least because it is reasonable to think of connectivity as an important, if not its most important, feature. Yet, like connectivity, infrastructure is a notoriously challenging concept, which eludes precision (Star, 1999) and poses well-known problems for scholars and analysts, both in terms of what it is—its ontology—and of how to study it—methodology. For Star and others, the study of infrastructures requires effort and determination to reveal their "embedded strangeness, a second-order one, that of the forgotten, the background, the frozen in place" (1999, p. 379). She thinks of information infrastructures as a "system of substrates" (p. 380) and an "installed base" (p. 382) with values inscribed into their "inner depths" (p. 379). Yet these materialist metaphors—railways and electricity grids are often evoked—have generally given way to relationist conceptualizations of infrastructure as arrangements and configurations of diverse elements (Monteiro et al., 2013). Following this perspective, infrastructures can be variously thought of as: a network with strong technology features; an institution with latent power and stability; in Foucault's terms, as a *dispositif* or apparatus (Foucault, 1980, p. 132); in Barad's (2007, pp. 145–146) notion of material-discursive practices; or as a Deleuzian *assemblage* of loosely related, continuously emergent and heterogeneous things, people, and ideas (see Buchanan, 2015).

Common to all these possibilities is the frequent call to study these messy aggregate and large-scale phenomena by focusing on the relations and connections between selected features of the world that seem to be mutually dependent and co-formative, and which tend only to be visible under conditions of stress. As Star puts it, we need "new methods to understand this imbrication of infrastructure and human organization" as a study primarily of overlapping relationships, not things (Abbott, 1995). Bowker et al. (2019) also see infrastructures in general in terms of their observable effects—what they do—rather than as "things". They can be known for how they "structure attention, shape decision-making and guide cognition", thereby configuring the thinking of those who participate in them. They also distribute and connect agencies and methods of evaluation across domains of action, generating ever new forms of defining, measuring, scoring, and tracking performance (Kornberger et al., 2017), even to the point of permeating "the barriers of the human skin".

Yet, if infrastructures and their connectivities are relations rather than things, then they are also perspectival, and both their theorization and representation reflect specific analytic and practice interests in making some features and relations stand out against others. There is therefore both an element of analytic- and domain expertise–relativity in defining infrastructures or apparatuses; they are relative to ways of seeing clusters of practices, and their dependencies. Hence, for a specific person or community, what counts as infrastructure, or as a taken-for-granted base, can be the primary focus of interest for another. The observability of infrastructure-like entities and connectivity arrangements is also methodologically challenging because it involves risky decisions about boundaries, which are always to some degree artificial and perceptual. Creative effort is needed in which some features must somehow be foregrounded. As Star implies, infrastructures need to be "dug out" from their organizational, informational, and social environments since they are often hidden in the shadows of more visible organizational forms and practices (Leonardi and Treem, 2020). But this "hiddenness" is itself an artefact of the specific relational lens.

The well-worn example of the railways in the United Kingdom in the 1980s helps with further explication. The privatization agenda of the Thatcher government proposed to separate the management of the railway system, or what was commonly called its infrastructure, from its use by independent, regulated, and competitive operating companies offering retail and freight services. The railway system provided, in a very literal sense, connectivity in the form of track for different applications and operations. It is far from our purpose to evaluate the efficiency of these arrangements, which have already been widely debated, but to draw from this example the duality of the connectivity potential of the track, on the one hand, and the connecting applications of train journeys on it, on the other. We might talk of this duality as being analogous to the difference between the "transportability", which is the materially enabled potential or affordance created by the connections of the railway network, and the specific practices of transporting provided by the operating companies. The former is a *type* of connectivity potential, which is a necessary but not always sufficient condition for the latter, understood as a *token* of flow or travel along the tracks (Kolb, 2008).

Platform and application in this sense are never entirely independent of each other; the underlying railway network can be enhanced or expanded by the demands of the operators; it is not a static thing in itself. Indeed, for railway engineers it is not at all "backstage" but front and centre of their concerns as something to be maintained, managed, and expanded, including being responsive to operating companies. Yet, for the train operators and their customers, it is infrastructure in that it is normally only visible in times of failure. Hence, abstracting artificially for the moment from the role of government and the significance of legacy systems, infrastructure-like connectivities—such as the audit trail—can be understood as *continuously enacted outcomes of a core recursive dynamic* between a system as "installed base" or platform and the applications/operations that it enables, but with much path-dependency driven by the former.

We should not overestimate the seeming ubiquity of connectedness in popular discourses. Connectivity may, at least in part, be more of a collectively imagined and desired outcome of capabilities for observing and representing processes *as if* they are connected in specific ways. In short, connectivity is often imaginary and projected in nature, which *accounting in its broadest sense performs and visualizes.* For example, supply chains, transport networks, and power systems cannot be experienced directly, as Latour rightly says, but they can be represented in diagrams and documentary form as more or less coherent assemblages of linked functions, technologies, and practices. Thus maps, family trees, organization charts, and many other artefacts can be created to represent connectedness and relations between territories, people, and processes, to mobilize actions and technologies and to create centres of power around these actions. An accounting document like a balance sheet is a summation of the effects of many transactions and can stand for an entire organization. The organization qua accounting entity is constituted by projected relations between collections of assets and liabilities, thereby enabling it to be connected to regulatory agencies, capital markets, and other centres (which are themselves constituted by a similar substrate of "organizing scripts"; Latour, 2013) (see Chapter 5 for a fuller discussion). Representational artefacts like a balance sheet provide what Latour (2005, p. 188) describes as the panorama, or big picture that "gives the impression of complete control over what is being surveyed". Yet he also suggests that while such panoramic representations enable scale and the "macro" to be constructed in specific locales, they also provide an illusory "excess of coherence" grounded in a desire for "wholeness and centrality" that may fail or not be fully realized. This is the essential tension between connectivity and its representation. Forms of connectedness may be fragile when their accounting manifestations prove to be defective. Hence such modes of connectivity as the audit trail must be understood to provide only what we propose to define as "evidentially sufficient observability" for different centres of traceability to believe and act *as if* they are connected. This "sufficiency" of evidence is grounded in collective belief and is institutional and cultural in nature, that is, it has evolved pragmatically and, per Chapter 1, is always contingently liable to fail, leading to shifts in what counts as evidence and changes in observability.

To summarize: connectedness and relatedness are always in some sense outcomes of acts of connecting and relating that are performed by specific agencies utilizing an array of seemingly mundane artefacts. The connectedness that is performed though audit trails as described in Chapter 3 is socio-material in nature. It is material in the sense of being grounded in technologies that produce material traces, including all manner of inscriptions, and it is socio- in the sense of being a temporary collective human settlement about the evidentiary sufficiency of observation it affords. The specific socio-material forms of connectivity that get created and maintained will depend in large part on cultural and economic investments in documentary (including digital) tracks and channels. We must therefore bear in mind that audit trail infrastructure exists in representational form as a panoramic depiction of connectivity that may vary in its performativity of connectedness depending on which agency is describing it and for what purpose. Just as organizations in supply chains may have different conceptualizations of the supply chain according to where they are in it and who their immediate neighbours are, so too may the representation of the audit trail and its connectedness vary depending on whether it is the sales office, internal auditor, audit committee, or regulator doing the panoramic representation. And in believing that there is an audit trail that corresponds to the accepted script for enabling observability, these different groups act in such a way as to confirm that belief and perform it. We need to consider this recursive process further.

Ruts in the Road

The argument so far proposes that the accounting audit trail is an important mode of infrastructural connectivity. Day and Lury (2016, p. 42), in a non-accounting study, show that, as traces accumulate, they turn "observations or traces made through data collection into tracks; [they make] data meaningful insofar as the traces are related, linked or connected to each other". On this view, the track/trail as a form of connectivity is an emergent infrastructure that is produced by the accumulation of traces. In the financial accounting setting, durable primary traces of transaction events are created to enable them to be observed and tracked for reporting purposes. The Day and Lury argument implies that as these traces become more organized, datafied, and processed, over time the audit trail coalesces as a "track" that links and connects the different levels of accounting representation. The accretive creation of the track by tracking and accounting practice in turn makes specific forms of traceability as observability possible (Power, 2021a). This is a very stylized argument, which we need to develop a little more.

The basic thesis is that tracks as *stabilized connectivity potential* are performed and generated by successive acts of connecting or tracking. The tracks and trails that materialize connectivity, including audit trails in accounting, are not typically thought of as cumulative sedimentations of tracking activity (Day and Lury, 2016, p. 57). So, to develop this idea further, we draw on the everyday metaphor used, among others, by routines theorists (Pentland et al., 2011, p. 1370) of "ruts in the road". Let us begin to unpack this metaphor by imagining a four-wheel cart as an "agency" engaged in moving across a terrain for a purpose, perhaps to trade with a distant location. The idea is that as this cart moves along the ground, it will create ruts from the friction of the wheels. If we assume the existence of other carts also engaged in this practice, they will not initially follow exactly the same ruts as the first, but gradually, perhaps as the ruts become deeper, a dominant track in the pathway will emerge. And, if they do not wish to break their wheels, the carts must use the dominant ruts.

For any specific driver of a cart, the track is experienced as an independently objective feature of the world—a "social fact" in Durkheim's sense. Yet, the "objectivity" of the track as a form of connective platform is nothing more than the compulsive power of the ruts that are the result of an accumulation of prior traces. Each time the track is used, the cart impacts the soil beneath its wheels and leaves a minor rut as a trace for the next one. At first the traces or ruts are weak and shallow but, as they accumulate, they become stronger and deeper and more determinative of an exact track. These accumulated traces are individually arbitrary, but collectively they produce and reproduce something with "objective" power. As the track crystallizes, it determines the actions that fall under it, like a grammar or logic. Each transit or use of the pathway is a specific *token* or instantiation of this "logic of the track", and any cart user must more or less conform to its normative force and, in so doing, reinforces it. In this way, the track and the uses it affords have a looping and self-reinforcing relationship to each other, which becomes weaker but never entirely vanishes as the track/logic becomes independently established as infrastructure and social fact for subsequent cart drivers (Jepperson, 1991; Marti and Gond, 2018). This is literal "path" dependency! The ruts analogy also suggests that if cart technology (e.g. axle length) itself changes, then the existing ruts may lose their institutional power and the formation of a new track and new connections may be set in motion, as we often see.

Unpacking this metaphor further, we can think of the specific transits of the carts as practices that generate the micro-foundations (Felin, Foss, and Ployhart, 2015; Barney and Felin, 2013) of the track. While there may be variation in specific cart transits, certainly initially, the track is an emergent form of connectivity that acquires considerable stability from use and becomes autonomous as an independent enabling platform supporting the movement of carts. And, even though late-comer carts will have little to no effect on the track, the latter is ontologically only the cumulative outcome of the traces produced by earlier carts. Following Latour (2013), we can say that the track is not a transcendental entity or organization that is above and outside the practice of tracking, although it can come to seem like that. Rather, it is explainable by the "piling up" of tracking events, of multiple acts of connecting for observing. For the "ruts in the road" model, tracking activities generate the track as infrastructure, a thesis with affinities to that of structuration (Giddens, 1999).

Let us now recall the definition of tracking provided in Chapter 2 as: *a trace-enabled practice by which an observer is connected to, and can act upon, as well as account for, an object of interest.* Tracking practices will vary in terms of their "observational reach" and connectivity across space and time. Overall, it is being proposed that traceification, tracking, and the track as latent connectivity are mutually formative. This claim may seem initially counterintuitive. After all, bridges and roads seem to exist independently of the cars and vehicles that use them, and are usually managed and maintained by public authorities. Such bridges as connectivity potential may also fail or be too weak for certain kinds of traffic. As I write these words, the Hammersmith Bridge in West London where I live has been closed to vehicles for many years, with significant consequences for traffic flow and ease of connectivity. Road surfaces also decay and new roads may need to be built to cope with expanded usage. Hence, to draw out the metaphor further, the empirical relationship between tracking practices and tracks such as an audit trail is not likely to be smoothly accretive, but it is still theoretically useful to think of them like this, at least as an initial baseline model, in order to envisage the dynamic nature of traceability complexes in which primary traces, tracking, tracks, modes of connection, and accounts are co-formative. And having established the baseline, we can now turn to some of its limitations and boundary conditions: disconnectivity, dependencies, and connectivity as value.

Disconnectivity

As already noted in this chapter, despite the seeming power of the "ruts in the road" metaphor, we should not take claims about audit trail connectivity at face value; they are aspirational; they are perspectival; they are made; and they are lost. The sufficiency of the observation that they enable today may prove to be insufficient tomorrow. Connectivity is therefore also always pervaded by disconnectivity (cf. Cooper, 2015). For example, in common with critical accounting studies (e.g. Hines, 1988), Day and Lury (2016) argue that the tracks that are the endogenous outcomes of tracking practices generate ambivalent forms of transparency, or what we call "evidentially sufficient observability" and reach. Indeed, they can be said to limit the scope of observation in a way that leads to a systemic "double form of blindness" in which we not only see what we want to see via the track/trail, but we also "don't see what we don't see". As Day and Lury argue, there are always gaps and errors, and the unseen lurks beyond the edges of tracks and trails. Indeed, a change in values and/or a crisis in assumptions about connectivity and traceability will often lead to demands for new forms of better connectivity, yielding new partial observabilities. Hence, notwithstanding our model of audit trail connectivity co-production, there is always a duality of connectivity and disconnectivity (Kolb, 2008), not least because the human agencies engaged in periodic acts of connecting may fail or exercise choice not to connect. The sufficiency of the observational capability that enables tracking is dependent on forms of connectivity that always hang in the balance. Existing tracks supporting connectivity may fail in times of crisis.

If we revisit the "ruts in the road" metaphor, it may be that the terrain is too bumpy. There may be rivers that need specific bridges or mountains that need the creation of passes. In short, interoperability and connectedness can be problematic. From this point of view, tracking practice is work, often hard work, to generate and maintain connectivity and traceability. We know that connecting may require a multiplicity of intermediate operations, such as bridge building, reconciliations, workarounds, and many of the other infrastructural adjustments identified by Star (1999). Yet such efforts at stabilization may fail not only for material technical reasons, such as electricity supply, but also inherently because tracks and connectivity are always partially disconnected (Strathern, 2005; Ratner and Plotnikof, 2022). The endogenous co-creation of traces, tracking practice, tracks, and accounts is therefore to be understood as continuous work to ground and maintain specific forms of connectivity and observability, actions that necessarily generate new disconnectivities via, for example, the reductive nature of primary traceification. Indeed, there may be active practices of disconnecting when actors explicitly prefer and value privacy and discretion in decision-making and work practices (Bernstein, 2012). This processual dialectic of connecting/disconnecting is especially evident in regulatory settings, as we discuss in Chapter 6.

Dependencies

As noted earlier, the "ruts in the road" metaphor, while helpful, can also mislead us into thinking of audit trails and tracks as discrete objects. In other words, tracks and the traceability complexes they assemble are dependent on multiple forms of social and technical connectivity, from information systems to fundamental material affordances such as the availability of electricity, well-functioning servers, and human expertise. When we look back to the "ruts in the road" metaphor, we see how this metaphor also abstracts from many such dependencies, including broader issues of geology and terrain that would concern anyone building a real track or road. Hence, common sources of disconnectivity are the failure of critical dependencies. Furthermore, these dependencies also pose a methodological challenge common to the study of infrastructures such as audit trails. As noted earlier, choices must be made about which of many dependencies to include and which to ignore.

Critical dependencies are sources of risk to connectivity. While tracks and their connectivity generate a certain sufficiency of observability, they also generate invisibilities and zones of ignorance. Tracking may generate tracks, but these tracks have "edges", and beyond such edges are things that may be important but which we do not notice. We become locked into the connectivity of the specific track, into the ruts in the road, and this lock-in is a source of risk. Indeed, audit trail connectivity can enable risks as contingencies to be made observable so that they can be tracked and managed (to be discussed further in Chapter 7). But the primary traces, and hence the nature of risk tracking, may ignore built-in critical dependencies and their vulnerabilities. Organizations and their leaders are often surprised by failures, despite investing in elaborate tracks, trails, and connectivity that support intense and granular risk-tracking and accounting (La Porte, 1996; Power, 2011b).

Connectivity as Value

If we recall the simple ABC model of accountability outlined in Chapter 1, then the B placeholder for accounts is that which makes the actions of A *observable* by C to some degree of agreed *evidential sufficiency*. A and C are connected via the accountability relationship, which reflects a value of reciprocity, a value that may be embodied in law, custom, or everyday expectation, and which is operationalized within the traceability-accounts nexus. Hence, socio-material forms of connectivity, like audit trails, are themselves value-laden to the extent that they participate in and enable accountability for connecting the value-purposes of quality, security, and discovery to specific traceability complexes. Indeed, there is an increasingly intense politics of connectivity in the digital age, in which privacy rights and concerns with intrusive surveillance are debated. The much cited example of a supermarket inferring pregnancy from shopping patterns is one of many that motivates pressure for restrictions on algorithmically driven forms of tracking.[1] The programming of discrimination into credit scores and insurance premiums is another example (Hurley and Adebayo, 2016). More generally, technology has always stood on both sides of these complex value-based pressures both to construct and to deconstruct connectivity. For example, widespread concerns about the extent of closed-circuit television (CCTV) in the United Kingdom have largely dissipated, while facial recognition technologies have emerged as a new area for contesting traceability (Egbert, 2019; Egbert and Esposito, 2024). And as I write these words, there is pressure for greater connectivity in supply chains allowing for the traceability of compliance with sustainability and human rights goals (see Chapter 5).

Centres of Traceability

The argument to this point has conceptualized the nature of connectivity as infrastructure, and has positioned the audit trail as a specific but significant mode of such connectivity, a mode that acts as a platform for accounts generation and traceability. To recap: primary traceification is the marking of things that enable them to be tracked and to become sources of accounting in its most general sense. Primary traces are thereby important boundary conditions of the many and various reports, metrics, lists, and rankings with varied scale and observational reach. In Latourian terms, it is the trail that enables traces and accounts to travel easily to the distant agencies that he calls "centres of calculation"[2]. These agencies can also use the trail "in reverse" to monitor, evaluate, and audit accounts of performance. In such circumstances, the traces that compose accounts are endowed with evidentiary and forensic status, which is the commonsensical understanding of traceability. We can think, in a manner

[1] See *Time Magazine*, 17 February 2012, https://techland.time.com/2012/02/17/how-target-knew-a-high-school-girl-was-pregnant-before-her-parents/.

[2] Latour (1986, p. 32) states, "The calculations themselves are less important than the way they are *arranged in cascades*, and the bizarre situation in which the last inscription is believed more than anything else" (emphasis added). Here, calculation for Latour is not specific since he is more focused on the gathering of inscriptions and the transitions they enable. The metaphor of the cascade is therefore central to his thinking.

consistent with the traceological inversion of the accounting/auditing relationship proposed in Chapter 3, of these connected observers and auditors as *centres of traceability* as much as centres of calculation. Indeed, this is what makes the trail an "audit" trail. All the acts of these different observational, monitoring, and account-producing agencies (which may be collections of humans in regulatory organizations but also machines and their algorithms) at different junctures of the audit trail are themselves performing its connectivity in the service of a traceability purpose. And in doing this work of mediation and connecting, they also change and further elaborate the trail. To repeat, connectivity is not a thing but a series of potentials that are activated by practices of tracking by different agencies.[3]

Notwithstanding the boundary significance of primary traceification, other intermediate inscriptions and metrics are also be produced along the trail, connecting to each other via shared or related accounting components. The connectivity of the audit trail is therefore a function of multiple operations of tracking in both directions that co-articulate with each other via their respective processes of abstraction/reduction and concretization. The audit trail has what Dourish (2001) describes as a "duality" of connectivity in that it is simultaneously both *technical* workflow and also the production of an *ability to account*, or account-ability in Garfinkel's sense of making things "observable and reportable" by *human* participants in the process (Garfinkel, 1984a [1967]; see also Suchman, 2002) (emphasis added). From this point of view, any process description of an audit trail by an operator in a centre of traceability is a form of script that prescribes a string or chain of connected activities to be observed and tracked. And equally, tracking and oversight practices generate process scripts that describe the connections and accountabilities that matter to their obligations to demonstrate and report on fulfilment. So while we have previously analysed the audit trail as a "technical" form of connectivity—a material "track" produced by successive waves of tracking practice—it also has an ideational or programmatic form embodied in scripted process descriptions of itself and the specification of its accountabilities. In other words, the audit trail is a socio-material and also a *moral* technology in which techniques and aspirational values cannot be parsed from each other.

Finally, Latour's (1999) notion of "circulating reference" is helpful in further theorizing the connectivity and dynamics of the audit trail. His anthropology of science takes aim at epistemologies that assume a gap between words and the world, and therefore generate a false philosophical problem of "reference". Reference is not to be understood as a kind of "glue" between words (traces,

[3] If the audit is the token, the audit trail is the type. And as routines theorists have come to recognize, the type/token dynamic is one of both continuity and change (Feldman, 2000).

inscriptions) and reality but, as Peirce and many post-empiricist philosophers suggest, is produced in a dynamic web of relations between many things arranged in chains of mutual transformation (see also Chapter 9). The idea of "circulating reference" denotes this movement, transformation, and flow of reports and accounts, and Latour is arguing that all knowledge is grounded in this ability—this "trace-ability"—to move back and forth, to circulate, along a track connecting concrete things and abstract accounts of those things at different levels. He is in effect suggesting, in a tantalizing manner not made fully explicit, that something like an audit trail, and what we call the "evidentially sufficient observability" that it supports, is a feature of all knowledge production as an unfolding process of abstraction and translation, from the material and concrete to the mobile and documentary. From the point of view of circulating reference theory, traceification and datafication are not distinct processes of producing distinct objects—traces and data—but sit along a continuum of to-and-fro transformation (Rheinberger, 2011). Referentiality, like evidentiality, is not a static given, but is emergent and endogenous to the work of connecting done by scientists, accountants and others who build knowledge. And if this implicit argument is plausible, it positions traceability complexes as sites of circulating reference and places a traceological theorization of accounts at the very heart of the sociology of knowledge.

Audit Trail Variation

The audit trail as a distinctive and dynamic mode of connectivity and knowledge-generation has variable characteristics that are important for the main thesis of this book, namely that there is an emerging shift in the nature of the accounts we live by. Indeed, if we think of audit trails as tracks, then it follows that they can be more or less crowded with agencies engaged in traceification, tracking, and oversight. According, to Kolb et al. (2008, p. 184) "the number of links between actors can be considered their connective *density*. We define connective density as the combined viable modes of social and technical connections between two or more persons or collectives". Drawing on this conception, we can understand the density of an audit trail in terms of the number of discrete agencies—centres of traceability—related to each other by the connective circulation of traces and accounts, and on which they are both dependent and which they produce. For example, in Chapter 6, we touch briefly on practitioner debates about governance and so-called "lines of defence". The question as to whether there are three or more such lines of defence is, in our terms, a question of audit trail density, that is, about the number of agencies within a trail that utilize it for discrete tracking and oversight practices (business lines, compliance departments, internal auditors, external auditors, executive boards, audit committees, and regulators). These different agencies may or may not be physically distant from each other, but it is their number and relatedness that are the important aspects of variation. The audit trail can in this sense be imagined as a specific kind of regulatory supply chain (see Chapter 5). This metaphor of the supply chain also implies another dimension of variation, namely *depth* or reach of the observational capacity it enables. Greater depth enables oversight by agencies that are more "remote" from contexts of primary traceification.

To develop these ideas further and to evaluate their implications, we need to revisit the distinction that was developed in Chapter 2 between *tracking-led accounts* and *accounting-led tracking*. By construction, tracking-led accounts are associated with less deep, less dense audit trails. An example would be a metric used by an organizational sub-unit to track its operations and monitor them for local quality-control purposes. In contrast, accounting-led tracking tends to be associated with deeper, denser audit trails spanning conventional organizational boundaries. An example would be the production of scaled-up accounts, such as financial statements for regulatory filing purposes. However, these differences should not be overstated, and care is needed empirically. A localized performance context, with many agencies acting independently to observe the work of others, would be characterized by dense but not deep audit trails. High reliability settings, such as air traffic control rooms, would be an example; airspace is made locally observable by technology. By the same token, there might be deep but sparsely populated audit trails across organizational boundaries, for example where inter-operative surveillance technology enables near-perfect observability, such as the tagging of legalized cannabis (Pflueger et al., 2019). Indeed, digital connectivity is generally leading to less dense audit trails with greater depth and reach.

Having postulated that density and depth are sources of variation in audit trail connectivity, we must also consider their *temporality* more explicitly. Notwithstanding the dystopian spectre of continuous connectivity and "everpresence" (Wajcman and Rose, 2011), there may be different temporalities of activated connection. Tracking practices and accounts production will vary in their frequency and rhythms, even within a discrete audit trail, from the real-time tracking of critical safety performance measures to periodic reports on safety culture metrics derived as combinations of such measures. But such distributed temporalities corresponding to different sub-processes can also change. During the financial crisis which began in 2008, *daily* liquidity tracking by banks dominated their *quarterly* reporting, and periodic internal audits. Thus, we can say that less dense, less deep audit trails will usually be characterized by relatively high frequency, even so-called real-time tracking and accounting, whereas agency-rich and deep audit trails will tend to have relatively lower frequency temporal rhythms (e.g. annual regulatory returns). Furthermore, different "regions" of an audit trail may be connected by evaluative agencies working to different temporalities and depths. Hence connectivity will often involve translations and transitions across different densities, depths, and temporalities.

We can now represent audit trails generically as connected sequences of trace processing and accounting, which "ascend" in scale (depth) and which are populated by different agencies (density) engaged in rhythms of tracking and oversight (temporality). To borrow again from Latour (1986, p. 17), while primary traceification has an important position in this scheme, "the phenomenon we are tackling is *not* inscription per se, but the *cascade* of ever simplified inscriptions that allow harder facts to be produced". The metaphor of the cascade, like that of "circulating reference", implies a dynamic of progression. Audit trails are certainly cascades but not in the sense of a chaotic "avalanche of numbers" (Hacking, 1982). They are rather the unfolding and continuous transformation and accumulation of materials into traces, which can in turn become "hard" accounts of ever greater scale. Figure 4.1 provides a visual representation of an ideal typical audit trail as a track or pathway that connects agencies. The vertical dimension of the map captures its density in terms of the number of discrete agencies or centres of traceability. The horizontal dimension defines its depth, the degree of abstraction, and temporal rhythm. Accounts production

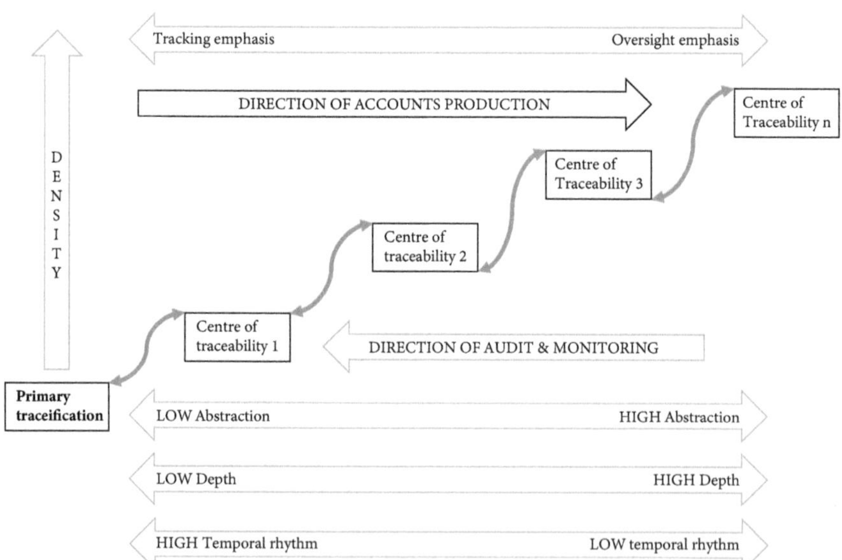

Figure 4.1 Audit trail elements showing variation in density, abstraction, depth, and temporality.

is the movement from left to right; audit and evaluation are movements from right to left. Furthermore, any specific audit trail may have "regions" that vary in how they emphasize tracking-led accounts and accounts-led tracking. By construction, the former are a feature of the lower density, lower depth, and higher frequency region of an audit trail; the latter is a feature of the higher density, higher depth, and lower frequency region.

We illustrate this audit trail model using the example of a food-production process. A specific foodstuff or chemical may be required to be tracked through a production process and tested for safety and quality reasons. The connectivity that matters here is that which enables the relevant primary trace of the foodstuff to be tracked, especially where it may be subject to further processes of transformation into an end product for sale. Here the process of tracking of the object to ensure its quality and safety is the traceability purpose, and there will be tracking-led accounts that reflect the fulfilment of this requirement, for example in the form of operational reports and dashboards for process-control purposes. At this point, we are deep in the production process itself and, assuming this is not a multinational supply chain for the moment, we are looking at the less dense, low-depth end of an audit trail. By assumption, the audit trail is internal to the production department, involving operational quality control only, and perhaps the gaze of the internal auditor from time to time. But while there may be only one centre of traceability in play, it may involve frequent reporting, depending on the precise nature of the system for tracking. Many different tracking-led accounts about the chemicals in the food will likely be produced regularly and close to decision-making and intervention points.

As the accounting becomes further elaborated, abstracted, and summarized for, say, use by food safety compliance departments, internal auditors, food standards regulators, and others, the audit trail becomes denser and deeper. These different agencies have an interest in and a mandate for observing and evaluating the tracking of food quality at the organizational level. Their needs for oversight via summative accounts generate pressure for deeper, denser audit trails that connect them to operational agencies and enable evidentially sufficient observation of them. Now the operational accounting (tracking-led) becomes further abstracted and aggregated into reports explicitly designed to enable a periodic oversight role. Regulatory agencies do not normally require hourly or daily reports, but rather meaningful summations that can nevertheless be verified and tracked back to the operational level. Hence, as the observational depth and density of connected agencies increases, accounting led-tracking becomes more salient, that is, specific reports and accounts are developed that enable such agencies to do their own tracking of the performance of the safety and quality system for an organization as a whole. Here, deeper audit trails make organizational operations "evidentially sufficiently observable" for evaluation and accountability purposes by various "centres of traceability". We might think of these agencies as stakeholders of a distinctive kind (i.e. they have a stake in maintaining the integrity of the audit trail in order to be able to connect and observe effectively; Comeau-Valee and Langley, 2020). Indeed, deeper and denser audit trails generate greater risks of disconnectivity simply because they are by definition composed of multiple agencies with different interests in traceability, temporalities of work, and degrees of discretion over whether to connect or not, and how. For this reason, the evidential sufficiency of observation by remote agencies is often operationalized in the form of due diligence protocols. Lacking stronger, more direct modes of observation, remote agencies rely on due diligence certifications further down the trail. In this way, audit trails as strings of devices to enable sufficient observability are at the heart of "making things auditable".

Formally bounded organizations are populated by many different audit trails with different depths and densities for different aspects of their performance. Hence, the empirical texture of traceability in any organizational setting is likely to be complex, multi-levelled, multi-agent, and contingent. Furthermore, not only should we be mindful of audit trail variability, but also when audit trail absence might be expected or desired. No "primary" traceification usually means no track, no accounting, and therefore no audit trail or connectivity. Such absence does not always reflect an intention to deceive or even an overriding value of privacy. For example, tracking an object directly via primary traceification can be practically challenging, both epistemologically and economically. In such cases, proxy traces are usually constructed for the main object of interest and its traceability. Thus, one likely reason why AML regulations focus intensely on the tracking of banking *customers* and their transactions, and on the second-order observation and oversight of this process, is because illicit *money* itself—the main object of interest—is difficult to track directly (see Chapter 6). If money could be "tagged", its biography and origins in criminal activity could in principle be tracked. But money is designed to be anonymous, especially so with the advent of cryptocurrencies. Hence, even where the values that mobilize traceability are strong, they must be organized pragmatically, to track and observe that which is economically and epistemologically possible to track. This is no surprise. As noted in Chapter 3, accounts are always partial and value-laden representations of organizational and individual activities. The old adage that "you manage what you can measure" can be adapted and extended to traceability and the architecture of the audit trail itself: "you *track only what you can traceify*!". The following vignette adds some colour to this proposition:

It is 9 a.m. on 26 July 2013 and the start of an additional audit committee meeting to consider some closure points for the half-year interim accounts. At the meeting are the chief financial officer (CFO), two non-executive directors (NEDs) who are the members of the audit committee, together with others attending by conference call. Yesterday, the company received a claim from the solicitors of an aggrieved third-party supplier. The question debated over the next hour is whether a contingent liability, as defined by the existing accounting standard, needs to be recognized or disclosed. In accordance with the rules of the time, the committee is not being asked to think of an expected value for the contingent liability. Rather, it must only consider whether, on the balance of the evidence, the company has at least a 51% chance of repudiating the claim.

The in-house corporate lawyer joins the meeting by phone (zoom, teams, and other forms of video conferencing do not yet exist or are in development and not widely used). All present have read the letter from the solicitors but they need his view. His professional opinion is that the claim is spurious, but he is seeking third-party legal advice. It's the holiday season so this advice may be delayed by a week. The external auditor has also been consulted, although he is not present at this meeting. He has seen the legal correspondence and has taken the view that the matter is too uncertain for the accounting recognition of a liability. On the question of disclosure, he says he is comfortable that no specific disclosure is required, and that anyway there is an all-purpose contingencies disclosure in the financial statements to the effect that the company may be "subject to non-material legal claims from time to time". He also takes the view that the maximum amount of settlement, should the company lose, is not material.

The audit committee discussion gravitates to the view that it should do nothing. It is also agreed that the minutes should reflect the reasoning. Since it is necessary to have closure for the interim accounts, it is suggested to the in-house lawyer that it would be good not to receive the legal advice until after the interim results have been announced. In any event, the question of provisioning would be reconsidered at the year end. After discussing a few other items, the meeting ends at 10 a.m., and everybody leaves.

The meeting described in this vignette seems very distant from the architecture of the audit trail discussed earlier in this chapter and in Chapter 3. Yet it is not untypical of many specific audit committee deliberations that focus on the reasonableness of assumptions, and on the estimates based on those assumptions, which permeate financial statements. The vignette suggests that estimations of future outcomes for accounting purposes involve collective interpretive work by many agencies—the CFO, the auditor, three non-executive members of the audit committee (one of whom is the author), the in-house lawyer, and a soon-to-be-contacted third-party lawyer. The litigants and their lawyers who have triggered the estimation discussion are "present" via their correspondence.

In this audit committee setting, we see that audit trail connectivity is not characterized by the mechanical tracing of transactions from their origins to accounts, but is an outcome of a deliberative process, a hermeneutic circle of consensus formation (Francis, 1994). First, the legal correspondence provides "evidentially sufficient observability" for tracking the potential liability and constitutes a time-series of documents as a form of "trail" that connects the relevant parties to an event in the past that is essentially absent. Via document-based primary traceification, the event is constituted in the present as an object and as a potential source of a future potential liability. Yet, this status is provisional and therefore its datafication for accounting purposes hangs in the balance. Second, this trail of documents counts as an evidentiary resource for the audit committee, enabling its members to exercise second-order "oversight" of the contingent liability control process, as well as for the CFO to determine the "correct" accounting treatment. In this example, the traceability of the potential liability is a necessary, if not sufficient, condition for the accounting decision, but it also makes oversight of that decision possible. The meeting also produces a record in the form of minutes, which traceify the decision process itself, enabling it to be added to the document history and tracked over time, including by a regulator.

Finally, all the activities depicted in this vignette are just components of one micro-event in the life of an infrastructure for governing the quality of financial accounting involving auditors, audit committees, professional institutes, and much else besides. It suggests that primary traces, audit trails, and tracks can be highly varied and idiosyncratic; tracks and accounts are often constructed pragmatically and opportunistically from available artefacts, both digital and non-digital in nature.

The Thinning-Out of Audit Trails

The preceding general conceptualization of audit trails and their variability matters for several reasons. First, it provides a reminder that tracks, trails, and connections exist as architectures of material elements subject to accepted process descriptions. In other words, the seemingly mundane technical features of audit trails reflect collective belief systems and values about what constitutes sufficient observability and accountability. Audit trails are therefore entanglements of technological elements and beliefs about their efficacy and connectivity. Second, it is proposed that under conditions of digital connectivity this entanglement is changing in emphasis; audit trails are becoming less deep, less dense, and characterized by higher-frequency tracking-led accounts. This postulated shift undoubtedly represents a potential for more efficient and direct observational capability by regulators and others. But it also provides a theoretical basis for contemporary disquiet about the accountability and oversight of digital technologies, namely the truncation, fragmentation, and *thinning-out* of the connectivities that enable human oversight. While the latter is undoubtedly imperfect and often ineffective—audit trails often break—it reflects an important ambition for human-based control.

Third, the conceptualization of the audit trail as we have developed it in the preceding also helps us to approach the question posed in Chapter 1 as to whether surveillance capitalism is a continuation and intensification of audit society or not. Audit society can be defined as, and is coextensive with, an expansion of second-order observation, involving the intensification of accounts-led tracking of performance, auditing, and oversight conducted by multiple centres of traceability connected in deep, dense audit trails (see Chapter 3). Surveillance capitalism, as Zuboff (2019) analyses it, turns this partly on its head. It posits an expansion of digitally enabled primary traceification and datafication for multiple operational purposes, involving tracking-led accounts of various kinds, such as document management. In audit society, reductive primary traces of performance were controversial but enabled tracking within dense audit trails populated by regulatory agencies seeking to "observe" organizations via multiple accounts. The denser, deeper audit trail connects, mediates, and makes performance observable and accountable to these agencies, which may be distant from first-order activities and operations. In surveillance capitalism, the expansion of trace production and tracking represents a dramatic intensification of connectivity but with at best less deep and dense audit trails in which oversight is largely operational and private. To anticipate Chapter 10 a little, it could be argued that in audit society, audit trails were "too deep and dense". They were intrusive, leading to both excessive and defective oversight practices. By contrast, in surveillance capitalism they are "too shallow and thin", with a consequent weakening of democratic oversight. Hence, it is proposed that *the humble audit trail turns out to be a point of inflexion between two powerful collective orders.*

Connectivity, Audit Trails, and Automation

To this point in the chapter, we have been concerned with the theme of connectivity, and with the "audit trail" as a distinctive mode of it. Yet with the advent of the digital age, connectivity in general has both become faster and broader in scope (Kolb, 2008). Studies focus on the consequences of this hyper-connectivity for increased behavioural visibility and traceability (Leonardi and Treem, 2020), for being "always on" and over-lit (Flyverbom, 2015, 2021), and for eroding productive spaces of privacy (Bernstein, 2017). The capacity for tracking as a form of traceification-enabled connectivity and behavioural observability has also greatly increased, and we see this in many different fields of activity, from inter-organizational supply chains to personal self-tracking and profiling (to be discussed explicitly in Chapter 8). These developments and their effects extend to the digitalization of audit trails, which, we now argue, is much more than simply the automation of an analog process.

Automation can be thought of as the replacement/displacement of human rule-following with machine rule-following. This "replacement project" has been underway for centuries and has attracted both enthusiasts and critics alike. Digital automation is no different in principle in this general respect. The rules or algorithms at the very centre of digital automation practices have attracted particular attention from scholars, even though the very category of "algorithm" is itself an object of dispute, having also a long pre-computer-age history (double-entry bookkeeping was in essence a system of algorithms to aid in accounting control; Daston, 2022). Studies of digital automation have shown that the very nature of organization (Alaimo and Kallinikos, 2020, 2024), regulation (Lodge and Mennicken, 2019), and management (Stark and Pais, 2021; Stark and Broeck, 2024) are being reshaped by algorithms, and for this reason they attract considerable academic, regulatory, and policy attention. This is known to scholars as digitalization in the sense of forms of digital automation that involve significant changes to work practices. Algorithms are imagined as new and powerful human-designed non-human actors at the heart of digitalization processes that are generating a level of moral concern about governance and control, and the displacement of human judgement and thinking, not least in the context of advances in machine learning and other forms of artificial intelligence (AI) (Clark, 2025).

Dourish's (2016) working distinction between algorithm and code is helpful for some conceptual navigation. The former is understood as the system of rules for processing data with different possible purposes and functions (e.g. process efficiency; profiling). In relation to this notion of algorithm, code is understood as the specific operationalization of algorithm into machine language. This algorithm-code distinction is easily challenged, but its suits the working purpose of our argument. As rules for automating and replacing or at least enhancing human activity, algorithms can be said to be features of *practices* even if such practices are difficult to observe and take place "inside machines". And taken as features of practices, they are not fixed in time or in nature but have biographies of development and use by humans (Glaser et al., 2021). Understood as strings of rules, algorithms in practice vary enormously from simple decision aids to complex machine learning–based decision-making.

Algorithms are involved in: the datafication of phenomena, and their representation as data; the pooling and connecting of data; and the production of patterns from these pools that have potential predictive and decision-enabling value (Puranam, 2025).

In principle, there is nothing to prevent audit trail connectivity from being automated using algorithms as rules for the primary traceification and tracking of relevant performance objects and events, and for the production of accounts at increasing levels of abstraction via rules of combination As such, the rules of transformation from trace to data to accounts/patterns also constitute the automated connectivity potential of audit trails that enables traceability applications of varying kinds, from data audits to journal entry checks, as well as accounts preparation.[4] Indeed, governance practices like auditing, to be discussed further in Chapter 6, have a long history of utilizing computer-based automation techniques to execute analytical review procedures. These early "computer-assisted audit techniques" (CAATs) were algorithmic in nature but also, by today's standards, relatively simple. However, even these early advances in computer technology and algorithmic power also generated problems of traceability and auditability. Auditors initially tried to audit "around the computer", dealing with inputs and outputs rather than the process (Dock et al., 1974). In this sense, computers were regarded as "black boxes", which was a pragmatic solution but which also generated much soul-searching about the quality of the audit trail. On the one hand, there was connectivity, even if the manner in which it worked could only be "sufficiently observed" by an expert programmer, on whom an auditor would need to place reliance. On the other hand, the audit trail could be said to be broken because, as a practice construct, the relevant human auditor could not test that connectivity directly but only indirectly via its inputs and outputs. This historical reflection suggests the potentially paradoxical nature of automated audit trails. The "black box" has changed in nature perhaps—now machine learning and AI are the governance challenge—but the problem of the human-machine-rule interface has not. It is proposed that when digitalized connectivity is extensive, the audit trail as a capacity for tracking with sufficient observability can itself become problematic. It all depends on the practice context, as the following examples of blockchain and machine learning suggest.

[4] There are a number of automated "audit trail" products on the market offering solutions to digital document and workflow control and security-supporting compliance with the standard BS-10008; see https://knowledge.bsigroup.com/products/evidential-weight-and-legal-admissibility-of-electronically-stored-information-esi-specification. For example, see https://apogeecorp.com/insights/audit-trails/ (accessed 22 January 2025).

The Paradox of Audit Trail Connectivity

Much has been written about blockchain technologies, first in their role as secure platforms based on cryptographic technology for trading crypto-currencies such as bitcoin, second in their later manifestations as platforms for multiple applications and smart contracts, and third in terms of their origination in the counter-institutional political imagination of decentralization. In general, blockchain has been the subject of considerable debate, not least because of its automated self-governance, defined by the motif of "code is law", and the claimed immutability of its transaction recording. Specifically, blockchain-based traceability is also the cryptographic guarantee of connectivity to an originating transaction or event that is permanently recorded. It is the idea of the complete connectivity of the "trail" in which all transactions are also of necessity self-authenticating. This ex ante control makes largely redundant the costly, regular ex post human activity of audit. Thus, in blockchain we see how the common sense of an audit trail is deconstructed. The pure connectivity of its infrastructural features crowds out and makes more or less redundant any specific audit or tracking processes that might use that infrastructure because all the assurance that is necessary has already been "designed-in", at least in theory.

Millo et al. (2024) study machine learning in practice and show how it "does not leave an easily examinable trail" (p. 1). Furthermore, a little like the computer black box of the 1970s, human understanding and capacity for interpreting its results are subordinated to the imperatives of the model itself. The absence of a humanly comprehensible audit trail is also correlated with the self-validation of machine-learning models by internally generated statistical measures of performance, measures whose variation cannot be readily attributed to clear causes. The model becomes a practice-in-itself around which humans organize themselves to facilitate its operations. Indeed, the opaque and self-referential nature of algorithms underpinning machine learning not only undermines accountability but also de-skills experts, including auditors, who are reduced to being facilitators of the model (O'Regan, 2024). This machine-learning context seems to be one of trace-ability as "data hunger" and production without evidentiary traceability. Hence there is no audit trail as commonly understood and no account-ability as discussed previously in this chapter. Even tracking-led accounts may reach their limits in machine-learning settings.

These two very different settings, in different ways, reveal the paradoxical nature of audit trail connectivity in the digital age of the early twenty-first century. On the one hand, blockchains for cryptocurrencies are contexts that promise near-perfect connectivity and in which the audit trail as transaction oversight is rendered unnecessary. On the other hand, machine learning is a setting in which audit trails as infrastructure for human oversight disappear as algorithmically defined connectivity increases in complexity. In both illustrative cases, the paradox is that as connectivity becomes more complex and opaque, audit trails as oversight applications become weaker to the point of non-existence. This paradox also suggests that whatever we used to understand by audit, assurance, and oversight, and their respective forms of evidentially sufficient observation, they are being reconstructed under conditions of advanced automation. Indeed, between these two posited extremes of redundancy and non-existence, automated audit trails are evident in many organizational settings as discrete platform-like functions on which tracking apps can run. Such apps can encode analytical and diagnostic capabilities enabling, for example, in the case of computer security, the tracking of who has logged on, of who has made changes to programmes, and where manual workarounds and adjustments have occurred. These trails and their applications are essentially specific manifestations of algorithmic management (Stark and Broeck, 2024).

This digitalization of the audit trail requires us to adapt the metaphor of "ruts in the road", which we used to theorize the emergence of connectivity. Automated audit trails and the tracking functions they support, such as so-called "regtech" applications, are more like the "service tunnels" or "hard shoulders" on multi-track highways. Built in parallel with, and part of, a main tunnel or road, they are used normally for specific maintenance and safety applications, and their connectivity is derived. The "traffic" on the road may be more or less continuous, but the maintenance tunnel/hard shoulder is a discrete parallel track that is part of the main highway and enables compliance with road regulations to be observed by specific apps, such as cameras and other sensors. Using this adapted metaphor, the "ruts in the road" model remains valid in algorithm-rich settings, but the audit trail is more like a derived and secondary "track within a track" that enables specific forms of app-relative observation (e.g. audits, compliance checks). This audit trail is still constituted by rules for the production of traces and their conversion into data and accounts, but these rules and the traceability they generate are produced less by recognizably discrete human agencies exercising judgement and forming opinions and more by algorithm-based apps, whose workings may themselves not be readily visible or understandable (see also Chapter 6).

This "appization" of the digital audit trail and the related algorithmic-based automation of oversight amounts to the tendency towards what we designate as "less dense" audit trails that support the expanded capability to produce traces at scale to enable the tracking of people, processes, and things. We are also likely to see growth and innovation in such tracking-led accounts with a strong operational and compliance focus. For example, multi-function information architectures, such as ERP systems, generate and store the digital traces of many activities. Dedicated "smart" auditing and financial accounting apps exist that are used to produce accounts, to track and validate transactions, and also to test the integrity of programmed systems for their logic. Integrated systems can in principle host a variety of audit trail-type connectivities, of which financial accounts production is but one. Audit trail flow-through becomes populated by fewer mediating human agencies, which are replaced by algorithms, even to the point where regulators can directly access, for example, the safety management system of an airline via a portal. Hence, we can theorize that audit trail connectivity, as trace-enabled observability, not only becomes deeper for quality, security, and discovery purposes under conditions of increased automation but also *becomes less dense and more distributed across multiple applications*, leading to more operationally specific forms of audit and assurance. Even in these more application-based settings, the earlier noted paradox reappears. Digitization increases connectivity in one way but decreases it in another; observability as tracking increases while observability as oversight is reduced.

We began this book with the example of a marathon runner tracked by GPS linking a smart phone app to a wearable device. This digital connectivity increased the observational reach of spectators, who might previously have been restricted to bodily positioning at various points along the course. Yet the nature of their observation capacity was changed, becoming more mediated and less experiential, while expanding its spatio-temporal reach. The digital traces produced by the wearable device not only enabled the runner to be tracked. It also enabled these traces—primary traces—to become data supporting tracking-led accounts of performance in the form of, times, splits, heart rates, and so on. This is a specific "audit trail" whose connectivity matters only to the runner and some spectators. In short, there is depth and real-time temporality without density. Yet, the runner's personal data, as with all self-tracking, may also in turn be co-opted as a valuable resource for further processing by tech companies, to discover more about the users of their apps, or to regulate its quality, fix problems, and make improvements (Lupton, 2016b). Here audit trail connectivity, as the pathway by which runner data becomes proprietorial data for an organization, is at best opaque. There is "trace-ability" without evidential traceability. Data security and privacy issues at stake in situations like this have led pressure groups and regulators to seek to reconstruct the trail and populate it with oversight agencies. In this sense, these groups are endeavouring to make the connectivity visible as an audit trail by increasing its density, thereby enabling human oversight of the use of personal data. In this simple and increasingly everyday example, we can see that audit trails and traceability are often partial and incomplete. There may also be multiple intersecting trails and non-trails serving different interests and purposes and with different depths, densities, and oversight potentials.

It was suggested earlier in this chapter that the audit trail is a moral technology and its automation is a potential site of contestation and negotiation about density and temporality, and hence about the nature of the oversight it supports. For example, while much is said about the advantages and efficiency of continuous auditing for the purpose of assuring process integrity and quality, there is also a loss of "temporal independence", that is, the ability for oversight practices to adopt their own temporal rhythm, to "stand back", reflect, and report. It has been said that "[t]o live in the digital ecology is to live within a chronoscopic temporality of the constant present. This is creating its own form of tyranny, the 'tyranny of real-time'" (Purser, 2000, p. 5; Hassan, 2003, p. 102). The general point is that the automation of tracks and tracking, which brings so many advantages to organizations, also has consequences for the temporal structure of oversight. We return to this issue when we discuss governance explicitly in Chapter 6.

In summary, we can see the audit trail mode of connectivity as an important site of fundamental transformations and shifts. But we also have to be careful. The audit society thesis suggests that ideals of accountability and oversight can overreach themselves when demands for evidential traceability are excessive and interfere with first-order operations and services. In addition, oversight structures and practices, like all regulatory projects, may be both mythical and ineffective (Scott, 1998). Hence, despite concerns about excessive surveillance and the erosion of human judgement, we should not assume that the tracking-led accounts and less-dense audit trails are without benefits. Far from it. Not only are the efficiency gains of automation often real, but digitally enabled tracking may also enable the development of varieties of powerful counter-accounts on matters of value, such as biodiversity. The potential for value-rich tracking with high observational depth displacing wasteful oversight, and therefore for new accounts to live by, exists in the evolving space between a return to audit society and the excesses of surveillance capitalism. However, practices in which machine learning and other forms of AI are significant, and whose operations escape human understanding and account-ability, also suggest that audit trail connectivity is not simply technical infrastructure but also a platform for ultimate human oversight and control. In time our sense of the human may change so much that we may come to doubt this.

Conclusions

It has been argued in this chapter that the audit trail is a distinctive and general mode of connectivity supporting traceability and accounts production. It is proposed that the tracking practices that do this connecting progressively generate structures of connectivity as sedimentations of repetitive action. In other words, we can think of audit trails theoretically as the outcome of repeated acts of accounting and auditing; connectivity potential is what makes and inheres in produced infrastructure. It follows that the audit trail, and the nature of the connectivity it produces, should not be conceptualized as having an independent ontology, even though historically it can be identified with observable architectures of documents and other artefacts. Rather, we must think of it as a continuously realized form of collectively perceived connectivity that is constituted and maintained by sequences of tracking and accounting activity. It is these practices of trail-making and accounting that bring traceability as a value to life, give it material form, and endow it with "explosive organizing potential" (Meyer and Rowan, 1977; Power, 1997, p. 96) even to the point where it is widely diffused as a model of knowledge (Strang and Meyer, 1993; see also Chapter 9). Variants of such tracks and trails are evident in many fields where traceability is valued and where tracking practices are mobilized by an interest in quality, security, and discovery. From computer security (e.g. Merconi, 2003) to genetically modified (GM) crops regulation (Lezaun, 2006) to palm oil production (Rival, Montet, and Pioch, 2016) to seafood (WWF, 2015; Lewis and Boyle, 2017) and flight safety practices (Gawande, 2010), tracking practices produce the accounts that define audit trail connectivity and which, as we see in Chapter 5, reach beyond the boundaries of the juridical organizational entity. Audit trails continue to be pervasive but are often implicit and specific structures of connectivity to be found in many fields of human endeavour.

The connectivity of the audit trail is one important building block for the *traceological theory of accounting* being advanced in this book. It is a theory that emphasizes the combinatorial and connective elements of accounting as a process. Audit trails also matter as an enabling basis for oversight as the second-order observation of operations. In this chapter, the general model of the audit trail has also been moderated to capture variations in their depth, density, and temporality. This variation matters because it requires us to address how different forms of digital automation are profoundly changing these characteristics, even to the point of eliminating the audit trail entirely. In simple terms, the thesis is that audit trails are becoming less deep, less dense, and higher tempo, and are more productive of what we have called tracking-led accounts at the expense of accounts for wider oversight purposes. Put another way, the portfolio of accounts that we live by is shifting towards tracking, with a corresponding "flattening" and "de-centrism" in the nature of governance. This shift is our focus for Chapters 5 and 6.

Chapter 4 Summative Propositions

The following propositions provide further elaboration of the variable architecture of audit trails and state the implications of digitalization for their connectivity:

1. **Tracks (trails) are connective structures or platforms that are co-produced by the tracking practices they host.**
2. **Audit trails vary in depth (observational reach), density (numbers of agencies connected), and temporal rhythm.**
3. **"You track what you can traceify".**
4. **The audit trail is a point of inflection between two powerful collective orders: audit society and surveillance capitalism.**
5. **Under conditions of advanced digitalization, audit trails are becoming less deep, less dense, and more frequent in their temporal rhythms. The mix of tracking-led accounts and accounts-led tracking is shifting to the former.**
6. **Blockchains deconstruct the "audit trail" into a self-checking platform or trail that makes audit/tracking redundant; machine learning deconstructs the trail itself, making human oversight impossible.**
7. **The paradox of audit trail connectivity: as digital connectivity and observational efficiency increase, the audit trail as a basis for human oversight decreases, to the point of disappearing entirely.**

5
Organizing Scripts and Governance Layers

Overview

Traceability and governance are deeply intertwined (Power, 2019; Muirhead and Porter, 2019). Practices of governance and oversight depend on connective structures like the audit trail, as discussed in Chapters 3 and 4. By linking and making observable the activities of multiple distributed actors and organizations via selective traces and accounts production, the audit trail provides the necessary, if not sufficient, conditions for practices of oversight. Furthermore, the quality of arrangements for oversight have come to be evaluated as an aspect of organizational performance in their own right. Such "oversight of oversight" reflects an inherent logic of expansion, in which practices of traceability must also themselves be made traceable and demonstrable (Power, 1994b).

This chapter focuses on the nature of governance as oversight in and between organizations and shows how it is enabled by modes of traceability that generate "evidentially sufficient observation" (Chapter 4). The argument begins at an ontological level, drawing upon established scholarship to argue that governing and organizing are not two distinct things. There is no entity that we would designate as an organization that does not involve some form of governing as oversight, even of a minimal kind. Furthermore, the stability and coherence of the entities we regard as organizations—what can be called their "organizationality" (Roth Smith, 2022)—is a function of many such governance-orientated practices—law and accounting, to name but two. Beyond this ontological level of argument, we argue that the specific modes of traceability that operationalize oversight practice must have some kind of microfoundational basis on which to operate, like the "tracks" of Chapter 4. Accordingly, this chapter draws upon the work of several scholars who emphasize the microfoundational and communicative role of documents and scripts, and how they generate connectivity, mobilize "acts of organizing", and "entify" organizations. We move away from the artefactual connotations of document, and adopt the notion of "script" that has theoretical utility despite being empirically imprecise. Scripts are the underlying prescriptive "software" of organizing. They are often cultural in nature, may be explicit or implicit norms, can be manifest in documents, may influence the myriad of communications that permeate organizations (Cornelissen

Economy of Traces. Michael Power, Oxford University Press. © Oxford University Press (2026).
DOI: 10.1093/9780197681527.003.0005

et al., 2015), or exist as invisible algorithms. While scripts are individually non-determinative of the actions at which they aim, they can be understood as agentic, at least to the extent that they are reference points in communicative exchanges (Cooren, 2004). The nature and shape of scripts as a whole are highly varied; they enable scaling and traceification and can be sources of de-centring, as much as hierarchy.

Building on this general thesis, the chapter develops the idea of governance as traceability, arguing that traceability makes ideals of transparency operational. Governance is understood as a traceification-dependent form of observation, organized and scripted in "layers" of "oversight" activities. This is what some practitioners call the "governance supply chain", and the chapter concludes by discussing supply chains in general where phenomena and metaphor have become indistinguishable. Regulatory efforts to generate the entification of supply chains over and above their discrete organization constituents illustrate how organizationality is in part an outcome of the dialectic and tension between forces of fusion and fragmentation. In Chapter 6, we illustrate and discuss this governance "supply chain" further.

Making Organizations Traceable

According to Meyer and Rowan (1977), formal organizations are embedded "sub-entities" of society. They are cultural products whose surface formality is generated by institutional environments that prescribe legal form, general purposes, and many other normative attributes. Institutional theories show how these "cultural scripts" flow into, shape, and individuate clusters of activities, conferring entity status on them as "organizations" (Powell and Rerup, 2017). In this sense, it is trivial to state that organizations are social entities—what else could they be? Yet creating and maintaining such discrete entities involve work to define and manage the boundaries between them and their notional environments that are positioned as "external" to organization. These environments have been variously conceptualized as sources of resource, of transaction costs, of uncertainty, of normative models, as noted previously, and much else besides. Regardless of these variations, some kind of duality of organization and environment has been essential not only to management theories, even seemingly very different ones, but also to management practice. The distinction between an organizational "inside" and "outside" has become deeply naturalized and juridified, even when we allow ourselves a more fluid view of organizational boundaries (Power, 2018). Furthermore, the institutions of law play a central role in the coding of organizations as discrete non-human actors endowed with both intentionality and the ownership of assets, allowing them to be further demarcated from an environment of other similar organizations (Pistor, 2019). Organizations as legal fictions contract in their own right; they own property and can be attributed with responsibilities, legal and otherwise. They have what has been called "actorhood" (Bromley and Sharkey, 2017).

Notwithstanding its continuing power, this juridical-realist conception lives uneasily with theorizations of organization that emphasize relations, alliances, and connectedness in human networks that are porous to normative environments. For example, Padgett and Powell (2012) show how organizations as "actors" crystallized from overlapping networks of family, church, and commercial interests. More generally, process scholarship increasingly focuses on organizations and their boundaries as contingent formations that are continuously "becoming" (Abbott, 1995; Hernes, 2014; Schatzki, 2006). And as theoretical attention has shifted from entities to relations, and from things to processes and connections, organizations have come to be understood more explicitly as the emergent outcome of multiple "acts of organizing" and of ever-changing relations between heterogeneous objects, people, buildings, machines, books and records, laws and regulations. As Abbott (1995, p. 860) puts it, entities are a sub-class of events, and an organization is "a set of transactions that are later linked into a functional unit that could be said to be the site of these transactions". Organizational boundaries emerge first as "sites of difference" (p. 862) produced by acts of differentiation that only subsequently become boundaries of an entity.

This processual and event-based view of organizations strengthens the sense that accounting practices in their broadest sense, and the traces that underpin them, are important aspects of boundary-formative acts of differentiation that generate organizations as entities. As already noted in Chapter 2, forms of accounting *for* organizational activities that presuppose an accounting entity also serve to constitute organizations *as* entities and define their boundaries and purpose (Hines, 1988). However, if traceification and datafication produce organization-constituting accounts and forms of self-observation, what are the underlying infrastructural conditions that facilitate these processes? What sets them in motion? One answer to this question points to the role of documents.

Documentality

Accounting is arguably a special case of "documentality" in general. For example, Ferraris (2012) argues that there are no "social" facts, like legal facts, without documents in the form of contracts, signatures, and treaties, which are more than paper and ink and which confer facticity and temporality on human interactions. As an ongoing assembly of such social facts, an organization depends for its continuing acceptance and existence, its organizationality, on such documents, obviously so in the case of constitutional-type documents, such as Articles of Association under UK company law, which perform legal corporate entities in shell form and encode the organization as a legally bounded aggregate actor. More generally, organizations are entities whose existence in general depends on being connected and projected in documents that transcend their transitory and fleeting moment of creation (Smith, 1984, 2001). As Abbott (1995, p. 873) puts it, the "central quality of an entity is endurance", and many documents, and the relations between them, sustain this durable entification. In short, scholars maintain that documents, at least an important sub-set of them that memorize and project, enable the complexification and layering of organizing activity over space and time.

Documentality theories emphasize the "textually mediated" nature of governing in which protocols for, and accounts of, acts of organizing are registered in documentary form. This self-observing and action-orienting nature of documentality is not an accidental, contingent feature of organizations. Rather, some documents are instrumental in constituting them. And once created, documents are:

> forms which externalize social consciousness in social practices, objectifying reasoning, knowledge, memory, decision making, judgement, evaluation, etc., as the properties of formal organization or discourse rather than as properties of individuals. (Smith, 1984, p. 60)

It has long been recognized that documents are never simply a representation of "what happened" (Garfinkel, 1984b [1967]; Van Maanen and Pentland, 1994; Hull, 2012a; Hull, 2012b). They are more like projective descriptions of possible action according to specific organizational or institutional purposes. There is "not initially an event or object that is subsequently given an objective record" (Smith, 1984, p. 65). Rather, it is argued that documentary processes are the source of the experienced facticity of the organization as a stable system, a facticity that is reinforced as documents, communication, and action are repeatedly intertwined (Ashcraft et al., 2009). The articulation of "facts" about an organization is made possible by the routine production and use of all manner of documents (Garfinkel, 1984a [1967]; Cooren, 2004; D'Adderio, 2008; Kaghan and Lounsbury, 2006). Many documents, including formal accounts, reproduce conceptualizations of organizations as entities that are more or less powerful in connecting, communicating, and motivating further actions under their schema:

> the formality, the designed, planned and *organized* character of formal organization depends heavily on documentary practices which coordinate, order, provide continuity, monitor and organize relations between different

segments and phases of organizational courses of action. (Smith, 1984, p. 66, emphasis in the original)

Documents, digital or otherwise, and the material devices through which they are produced, are therefore important relational material of organizing. They can also embody *dual temporalities* (see Chapter 7), on the one hand, by tracing and memorizing past organizational activities and events and, on the other hand, by projecting possibilities for future action and connections. Documents, including especially those of an accounting nature, are thereby "front-loaded with the habits, intentions, and rationales held by the agencies by which they have been created, adopted, and adapated" (D'Adderio, 2011, p. 207).

Documental theories of organizing are compelling and have the potential to enrich traceological theories of accounting. Provided that documents continue to exist and are not erased (as many are), they make organizations traceable. The physically and visual form of documents has undoubtedly been an important aspect of their contribution to theories of organizing, not least those that adopt a "governmentality" lens on organizing. Furthermore, in digital form, documents provide the primary data for forms of AI, such as Large Language Models. However, scholarship has tended to anchor documentality by default in an analog world of books and records.

Scripting

One of the problems with the concept of document is its ambiguity between material form and content. In the founding terms of routines theory, this means that the notion of document blends its artefactual (material) and ostensive (prescriptive) features (Feldman and Pentland, 2003). In contrast, the notion of script is broader and more clearly focused on prescriptive content rather than its form. However, scripts and scripting can be thought of in many ways. As noted earlier, Meyer and Rowan (1977) theorize cultural scripts as symbolic resources and templates in organizational environments, which can be drawn upon in specific organizational settings. Goffman's (1959) dramaturgical sociology generalizes the actor's script, which defines his or her role in the context of a play. Actors may improvise to some extent, but they are also governed more or less by the text. And Latour (2013) has yet another take on scripts, arguing that they are the prescriptive basis for what he calls "acts of organizing". He claims that organizations as we know them are nothing beyond a piling-up and cross-referencing of scripts that make them somehow legible, traceable, and durable, and which prescribe varying degrees of (imperfect) actionability.

Latour (2013) begins from the idea that that the notion of "organization", like those of society, economy and capitalism, has been over-substantiated, meaning that it has come to be regarded as an independent entity in what he calls a transcendental sense. Rather, with the empirical eye of the ethnologist, he argues that there are only what he calls "scripts" that he understands as action-orienting, prescriptive, and projective plans and protocols, and which underwrite and facilitate multiple ways of acting and communicating "organizationally".[1] This adverbial and event-based turn in thinking about the ontology of organizations requires us to accept that these multiple scripts have action rather than representation as their primary purpose. However, scripts also vary a great deal in their purposes. For example, some of them enable more aggregated framings and positioning of organizations as bounded entities. Latour refers to these scripts with framing and entification power as providing "mini-transcendences" in level. For all this, they are not at all indications of a hidden master entity called an organization. It is these continuously circulating and connecting scripts and their capacity to frame, and to give meaning to, the actions taken according to their prescriptions, which enable organizations and organizing to be what, in Latour's version of processualism, he calls a "mode of existence" rather than a domain of reality that stands over the individual and under society.

If we accept the general direction of Latour's thesis, organizations are not entities that exist independently of multiple and varied scripting processes that embody expectations and shape the terms in which actions are described. Organizations are real for Latour in that they are "made up" as humans perform these organizing acts and communicate in accordance with the scripts that frame and categorize them as acting organizationally. For example, many such scripts will invoke and project the culturally engrained duality of organization and environment. Indeed, for all the theoretical shifts in contemporary organization and management theories, and the centrality of relational and processual thinking in these shifts, this dualism of organization and environment, like that of mind and body, has remained remarkable durable, deeply anchored in everyday discourses. The relevant issue is not whether organizations "really are" fluid and relational, or a nexus of contracts as Coase famously put it, but how a relatively coherent, stable, and bounded "organizationality" is produced and sustained over space and time. Latour's anthropology points us towards the answer in the form of scripts, some of which embody cultural ideas supporting discrete entification. Hence, organizational entities and the organization-environment duality are enacted in the connections generated by multiple scripts across different

[1] Abbott (1995, p. 876), argues that we should "think about such scripting as a phase in the construction of entities . . . scripting cannot be seen as independent of boundaries".

"sites" of organizing (Schatzki, 2005; Bailey et al., 2022). And as we see in the following, they can be de-entifying to some degree.

The notion of script as Latour uses it seems to be much broader in scope than that of document as text. Scripts understood in more explicitly prescriptive terms as protocols, rules, and purposes that generate expectations and that orient many different "acts of organizing" may be encoded in, and have, a documentary basis. But equally, as Garfinkel, Goffman, and Meyer and Rowan show us, they can be implicit, shared understandings of how to act appropriately. Hence, not all scripts are documental in form; many are implicit norms and oral in nature. Some may even be intended to be deliberately deceptive, and to leave no trace of their script. Secret organizations with scripts but no, or only minimal, documents are not uncommon. And scripts with legal, regulatory, and operational content also give rise to the problem of how formal prescriptions relate to the script "in action" as it features in organizational communications and actions. This is an issue that has animated both socio-legal scholars (Halliday and Carruthers, 2009) and routines theorists, who observe practice and inductively elicit the revealed "true" script and its grammar (Pentland and Rueter, 1994). Scripts may encode normative purposes into standard operating procedures in order to mobilize an ongoing stream of actions that they recursively constitute as being "instances" of the official routine. This fit between normative guidance and action sequences is never perfect and tight. But, rather than being a deficiency, such essential looseness allows for improvisation and for a view of practices as unfolding patterns of action and communication. Scripts as prescriptions that aim at action always require continuous work, often hidden, to maintain the status of events as being more or less in accordance with the prescription (i.e. compliant with a rule). Thus, what counts as "enacting" a script is itself a communicative construction from patterns of actions and interactions that are not rigid and uniform. A formal script may exist in a loose relationship to the revealed "grammar" or logic of its operationalization in a "narrative" structure, a structure that highlights its points of inflection, stability, and change (Pentland et al., 2011).

Latour's conception of scripts allows for variation in their projections of "scale" in that they operate at, and encode, different "levels" in relation to each other. For example, some scripts are manifested in documental forms such as diaries, memos, time sheets, questionnaires, checklists, and log books, as well as basic formal accounting records (Wheeler, 1969; Riles, 2006). They may operate at the relatively "low" level of "primary trace" production by prescribing how events are to be traceified, how they are marked for inclusion, circulation, and accounting within an organization. In Chapter 3, we noted that the making of a mark on the clay tablet was an act of both organizing and accounting. The tablet also encodes an implicit script, which is agentic in that it defines the mutual obligations and expectations of one or more parties and defines a space for communicative exchange.

The agentic properties of scripts can be further dramatized by the case of the flight readiness protocol/checklist discussed in Chapter 3. There is a documentary underpin or medium that may be paper or digital in nature. There are also many mini-scripts, in the form of questions/instructions for a specific routine (e.g. testing procedures for wing flaps and recording that this has been done as an "act of organizing" that connects a single operation to many others like it). The instructions and the production of traces of compliance are the prescriptive content of the checklist. Overall, the flight readiness protocols are low-scale scripts that are at the centre of, and necessary for, the communication between the pilots and ground staff. Furthermore, the script is the prescriptive feature of the checklist in the form of instructions for producing the primary traces of aircraft safety and readiness prior to take-off. Earlier chapters may have implied that the production of primary traces of relevance and interest just happens. It does not. Scripts for traceification, like the checklist, provide the protocols by which primary marks are created and are drawn upon by other "higher-scale" scripts. These scripts for primary trace production reflect choices, both cultural and technical, about what is and is not organizationally relevant. In this sense they are value-laden.

In general, small-scale scripts like the take-off protocol can be connected to others in audit trails to generate mini-transcendences in the form of larger-scale, more abstract, scripts for representations of the organization. As Latour (1986, p. 29) puts it, "In order to exist . . . entities have to be summed up somewhere". For example, financial accounting practice, as discussed in Chapter 2, is a complex web of scripts that aggregate and "sum up" transactions. This leads to powerful high-level panoramas of the organization that can be made to seem as if they refer to it as a pre-existing entity. Indeed, trainee accountants are always taught that financial accounting is dependent on the entity assumption. Yet, it is an assumption that accounts continuously perform via a myriad of scripts, such as the rules of double-entry bookkeeping. Organizations must therefore be understood as "entities" that are nothing more than temporally produced and changing outcomes of "scripting processes" that establish and sustain action-orienting and communicative relations between human actors. Where an organization begins and ends, the boundary between the inside and the outside, between an organization and its environment, is itself an outcome of these processes, of how they are scripted, and of what counts as an act of organizing and differentiating (Abbott, 1995). Many of these scripts are deeply engrained, cultural norms about the organization as an entity. From this point of the view, the entrepreneurial work to, say, transform a "movement" into something we would call an organization necessarily involve inter alia a shift in the dominant scripts and related communicative practices (Hedberg and Lounsbury, 2021).

To summarize, we have selectively reviewed two streams of adjacent scholarship—on documentality and scripting—which are relevant to what we might call the "microfoundations" of organizing. For many reasons, it is tempting to avoid placing too much theoretical weight on the metaphor of the script. Yet it also remains a compelling concept because (a) it is a digitally neutral notion that can be developed in algorithmic terms—scripts are organizing software, both human and non-human; (b) it references non-deterministic prescriptive processes within wider communicative contexts (e.g. Cornelissen, 2004; Cornelissen et al., 2015; Cooren, 2004); (c) scripts provide the raw material for making organizations traceable; and (d) some scripts are specifically recipes for traceification and underpin the self-observation capacity of organizations. For these reasons, the concept of the script remains attractive and suggestive as a theoretical reference point, even when it is difficult to specify empirically. Importantly, scripts relevant to accounting are generative of organizational capacities for self-observation, enabling the tracking of operations.

De-centring the De-centred Organization

The thesis to this point is that organizations require some self-observation capacity to persist and endure, and the microfoundations of this capacity are to be found in sub-sets of scripts, notably those that enable tracking via the traceification of events. However, this thesis is expressed at the general level of organizationality as such. It is also neutral as regards the matters that typically engage scholars of organizations, such as design, structure, control, and much else where we find observable empirical variety in the quality and nature of self-observing capacity. Our proposition is that organizations as manifestly diverse as universities, banks, charitable trusts, and oil companies must, as a minimal condition of being more or less coherent entities, be able to observe, memorize, plan, and control actions over space and time. In this way, the argument aspires to establish the internal relations between traceability, accounting, scripting, and organizationality.

In this section, we consider how this theorization of organization remains foundational under conditions of intensive datafication, and as organizations become what scholars and practitioners describe as increasingly "data-driven" (Quattrone, 2016; CGMA, 2016). As noted already, digital algorithms can easily be understood as embedded scripts of varying complexity to support/enable prediction and decision-making. They have also become vehicles for realizing dreams of "data-driven" organizations, which are more efficient, more intelligent, more sensitive to changes in their operating conditions, and capable of greater precision and predictability in employee control. It is no doubt tempting to regard the notion of being "data driven" as hype and cliché, and this may be so in many instances. Indeed, the theory of organizing developed in this chapter suggests that organizations have always been, to a greater or lesser extent, script-driven, and this includes scripts for defining and producing data. The data-driven nature of older organizations may have been "weaker" by contemporary standards, but there was always some data (e.g. about transactions), which informed management actions to some degree.

However, for all these continuities, there also seems to be a step-change in the epistemology of organizing in the form of a digitally intensive empiricism that is reconstituting capacities for informedness and observation, as well as the very nature of organization. According to Alaimo and Kallinikos (2024, ch. 6), this step-change marks a shift to a more explicitly "de-centred" organizational topology (Stark and Broeck, 2024). The thesis is that data, far from being just an *input* to information systems about their nearby operations and transactions, is now deeply implicated in forms of discovery and control based on gathering and processing heterogeneous sources well beyond the traditionally inscribed organizational boundaries and conceptions of their neighbourhoods. In the terms of the preceding analysis, the scope of organizational self-observation has greatly expanded.

For Alaimo and Kallinikos, "datafication", as described in Chapter 2, has a rich and contingent texture, consisting of the primary capture mechanisms that we call traceification and subsequent statistical clustering processes that generate categories and relations of similarity and difference. In settings such as recommender platforms, this is a granular bottom-up process of category production and grouping that implicates new forms of human expertise and new modes of power and sociality (Fourcade and Healy, 2024). Importantly, the distinction between the technological means to capture and utilize traces generated beyond formal organizational boundaries and the very nature of organizing itself becomes blurred. The data-driven organization in this theoretical sense is potentially unbounded.

If we think of this de-centring of organizations via the notion of the script developed in the previous section, we can make a number of observations. De-centring can be theoretically reconstructed as a systematic shift in the mix of such scripts, namely a shift from those that aim at aggregation and scaling up and that generate orientations to a controlling centre and hierarchy (actorhood), and those that are more operational in ambition, oriented to the processing of data and tracking all manner of objects. In terms that have already been expressed in Chapter 2, we can think of the de-centred organization as one in which data-driven tracking is displacing/diluting those scripts that articulate and promote capacities for oversight as the view "from above". In short, there is a *flattening* of organizations in terms of their levels and scale—what Latour calls their "mini-transcendences". And we should remind ourselves of the dynamic nominalist insight here. If organizations are at least partly realized via the enactment of their scripts, then, in the absence of compensating communicative practices, a change in the portfolio of these scripts necessarily changes the "reality" and topology of organization, even to the point of the weakening of entification, or as Alaimo and Kallinikos put it, de-centring. We return to this issue in Chapter 6.

The purpose of this section has been to explore the microfoundations of organizational self-governance. In the notion of the script as organizational software we find at least one important component of these microfoundations. The overall argument is that there is not first an organizational entity that has to be governed. Rather, governance, in the sense of minimal coherence and capacity for self-observation and tracking, is essential to, and co-emerges with, the acts of organizing that stabilize entities in waves of scripted actions. In this sense, Latour would argue that organizations have always been more decentred and less "modern" than we might imagine, despite having boards of directors, organization charts, job descriptions, incentive plans, discrete buildings, financial accounts, and much else besides. This is because such "centres" of organizational control and traceability are themselves artefactual and communicative outcomes of the ongoing piling-up of centralizing scripts in his sense, which build rather than presuppose the centre/periphery distinction. Indeed, this view is consistent with established theories of organizations as loosely coupled systems (Meyer and Rowan, 1977; Orton and Weick, 1990). However, technology-based transformations in the nature and role of data have also led to further de-centring by de-authorizing the scripts that sustain organizational boundaries and hierarchies (Alaimo and Kallinikos, 2024; du Pont, 2024). The organization as an entity becomes in effect "dividuated" (cf. Chapter 8 on the self) or subject to de-entification pressures. It exists and is governed through multiple manifestations wherever and whenever technology enables datafication to occur.[2] Although it may not seem so, this de-centring and flattening has major implications for how we think of governance, assurance, and much else in the digital age. We now turn our attention to this idea of self-observation, or what we can call in more familiar terms "oversight" (Edelman, 1990).

[2] See Bailey et al. (2022) for a similar argument, which develops a relational perspective on emerging technologies and organizationality.

Governance as Traceability

What is governance? We can think of it in its more traditional sense as essentially relational in nature and oriented to behaviour modification for a purpose. In this broad relational sense, something or someone C may be governed by something or someone else—A—often using a means or instrument of some kind—B. As already discussed in Chapter 2, there are many different theories of this relationality and of the content of the ABC triad that operationalizes governing as practice. Principal-agent theory is perhaps the historically dominant model and in its various forms emphasizes contractual or quasi-contractual relations between the governed (C), known in economics as "agents", and the governing (A), known as "principals". The approach focuses especially on the design of "incentives" for agents to align their actions to the interests of principals as far as possible, and on the design of optimal information systems (B), like accounting, to enable principals to monitor agents. Economists know full well that these arrangements are always costly, imperfect, and frictional. They also raise fundamental questions about which aspects of agents' activities can and should be monitored and how: inputs, processes, or outputs, and with what degree of precision and transparency? Theories also variously analyse markets for corporate control, auditing, regulation, and remuneration design as institutional mechanisms that underpin the dynamics of governance as a temporally structured process of principal-agent interaction and optimal alignment. Empirical studies have identified many other variables associated with the quality of these aspects of governance, including leadership style, organizational culture and values, and board composition, to name a few. In general terms, principal-agent theory presumes that governance depends on leveraging forms of self-control via incentives design. Indeed, it has become self-evident across both economics and sociology that organizations, to varying degrees, necessarily participate in their own regulation.

In thinking about governance in terms of principal-agent theory and the ABC triad, it may often be assumed that the incentives and resources of A and C are given and B is the design variable directed at the reduction of agency costs. Yet, it is also recognized that B generates agency issues of its own, leading to the prospect of chains of principal-agent issues and complexity in contract design. Processual theories of organization put Bs, understood as socio-technical devices like accounts, in a more central and agentic role from the outset, even to the point of shaping the behaviour and expectations of As and Cs. Such a theoretical positioning of Bs moves the analysis of governance towards Foucault's influential notion of "governmentality". The latter is already de-centred in its theoretical emphasis because it grows from a focus on practices and their devices rather than organizations as such (Raffnsøe et al., 2019; Mennicken and

Miller, 2014). The notion of governmentality captures the sense of the pervasive and constitutive forms of self-governance grounded in assemblies of ideas, documents, and devices. Governmentality studies also emphasize how such forms of self-governance and regulation via registers, accounts, and other documents are understood in constitutive and not just disciplinary and hierarchical ways (Rose et al., 2006; Dean 2009). At the extreme, governmentality is pre-emptive because it aims to "programme out" deviance from norms in advance (Bogard, 2006), in part by generating a "governable self" (Miller and O'Leary, 1987). Travelling a similar path, socio-legal and regulation scholars have come to recognize that purely hierarchical models of regulation of the command-and-control style—which we might label as centrist in their assumptions—are rarely empirically descriptive. Their focus has shifted from the primacy of law on the books, notwithstanding its continuing significance as a source of organizing, to governing and regulating as multi-actor networks in which private organizations and a multiplicity of "soft laws" are pivotal. These shifts have resulted in increased scholarly and practitioner focus on how organizations "naturally" self-regulate, as well as how they responsively internalize, and therefore re-script, a great deal of the apparatus of imposed regulation (Ayres and Braithwaite, 1992; Edelman et al., 1999; Power, 2007, ch. 2).

The nature and extent of these broad shifts in the style and centre of gravity of regulating towards organizing and self-governing are much debated. There are those who see the law as continuing to have a distinctive role in this apparatus as a "master" script, in contrast to those who see it as just one source of normativity among others. Furthermore, while so-called neoliberal ideologies have been premised on notions of market-based governance and de-regulation, in fact the very opposite seems to have occurred in the neoliberal period, in that there has been a conspicuous expansion of organizing scripts in the form of policies and normative frameworks with associated information and compliance requirements (Gray and Silbey, 2014). Within this broad shift, states also reinvented their steering role by creating specialized bodies, such as regulatory agencies, whose purpose is to produce scripts for other organizations in the form of broad frameworks, templates, and principles within which formal organizations might write their own detailed versions. This de-regulatory intention resulted in the amplification and elaboration of scripts not only for organizing but also for making organizations more traceable, legible, and auditable to third parties. These regulatory scripts in turn presuppose and demand new roles in the form of multiple compliance professionals in law, accounting, risk management, internal audit, and many others, whose role is to service what Huising and Silbey (2021) call "accountability infrastructures". Their practice involves the further elaboration and intensification of organizing and traceifying scripts. In this period of what has been called "regulatory capitalism" (Levi-Faur, 2005) regulating, governing, and organizing became more intertwined than ever. However, we should also be cautious about taking the notion of regulatory "internalization" too much at face value, since it already presupposes the inside/outside distinction as given, whereas we have argued that this is a function of scripting. So we should retain the notion of internalization only as a proxy label that references a particular mode of constituting governance in the form of practices of self-observation—oversight—enabled by intensified traceification.

The expansion of audit and audit trails (Power, 1994b, 2021a) is a specific manifestation of these wider developments in governance practices as forms of second-order observation or oversight. Organizations were already being decentred by these developments in the specific sense that their operations were being "turned inside out" and made visible to, and trackable by, agencies beyond their formal boundaries. Scripts for "self-governing" processes were being made explicit with the aim of making organizations auditable and "ready for inspection". Corporate policies, codes of conduct, and oversight committees multiplied for all manner of issues, such as conflicts of interest, and internal systems of control became more elaborated and overseen by internal auditors and others who report to audit committees. In addition, risk moved to the centre stage of organizational governance with requirements to maintain and evaluate the quality of risk management. As the scope and reach of risk-thinking expanded, so too there was a conspicuous expansion of the scripted "riskification" of organizations (Hardy and Maguire, 2016). It was as if every aspect of organizational life could be seen through the lens of risk—the risk management of everything (Power, 2004a) (see also Chapter 7). These trends in governance were also being mobilized by an unquestionable ideal, namely that of "transparency" as a concept, which itself presumes the duality of observer and observed.

Transparency and Traceability

The ideal of transparency is never far from discussions of governance, regulation, and accountability. As Christensen and Cornelissen (2015) argue, transparency has a long history, reaching back at least to the Enlightenment and to the origins of perceptivist metaphors of knowledge as a "mirror" (Rorty, 1980). It is a deeply embedded myth that mobilizes and underpins not only science but also discourses of governance and governing. Transparency is a value that is almost impossible to be against, and calls for more transparency in economic and political life are rarely contested. The cultural power of transparency is that it is "somehow sheltered from critique" (Christensen and Cornelissen, 2015). Many regulations, including accounting requirements, have their origins in ideals of transparency and disclosure, which make the "inner" workings of organizations and the activities of agents visible to outsider-principals, thereby enabling leaders and others to be held to account for their actions. The transparency of their actions to others is argued to modify their behaviour in desirable ways. In short, transparency as trace-enabled observability is imagined as a mechanism of principal-agent alignment in many fields of human collective endeavour.

This implicit and deeply institutionalized belief in the value of transparency and its power as a form of control reaches back to Bentham's dictum that "the more we are watched, the better we behave". Yet this ideal of behaviour modification through transparency has always been fragile and problematic in both theory and practice (Christensen and Cornelissen, 2015). Behavioural economists and others argue that full visibility of this kind, even if it were possible, is undesirable because it may lead to perverse behaviours, feelings of being mistrusted, motivational crowding, and value-damaging conformity (Prat, 2005; Frey and Jegen, 2001; Falk and Kosfeld, 2006). In principal-agent terms, a degree of agent non-transparency is widely regarded as optimal, an insight that Bernstein (2012) describes as the intra-organizational "paradox of transparency". If more visibility and control can have negative effects on innovation and experimentation, then transparency as a value should always be considered in relation to the value and benefits of privacy. In some settings, the creation of "zones of privacy" for teams can increase their productivity (Bernstein, 2017). Others adopt a more critical view, arguing that transparency requirements of regulatory compliance and performance management are a form of "tyranny" that distort and blind organizational agents (Tsoukas, 1997; Strathern, 2000b; Roberts, 2018). In particular, the ideal of transparency is itself a kind of cultural script that aims at "explicitization", a goal that is self-defeating because it is based on mistaken assumptions about how organizations really work (Strathern, 1995). Change projects to make organizational processes more explicit may create platforms for audit and evaluation, but are known to damage and devalue the tacit capabilities that underpin operations.

Transparency, for all its mobilizing power as an idea and virtue, is not a single thing. It is manifest in different ways (Hood and Heald, 2006), must be managed (Flyverbom, 2015), and involves significant work to bring about (Hansen and Flyverbom, 2015). Thus, accounting disclosure and freedom of information regulations are very different instantiations, and operational scriptings, of transparency.[3] The former conceives of transparency as the managed disclosure of information, while the latter sees it as rights of access for publics external to the organization. In short, transparency has many faces, and it therefore makes sense to enquire less into what transparency is, as if it were a singular property of things, and more into how the idea is scripted by different actors

[3] See Bernstein (2017), who draws attention to the different ideas and practices that are often discussed under the notion of transparency (i.e. monitoring, process visibility, surveillance, and disclosure).

and communities (Heimstädt and Dobusch, 2020). As we do so, it is clear that transparency practice is highly mediated in nature. Furthermore, for agents of transparency, such as inspectors and auditors who report on organizational conformity to rules, transparency must be translated. It must become *traceified*; to make things and people observable. They must be somehow "marked" to enable them and their actions to be tracked across space and time. Hence, a key proposition for this chapter is that *transparency as an abstract value of observability by others is often realized as, and mobilizes, traceability.*

The idea of traceability draws from the same well of values as the myth of transparency, but it also transforms them. Transparency leverages perceptivist metaphors of revealing that which is hidden to observers, of looking-through or disclosing the "inside" of things to "outsiders". Yet transparency in this sense is rarely realized as unmediated capacity to see how things really are, as critical accounting studies emphasize. In contrast, traceability is observation enabled by traces and *connections*, as discussed in Chapters 3 and 4. The primary epistemological orientation is not that of *revealing* but of *marking and tracking* (Bernstein, 2017). Understood in this way, traceability is not so much a version of transparency as its material foundation and condition of possibility. When we analyse transparency in action, we find that it depends on traceability or, more precisely, on the traceification of things and events to make them observable.

In summary, this section has developed the close linkages and practical convergences between governance as a form of oversight and traceability. This convergence reflects the expansion of scholarly and practitioner interest in organizational self-governance and internal controls, itself in part a function of the reconfiguration of state-based regulation in the form of regulatory capitalism (Power, 2007, ch. 2). It has also been suggested that ideals of transparency and traceability have some co-dependence. In neoliberal settings in which there is consensus that regulation must be a hybrid of self-governing and state-agency oversight, transparency values can be realized concretely as the script-enabled traceability of organizations. Furthermore, traceability complexes are often mobilized by, and draw their legitimacy from, the same ideals of transparency. With this transparency-traceability entanglement in mind, now we explore the nature of oversight in more depth.

Oversight, Layering, and Connectivity

Auditing procedures are a paradigm case of organized oversight. We may think of auditing as a specialized form of second-order observing of first-order observing practices encoded in, and enabled by, management systems: "it is the material traces of the management system and its associated forms of documentation which are the conditions of possibility for audit protocols, checklists and questionnaires" (Power, 1996, p. 303). The traceification of primary objects that makes tracking as first-order observation possible also enables and supports evidentiary oversight practices like audit. Audit is one formalization of a core feature of organizationality; namely, it is a mechanism by which entities make themselves formally observable by (notionally) internal and external agencies (Power, 1996, 2021a). The relations between these agencies, their responsibilities for enacting oversight, and their reliance on the work of third parties like auditors can be imagined in terms of the metaphor of "layer".

Levels and Layers

Governance as traceability involves the scripting of connected "layers" of observation or oversight. Latour's vision of organizations, and indeed of society in general, as essentially "flat" and consisting only of scripted relations among actors of various kinds, has been outlined earlier in this chapter and it is a compelling one. Yet, it must also explain why such an idea of flatness is stubbornly counterintuitive and why we cannot help but think of organizations in terms of hierarchies and levels. Part of the answer to this puzzle, already suggested in this chapter, is that there is a class of organizing scripts that function to generate a sense of what is "above" and "below" a current role position. In other words, it is these levels, rather than flatness, which are performed and generated by repeated actions, and by communications according to specific scripts, and this is important to our current conceptions of governance and oversight. These levels seem hard and durable. They are experienced as organizational and social facts, until they collapse due to scandals, economic failure, and other events.

The metaphor of "oversight" implies a second-order observational capacity to look "down and over" an activity from a (vertical) distance, to see it in its essentials, and to determine if the activity is happening as it should. Thus, "higher" layers within and beyond organizational boundaries, such as board audit committees in the case of financial accounting, embody more or less implicitly the mythical grammar of the panorama, the view from above, by which they can oversee "lower" executive or business functions. The so-called audit explosion in the United Kingdom in 1980s was in essence an oversight explosion in the sense of the creation and scripted elaboration of such layers that could be connected in audit trails and thereby constitute practices by which "higher" levels observe and track "lower" levels (Power, 1994b). In UK financial services, borrowing from the language of safety and security, this metaphor of layers came to be further developed figuratively as "lines of defence", leading to debates about how many such lines or layers there "really" were or should be (Davies and Zhivitskaya,

2018).[4] Three lines of defence—business line, risk management, internal audit—emerged as a conventional model, yet independent directors of boards, external auditors, and even regulators could equally be conceptualized as lines of defence in this sense, albeit "outside" of the conventionally constructed boundaries of an organization (Turner, 2022). Lines of defence can be imagined as centres of traceability, as described in Chapter 4; they are the agencies that are often connected in and by audit trails.

There seems to be no limit in principle to this script-generated hierarchy of layers within and across conventional organizational boundaries or to the elaboration of oversight roles and agencies. The theory of the audit society draws attention to this apparent multiplication of oversight layers, which is only partly explainable by a systemic decline in trust. And there seems to be no limit to this layering of agencies involved in organizational oversight.[5] For example, in the United Kingdom in 2022, improvements to the oversight of the work of audit committees were proposed as part of broader reforms to the market for auditing services.[6] And a sub-set of these oversight agencies have also been theorized explicitly using another metaphor, namely that of the "gatekeeper", which references how they lend their reputation to the oversight function and, in some cases, can exercise veto rights as part of it (Coffee, 2006). In this sense, overseers do not only oversee—they also have options for action, depending on the institutional setting. The general point is that what we currently call governance is increasingly imagined and formally scripted as a layered and multi-agent hierarchy of oversight practices that are mobilized to solve a variety of principal-agent issues. Oversight is a core mode of human organizing, facilitated by accounts.

This elaboration and extensive rationalization of governance in the form of layers of interdependent oversight practices demands that first-, second-, and n-order forms of observation are *connected* (see Chapters 3 and 4). Furthermore, these connections, real and perceived, have an evidentiary quality in that they enable lower layers of oversight practice to be able to provide *evidence* of their oversight to higher layers. In practice, this means that governance requires that the relevant actions of each layer can be tracked by the next layer with "evidentially sufficient observability". In many empirical cases, such actions, like the

[4] This lines of defence model is also loosely counterpoised to another—the "Swiss cheese" model, which became popular in safety management (Reason et al., 2006). Both metaphors suggest layers to governance and control, but whereas in the former non-alignment provides extra security, in the latter the "holes" are aligned and continuous with each other, thereby enabling systemic problems to be transmitted through the layers. One might say that lines of defence provide a solution to the "Swiss cheese" problem.

[5] For example, in private correspondence I learned that a significant world-level governance body has created a function to oversee the work of the audit committee, itself an oversight function.

[6] See FRC, *Audit Committees and the External Audit: Minimum Standard*, UK Financial Reporting Council, May 2023, https://media.frc.org.uk/documents/Audit_Committees_and_the_External_Audit_Minimum_Standard.pdf (accessed 27 December 2024).

take-off protocols for airline pilots, are evidenced by the completion and certification of a checklist-like instrument, known more generally as "due diligence". Accordingly, organizational governance has co-evolved with the technical production of connectivity in the form of "audit trails" that link different layers of oversight—centres of traceability—often in chains of certification (see Figure 4.1 in Chapter 4).

This model of governance as oversight intensifies the traceification of events considered to provide evidentially sufficient observation. As we see in Chapter 6, specific regulatory programmes can be conceptualized in these terms as layered scripted oversight practices, which drive trace production. Traces of activities are produced to support bespoke measures and indicators that make it possible for the "performance of governance" by organizations to be itself subject to oversight by specific agencies, such as auditors and inspectors. This is not to assume that such oversight practices are perfect or never fail. The sufficiency of observation can be challenged and subject to change; centres of traceability may be incompetent or corrupt; and there may be means-end decoupling by which audit trails as a mode of connectivity take on a life of their own and fuel excessive oversight (Bromley and Powell, 2012). The argument is rather a theoretical one, aimed at revealing the logic and internal relations between governance and traceability, drawing upon the metaphor of the "layer". There is also another important metaphor that is visible in practice discourses and which plays a similar role to that of the "layer". This is the "supply chain", the discussion of which completes our theoretical exploration of traceability and oversight.

The Oversight "Supply Chain"

Financial reporting, taken as a whole within and across jurisdictions, has been described as being not only an "eco-system" (Center for Audit Quality, 2021), or an infrastructure (Ball, 2001), but also a "supply chain" (Knechel et al., 2020). This chain connects auditors, professional institutes, taxation advisers, company lawyers, standard setters, corporate governance bodies; and capital market actors like analysts, all of which have evolved over time (Power, 2021b). A chain is an especially powerful metaphor to express connectivity because it is so familiar that it hardly seems like a metaphor at all. Each "link" in a chain is a discrete element that is connected to its immediate neighbours. The chain as a whole—so the saying goes—is as "strong as its weakest link". There is therefore mutual dependence between the links, and the chain has no function unless it connects these links. Chains are not usually, except perhaps in pure mathematics, infinite. They have a beginning and an end, or rather they have two ends that are most likely attached to other objects. The chain is a series of linkages, but it is also something whose function is to connect—a ship to an anchor, a broken-down car to a rescue vehicle, a prisoner to a chair, and so on. Material chains in this sense are primitive forms of governance and control. Chains are a species of infrastructure; they are often ignored and taken for granted until they fail, until a link breaks or was never there but only imagined to be.

"Supply" chains are depicted and imagined paradigmatically in textbooks as connections or networks linking multiple producers to the end-consumers of goods, often across large distances. Such supply chains may depend on material infrastructure, not least in the form of physical pathways for goods to travel from origin to destination. For example, the various "silk roads" connecting East to West Asia surely began life literally as "ruts" formed in the terrain that hardened into tracks with repeated use, as discussed in Chapter 4 (Frankopan, 2015). The organized movement of goods along these pathways came to involve the production of specialized documents—bills of lading, manifests, despatch notes, and many more, some of which moved physically with goods and the merchants transporting them. Supply chains in this sense can be both flows of goods and also flows of their primary traces or "tags", devices that enable both the tracking of the goods (first-order observation) and the indirect oversight of the track as a system (second-order observation). Such commodity supply chains, which might or might not involve further processing of products, have been mainly imagined and problematized in terms of their logistical challenges and specific issues of coordination, such as storage, transport (especially container freight by sea), refrigeration, as well as the security of supply, quality, and many other factors. Operational and logistical sciences have advanced greatly over the years, and supply-chain management has become a sub-field in its own right, drawing in large part on operational research techniques and their variants (e.g. Stevens, 1989; Mentzer et al., 2001). Supply chains have also come to be imagined as multi-organizational "value chains" in which the economic value added at each point of transition in the chain can be explicitly managed and, sometimes, re-engineered (Kaplinsky and Morris, 2000). Industries, such as car manufacturing, have been transformed by the rational management of their supply chains, from parts production to assembly to distribution. The aim is to create smooth, cost-efficient connections of both real goods and information across and between critical links in the chain, via designs such as vertical integration, outsourcing, and strategic alliances (Rothaermel et al., 2006). Hold-ups, delays, and other contingencies must be minimized, and supply chains have, like many other areas of management, become primary objects of risk management. As the 2020 blockage in the Suez Canal demonstrated, chains are indeed only as strong as the weakest link.

For the most part, consumers at the end of many supply chains have tended not to worry about the chain in totality, provided that goods of required quality are delivered. Indeed, supply chains were initially conceptualized primarily as an engineering problem for specialists. How goods were produced and the pathway by which they reached the end consumer have, until recently, been largely unproblematized. In this sense, supply chains have been an example of "out of sight and out of mind" in which the effects of their connectivity on people, habitats, animals, and things were largely invisible or understood only according to engineering values within the belief system of globalization. However, product supply chains have never been fully immune to a politics of their mode of connectivity and traceability. Indeed, different forms of connectivity and disconnectivity can exist at the same time. For example, Mintz (1986) provides a critical narration of connectivity and its effects in the sugar supply chain.

Recent analyses by both scholars and activist groups document the effects of supply chains on their natural and human environments, specifically highlighting issues of worker exploitation and slavery at remote points of the chain (Doorey, 2011). Indeed, it can be argued that the links in such supply chains have come to be logistically strong only because other values and concerns have been weak and powerless. As suggested in Chapter 4, every form of connectivity is partial, and disconnectivity is always in play. Particular events have intensified this supply-chain politics, and organizations like supermarkets and clothing manufacturers have been surprised to have previously unthinkable responsibilities attributed to them. Questionable aspects of connectivity have been made visible by movements, by nongovernmental organizations (NGOs), and by policy reaction to major disasters, such as Bhopal and Rana Plaza. Accordingly, critics seek to reconstruct and moralize the connectivity of supply chains as a focus for a new politics of consumption and the traceability of labour practices. Underlying this politics, the supply chain is being reimagined as a newly responsibilized entity in need of improved governance and oversight (Schilling-Vacaflor, 2021). Demands for traceability are no longer limited to the tracking of operations and the oversight of their efficiency, notwithstanding the great impact of digitalization on logistical practice. Supply-chain participants are also being required to know more about, and be able to observe, the impacts of activities elsewhere in the chain, especially upstream.

Individual organizations might only be fully engaged operationally with their immediate neighbours in a supply chain. Hence, the chain as a totality is not itself visible and legible as an entity, other than in stylized diagrammatic forms. However, oversight requirements in the name of sustainability and justice are creating pressures for expanded traceability and observability and for the postulation of a "responsibility chain" in which each discrete link has oversight capability for the whole and can understand its own role and impact throughout the chain. Any such arrangement, whether within a globally integrated corporate group or pertaining to the activities of a single organization with independent suppliers, depends on the successful primary traceification and observability of the performance value of interest, such as fair employment conditions, and its connectivity within an audit trail design to enable the oversight by each supply-chain member. Such an attempt at the moral reimagination of supply chains is visible in the European Union Corporate Sustainability and Due Diligence Directive (CSDDD) issued in 2024 (Bueno et al., 2024).

Efforts to responsibilize supply chains implicate a dialectic and struggle between pressures to expand the boundary of formally constituted organizations and prevailing interests to limit it. This is a dynamic of countervailing forces for fusion/connectivity and fission/disconnectivity (Enfield, 2017, p. 13). It is also a struggle over boundaries and hence over "entification" (Abbott, 1995). On the one hand, supply chains connect discrete formal organizations and make explicit the logistical relationships of supply and dependency that span the determinate and intensively scripted boundaries of those organizations. From this point of view, the idea of the supply chain remains grounded in, and does not fundamentally change, existing juridical notions of the organizational entity (Power, 2018). On the other hand, efforts to responsibilize supply chains, making their impacts traceable, seek to project them as new proto-entities, as meta-organizations composed of organizations that account for themselves primarily as parts of the whole. As meta-organizations, supply chains can be understood as partial but emergent forms of an organization whose members are other organizations (Ahrne and Brunssen, 2008). Even vertically integrated global corporate groups can be imagined in this way, often lacking the coherent entification that consolidated accounts attribute to them. The general point is that supply-chain connectivity is becoming more explicitly articulated in ethical terms. The juridical boundaries of participant organizations exist uneasily with the responsibilization of the supply chain as a meta-organizational entity (Cowen, 2010; Elyachar, 2017).

How does a chain of things become a new singular thing? From the earlier arguments of this chapter, we can infer that any new organizational entity will have to be intensively scripted by multiple actors, such as pressure groups, trade bodies, regulators, legislators, and academics. For example, stakeholder organizations like NGOs are likely to create scripts of connectivity that, like Mintz (1986), challenge the assumed moral and operational autonomy of distributed agents in chain-like relations with each other. Furthermore, digital technologies, mobilized by ideals of interoperability, are also expanding the capability for the tracking and oversight of supply chains as a whole. However, building sufficient consensus for entification, especially cross-border, will be pervaded by frictions and will involve considerable political work. In general, we can theorize product supply chains as continuously co-evolving triads of: formal organizational entities; varied socio-material connections linking them; and practices of digitally enhanced traceability that enable them to be observed and governed as a whole to some degree. Following Abbott (2005), we can hypothesize that as these connectivities and linkages between formal organizational entities in supply chains increase and become denser, so too does the potential entification of the supply chain increase. The process is partly one by which the externalized relations of discrete entities become re-internalized as part of a single one.

The supply-chain metaphor is widely diffused. The layers of oversight practices described in the previous section have also come to be imagined as a kind of governance "supply chain" in which parts of the chain, such as regulatory agencies, delegate responsibility and necessarily rely on other parts. For example, practitioners and scholars refer to the notion of a financial reporting "supply chain" (Knechel et al., 2020; Power, 2021b). As we have argued in the discussion of levels and layers, there is general institutional expectation for different organizational agents whose roles exist in chain-like relations to each other (centres of traceability) to be able to "look through" and observe and track relevant activities beyond their conventional organizational boundaries, and to understand other relevant agents upon whom they rely in the chain. Organizational leaders, such as company directors, have in many jurisdictions been responsibilized to govern supplier relationships beyond the formal juridical boundaries of their organizations. To do this, they must construct appropriate and acceptable audit trails that connect them to "third parties" and allow them to track activities relevant to their oversight function, and account for them in the form of certifications. Under these conditions, supply-chain governance crystallizes as chains of certification that can be said to constitute a responsibility chain linking different oversight layers.

The question of how much oversight capability provides "evidentially sufficient observability" across all supply-chain-type arrangements has no determinate answer, as we saw in the discussion of the audit trail; it is always variable and subject to changes in resource and technology, as well as shocks. What counts as being "connected" and traceable across organizational boundaries is often pragmatic, partial, and value-laden. Indeed, organizations may outsource the provision not just of goods and services but aspects of oversight itself. While there are economic rationales for such outsourcing, it is also somewhat paradoxical by increasing requirements for the *insourcing of the oversight of outsourced oversight* and thereby generating ambiguity and contradiction in the scripts that sustain organizational boundaries. For example, in the United Kingdom, Carillion plc, which was liquidated in 2018, had "out"-sourced its "internal" audit function. This is a common practice and is readily understandable via the lens of transactions cost theory. But it also has implications for the nature of organizationality insofar as it blurs and renders fluid the distinctions between what is inside and outside, leaving—by ideological design in many cases—only a nexus of specific contracts around which any boundary seems increasingly arbitrary.

Furthermore, outsourcing like this is offset by pressures to "insource" responsibility and capability to support and demonstrate oversight of supply-chain risks, the management of which seemed to be deficient in the Carillion case (House of Commons Business, Energy and Industrial Strategy and Work and Pensions Committees, 2018). Hence the de-centring of organizations is not only a theoretical thesis about their essential grounding in scripts, or an outcome of data-driven imperatives as argued in earlier sections of this chapter. It is also a practical matter as formal organizations continually experiment with their boundaries, re-scripting what is considered to be inside and what is outside, often in contradictory ways.

Conclusions

In this chapter, we draw on the notion of script to characterize the ontology of organizations as self-observing entities. Scripts are defined as prescriptions that may or may not be documental in form, and that specify "acts of organizing" according to various temporalities and scales. Some culturally grounded scripts may be fundamental to the constitution of organizations as entities that can endure over time, can plan and track their operations, can be attributed with intentionality, actorhood, and boundaries, and in all these respects can self-govern, at least in the sense of minimal self-observation. More operational scripts may determine the nature of the traceification processes that enable organizational self-observation as activity tracking over space and time.

It has also been argued that governing and traceability are mutually constitutive and co-dependent. We developed a specific reading of governance as multiple, linked, and interconnected practices of oversight, understood formally as the scripted second-order observation of first-order observation and tracking practice. The thesis of this chapter is that governance as oversight involves the organization of traceability as a system of connected agencies (Power, 2019; Muirhead and Porter, 2019). It is not just that governance utilizes traceability practices, but that traceability as a logic of the audit trail is its operating principle. We might go as far as to say that to govern is to track, a phrasing that implicates governmentality theories of organizing.

Several metaphors have been employed to aid the analysis of oversight and to provide more texture to the notion of second-order observation: layers, gatekeepers, and supply chains. As metaphors, they can be performative in that they are embedded in, and reproduced by, scripts that mobilize the practices which make them real and concrete; in this way they can become social facts for practitioners. Metaphors are ways of seeing objects that may come to shape and naturalize those objects such that they seem to be non-metaphors. Hence, the notion of "supply chain" is both a metaphor for governance and also a referent for the reality that it constructs through its organizing scripts. The supply chain is thereby both context and outcome.

Finally, we argued that connectivity in supply chains (and audit trails) is much more than logistical and technical in nature, as the politics of food supply demonstrates. There are widespread regulatory efforts underway to responsibilize organizations within supply chains, both for their direct and indirect impacts on labour and the environment. We conceptualize the challenges of such a programme in terms of (a) generating evidentially sufficient observability between connected entities and (b) generating the moral entification of the supply chain itself. The programme is a collective project of constituting a thing-based metaphor into an entity that can be acted upon and governed. It involves thinking of how flows of goods and services are intertwined with flows of oversight and tracking. As we discuss next in Chapter 6, there is both empirical variation and commonality in this organization of traceability for governance as oversight.

Chapter 5 Summative Propositions

The following propositions address the relations between organizing, governing, and traceability:

1. **There can be no organization without minimal capacities for governance, understood as self-observation and traceability over time and space.**
2. **"Scripts" can be defined as prescriptive protocols, rules, and norms that influence communication and mobilize actions. Scripts can take documental form but can also be implicit and cultural in nature.**
3. **Organizations are constituted as bounded durable entities by a sub-set of scripts that enable self-observation and mobilize the traceification of phenomena to be tracked.**
4. **Governance as traceability consists of layers of oversight connected in and by audit trails; transparency as an ideal of governance is generally operationalized as traceability.**
5. **The "evidential sufficiency of observation" that defines oversight is always contingent and subject to change, usually in the direction of intensification.**
6. **Supply-chain governance is characterized by tensions between the aspiration to constitute the chain as an entity and the autonomy of its constituent organizations.**

6

Traceability Lost

Oversight and Platformization

Overview

This chapter moves from the general reflections about organizing and governing in Chapter 5, to a more specific comparative analysis of regulatory systems, using the elements of the traceability complex (Chapter 2) as a template.[1] A number of illustrations from within financial services and beyond are provided. The benefits of this comparative approach are two-directional. While the model of the traceability complex provides a distinctive optic on governance and oversight in diverse settings, these settings can also be used to demonstrate its theoretical purchase and analytical utility. In this way, the credibility of the model is strengthened from its encounters with cases, enabling it to become a "way of seeing and problematizing" a domain for further enquiry. The comparison of the settings draws out important variations in the elements of traceability complexes, namely their value-purposes, tracking as first-order observation, oversight as second-order observation, and accounting. This comparison, though stylized and not empirically systematic, shines further light on how the mix of tracking and oversight mentioned in prior chapters is a critical point of inflection within the new economy of traces.

Following this relatively static comparison of traceability complexes, the chapter turns to the unfolding dynamics of governance and oversight in the digital age. It is proposed that while platforms as specific organizational forms have received considerable attention from many scholars, "platformization" can be understood in a more general way as the processes by which governance and oversight activities, like auditing, become portfolios of "self-certifying" apps with a primary focus on operations (Power, 2022, p. 12). Indeed, the digitalization of organizational processes erodes the governance/operations distinction. This critical proposition is explored in more detail in a specific context,

[1] In this chapter and the book as a whole, and at the risk of offending regulation scholars, no attempt is made to be analytically precise about the difference between regulation and governance since it is not germaine to the analysis. Both are in some sense systems of rules that seek to modify human behaviour, and both can be characterized in terms of traceability issues. On balance the category of governance is preferred for its greater scope and generality.

Economy of Traces. Michael Power, Oxford University Press. © Oxford University Press (2026).
DOI: 10.1093/9780197681527.003.0006

namely debates about algorithms and their auditability. The analysis points to an inversion of audit society dynamics. Rather than organizations responding to *external* institutionalized demands to make themselves auditable and traceable, it is argued that, under conditions of platformization, governance practices like auditing adapt to data-driven organizing and algorithmic management by becoming platform-like themselves. This potential reconfiguration of the topology of organizing greatly increases traceability as the ability to *generate objects* for tracking and further processing. Yet, it also greatly reduces traceability in the sense of capacities for traditional forms of human oversight based on traces as *evidential elements* in audit trails. The chapter concludes by exploring the prospects of "traceability lost" and its implications for the accounts that govern us and that we collectively live by.

Traceability in Context

Building on Chapter 5, governance and regulation regimes can be reconstructed as traceability complexes consisting of audit trail-like connections that enable oversight. These complexes have their own distinctive sub-purposes, trace-enabled tracking practices, and forms of accounting. It has already been proposed that tracking and oversight practices are always found together in one form or another, but their precise combination and configuration in any specific regulatory architecture will vary in terms of the "levels" of observation. To extend this analysis and to bring out aspects of this variation, we now consider a number of more specific examples.[2] They are: anti-money-laundering (AML) regulation; the UK senior managers and certification regime; the US Sarbanes-Oxley legislation; the regulation of interbank lending; the 2020 pandemic; governing fisheries and agriculture supply chains; the legalization of cannabis in the state of Colorado; and the governance of cryptocurrencies and blockchains.

Anti-Money-Laundering (AML) Regulation

AML regulation has grown in significance over two decades, not least because the links between crime and the funding of terrorism have become evident. Money laundering is often referred to under the broader heading of "financial crime", and the purpose of regulation is primarily that of *security*, in the sense of

[2] The choice of these examples is opportunistic and idiosyncratic; it is not based on any formal sampling method and is partly reflective of my experience as a director in the UK financial sector, which is also evident from the choice of vignettes elsewhere in this book. No doubt different examples could have served equally well. However, those chosen are sufficiently rich to support a suggestive comparative analysis of traceability, which highlights variations in, and dynamics of, the traceification, tracking, and oversight mix.

preventing the financial system from being used to launder the proceeds of financial crime and/or be used to fund terrorist activity. Since money is essentially fungible, this purpose presents significant operational challenges in detecting and tracking illegally sourced monies as they flow in banking systems. The very point of "laundering" money is to make tracking it impossible and to obfuscate, if not destroy, the connectivity that could support such tracking. The regulatory task is to create capacity to observe a monetary "laundering supply chain" originating in criminal activity and ending in legitimate usages. Making this illicit supply chain even partially visible requires coordination between a mix of private and public actors (Djelic and Sahlin-Andersson, 2006). In effect, while security and police services focus on the origins of financial crime and engage in elaborate forensic tracking practices to frustrate criminals and bring them to justice, another "layer" of preventative defence has been delegated to banks, which are enlisted to perform a range of checks on customers and their transacting activity. In this system of distributed responsibility for financial crime, commercial banks act as agents of the state in a process that begins with adapting Know Your Customer (KYC) checking processes at the point of onboarding new clients (Favarel-Garrigues et al., 2011). In this way, proprietary data about clients are leveraged, explicitly traceified, and enrolled into the AML traceability complex. The relevant primary traces of such checks include proof of identity in the form of passports, explicit tracking of persons using specialist investigative agencies, and (often self-declared) evidence of sources of funds for transactions, especially if they are large and unusual. Banks also process customer data to generate AML-related risk profiles of their customers, based in large part on their declared country of residence. Any bank employee with concerns can initiate suspicious activity reports (SARs), which are submitted to the police authorities. Individual banks have limited forensic capacity to track monies deposited with them to their ultimate sources; they can only make inferences and report suspicions.

AML regulation is field-wide and multi-organizational (see also Muirhead and Porter, 2019). It is mobilized by a security purpose and generally requires the elaborate production of traces (traceification) to enable first-order observational practices of transaction tracking and identity verification. It also involves the generation of audit-trail modes of connectivity within banks and across the relevant actors—banks, regulators, and their clients—in order that conformity with AML requirements can be evidenced for boards and regulatory inspectors. And it involves the production of accounts in the form of Money Laundering Reporting Officer (MLRO) reports, risk assessments, and much more. This mix of tracking and layered oversight begins in the so-called "first line of defence" at the point when new banking customers are acquired and are subject to due diligence checks. In turn, boards also rely on second-order observation by compliance teams and internal auditors to test and audit the quality of tracking. Boards can be sanctioned if the regulator finds deficiencies in the application of AML rules and their oversight. Furthermore, the boundary of AML responsibility extends beyond the legal entity. This raises the question for overseers as to how much observability as traceability is sufficient when an organization relies on the AML practices of other group companies or third-party suppliers.

Finally, AML processes and their governance and oversight are continually developing, not least to ensure that practices are auditable and fit for inspection. In the face of some notable scandals (Huang, 2015), individual organizations and banking groups have had to evolve their tracking and reporting practices to support changing AML accountability requirements. So-called "Regtech" markets have also expanded for products that offer to automate and integrate AML compliance (e.g. Kurum, 2023).

The Senior Managers and Certification Regime (SM&CR)

The UK Financial Conduct Authority requires financial services firms to specify the critical control and decision-making roles of senior personnel, supported by clearly defined job descriptions.[3] The regulations are the latest in a series of efforts to define the responsibilities of senior management thereby making roles more explicit, codified, and auditable. Via the elaboration of job description scripts, executives can be made more precisely accountable for the key control functions that they are required to perform. The purpose of the regime is a hybrid of quality assurance—to ensure that only "fit and proper" persons have key roles in financial services—and security, to ensure that the financial system is safe and free from behaviours that might cause excessive risk for retail clients and for the system. Relevant primary traces that operationalize these purposes include new job descriptions for senior managers, formal curricula vitae, proof of qualifications and continuing professional education, and evidence of any prior regulatory sanctions. These items already exist in some sense as data, but they become *traceified* and acquire evidentiary status within the new regime, enabling the regulatory object (i.e. the fitness and propriety of senior managers) to be constituted, observed, and tracked.

Primary documentary traces support second-order observation and the production of regular regulatory returns (accounts) and certifications. As in the case of AML, there is a layered audit trail that connects these various primary traces of individuals and their presumed propriety to a summative and aggregate overall assessment for all relevant staff. And this trail connects to further layers of oversight practices that test compliance with the requirements, in part

[3] See https://www.fca.org.uk/firms/senior-managers-certification-regime.

to reassure boards of directors that the organization is fit for regulatory inspection. The SM&CR system can therefore be analysed as an intensively scripted organization of traceability that enrols and connects a sub-set of senior employees for security and safety purposes by tracking and producing accounts of their integrity and capability. The SM&CR arrangements are structurally similar to AML; they are both forms of regulatory outsourcing whereby system objectives are transferred first to organizations and then to the self-reporting of responsible individuals. The SM&CR audit trail is also a regulatory supply chain (Chapter 5) with multiple layers of oversight and checking along the way, both within an organization and between an organization and the regulatory team at the UK regulatory agency.

The US Sarbanes-Oxley Legislation ("SOX")

It is well known that the Sarbanes-Oxley legislation in the United States, first passed in 2003, was a response to a perceived crisis in financial reporting quality following major corporate collapses, notably those of Enron and WorldCom (Brickey, 2003; Coffee, 2006). The legislation is wide ranging, but one of its specific purposes is to make senior management responsible for the quality of internal controls over financial reporting, thus making explicit and formal what had been until that point implicit and proprietorial. CEOs and CFOs are required under the legislation to attest that internal control systems contain no "material irregularities", and their attestations must be themselves independently audited. The requirements triggered extensive investment in controls whose performance could be tracked (Economist, 2007), which included the creation and detailed scripting of processes involving the production of primary traces of control, much like the aircraft take-off protocol discussed in Chapter 3. Unlike AML and many other regulatory developments, this intensified architecture of controls over financial reporting had to be rapidly generated by organizations, even to the point of unnecessary amplification and intensification, according to some commentators (SEC, 2005; Linck et al., 2009). The avowed purpose of the regime was to improve the quality of financial statements, and thereby the security and integrity of capital markets, by addressing control problems at source with a view to "getting things right the first time". Existing control data were traceified for this purpose, while new traces for controls were also created and datafied to generate an enhanced and more granular empirical base for demonstrating control. Existing audit trails linking all this data to assertions about the quality of controls were also reformed, in order to give senior officers the confidence to make the required public assertions. The quality of these controls as newly created objects of regulatory oversight and intervention was in theory to be subject to second-order observation in the form of testing by internal (so-called "third"-line defenders) and external auditors. SOX public "accounting" operates in conjunction with financial reporting itself and consists of management certifications and auditor certifications of those certifications. Like AML, SOX can also be conceptualized as an intense and multi-organizational traceability complex, involving trace production (of controls), tracking of these scripted control actions to observe them in action, and layers of oversight and related accounting.

Interbank Lending

In the years prior to the financial crisis of 2008, the focus of banking regulation was primarily on an organization's individual risk profile in terms of its size, capital strength, and governance as a separate entity. Banks and related financial institutions developed elaborate systems to track, oversee, and provide accounts of calculative objects such as "regulatory capital" and solvency under so-called "Pillar One" rules. National bank regulators engaged in extensive practices of second-order observation of these banking organizations. Though complex in many respects, the 2008 financial crisis was in effect a "run" by banks on each other due to loss of confidence in the ability to honour inter-company obligations. It is now well known that this in turn created profound liquidity problems, resulting in notable failures (e.g. Lehman brothers) and state intervention in both the United Kingdom and the United States. The interconnectedness of banks in the form of inter-bank lending for short-term, often daily, liquidity and treasury-management purposes was known but at best weakly understood (Haldane and May, 2011). It was in principle possible to track this interconnectedness, but it was not done to the same degree or had the same prominence as regulatory compliance requirements at the formal entity level. In other words, the risks to the banking "system" were predominantly imagined, theorized, and scripted by regulators as the sum of its parts. As a result, the meta-entity of the interbank lending market as a multilateral system for short-term liquidity management was, with the wisdom of hindsight, not made sufficiently observable and subject to oversight to the same degree as the focus on individual banks. The security of the financial system was primarily thought of in terms of asset quality and leverage, rather than the interdependence of interbank credit, which was long regarded as more or less risk free. In short, a traceability complex for system safety dedicated to tracking and overseeing these interconnections and their systemic risk implications was at best partial. The representation of the interbank system in a way that could support the tracking of interbank credit risk was far less developed than the accounting-dominated, regulatory tracking of own-risk capital by individual banking entities using value at risk (VAR) modelling and similar techniques.

The example of interbank lending regulation is important because it demonstrates how systems of governance and regulation, which can be readily understood as traceability complexes, may generate elaborate connectivities, intense tracking, and a certain style of entity-based oversight and accounting that nevertheless fail to capture other important relationalities, dependencies, and vulnerabilities. Banking regulatory practice emphasized one form of performance traceability at the expense of another, thereby providing a dramatic example of how connectivity and disconnectivity go hand in hand (Chapter 4). Haldane and May's (2011) proposal to correct this entity bias in financial regulation involved the development of an "epidemiological" model of financial contagion. This turn to epidemiology for inspiration to rethink financial contagion is full of irony. A decade later, epidemiology would no longer be a clever source of analogical thinking to stimulate financial market reform. The world faced a different systemic crisis that provided a sobering reminder that any financial market presupposes healthy human beings able to make it work.

The 2020 Pandemic

The experience of the 2020 pandemic demonstrated both the necessity and difficulty of tracking the human and animal carriers of contagious viruses like COVID 19. In these circumstances, traceability had to be rapidly constructed at scale, building on an existing organizational and regulatory landscape, in order to generate new connectivity and oversight in fragmented public health systems. The political purpose in addressing the pandemic was initially clear-cut in most countries in terms of the security of nations and the health of every individual in them. Yet, during 2020 and 2021 a more complex political economy of traceability emerged from the tension between the protection of individuals, especially those deemed to be vulnerable, and the need for economic security and the resumption of normal working. Initial efforts to track and trace early carriers of the virus, in order to prevent spreading by isolating them, quickly began to fail, and many countries moved at different speeds into various degrees of lockdown (Wang and Mao, 2021). Lockdown itself is a symptom of traceability failure that implicated entirely different approaches to restrict the movement of humans (Min et al., 2024). Initiatives in virus tracking were too slow and varied compared to the diffusion of the virus itself, largely because candidate primary traces in terms of observable symptoms were always *lagging* indicators of infection (see Chapter 7). Metrics, and therefore primary traces, shifted their ground over time, from infection rates in general to hospitalization rates, as an indicator of risks to the health system, and then to death rates. The latter may have been understated because they relied on death certificates that cited the virus as a cause. In short, there were multiple emergent, often competing, tracking-led accountings for the pandemic and its effects (Yu, 2021; Olofsson, 2025).

As conditions for strict lockdown were eased, there was considerable institutional experimentation and change. In the United Kingdom, efforts were made to operate a self-reporting "track and trace" system based on mobile phone apps. In a related innovation, individuals might be notified ("pinged") if they were in the vicinity of someone who had tested positive, and isolation was required/recommended. Yet the production of relevant primary traces of the presence of the virus in this way was always incomplete (individuals could switch off any app) or non-existent (the app was finally decommissioned in April 2023). Key elements of infrastructure for tracking the incidence of the virus were therefore critically dependent on rapidly developed apps and, at least in the United Kingdom, on voluntarism in reporting lateral flow test results, registering at venues, wearing masks, and responding to results with the necessary forms of isolation. Hence, virus traceability (via infected humans) was imperfect, at best partial, and could not prevent, although it may have mitigated, a second wave of cases as lockdown eased. The advent of extensive vaccination programmes, themselves highly controversial and many months in development, began to change the incidence and severity of infection, and shifted the focus of traceability from the virus to humans and from death to vaccination rates as a key metric for the state. Individuals were incentivized to be vaccinated and tested to some degree by the introduction of "COVID passports" for travel purposes. The rules began life in complex and contested form, but in essence were intended to ensure that only COVID-free individuals could travel. More significantly, a new politics of traceability quickly emerged from opponents of vaccination, including prominent public figures. Tracking vaccination history at the individual level proved to be technically successful, but the "unvaccinated" found themselves stigmatized to varying degrees.

In the United Kingdom, the pandemic response experience was extensively criticized for various reasons—acting too late, technologies that did not work, widespread non-compliance and violation of rules, not least and infamously by members of the UK government itself. The hastily assembled practices to track the virus represented at best a fluid and fragmented collection of traceability complexes in the making: purpose(s) were unclear and contested over time; there was defective and contested primary trace collection with limited tracking (except for quarantined travellers) and heavy reliance on self-accounting. Accounts in the form of national data for COVID-related hospital admissions and death rates were built up from below and were only as good as their source data. Later systems for tracking vaccination rates were more operationally successful. Studies also show how the policies and actions to manage the pandemic varied both geographically and across time, with China being acknowledged as having the toughest regime, characterized by strongly enforced lockdown practices and compulsory vaccination. Yet, notwithstanding variation in policies and enforcement, the underlying need for the traceability of people was much the same. In all contexts, there was an ambition to capture relevant primary traces—digitally or otherwise—in order for tracking and accounting to happen (Gkeredakis et al., 2021).

In prior chapters we have emphasized how tracking is crucially dependent on generative traceification, which may be provided voluntarily by individuals or via devices, and therefore on interfaces between human bodies and technologies, such as thermometers and smart watches (see also Chapter 8). While the virus itself was more resistant to being tracked prior to the manifestation of infection, something that led to restrictions on human movement, eventually it was the incidence of vaccination that was much easier in principle to track and account for. This is an example of risk *translation* or shifting (Hardy et al., 2020). Yet, the pandemic setting also reminds us of the sociology of the trace (Chapter 2) and the critical counter-accounts that try to give voice and visibility to suffering beyond the official statistics and to enable mourning that has been suppressed (Yu, 2021). In effect, the formal metrics and accounts developed to manage the pandemic did not correspond to the accounts many people lived (and died) by (Arjaliès et al., 2021).

The intention of this illustrative case, as with each of the others, is not to judge the success of failure of the United Kingdom's or any other country's response to the pandemic, or to judge its morality and the suffering that enforced lockdown caused—many others have done that (e.g. Scally, 2024). Rather, it points to a different kind of challenge to that of interbank lending, which, as noted, involved elaborate traceability of the wrong object. The operational challenge in this setting was to construct, mobilize, and scale tracking more or less from scratch, despite the prior existence of emergency plans. The pandemic case highlights how the elements of a traceability complex in the making can be fragile, revealing fragmentation, contestation, and failure, rather than something that might qualify as coherent and connected. The *purpose* of various initiatives shifted from early clarity about health to the need for economic security; practices of *tracking* the incidence of the virus were eventually displaced by practices to track vaccinations, and relevant *accounts* and key metrics shifted with conceptions of the primary risk. As the pandemic in the United Kingdom progressed, in addition to COVID-related deaths and "R" as key metrics (Miller, 2021), hospitalization and vaccination rates came to be regarded as significant lead indicators for the possibility that the health system might be overwhelmed. In the pandemic case, emergency epidemiological management was always intertwined with other critical systems, such as food supply and financial support to avoid hardship for individuals and businesses. Virus tracking was at best one initial and temporary manifestation of traceability needs within a broader network of interdependent functions subject to stress. The "case" is therefore several in one and is suggestive of a field of epistemologically diverse and loosely connected forms of tracking, oversight, and accounting practices, rather than anything approaching a coherent traceability complex (Olofsson, 2025).

Fisheries and Agriculture

Regulatory and consumer pressures for enhanced supply-chain management in the fishing industry have grown due to concerns about fraud, the sustainability of fish stocks, and evidence of labour exploitation (WWF, 2015; Lewis and Boyle, 2017; Charlebois et al., 2024). In effect, as noted in Chapter 1, the concept of "purpose" in many food settings has expanded to include sustainability as part of what is meant by quality. Logistically, the tracking of fish has been made possible by digital technologies that capture their "point of harvest". In addition, vessels maintain electronic log books and use interoperable software across supply chains, enabling fish processors and retailers to track and have oversight of catches, and to determine their compliance with standards and regulations for sustainable fishing. Pressure groups and NGOs like the World Wildlife Fund (WWF) seek to hold agencies in food supply chains to account by making a whole range of issues traceable and reportable, from harvest to the table. Sustainable sourcing, fair wages, and energy consumed in getting to the shops are all features of the new interest in traceability, which, as we discussed in Chapter 5, expands the conception of supply-chain governance beyond logistics. Advances in technologies, such as GPS, digital tagging, digital mapping, and visualization of seas and farms, have increased the possibilities for the tracking of fish and vessels, generating new "accounts" of their origins, quality, and ethical impacts. These technologies also generate capacities for the oversight of supply chains whereby organizations downstream can monitor and influence upstream practices for compliance with norms. Accounts in these diverse settings can take many forms, for example: due diligence audit reports; certifications of sustainability of sourcing; certification of chemical validation and testing of contents; and sustainability audits (Sander et al., 2012; Lezaun, 2006). All in all, a growing politics of food sustainability is generating new markets for traceability, for tracking foodstuff itself and also for oversight of the supply chain, both in part and in whole (Canavari et al., 2010; Rival, Montet, and Pioch, 2016). Food supply chains have become fertile grounds for advisory work, especially soft law initiatives, to improve within-chain connectivity in the form of audit trails that enable both first- and second-order observation, tracking, and oversight, respectively (Porter, Baker, and Agrawal, 2011).

Legalizing Cannabis

A second supply-chain illustration concerns the formation of the legal market for cannabis production and consumption in the US state of Colorado (Pflueger et al., 2019). This market takes shape under strong regulatory guidance about its boundaries in the form of prescriptions about what is within the market and therefore legal, and what is not within the market and therefore illegal. Martinez et al. (2022) draw on Deleuze's notion of assemblage to theorize the emergent relations between technology, market actors, and cannabis plants. This assemblage displays features of a traceability complex under construction. Its *value-purpose* is not only to ensure the *quality* of product, as in any agricultural food chain, but also to *secure* the boundaries of the legal market itself. A system based on the primary traceification of plants in the form of digital tags is used flexibly to track plants and to enable oversight of the entire supply chain. The digital audit trail that *connects* growers to distributors enables *accounting* in the form of certifications of legality and quality for the end user. The case is especially salient in demonstrating that the regulatory work of creating and maintaining traceability as oversight can be coextensive with the generation of a novel market. The legal cannabis as an object and its traceability cannot be separated. Hence, this example shows clearly the duality of traceability (Chapter 2) as being both constitutive of the regulated object and evidentiary in generating an audit trail that connects cannabis plant production to the market regulator.

Cryptocurrencies and Blockchains

Beyond their potentially addictive properties, the similarities between cannabis and cryptocurrencies might not seem obvious. However, traceability is a constitutive feature of their respective constructions of novel markets. Cryptocurrencies, in the form Bitcoin, were initially understood as synonymous with blockchain. Yet, cryptocurrency trading has come to be framed more explicitly as an application that uses blockchain technology as a platform (this platform/application duality is more evident in the case of Ethereum). It is well known that blockchain was conceived as an engine for radical empowerment involving the disintermediation and decentralization of currency. It was intended as a technology for secure transactional capability beyond the reach of central bank control.[4] Yet, this quasi-anarchist agenda faltered, not least because

[4] See Schneider (2019) for a comprehensive critical review of decentralization. It is argued that blockchain architectures may seem decentralized, but their logics are not. Protocols become mechanisms of continuing central control.

of prominent "failure" events that have problematized blockchain governance and have called into question the mantra of "code is law" (Pflueger et al., 2022; DuPont, 2017).

Much has been written about the economics of blockchains, cryptocurrencies, and their potential uses. The technological heart of any blockchain, which distinguishes it from a distributed database, is the cryptography of "hashing" transactions and events, that is, giving them unique unchangeable digital references, bundling them together in "blocks", and chaining these blocks together in a system that is, at least in theory, immutable because of a validation process or "consensus protocol" for the hashing process, thereby avoiding the double-spend problem that destroys any monetary system. Crypto-transaction history is designed to be unique, permanent, and common to all human participants in the blockchain whose computers occupy nodes in an anonymous network. Blockchains so imagined are simultaneously traceification, transaction enablement, tracking, and accounting (Pflueger et al., 2022). Their digital currencies have been referred to as "data money" (Caliskan, 2020), although we might equally think of them as "trace-monies", since their value is grounded in their digitally inscribed "tokenality" and in the traceability of these tokens, like the cannabis case.

The purpose of blockchains as platforms for the exchange of traceified objects is generally to guarantee the authenticity and *security* of a crypto-transaction in the form of a distinctive digital trace, namely a hash or token as a unique and unalterable primary index or referent to whatever the application running on the blockchain may take as its transactional object, whether cryptocurrency transfers, interbank settlements, insurance payouts, land transfers, or movements in any other asset class. These currency and non-currency uses of blockchains are emerging where demands for traceability in the form of quality assurance or security of identity are high and cannot be easily and cheaply provided by other means. Thus, wine labelling as a mark of quality and origin has been subject to fraud, and this has incentivized some actors in wine supply chains to explore blockchain-based forms of grape and vineyard authentication (Malisic et al., 2023). Other examples include diamonds trading and land registration and any system where there is a high demand for proof of ownership and quality. Markets for non-fungible tokens (NFTs) have also emerged as forms of cryptographic proof of ownership for digital assets (Chalmers et al., 2022).

Human transactors using digital money may themselves be untraceable. Indeed, this is a feature of money in general. But the anonymized history of transfers of, say, Bitcoins is a matter of permanent record in what is called a "distributed ledger" and can in principle be tracked by any member of the network. As in the example of cannabis, blockchains promise the secure traceification of objects for trade. Traceability is therefore a constitutive feature of both the digital object and market infrastructure, which approaches a "pure" form of an economy of traces. Both digital monies and NFTs rely on a critical threshold of users who make their markets more or less liquid and also produce and sustain the facticity of their asset value, as a belief system. This facticity, which is certainly not universally accepted, may be fragile and is damaged by failure events such as bubbles and fraud (Conlon et al., 2023). In such cases, the human communal underpinning of blockchain applications goes to work, developing off-chain governance solutions, such as so-called "hard forks" (DuPont, 2017).

In summary, cryptocurrencies and the blockchains that operate them can be imagined as tightly integrated traceability complexes for tracking and accounting whose purpose is to secure transactions independent of central authority. They are characterized by: trace production in the form of "data monies" or tokens generated by algorithms, transaction validation by consensus protocols; connectivity of participants to enable oversight of all by all; and accounting in the form of an immutable public ledger.[5] Yet the perfect accounting traceability promised by immutable blockchains as "procedural-truth finding" (Pflueger et al., 2022) has the paradoxical effect of making redundant and unnecessary practices of actual tracking beyond initial transaction validation. It is a so-called "trustless" system in which the security of a transaction is guaranteed by algorithmic design ex ante, and in which code is law pure and simple. It does not require the regular production of trust ex post in the form of human oversight and auditing. Blockchains for the production of cryptocurrencies therefore seem like limit cases of a traceability complex in which "governance" is temporally and operationally coextensive with code as script. That said, as noted earlier, the stable functioning of the underlying code requires governance by "off-chain" human control (Zachariadis et al., 2019; Pflueger et al., 2022; DuPont, 2017).

Finally, blockchains beyond crypto have also been imagined as a basis for new forms of collaborative and relational governance that are less dependent on contracts to produce trust (Wang et al., 2022). There has been much debate about the hidden governance of blockchains themselves, the continuing need for human-centred oversight of code design and functioning, and for re-centralizing so-called blockocracies (Kavanagh and Dylan-Ennis, 2020; Du Pont, 2017). We consider these issues further in this chapter, since they suggest how novel forms of digital automation like blockchains significantly shift the tracking/oversight mix and with it the accounts we live by.

[5] "The two main features of blockchains—decentralized consensus and machine-based automation—enable an original combination of appealing functionalities, such as information immutability and reliability, transparency and traceability of records, and autonomous enforcement agreements" (Lumineau et al., 2021, p. 503).

Governance as Traceability Revisited

We have described a number of cases that illustrate the entanglement of governance, oversight, and traceability in: financial services, financial reporting; interbank lending; pandemic management; food supply; and cryptocurrency trading. The concept of traceability complex was used to organize these mini-case descriptions broadly in terms of: purposes; traceification and tracking (first-order observation), and oversight and accounts (second-order observation). The different cases suggest that traceability complexes have fuzzy boundaries, as discussed in Chapter 2. For example, governance as traceability in the AML and food-supply-chain settings involves multiple organizations and geographically distributed agencies. Which agencies count as part of the complex and which do not depend in part on the analytic interest and focus. In most representations of AML regulatory systems, banks are core actors, and law-enforcement agencies involved in tracking illicit funds and prosecutions are external recipients and users of suspicious activity reports (which may count as primary traces for them). And in the case of food-supply-chain governance, different NGOs may feature in different ways. They can count as internal agencies when they engage in monitoring or certification practices, but they may also be positioned externally as sources of pressure for change at the level of purpose. A related key point of variation is the extent to which end users and beneficiaries of tracking are, or are not, to be considered within the boundary of traceability complexes. Individual consumers of food seem to be external to supply chains, on whose behalf traceability is organized, but consumer groups can also be part of oversight practices involving certification. Furthermore, as we shall see in Chapter 8, users of digital platforms are often co-opted as sources of traceification.

These boundary issues arise partly from the use of the traceability complex as a broad template to guide description. There is therefore always a tension between the template and empirical settings where fuzzy boundaries and overlaps may be evident. For example, the SMR&C regime in the United Kingdom clearly operates in parallel with many other "conduct of business" regulations, and they are likely to be managed at the organizational level by teams operating with similar scripts and working within "accountability infrastructures" with shared operational logics. Furthermore, the pandemic example strained the singular applicability of the template; it is at best a case of multiple traceability complexes emerging, competing, and interacting. While the notion of traceability complex may not qualify as a fully coherent unit of analysis, it can nevertheless be a useful abstract summation of linked practice bundles for tracking and oversight. Furthermore, traceability complexes in many empirical settings generate their boundedness and operational autonomy via the scripted elaboration of structures and roles, not least in the form of discrete bodies of expert practitioners and "officerships", like the MLRO and Chief Risk Officer (CRO) (Power, 2005). In other words, traceability complex boundaries may be fuzzy and relative to analytic interest, but they can be sharply formed by regulatory and governance practitioners as a response to events. With this in mind, Table 6.1 visualizes and summarizes the examples discussed in the previous section using the traceability complex as template, and enables some broad comparative observations to be made.

Table 6.1 Traceability Complexes Compared

Traceability Complex	Primary Value-Purposes	Traceification and Tracking (First-Order Observations)	Oversight and Accounting (Second-Order Observations)
AML	Security: financial security; prevention of financial crime	Passports for client identity; declarations of source of funds; specialist tracking of persons and monies (e.g. Experian, Kroll); risk profiling of banking clients	Risk profiling client banks; sources of funds; AML officer routine reporting and MLRO report to regulator; audit-trail-enabled oversight of AML process by board and regulator
SM&CR	Quality: management capability and responsibility	Responsibility scripted by organizations; trackable CV and qualifications; evidence of relevant training; self-declaration of legal and credit issues Self-declaration of "fit and proper" status	Audit trail enabled oversight of process for "fit and proper" compliance; organization-level self-certifications of "fit and proper" compliance; regulatory visits and inspections
SOX	Quality and security: financial reporting quality for capital markets	Scripting of material controls over financial reporting; primary traceification of new control actions; tracking of control-process quality and compliance	Audit-trail-enabled oversight of internal control system as a whole; board audit committee; assertions by management (disclosure of material weaknesses if necessary); audit certifications of management assertions

continued

Table 6.1 *continued*

Traceability Complex	Primary Value-Purposes	Traceification and Tracking (First-Order Observations)	Oversight and Accounting (Second-Order Observations)
Interbank lending (pre-2009)	Financial system security	Weak primary traces of liquidity risk at firm level; tracking capital quality mainly at bank level; failure to track aggregate interbank credit risk	Weak regulatory mapping of interbank lending and risk analysis; overemphasis on oversight of individual entity; insufficient emphasis on short-term liquidity
Pandemic (emer-gency)	Security: population health and economy	Multiple primary traceification efforts; self-reporting apps; tracking persons; tracking hospital admissions; causes of death registers; vaccination rates	Fragmented oversight; multi-organizational; local and national infection rate databases; "R" number reporting; politics of vaccination rates; death rates
Fisheries and agriculture	Quality: foodstuffs; sustainability, labour justice	Labels, tags, point-of-harvest data; tracking products through supply chains; quality testing of food processing; traceification of sustainability-related data	Multi-organizational oversight of parts of supply-chain processes; certification processes (e.g. CSDDD); critical voices; the role of movements
Cannabis	Security and quality: safety and control of supply	Digital tags on "legal" plants; tracking of product from supplier to customer	Regulation of entire supply chain; certifications of origins
Crypto-currencies and blockchains	Security: reliability of transacting	Unique primary traceification of asset class (crypto; NFT); immutable transaction records (blockchains)	Trustless system—oversight, audit unnecessary? Forking practices; crypto-community oversight

Value-Purposes

As one would expect, each governance setting varies in terms of its purpose(s). Table 6.1 suggests that specific governance systems are primarily concerned with variants of quality and security. Yet the third generic value-purpose of "discovery" is indirectly evident, for example in the regulatory generation of a new legal market for cannabis or customer risk profiles for AML. Furthermore, the pandemic generated emergency investment in vaccine development, a process in which governance for quality, as safety, and science as a commitment to discovery are found necessarily in combination. Yet, these different purposes vary in their institutional foundation and stability in terms of whether they are grounded in formally enforceable law, in privately developed norms, or, as with many of the cases, a hybrid of the two. Relatedly, the purposes and values on which specific arrangements of governance as oversight are founded may be implicit, emergent, and even contradictory. Thus, the pandemic case shows how purposes may be hybrid, involving trade-offs that can shift in the face of contestation. A politics of traceability will tend to be visible in settings like this where different values are at stake, not least the competing values of freedom and control.

Traceification and Tracking

People, processes, and things must initially be traceified in order to constitute and datafy them as observable objects for tracking purposes. In the cases of AML and the SM&CR regime, for example, pre-existing documents—passports and curricula vitae—are traceified (i.e. they acquire "trace-of . . ." status relative to the specific governance practice) and are enlisted into the organization of governance as traceability. Yet in others, for example the case of legalized cannabis, the digital traceifcation of plants in the form of barcodes generated new data for tracking purposes. Whereas in the former example, traceification builds observational practices from existing data, in the latter case, new data are produced from digital traceification to make an object capable of being tracked—a "data double" of the material thing is created that is the focus of its first-order observability. In the pandemic case there is a more fluid landscape of traceification. Existing information systems on hospital admissions are utilized, while efforts are also made to create enhanced systems based on traces of infections and of vaccination practices. Traceifcation can be risky because it involves decisions about what to track and how to track, decisions that may prove in hindsight to have been mistaken. From this point of view, as already noted, the governance of cryptocurrency trading by blockchains provides a limit case in which we might say that the trace of a currency as it is transacted in the form of a unique cryptographic identifier is part of its nature as an object. In this mini-case, datafication and traceification are indistinguishable—"data money" or "trace money" are labels for the same object that exists only within, and can only be tracked by, a shared ledger. To repeat, for both cryptocurrency trading and legal cannabis tracking, the connectivity that supports traceability also constitutes their markets; there is no market without tracking-enabled governance.

In general, Table 6.1 suggests that the construction of what we call first-order observation or tracking varies in terms of the kinds of objects and events that are traceified. Modes of traceification also vary between those that support the tracking of a person or thing, which is more or less unchanged by the tracking process, and those in which the object of tracking is part of a composite and may be mixed and transformed into new things and products. Wine, people, and cryptocurrencies would be examples of the former; they can be "tagged" and tokenized in order to track them spatially and transactionally. The cases of cannabis and many agricultural products, including GM crops, are of the second kind, involving, in many instances, the need to trace (i.e. discover) chemicals as they are processed (Muirhead and Porter, 2019). In general, tracking a substance through transformative processes will require specialized and costly apparatus. In such settings, traceification as regulatory object construction will often involve second-best, feasible strategies on grounds of cost and/or technical feasibility. AML regimes operate by substituting the tracking of unique persons for the more elusive problem of tracking money. Similarly, "fit and proper" persons are made traceable by focusing on qualifications, job descriptions, and prior sanctions as proxies. Thus, tracking practices will be shaped by pragmatism.

Oversight and Accounts as Second-Order Observation

Governance as traceability also varies in terms of the agencies organized in *layers* of connected observational practices, and which enable oversight (Chapters 4 and 5). Such layers can be extensive or minimal in nature. The more elaborate they are in terms of the number of discrete oversight agencies (audit trail "density" per Chapter 4), the more potential there can be for fragmentation in their connectivity. Hence, oversight, as we have conceived of it metaphorically in terms of layers, spans a continuum. On the one hand, as the pandemic and food examples show, it can be multilayered, dense but prone to non-integration, or on the other hand, like cryptocurrencies, it can be light and highly integrated. Layers as structures also vary in terms of their connectivity via audit trails. From Table 6.1, the cases of AML, SM&CR, and Sarbox suggest deeper, denser audit trails populated by different connected agencies and centres of traceability. The cases of interbank lending and the pandemic suggest more complex and less coherent audit trail connections at times of emergency, either because the "business as usual" governance was focused on the wrong risk or because of fragmentation and disorganization. The example of fisheries and agriculture supply chains are contexts with highly developed logistical connectivity and advanced forms of quality assurance. Organizations in these supply chains are now also responding to pressures to generate new audit trails in order to track ethical issues.

Table 6.1 has been constructed using the traceability complex as a template for comparative analysis. It is therefore hardly surprising that it reinforces a traceological theorization of accounting that begins with traceification-enabled tracking. Yet it also usefully reminds us that not only do traceability complexes vary in terms of the accounts that they produce, but also that some of this variety relates to differences between whether accounts are part of first-order observation and tracking or more a feature of second-order observation and oversight. The former feature a variety of metrics, checklists, declarations, and digital tags that are the traceified proxies for an object of interest. The latter tend to include summations and aggregations in the form of reports and certificates for consumption by oversight agencies.

In prior chapters we have developed a distinction between tracking-led accounts and accounts-led tracking. Given that the different cases are designed to illustrate variation in governance as traceability, where there are often legal mandates, it is no surprise that accounts-led tracking is prominent. Hence the traceification of professional qualifications under SM&CR supports the ability of the organization to provide a summative account of how its relevant employees are "fit and proper". Management certifications under SOX perform a similar role in order for CEOs and CFOs to demonstrate conformity to the law. In these contexts, traceification and tracking are developed explicitly to enable oversight and related forms of accounting. They are the *means* to the accounting *end*; this is accounts-led tracking as developed in Chapter 2. It is broadly aligned with, and is a feature of, oversight. The outlier and limiting case in Table 6.1 is that of cryptocurrencies and blockchains in which accounts in the form of immutable transaction records are tracking-led (i.e. perfect transaction tracking as potential is an end that constitutes digital money). In theory, the need for oversight has been "designed out".

From this brief analysis, we can propose that the distinction between tracking-led accounts and accounts-led tracking is not inherent in any specific device or technology but is a matter of their function within any specific traceability complex, its purposes, and the accounts that serve those purposes. Sociology also reminds us that technologies—auditing and accounting included—can develop their own autonomy and purpose, shaping the contexts in which they operate and becoming decoupled from their formal purposes (Bromley and Powell, 2012). This is means-end decoupling that, in the context of Table 6.1, suggests that tracking practices can begin to drive accounts production by default. In the case of Sarbox, there is some evidence that tracking-led accounts of control led to excessive elaboration of process. Means-end decoupling like this can arise because the agencies responsible for tracking are usually different from those responsible for oversight further along the audit trail. It can also arise, as the case of the pandemic shows, in an emergency, when the need to track and control something is more urgent than periodic oversight. Hence, while Table 6.1 is a useful re-description of specific governance regimes, traceability complexes are not static. One significant horizon of change is the effect of digitalization and how it is shifting the tracking-oversight mix.

The Tracking-Oversight Mix

From the preceding static descriptive comparisons, the key focus is on how the organization of traceability blends tracking and oversight in any specific setting. This variation matters because there appears to be a systemic direction of change that Table 6.1 does not capture. The production of primary traces and the tracking practices they enable are shaped by advisory markets and the use of standardized information systems, such as ERPs supplied by vendors. In addition, the practices that we identify under the category of "tracking" necessarily include an element of operational supervision and oversight. We might think of this oversight as the "first line of defence" populated by line managers, supervisors, and accounting devices like "dashboards" designed to enable operational tracking and intervention. For example, front-office workers in banks will have detailed procedures for "onboarding" and checking new clients. Their work will be overseen by a supervisor or by a programme, suggesting that what we call tracking already includes some form of operational second-order observation. If we think back to the checklist discussed in Chapter 2, it functions as *both* the tracking and accounting of actions and *also* the enabler of oversight by pilots of themselves. In short, the checks in the checklist are both generative and evidentiary.

From Table 6.1 and the related discussion, it becomes clear that tracking is the foundation of oversight in most of the examples considered. There can be no governance as oversight without being grounded in tracking practices and their sub-accounts. It follows that audit trails as modes of connectivity between centres of traceability are only as good as their primary traceification of objects and related tracking. Traceability complexes are therefore fertile ground for means-end decoupling in which tracking practices become powerful determinants of the other constituent elements. It is proposed that advances in digital technologies are driving such a shift. If governance as traceability drew on the metaphor of layers to characterize its mode of oversight and connectivity, then the rise of tracking suggests the inverse, namely *de-layering* or *flattening*.

De-Layering Governance?

The audit society was characterized by an excess of external oversight that was at best pointless and at worst a form of "crowding out" that damaged professional morale. Yet, judged by the concerns being articulated about digital capabilities for surveillance and the trajectory of AI, it could be that we are transitioning to a world in which oversight as *second-order observation capability* is being radically *de-layered* and emptied of intermediate agencies acting as *centres of traceability*. In the case of legalized cannabis, regulators have observational capabilities to track plants directly without the need for intermediate agencies. Cryptocurrencies, and the blockchains on which they operate, are built on a promise of "trustlessness". They are a case that implies the non-necessity of conventional audit and oversight.[6] In other words, in these settings first-order transactional tracking is in design a form of auto-governance in the sense that it also observes and accounts for itself.

Blockchains for cryptocurrency exchange provide a limiting case of governance as traceability in which first- and second-order observation are de-layered and merged into each other, reducing audit trails to linked "blocks" with near-zero human density (as defined in Chapter 4). In this setting, the traditional duality of governance and operations dissolves, and governance is reduced to a code-based auto-checking reflex of tracking practice (code is law). This operates until it fails, at which point human contestation and critique overflow into the supposedly de-humanized blockchain world (DuPont, 2017). This de-layering of oversight in the blockchain model is a general effect of digitalization in which human-centric governance and accounting are becoming "platformized".[7]

The Platformization of Governance

Platforms as organizational forms are widely discussed and analysed by scholars (Poell, Nieborg, and van Dijck, 2019), yet there is no precise consensus as to what they are. They are variously understood as "multi-sided" markets, infrastructures, new organizational topologies, and new modes of controlling

[6] The same is not true for the many crypto-exchanges that provide retail access to cryptocurrency trading. Regulation here is evolving since the FTX scandal and bears a closer resemblance to that of other exchanges to ensure transparency and fair trading.

[7] De-layering has a longer pre-digital history. For example, early quality movements in manufacturing and medicine were premised on the advantages of "getting things right first time" in design and in the so-called operational first line of defence, rather than relying on layers of ex-post oversight and correction (Price, 2017).

labour.[8] Notwithstanding these different optics on, and conceptions of, platforms, there is agreement that they disrupt more traditional andinstitutionalized conceptions of organizational boundaries. They internalize so-called external users of services—both suppliers and clients in two-sided markets—via processes that traceify their activities (see Chapter 5). Despite these de-centring effects, they are also powerful centralizing organizations in their own right—eBay, Uber, Airbnb, and many others—whose purpose is to provide relational infrastructure to host and support services to platform-defined users. For this reason, and their multi-sided nature, they also pose complex questions of their accountability (Rahman et al., 2024).

The process of "userfication", of internalizing and co-opting humans as users, is both a form of old-fashioned customer acquisition essential to the scale economics of platform organizations and also a source of valuable traces that can be datafied, stored, retrieved, and used for tracking and further analysis. As Alaimo and Kallinikos (2024, p. 137) put it, platforms are highly administered organizational forms but have an "outbound orientation [which] confers platform operations [with] specific, unique, recognizable features that are absent from most known types of organizations". Similarly, Kornberger et al. (2017) argue that an important outward-facing application enabled by many platforms is the enrolment of users in evaluation processes in the form of ratings and feedback. In theory, consumers of a platform-provided service become users and evaluators of services and of other users. Their actions are a source of platform governance as well as of data via the primary traceification of their satisfaction in feedback mechanisms (Power, 2011a; Scott and Orlikowski, 2012; Jeacle and Carter, 2011, 2022; Orlikowski and Scott, 2014). Platform organizations are thereby "generative" of evaluative communities with a distinctive human-machine character (Kornberger et al., 2017; Fourcade and Johns, 2020; Mennicken and Kornberger, 2021). In turn, service-providing organizations will track and aggregate individual user evaluations and will develop strategies to respond to them if they are beyond certain levels of tolerance. In this way, the reputation of service providers, like hotels or car rental firms, shifts from being an object of periodic management concern, often driven ex post by visible failures and scandal, to being something continuously and granularly monitored as an ex ante lead indicator of economic risk (Alaimo and Kallinikos, 2017).

Platform organizations are "centres of traceability" with fluid boundaries defined by the limits of their traceification capabilities. Their purpose is hybrid. It is primarily "security" in the sense of securing both economic performance

[8] See Rochet and Tirole, 2003; Kornberger, Pflueger, and Mouritsen, 2017; Plantin et al., 2018; Ciborra, 1996; Casilli and Posadi, 2019; Stark and Pais, 2021; Frenken and Fuenfschilling, 2021; Kellogg, Valentine, and Christin, 2020; McDaid, Andon and Free, 2023.

via user retention and also the operational integrity of data and transactions. It is quality in the sense of quality assurance about the goods and services provided by users and by themselves as platform operators, including the quality of the experience of being a user. And it is discovery in the sense of enabling users to discover their preferences through engagement with the platform and its evaluative structures. They achieve all this via the primary traceification of user behaviour, whether in the role of buyer or supplier. The category of "consumer" as the historic external target of advertising campaigns has now become reconstructed as platform user, and the traceification of their actions enables their behaviour to be tracked and subject to further algorithmic processing and accounting in the sense of discovering patterns and profile generation (Constantinou and Kallinikos, 2015). What we describe in Table 6.1 as "first-order observation" to enable tracking is really a core capability of the platform business model. Connectivity to platform users to enable this tracking is supported by machine-human interfaces (e.g. mobile apps). While platform organizations have administrative control centres to oversee the design and running of operations, to produce financial statements and pay taxes, they also have non-hierarchical, de-centred features in that any user may in principle be enabled to evaluate any other. Indeed, platforms enable and encourage users as consumers and suppliers/sellers to compete for good ratings and feedback (see Chapter 8). Furthermore, while many of the "accounts" produced from these user traces take the form of proprietorial analytic summations for platform management and strategic purposes, many consumer ratings and feedback ratings are also made visible to other users, generating an evaluative network.

Taken literally and realistically, a platform, like a stage, enables people to stand on it, to speak according to scripts, and to be seen. It supports various activities—music, theatre, public speaking, and so on—which can be enjoyed by audiences. A platform in this material form is relational: it brings together performers and spectators who are each, in different ways, its "users". We also know that in many instances such platforms can be adapted—raised, lowered, extended. They can be flexible and modular, permitting a variety of usages, scenery applications, and stagings. They are never fully static structures, and multi-use flexible platforms are common in modern cultural venues. There are many examples.[9] Furthermore, actors and their audiences don't really notice a good platform; it is often out of sight. They don't come to see the platform itself, yet the platform is at least a necessary condition for the success of the activity of interest. They might only

[9] The O2 Arena in East London, UK, can be thought of as a platform like this: I have attended conferences there, but also music concerts and basketball. As a platform it is flexible and modular in design and can be reformatted for new purposes, yet there is also an organization that manages the platform. It has a centre.

notice the platform if something went wrong, if it collapsed or if some aspect of it, like scenery changes or sound systems, failed to work.

The entities we designate as formal organizations have always had platform-like infrastructural characteristics to a greater or lesser extent (see Chapter 5). The scripts that provide the protocols for organizational routines and accounting systems are platform-like in that they underpin and mobilize multiple, connected "acts of organizing" and thereby constitute the very organizationality of organizations. Platforms can therefore be conceptualized in much the same way as the "tracks" discussed in Chapter 4, and platform administration is a kind of track management. In general terms, platforms refer to relatively stable but flexible configurations of technologies that connect and support relations among, sometimes well-defined, sets of human actors engaged in a variety of practices, including selling and buying but also many other performances.

Notwithstanding the economic significance of platforms like eBay, Airbnb, Uber, and many others, and the seemingly novel organizational forms that they represent, they can also be seen in an expanded way as instantiations of a more widespread and pervasive process of *platformization*. This notion does not only reference changes in traditional organizational boundaries and the formation of new relational topologies of organizing, such as "userfication" (Stark and Pais, 2021). It also refers to a mode of organizing in which the tracking (voluntary and involuntary) of users is central and dominant. The notion of platformization is thereby broader than the organizational forms that have come to be called platforms, and encompasses a more general mode of operation that includes the tech companies in general—such as Google, Amazon, Facebook, and Apple—and their clients. These mega-companies have attracted considerable critical commentary largely because they pose multiple questions of governance in terms of their size and scale, their mode of operations, and their general influence on our lives, on democracies, and on the nature of capitalism (Zuboff, 2015; Power, 2022). To theorize the stakes in these debates and concerns, we view platformization as the de-layering and flattening of human governance practices, specifically in terms of shifting the mix, evident in Table 6.1, between "tracking" and "oversight". Algorithms are at the centre of this de-layering and flattening process.

Governing Algorithms

Algorithms used to be of interest only to computer scientists. Yet, we can think of them as the invisible rules that we have always lived by (Daston, 2022) and increasingly so. As algorithms have come to play a significant role in many areas of social and economic life, they are both celebrated as sources of efficiency and benefit and also problematized as objects of concern. Issues to do with privacy, secrecy, labour control, discrimination, and general lack of transparency have animated an extensive and growing critical discourse (Kellog et al., 2020: Newlands, 2021). It is argued that algorithms increasingly control many aspects of our lives and are infrastructural features of new governance and security techniques, yet are themselves argued to be ungoverned and opaque (Busuioc, 2021; Bellanova and DeGoede, 2022; Grote et al., 2024; Lavie et al., 2025). Algorithms represent a fracture point where generative traceability and evidential traceability part company with one another. Political scientists, lawyers, and sociologists are increasingly preoccupied with the prospective automation of decisions that were previously deliberative (Yeung, 2018; Lodge and Mennicken, 2019); with how an algorithm and its logic can be subject to oversight and governance (Goodman, 2016; Gellert, 2022); with the emergence of new elites and algorithmic orders (Burrell and Fourcade, 2021); and with the paradox of transparency-enabling algorithms that are not themselves transparent (Burrell, 2016; Annany and Crawford, 2018). Indeed, what happens to human jurisprudence and hermeneutical practice when oversight is in effect delegated not only to expert coders as hidden governors (Ulbricht and Yeung, 2022) but also to machines that learn and programme themselves?

These questions have generated calls for new forms of human-centred governance, accountability, and regulation. Yet, much like accounting, as discussed in Chapter 3, algorithms also seem to have their own "authority", power, and aura (Lustig and Nardi, 2015). Understood in their most general sense as logical sequences of "if-then" rules to make or support decisions and actions, they are not especially new. What is new is the computing and coding power that gives them not only speed and reach, but also the capability to become complex and self-adapting. We can think of algorithms as applications that rapidly generate their own "ruts in the road", as discussed in Chapter 4. However, such ruts or pathways have a biography of co-formation with the human agencies that adapt, resist, extend, and operationalize them. In this sense, algorithms are not static stand-alone objects with hegemonic agency but are enmeshed in practice settings as changing configurations of humans and machines (Stark and Vanden Broek, 2024). Like accounts, they are not things but "phenomena-in the-making" (Scott and Orlikowski, 2025) that have been progressively shaped and rewritten in the face of successive applications, learning, and development (Glaser et al., 2021). This also means that the coding, which enables the logic of algorithms to be written in a programming language that can execute its rules is, like accounting, infused with procedural norms. Writing algorithms is a process of the decomposition, reduction, and reconstruction of a non-algorithmic process, such as an "expert" decision or diagnostic setting, into a series of "if-then" steps and sub-steps (Henman, 2020).

The abstractive character of algorithms positions them as a further inflexion in the history of apparatuses of "governing by numbers" (Miller, 2001; Rose, 1991; Fourcade and Healy, 2024). Puranam (2025)conceptualizes the algorithm-driven transformation process as having three stages. First there is the production of representation via traces that become data. Second, there is the generation of connectivity by which data can be pooled. Third, there is the advanced level of aggregation in which meaningful patterns and predictive potential are created. Puranam's threefold conceptualization has parallels with that of the traceability complex template, in which traces are connected in audit trails and produce aggregate accounting summations. This should not surprise us since accounts construction is also based on rules for data transformation (i.e. from transaction to invoice to annual sales; Chapter 2). But the obvious difference that makes a difference is that the observability enabled by the audit trail is at best opaque for most digital algorithms.

Even though there is a growing consensus among scholars that algorithms are not simple, well-bounded objects, there is also tendency to treat them as "black boxes". Dourish (2016) positions algorithms within broader digital assemblies as "pseudo-code", which are only promissory or programmatic and must be transformed into formal code for specific operations, which may include many other things, including rules for interfaces with machines. Hence, the boundaries between algorithm, code, and programme are not always clear-cut and are continuously being worked upon by groups of human actors. Given this practice-contingent fluidity, it is often difficult to read, and therefore audit, the algorithm as distinct from code. Algorithms as objects-in-making do not present themselves in a straightforward way and may be distributed and fragmented, such that they dissolve into their constituent elements on closer analysis, elements that are necessarily embedded in the socio-materialities of devices and their human operatives.

Given this complexity and fluidity in the ontology of algorithms, the question of how they are to be governed by the humans who use and are subject to them is equally fluid. At the extreme, as articulated by some proponents of blockchains, the code that gives algorithms power is in principle visible to all willing participants; it is de facto law and cannot be "in error". Yet, various blockchain crises have demonstrated that this ideal is problematic; governance *by* algorithms does not exhaust the problem of the governance *of* algorithms—quite the opposite (Pflueger et al., 2022; DuPont, 2017). Though evacuating flesh-and-blood humans from transacting, they inevitably come back into play during periods of transactional crisis. Debates about governance have acquired additional intensity in the face of developments in machine learning and advances in artificial intelligence (Millo et al., 2024). But if there is agreement that algorithms must be governed, what exactly does that entail, and for what overall purpose or value?

Pasquale (2015) calls for more openness in the face of the inscrutability of algorithms; they need to be "audited". However, Burrell (2016) argues that the very notion of the opacity of algorithms is itself in need of clarification. She distinguishes between intentional corporate secrecy, in relation to proprietary algorithms, and opacity in the sense of expert capacity to understand algorithms, which by definition is not widely distributed in human populations. In both cases, algorithms are not opaque in principle and could be made auditable.[10] In other words, there could be an audit trail by which the components of an algorithm and its "neighbours" are all connected, and this connectivity and traceability could in principle enable checking by a third party.

Burrell (2016) distinguishes these two cases from a more radical form of opacity associated with machine learning. She proposes that there is an irreducible gulf between advanced algorithmic processes and human interpretability (cf. Amodei, 2025). This gulf points to an adapted form of human governance that gives up on understanding and auditing "how" and "why" algorithms do what they do, in favour of focusing on "what" they do and their impacts (e.g. the forms of classification they produce in specific settings, such as credit ratings). Ironically, such an approach of auditing "around" the algorithm resembles 1970s strategies of financial auditing around, rather than "through", computer systems (see Chapter 4). Furthermore, as work by Sandvig et al. (2014) and Diakolpoulos (2020) suggests, audit as a research-based evaluation of algorithms must itself become algorithmic in nature. Auditing practice is a specific setting in which the paradoxes and tensions of governing algorithms are evident (Busuioc, 2021). It is a kind of "knowledge-work" that is always colliding with new technologies, and this has given rise to varieties of black-boxing and reworking of practitioner-technology relations over its history (Anthony, 2021).

Auditing and Algorithms

Double-entry bookkeeping, which was discussed in Chapter 3, is a kind of algorithm in Dourish's (2016) sense of pseudo-code (i.e. it is expressive of purpose and rationality; Espeland and Carruthers, 1991), but it needs much more real "code" in the sense of practical instructions and protocols to make it work as a script. Double-entry bookkeeping is therefore entangled in the specific context of the books and records within which it is operationalized, and is subject to error, adjustments, and human workarounds via "journals". Importantly, Double-entry bookkeeping requires primary traces of transactions as input for

[10] Based on an ethnographic study, Rostain and Huising (2024) show how it can be possible for non-programmers to breach and challenge computational opacity when it is out of line with their physical world and its representations.

their datafication in an accounting system. The key question for critical accountants has always been about how such data are not simply "input" but are, over time, shaped and classified by the demands of the algorithm and constituted to be processable according to its logic. Hence, Double-entry bookkeeping as an algorithm sits within an assemblage of related functions and devices that shape both what counts as proper input for accounting practitioners and the nature of the output (i.e. the accounts).

The governance "problem" for Double-entry bookkeeping has the same duality as for digital algorithms. On the one hand, DEB is a source of governance via the accounts that are produced according to its rules. On the other hand, it must also be governed itself. In the first instance, this governance was enacted by human merchants themselves and their social rules, standards, laws, and beliefs (Matringe and Power, 2024). DEB as an algorithm leaves traces of itself—an audit trail, as discussed in Chapter 3—and this enables the operational logic of DEB and the inputs to which it is applied to have "sufficient observability" for merchants and others for checking purposes. And just as there are debates about whether algorithms encode systematic biases and classificatory discrimination, critical accounting studies have also functioned as a kind of "audit" that seeks to expose the partisan nature of accounts and the significance of what they omit and make invisible (Hines, 1988).

More generally, comparing financial and algorithmic auditing helps to sharpen some of the issues at stake with the latter. What exactly is to be governed (scope) and subject to oversight in the form of audit? How is this auditing to be done (standards), and what would be reported or certified? For example, while code development is subject to oversight by coders themselves, working continuously to test and identify errors and bugs, the audit debate is largely mobilized by concerns with public policy issues, such as discrimination (Goodman, 2016; Bandy, 2021). Not only is discrimination itself an imprecise category and audit objective but, for the reasons Burrell (2016) states, algorithms, especially meta-algorithms for machine learning, are in principle difficult to make transparent and auditable.

Given that debates about the audit of algorithms are multifaceted (DRCF, 2022), it is useful to distinguish between (a) long-standing but specific ambitions to automate aspects of auditing and risk-management practice, including the deployment of algorithmic procedures to audit companies, and (b) the larger problem of the auditability and governance of algorithms themselves, for example blockchains. These two problematics overlap but have different institutional histories. Regarding the former, the history of financial auditing practice can be seen as one of a continuous search for process efficiencies via new technology. Indeed, as suggested already and in Chapter 4, experiments in automating aspects of the audit process, and in embedding auditing programmes in information systems, reach back many decades and have generated heated debates about the importance of situated professional judgement—the so-called structure-judgement debate (Power, 2003). These debates about judgement have increased in salience as audit firms seek to deploy artificial intelligence in their audit work (Samiolo et al., 2024). Developments in digital technologies promise to realize the long-standing dream of an audit process with predictive power, a dream that led to the development of risk-based models in the 1980s (Robson et al., 2007) and now takes the form of data-driven auditing and risk assessment (e.g. Singh et al. 2019; Demortain, 2023). These aspirations and developments in auditing are consistent with broader shifts towards "design-based" governance, understood as digitally enabled ex ante strategies of behaviour modification commonly understood as "nudge" (Gritsenko and Wood, 2022), as well as the use of predictive analytics to extend the power of risk-based regulation (Lodge and Mennicken, 2019). Developments in financial auditing are symptomatic of the digitalization of governance and regulation.

The second related problematic of the auditability and governance of algorithms in use in different technology settings, such as blockchains and AI, raises fundamental issues of expertise, scope, process, reporting, and standards. On scope, there are serious questions about what is to be audited and why: the quality of the ecosystem within which algorithms are developed and revised; the integrity of specific datasets; or the quality of the algorithms themselves and whether they perform as expected or discriminate in some way (Birhane et al., 2024; Sandvig et al., 2014; Mainelli and Leitch 2017)? Goodman (2016) draws an analogy between algorithm audits and safety audits, noting that the former are largely conducted by academic researchers. There is no clear institutional framework or standards for such work, nor is there a unified body of human practices, assuming this would be desirable. There are also calls for holistic approaches that combine technology- and process-focused audits in the context of AI (Moekander, 2023; Mokander et al., 2023). In general, despite the efforts of bodies like the Digital Regulation Cooperation Forum (DRCF), the emerging field lacks the kind of standardization that is evident in financial auditing, and the different possibilities and concerns that motivate the audit of algorithms implicate different bodies of expertise, stakeholders, and methodologies. And underlying all of these initiatives remains the problem of how to generate credible second-order observation—"evidentially sufficient observation" of how algorithms work, in the form of third-party audits. It demands not only specialist and context-specific knowledge but also a high degree of epistemic dependence on the very phenomenon being audited (Amodei, 2025). This is an indicative feature of platformization; it implies that the audit of algorithms must, at least in part, be algorithmic in nature, and thereby more of a self-auditing model (Power, 2022).

What can be generally concluded from these reflections on the audit of, and with, algorithms, and their implications more generally for the nature of governance as oversight? First, capability and expertise gaps are not new to auditors and other governance agents. External financial auditors have always placed reliance on technical experts in different fields (e.g. the valuation of land or pension liabilities) in order to support their opinion on the accounts of complex entities (Power, 1996). In this sense, the audit itself has always been more of a networked and de-centred practice, an assembly of discrete routines and reliances, rather than a unitary, single-agent control function. However, it has always involved groups of humans coming together, utilizing technologies to make some kind of sense of an object.

Second, algorithms present challenges of scope as to what exactly it is that is being audited and thereby governed. As discussed in Chapter 4, auditors in the 1980s used to treat computer processing as a black box and tested inputs and outputs rather than the process. Then they moved to a more "systems"-based audit in which the control environment of computer systems and the design and operations of specific controls (e.g. access controls, programme change controls etc.) became a critical audit focus. For algorithm audits we go further in this direction, but the audit object(ive) is becoming less clear and more plural. Is it the human-rich control environment for algorithm development and usage? Or is it the algorithm "itself", an elusive phenomenon-in-the-making? Here the question is whether the audit and governance questions are to do with the quality of the design of the algorithm or its operationalization in code (the risks of bias or bugs). In all these possible purposes and scopes of auditing, expertise issues begin to bite, especially in the setting of artificial intelligence, where there may be multiple potential objects of audit interest.

In the light of these questions, we need to adopt a more fluid view of auditing and what it is to govern and provide assurance. While there are still many continuities with the audit problematics of an earlier time, demands for algorithm governance are also reconfiguring and *multiplying* the very notion of audit and the assurance it claims to provide. Indeed, the verification that auditors provide is just one model of the production of assurance and accountability—there are many others that are less information- and transparency-oriented (Donia, 2025). Furthermore, what is deemed to be evidentially sufficient observation for oversight has always evolved throughout the history of auditing. Algorithms signify much more than another shift in method and technique. They reconfigure auditing and auditability itself as part of the general shift away from the hierarchical model of "layers" and supply chains to one in which governance in general and auditing in particular become "platform-like". As auditing turns to data analysis methods and artificial intelligence, it not only represents a form of governance of algorithm by algorithm, but also begins to be reconstituted and de-centred as a network of apps with specific objects and scopes built into operating platforms. In effect, platformization shifts auditing practice more explicitly towards a multiplicity of specific applications, including but not restricted to financial statement audit, in which traditional distinctions between internal and external auditing are eroded.[11]

While anticipatory and preventative regulation has a long history, technology has provided further stimulus towards such designed-based governance (Gritsenko and Wood, 2022) in the form of specific applications. Many aspects of rule compliance in AML, financial reporting, treating customers fairly, and other areas have lent themselves to automation, beginning with smart contract applications. Lower cost, "labour-lite" compliance is attractive to many businesses, and markets for *Regtech* products are large and growing (Anagnostopoulos, 2018). Programmed governance like this is attractive to regulators too, allowing them to target inspections and avoid the cost of unnecessary site visits. Indeed, not only may there be no site to visit, but regulators themselves are becoming platform-like organizations.[12]

It is proposed that the emerging platformization of monitoring and auditing practices constructs them as one "app" among others. Governance agencies, like auditors, become conceptually just another platform user. Understood thus, platformization inverts previous theories of auditability at the heart of the audit society thesis. Rather than a model of organizations reacting to institutional pressures to make themselves "auditable" via controls and performance metrics (Power, 1996, 2021a), it is more the converse; practices of auditing and evaluation become reconstituted as adjuncts of platformized and de-centred organizations. Such developments necessarily blur institutionalized distinctions between internal and external audit and oversight (Chapter 5). Indeed, the very conception of "external" scrutiny becomes problematic, not because of issues to do with the auditor's motivational and structural independence—the historical obsession of regulators and critics of the audit profession—but because of its topological and epistemological constitution as a user app running on the platforms they audit.[13] The algorithm-generated platformization of auditing symptomizes this trajectory towards general de-layering and "appization" of auditing and oversight and towards a flatter topology of operational governance

[11] It should be noted that traditional internal auditing has tended to have multiple, project-specific scopes and was always more "app-like" in conception.

[12] For many years, the Civil Aviation Authority in the United Kingdom had direct access to the safety incident recording system of many airlines under its jurisdiction—an early example of regulatory platformization that blurred organizational boundaries, enabled near real-time monitoring, and rendered costly forms of ex post second-order observation checking and oversight less necessary, if not redundant.

[13] Although it should also be noted that financial auditors have always been dependent on client systems and have had to adapt their procedures as these systems changed.

functionalities.[14] Such a reduction of oversight to a series of apps would truncate governance as a collective process of sense-making and interpretation.

It is in these debates about the audit of, and with, algorithms that the general implications of platformization for governance as oversight become visible. As organizations, including formal platforms, become more manifestly de- and multi-centred relational configurations of human groups, technology, and data curation, there always remains a need for second-order observation for quality control of operations to ensure that trace production, datafication, and higher-level analytic processing are working as they should. Thus, it is proposed that operationally focused audits and quality-control processes in the first line of defence constitute a space in which a more dividuated, focused, and distributed governance model takes hold. In such settings, oversight is increasingly reconstructed as multiple, functionally specific forms of operational self-certification of tracking processes (Cohen, 2019). This self-certification could be performed by what we presently call an "internal" audit, but it is more likely to be a feature of the first-line operational level itself, which self-audits critical processes. On the one hand, there is nothing new about quality control of this kind, whether we call it an audit or not. On the other hand, this reconfiguration, platformization, and de-layering of governance practices has larger implications for the very idea of traceability-based oversight, which we now consider.

Traceability Lost?

The idea that platformization reduces governance, oversight, and auditing to a portfolio of operational applications that self-certify is undoubtedly overstated, but it has been proposed to characterize an implicit trajectory and an emerging topology of operational governing. The earlier discussion of algorithm audits also suggests that oversight is becoming more fragmented and application-dependent. Indeed, rather than the organization being shaped by auditing and regulation, both organizationality and auditability are becoming dependent on algorithmic processes—are being digitalized—which utilize the traces generated by a multitude of devices from many sources. Should we therefore conclude that developments in algorithm-based regulatory technology are creating a crisis of oversight as the core of what we mean by governance?

We should be cautious about making this inference too quickly, notwithstanding the implications of prior arguments in this book. First, algorithmic practices

[14] It may not be so fanciful to imagine that AI could also in time perform a sense-making form of oversight role that is more than the sum of opinions on specific operations. How might humans make sense of this non-human, non-group-based sense-making? I owe this point to Ted Schatzki.

could in fact enable a productive and beneficial shift in the "governance mix" from costly ex post monitoring and enforcement to cost-effective ex ante, predictive, and design-based forms of regulation. This shift could address many of the present frustrations of regulators and provide further impetus for risk-based approaches (Lodge and Mennicken, 2019). Much is also made of the control benefits of "real-time" surveillance, not least the possibility for enhanced anticipatory control (Flyverbom and Garsten, 2021).[15] And there is the prospect of eliminating expensive layers of regulation and of realizing the ideal of getting things right the first time. Second, as the audit society thesis implies, the layers of governance and lines of defence models should not be assumed to have been somehow functionally superior scripts for governance architectures. The benefits of multiple lines of defence—the so-called Swiss cheese model (Reason et al., 2006)—were perhaps overstated; most regulatory and governance assurance exists in the so-called first line where the operational self-control enabled by tracking happens. Indeed, algorithms could not only enhance the tracking and surveillance aspects of hierarchical oversight, but also generate new bodies of regulatory and organizational knowledge. Third, multiple, automated audits could increase the overall scope and objects of the portfolio of audits, avoiding some of the myths of assurance that have given rise to "expectations gaps" in the financial auditing setting. In sum, the benefits of platformization for targeted anticipatory and efficient governance seem to be considerable. So why is there so much unease, as revealed in the continuous moral debate and near moral panic about algorithms (Edmonds, 2024)?

First, for all its imperfections, the idea of some kind of *independent human oversight* by auditors, inspectors, or even the general public remains an important imaginary of organizational governance as essentially human-centric (Puranam, 2025). Usually this independence is framed as a moral quality, but it is also epistemic and cognitive in nature (i.e. it is the idea that an independent, expert third party can reach conclusions that are understandable, interpretable, and communicable in human terms). In other words, governance is essentially human group activity, in conjunction with technology. It involves human capacities to demonstrate matters that can be understood by other humans. Hence, there is unease about governance by algorithms that are not, or seem not, themselves to be governed or easily subjected to oversight by humans. The audit society may not have generated trust, but it embodied an empirical-juridical ideal of demonstrability, namely a commitment to making organizational and

[15] However, in a comparative study of ERP systems, Quattrone and Hopper (2005) show how the implementation of real-time information flow, which collapsed the distance between centre and periphery, did not enhance traditional HQ control but led to fluid loci of control. Brivot and Gendron (2011) reach a similar conclusion, arguing that the control metaphor of the panopticon must give way to more lateral and fluid networks of control.

individual performance observable and "legible" (Scott, 1998) by third parties. In contrast, platforms are themselves infrastructures that enable, but which increasingly place themselves beyond, evaluation (Kornberger et al., 2017).

Second, notwithstanding the theme of this chapter, oversight is more than just traceability and observation. It also invokes ideas of critical dialogue between human overseers and overseen agencies, or what have been called "regulatory conversations" (Black, 2002). Platformization, as we define it, limits the possibilities for such deliberative processes that are central not only to organization-level governance but also to democratic processes in general. When auditing and evaluation become a series of applications, there may be considerable efficiency and diagnostic gains, but there is also loss of institutional capacity to take an overall, and even critical, view. The latter is an implicit value in the very idea of governance and motivates the demands for practices of oversight by skilled humans. Furthermore, the panoramic forms of accounting that are produced for oversight purposes may be simplifications, even myths, but they are valued precisely because they provide representations of organizations or activities that inform collective human sense-making. In contrast, platformization seems to lead to more "seeing without knowing" (Ananny and Crawford, 2018) and to the potential operational governance of parts without a sense-making governance narrative of the whole. Such synoptic forms of sense-making, which can somehow stand outside and over these developments in intensified trace creation and tracking, are increasingly displaced by operational dashboards of metrics and dispersed visualizations of performance. The digitally enabled dashboard has become a paradigm for focused tracking and accounting control using a range of near real-time "indicators" for operational oversight. As more dimensions of organizational performance become measurable and trackable, dashboards and their metrics, which reach back in conception to the balanced scorecard and beyond, have evolved. Dashboards measure and visualize in new ways, which gives them enormous facticity and attention-generating power (Quattrone, 2017; see also Chapter 3). They have the potential to prevent overdetermination by a single tracking metric and can be understood as forms of macro-script (Chapter 5) that do in fact enable a mode of oversight of operations.[16] Yet, dashboards that enable this organizational self-observation also contribute to de-layering and flattening in which governance-related metrics may become one category among others. To repeat: platformization weakens, if not collapses, distinctions between operations and oversight.

Third, these developments have important implications for traceability as a value. In Chapter 1 we began with the duality of "trace-ability" as the ability to

[16] Whether dashboards and scorecards really embody this balance of indicators is an open empirical question. For a critique, see Norreklit (2000).

generate traces, on the one hand, and the ability to exercise control and governance by making things, people, and processes traceable, on the other. Under conditions of platformization, the two senses of traceability exist in increasing tension with one another. The rise of the former, which is data- and algorithm-driven and which expands connectivity and behavioural visibility, also changes traceability in the second sense. even to the point of making it impossible. Without strong human counter-controls, algorithms are engines of the former and problematic objects of the latter. This is the ironic "over-lit" society phenomenon (Flyverbom, 2021), so bright that we cannot "oversee" many decisions. It is so connected that we are disconnected. And it is so full of traces that we cannot trace where decisions come from and how they are produced. Algorithmically constituted traceability complexes are likely to multiply numerically and intensify, but they will become smaller, shorter, and less dense, even to the point where they disappear from human comprehension. We may not yet be in this world—governance as an archipelago of apps—but advances in artificial intelligence are rapidly taking us there.

Once again, we should be careful before embracing too dystopian a view. While developments in social media have been much debated, not least as a source of falsity, in principle they also provide channels for new capabilities and critiques of corporate conduct. Anonymous employee reviews on platforms like *Glassdoor* have generated interest as independent sources of information on value and conduct, and constitute a node of decentralized governance beyond the traditional hierarchical model (Campbell and Shang, 2022). Employee-generated texts may or may not be trustworthy and informative, but they are new and emerging forms of traceification, scripting, and oversight "from below" (Brivot and Gendron, 2011). Hence while platformization may fragment and de-layer governance as we know it, it can also create new mechanisms for human voice and critique (see also Chapter 8)—all of which shows that an apparent crisis of human oversight and traceability must be offset by new human-technology alliances and formations (Acemoglu, 2025). And if we must broaden our view of what counts as accounting (Chapter 1), consistency requires that we extend that breadth to our conception of governance and the very nature of assurance in a digitalized world.

Conclusions

In this chapter, we have examined the traceability-accounts nexus as it bears upon regulatory and governance practices. Traceability is at the heart of modern ideas about organizational and societal governance, constituting forms of connectivity and regulatory oversight in many different fields, from anti-money-laundering (AML) to fishery supply chains. These and other examples help to strengthen the model of the traceability complex as a framework for comparative analysis. In particular, the different mini-cases provide prima facie support for conceptualizing traceability as a mix of two overlapping practice modes—tracking and oversight—and their respective epistemic orientations—generative and evidentiary.

It has been proposed that this mix of elements, which constitute organized forms of traceability, is changing under conditions of societal and organizational digitalization. In effect, the digitally enabled expansion in the nature, scope, and power of tracking is having a reconstitutive effect on governance. Hierarchical layers of oversight or control of control, which were emblematic of the audit society trajectory and of regulatory design in general, are being "flattened" and dispersed into specialized operational evaluations, which become applications sitting alongside others. Since organizing, as argued in Chapter 5, is to a large degree shaped by powerful scripts that enable governance as self-observation—books and records in the pre-digital past and now algorithms—this shift in the traceability mix also has implications for the topology of formal organizations. It is a process of change, conceptualized here as "platformization" (Power, 2022), which is both institutional and technical in its effects, blurring governance and operational control and reshaping, as an indicative example, the very nature and scope of auditing.

Trends in governance and regulation towards the enrolment of soft law, voluntarism, enforced self-regulation, meta-regulation, and many similar notions reach back many decades (Baldwin et al., 2011). All these notions stress, in different ways, the importance of what we have called first-order observation or tracking as a resource for operationalizing organizational-level governance and as a resource for a myriad of state-backed regulatory agencies. It is proposed that platformization radicalizes these trends, leading to an emphasis on multiple forms of operational tracking and de-layering. As tracking and related accounting practices expand, and are constituted by increasingly ambitious algorithms, they become more generative and predictive in nature, and the audit trail as a mode of connectivity supporting oversight becomes weaker and shorter. While there are undoubtedly many benefits to this promised de-layering of costly oversight and "control of control" architectures, in effect the unwinding of the audit society, there is also a decline of organized collective oversight potential that leaves critical second-order observation to ad hoc groups of academics, journalists, commentators, philosophers, and other outsiders who endeavour to provide accounts that counter the loss of traceability and voice in algorithmic culture. The emergence of social media outlets like "Glassdoor" as critical channels is both a symptom of, and compensation for, a decline of formal oversight structures and signifies the rise of multiple sources of governance and control beyond traditional organizational boundaries.

Finally, a new politics of traceability is visible in these developments focused on the far-reaching reductionism of digital traceification and datafication. In audit society, that which was non-reduced and non-commensurable could still be observed and conceptualized. Under conditions of advanced datafication, the world of the incommensurable, non-reducible, and idiosyncratic, the residual waste of the audit society, is becoming its very object—via big data analytics and other technologies. The formerly incommensurable material of social life is being pulverized and traceified in order to be turned into data, tracked and formed into new objects of predictive economic interest (Alaimo and Kalinikos, 2019). In short, primary traceification as the fundamental act of organizing within traceability complexes is the frontier for a politics of traceability and tracking. Governance concerns about the invisibility of the radical reductionism and value-bias inherent in digital traceification, which aims at making everything but itself observable, must confront the growing enthusiasm for its generativity, creativity, and demonstrable benefits. The maturity of this politics will depend on whether it retreats into crude dualities of resistance and support or develops forms of discourse and governance practice that can navigate these changes, retaining both their evident benefits and possibilities for human-based oversight. The recent history of new technologies is not very encouraging on this point.

Chapter 6 Summative Propositions

The following propositions address variations in governance regimes and the implications of digitalization for auditing and practices of oversight.

1. **Governance regimes can be re-described as traceability complexes that combine tracking as first-order observation of relevant actions and audit-trail-enabled oversight practices as second-order observation.**
2. **Between limit cases of disorganized and highly integrated traceability complexes, specific regulatory/governance regimes vary in terms of: clarity of purpose; the nature of their traceification and tracking; the depth of their oversight practices; and their forms of accounting.**
3. **The digitalization of economy and society is leading to a shift in the mix of tracking and oversight. Oversight is being de-layered and platformized.**
4. **Platformization is characterized by: userfication that blurs the personal-organizational boundary; the centrality of algorithm-enabled tracking and analytics; the erasure of the distinction between**

operations and governance; de-layering of oversight functions into stand-alone apps; increased self-auditing; accounts as dashboards.

5. **The audit and governance of algorithms is reaching the limit of human understanding, leading to a weakening of evidentiary traceability. Trace production is overwhelming and reshaping the nature of trace usage for assurance and oversight.**
6. **Despite the great benefits in efficiency associated with digitalization, the economy of traces governs and monitors itself through algorithms that are increasingly beyond human oversight and interpretation.**

7
Traceability, Temporality, and Risk

Overview

In 2005 I was appointed as an independent, non-executive director of a large UK public company in the financial services sector. My very first task was to chair what was then called a "compliance committee", which reviewed the internal assessments of compliance across a wide variety of regulatory requirements, mainly, but not exclusively, conduct of business rules. Capital adequacy issues were reserved to the audit committee. From the outset I had the impression that senior executives attending the committee were not especially engaged with compliance issues. There was a sense that much of it was needlessly bureaucratic and unrelated to the "front end" of the business. The first meeting was somewhat flat. At the beginning of my second meeting as chair, I gave a short introduction, which proposed that compliance metrics taken as whole are the pulse of the business and an early warning system for potentially deeper issues. Thus, a spike in complaints or regulatory breaches could mean many different things, but might also suggest that operations were overheating in pursuit of new business. The committee agreed that there should wherever possible be a "root cause" analysis of any material variance in compliance indicators and continuous review of what represented tolerable non-compliance. Over time, and especially in the wake of the 2008 financial crisis, the UK regulator's own tolerance for non-compliance shifted, and more granular reporting was demanded. Its evidentiary demands increased, and audit trails for compliance became more detailed and elaborate. With the support of the chief risk officer, it became clear that compliance needed to be understood explicitly in terms of business risk and not only regulatory risk. At the same time, the compliance committee was re-designated as a "Risk Committee" with an expanded agenda. This riskification of the very category of compliance was more than a change in label. It was also a change in its temporal orientation, namely from being about what had been done and whether it was compliant, to becoming more explicit about what might happen in the future. Compliance data were thereby subject to progressive reframing as "traces of the future", not just of the past.

Chapter 6 explored the significance of traceability for governance, understood in hierarchical terms as "layered-oversight". It was argued that these layers, as connected agencies in an audit trail, are being "flattened" and "de-centred" under general conditions of digitalization and platformization, a trend which suggests

Economy of Traces. Michael Power, Oxford University Press. © Oxford University Press (2026).
DOI: 10.1093/9780197681527.003.0007

that traceability is being eroded and even lost. It was also noted that governance practices are designed and mobilized more or less explicitly to contribute to the management of risks to values. Hence the broad "value-purposes" of traceability outlined in Chapter 1 can be credibly reframed in terms of managing risks to the valued goods of quality, security, and discovery. In this chapter, we adopt this risk lens explicitly as a way of exploring the temporal character of traceability.[1]

The chapter follows an "arc" that describes the entanglement of traceability, temporality, and risk across three levels and problem clusters—the ontological, practical, and cultural. The ontological arguments begin in the next section by drawing on Stiegler's (1998) thesis that the trace is a point of exteriorization and projective deferral that emerges in the encounter between the human brain and the simplest hand technology (from our modern point of view), namely a stone flint. This onto-biological reading of the trace establishes its centrality to temporality and historicizing, and, by analogical extension, to the temporal nature of organizing (e.g. Hernes, 2014, 2022). For organizations to be relatively stable entities, Chapter 5 argued that they required minimal self-observation capacity grounded in varieties of scripts, oral and documental, cultural and operational, which make an organization traceable as an entity both forwards and backwards in time.

From these more abstract considerations of temporality and traces, the argument shifts to consider how the future is made traceable as a matter of practice. Specifically, risk management is framed as a family of practices that process traces of future harms and benefits in the present. Here we develop a series of arguments, drawing upon the social construction of risk objects in Hilgartner's (1992) sense and emphasizing the importance of indicators that anchor the causal relations between an object and the harm attributed to it. We also consider the design of so-called "lead indicators" of risk and the ways in which they encode varying degrees of temporal depth in relating risk objects to something valued and at risk. The greater the depth, and the seeming temporal distance of the harm, the more contentious is the design process. Drawing upon prior work (Hardy et al., 2020), we then zoom out from the indicator level to consider how risk-management practices combine varying temporal orientations—prospective, real time, and retrospective. In particular, we identify the phenomenon by which prospective, future-oriented risk management can

[1] This chapter will focus primarily on risk as contingent future harm. It would have been equally possible to explore the traceability-temporality-riskification nexus in terms of benefits and opportunities. Such an emphasis would have taken the discussion in this chapter more into the strategy, entrepreneurship, and planning literature (e.g. Garud and Gehman, 2019) rather than, as here, risk-management studies. It is acknowledged that this gives the analysis a more asymmetric treatment of harms and benefits than is found in other bodies of work. See also Jarzabkowski et al. (2025) for a synthetic review that overcomes this asymmetry.

be shaped by a retrospective, defensive orientation. This analysis opens up the theme of riskification.

The third movement of the arc of the chapter considers the cultural aspects of risk and temporality. Riskification is understood as a cultural phenomenon by which many practices come to be organized explicitly according to a master-script of risk management and must be traceable and auditable according to that script. As discussed in Chapter 5, organizational governance has been riskified in this sense. Riskification also extends to the idea of the traceability complex, which can be reframed in risk-management terms, emphasizing the tracking of risk objects. Finally, the chapter considers the more general implications of digital transformations for temporality and traceability. The motif of the *archaeology of the future* is proposed, and three indicative themes are developed. First, it is argued that traceability as an expanded capacity to track has itself become both a new risk object and a value at risk. Second, platformization processes (Chapter 6) and related aspirations for big data and predictive analytics embody implicit dreams of eliminating so-called "Knightean uncertainty", understood as the space for creative, entrepreneurial humans confronting uncertain futures. The temporal orientation of what we call digital "archaeologies of the future" is that of the moving horizon of a data-saturated present that absorbs both the past and the future. The implicit teleology of such archaeologies is the elimination of uncertainty that runs counter to human projective capabilities. Third, the chapter suggests that this dilution of human projective capability (Emirbayer and Mische, 1998) changes the accounts we live by and hence the nature of self-hood, in which more is at stake than privacy. This will be the subject matter of Chapter 8.

Traces and Temporality

The nature of time and temporality has puzzled philosophers, scientists, and many others for millennia. Perhaps more than in any other case, the noun form "time" gives a false sense of its nature. The notion of "temporality" is usually preferred by organization scholars for its processual nuance, but this hardly limits the extraordinary range and diversity of analyses and approaches that are attached to it. Since at least the philosopher Kant and no doubt earlier, we know that our experience is essentially temporal in nature. He reminds us of the fundamental role of time as a "*form* of experience", meaning something without which experience as we know it would be impossibly fragmented and diffuse. Time is therefore not an object among others; it is a "transcendental" condition of possibility for everyday experience of a world—"we live in time". Kant's insights have been challenged, but they have also greatly influenced many subsequent schools of historical hermeneutics, especially the phenomenology of Husserl and Schutz.[2] Thus, when we pay close phenomeno-analytic attention to the manner in which the world appears to us in our own experience, its underlying temporal organization is generated by our combined capacities for the *retention* of traces of fleeting moments and their *protention* as the formation of expectation. This conjoined process of memorizing and projecting is insistent and unavoidable. As stable, habitual, and consistent our experience may feel, there is always continuous change in time in the sense made popular by Heraclitus's dictum that one can never step into the same river twice. Without the fundamental structuring properties of temporality, experience would be mere succession and effluxion, which is no experience at all, or at least no experience of the kind that we could understand, or would not regard as in some way pathological.

Stiegler (1998) steers away from phenomenology, drawing on evolutionary biology. He argues that the trace, as discussed in Chapter 2, is inherently paradoxical, being both meaningless material mark and meaningful sign. He understands it as referencing the point at which otherness and exteriority, including temporal exteriority of past and future, emerge from the ongoing encounter between brute matter and the evolving cortex of humanoids. Traces in this sense point to the process by which the human brain evolves in conjunction with raw matter become hand-held tool (i.e. the flint). This process marks the origins of intention, reflection, temporality, and of meaning itself. The flints as lying "ready-to-use", in Heidegger's (2013 [1954]) sense, enable something to come from nothing, and for the human to emerge from the non- or pre-human. For Stiegler, retention and protention as concepts in transcendental phenomenology become repurposed with an onto-evolutionary meaning. He draws on Derrida's notion of the trace (see also Chapter 2) to highlight the evolutionary significance of *différance* as not only difference as otherness (e.g. what is not me), but also deferral, of what is absent and not yet, which implicates the temporality of the human, and a space of uncertainty. Where Heidegger distinguished between organized and authentic time, Stiegler prefers Derrida to support his argument that there is no temporalization that is independent of technologies that generate *différance*. Tools imbued with purpose and an essentially temporalized, intentionalized, humanity co-emerge over millennia via brain development. From this point of view, the trace is fundamental to the "horizon of otherness" and meaning that emerges within the transition from undifferentiated phenomena to the temporalized human capable of memory, reflection, and planning (cf. Barad, 2007). The critical feature of this argument is that technology does not stand outside of the human, as an artefact of human intention and invention. It produces distinctions inter alia between human and non-human, just as it is also produced

[2] Kant (1978); Husserl (1970); Schutz (1976).

by humanity; it is what we live by and what lives through us collectively. We shall draw further on Stiegler's relational theory of self in Chapter 8.

Traces and Histories

These onto-biological arguments about the nature of temporality point to the importance of traces and traceification for understanding history, not just as the basis for recording events and traces, but also in constituting the very nature of history as enduring beyond the limitations of human memory. Notwithstanding that the nature of history is widely debated, it can be understood generally as the sum of diverse narrations of pasts, grounded in varieties of cultural objects, artefacts, and inscriptions (i.e. traces)—which form the basis for historical data and fact-building. History in this sense consists of plural, often contested, and selected sense-making structures in which the seemingly personal, collective, and technical are necessarily intermingled. Individual and collective human capacity for memory is limited but has come to be augmented by, and co-developed with, many prosthetic technologies, including accounts, books, and archives that, insofar as they reach and endure beyond finite individual biological lives, are necessarily collective and relational in nature (Eisenman and Frenkel, 2021). Hence, as paradoxical as it sounds, the capacity of organizational memory exceeds that of any individuated human being.[3]

As discussed in Chapter 2, histories small and large can take a critical form by seeking to recover traces and generate narratives that might otherwise be lost or suppressed (e.g. of slavery, of injustice, of hope). Historical understanding and collective memorizing are therefore implicitly or explicitly agonistic. This is not only the case when the history of the "victor" or colonialist is explicitly disputed, but also, as many studies reveal, for more seemingly mundane forms of accounting and the power relations that they embody. As outlined in Chapter 3, accounts in all their variety are memorializing practices that are not neutral and objective, but which encode values and power (Quattrone, 2015). They contribute to, and reflect, specific temporalities of organizations and organizing. In short, the "accounts we live by", even and especially when they take digital form, are saturated by both histories and imagined futures (Beckert, 2013, 2021). In whatever way we choose to think about the nature of history and about specific practices of memorizing, they both depend fundamentally on the production, deliberate or otherwise, and preservation of traces of actions, events, and people. These are

[3] In their classic paper, Walsh and Ungson (1991) remind us that memory is used metaphorically when applied to organizations and that they do not remember independently of human practices of storage and retrieval, which we might call the accounting system in a broad sense.

at least the necessary, if not sufficient, conditions for the interpretative, inferential, and connecting work of historians, accountants, and others. We know that much of this material basis for history, whose knowledge paradigm is the archive, is lost or incomplete. Ancient libraries have been destroyed, books have been burned, and relics may be buried. In other words, in the analytic language of this book, traceability in the form of primary traces, audit trails, and accounts is always partial and incomplete. Dreams of the total archive and complete and perfect history are futile, as Borges reminds us in his *Library of Babel*, but this has not extinguished the fascination with this dream, which is also evident in contemporary discussions of big data and AI.

The idea of the trace is fundamentally temporal in that it registers and marks an event at the time of its happening, it endures over time, and its retentions ground the possibility of protentive and projective historical narratives. These narratives in turn constitute some traces as historical "data" and consign others to oblivion. Traces are not in this sense objective and given; on the contrary, their production and non-production is motivated by many interests and values, and their "datafication" (Chapter 3) can be disputed, especially in forensic settings (Weyermann and Ribaux, 2012). Yet this traceification of objects, texts, and ideas produces the primary registrations that are fundamental to the construction of histories as specific narratives and accounts. There can be many different possible "ruts in the road" of history, and primary traces must be used, datafied, narrativized, and must compete with others in order for the histories that they constitute to acquire centrality and cultural significance. This narrational competition over the "facts" of history is as brutal as it is also often invisible, for both substantive and methodological reasons (Clemens, 2007). Most traces, and therefore potential histories, are lost and never become institutionalized as data. They are mere marks and the exhaust and waste of history. Such traces can admittedly make a comeback, can be dug up and re-datafied, provided that they are not fully and completely extinguished. And new techniques have emerged to recover such traces and create new history potential. Yet the general point remains: without trace production in general as the generation of durable marks of human activity, there is no possibility of anything other than oral human history, bounded by the limitations of memory and biological life.

Common sense would suggest that a "trace of" something normally references an event that is past; it is the residue of that which has happened and is over. On this view, the temporality of traces—what we may call their temporal reference—seems simple and even objective. They are traces of the past, and their ontology is essentially that of historical residue. Indeed, it is exactly this quality that underwrites their forensic status and permits them to count as "evidence" or signs of something that has happened, or to be a trace of the past of an object or person. Traces in this sense point to a dead past, which would be spectral and fleeting without the survival or cultural retention endowed by the trace. More generally, what we call "culture" is coextensive with this variety of organized meanings enabled by the material traces of things, people, and processes. However, our brief onto-biological excursion also suggests that history and memorizing do not just "refer backwards". Historiographical studies remind us that historicizing is deeply implicated in projects of cultural projection. We should therefore conceive of temporality as hermeneutic philosophers have done, as the continually unfolding backward-and-forward horizon of a trace-producing present (Gadamer, 2013), the continuous emergence and stabilization of social order (Clemens, 2007, p. 532). This deep imbrication of human memory, the technologies that augment it and temporality, generate rich and varied forms of projection and prognostication. And, while it has become philosophically and sociologically unfashionable to suggest that there is any kind of essence to being human, a reasonable case could be made for defining such an essence in teleological terms, that is, as an orientation to, and the imagination of, possible but uncertain futures fabricated from traces of the past. Phenomenological philosophers like Brentano, Husserl, and Schutz want to ground these projective capacities in something more fundamental, namely the essential *intentionality* of humans for whom action, communication, and projection are mutually constitutive, a theme that is also characteristic of American pragmatism, discussed briefly in Chapter 2.

Intentionality as future orientation can take many practice forms, not least in explicitly strategic contexts. And while it can be an engine of inventiveness and creation in the face of uncertainty, when severed from action it also points to the human condition as one of permanent waiting. In Samuel Beckett's famous play, his characters wait for "Godot", who never comes and is nothing but a temporal vanishing point of existence. On Beckett's view, found to some degree in the work of Heidegger, waiting is the essential tragic condition of being alive. It is a notion of human intentionality without object(ive)s, which yearns to be infused with purposes but whose substantive emptiness is nevertheless always latent and periodically visible. These sensibilities have informed stoic philosophies and more nihilistic variants of existentialism, but they also appear in theologies of hope and purpose.

The projection capabilities that characterize individual and collective agency (Emirbayer and Mische, 1998, p. 971) can take many specific practice forms, not least as organized imaginaries of possible futures, from organizations with social purpose, to technologies like blockchain or accounting, to science itself (Jasanoff, 2015; Taylor, 2004; Valk, Preda, and Xu 2023). Thus, tragic or otherwise, collectively and individually, human life is teleological, meaning that we have plans, strategies, purposes, goals, and all manner of projects that orient themselves to futures (Palermo, 2018; Giraudeau, 2012a, 2012b; Schatzki, 2020. These issues of temporality and the human condition emphasize how humans are immersed in practices oriented to shaping futures and their variable temporal "textures" (Flaherty, 2011; Esposito, 2011, 2024). In particular, as we now discuss, formal organizations can be understood as culturally specific manifestations of projectification and as "engines of imagination" in the face of uncertainty (Beckert, 2021).

Organizations in Time

Processual theories of organization focus explicitly on the work by which the temporal flux and flow of human activity are structured (Langley et al., 2013; Hernes, 2014, 2022; Bansal et al., 2022). Distinctive rhythms and sequences of actions provide essential stability and repeatability to organizations, and constitute the temporalities of the practices through which they are enacted (Kirsch, Moeen, and Wadhwani, 2014). Broader historical and sociological studies have focused on the clocks (Landes, 1984), timetables, time sheets, diaries, and many other material devices through which we give form and organized structure to temporality and through which time is made observable, controllable, and can be "assetized" as a scarce resource (Birch and Muniesa, 2020; Ericson and Wajcman, 2022). Notwithstanding the evident variety of these many practical and material orderings of time, it is plausible to propose that there is no organizationality, in the sense of a self-governing capability and minimal identity, without scripts that aim at some form of temporal structuring (Orlikowski and Yates, 2002). Hence, if organizational substantiality and agency are a continuously reproduced fiction, theories of temporal structuring remind us how the reproduction of these fictions enable organizations to have an institutionalized presence independent of the limited memories and experiences of their changing and transient human members.

The scripts that pervade organizing, and which produce strings of actions, encode different temporal rhythms—daily, monthly, annually—and "depths" of temporal orientation to the past and future (Reinecke and Lawrence, 2023). Specific organizational temporalities are "enacted" (Orlikowski and Yates, 2002); time does not have an independent existence or structure.[4] It is difficult to imagine that an entity could count as an organization without some temporal rhythm of accounts production, understood in the minimal sense of the scripted self-narration of transition between past and present. At its simplest, there could be no credit or indebtedness without enduring records for tracking obligations

[4] From a Latourian point of view, both spatiality and temporality could be said to be ontologically "flat"; the future and past are always modes of reference in a documentary present.

over time. While the clay tablets discussed in Chapter 3 emerge much later in human history than flint-based hand tools, the mark on the tablet as trace can be understood as encoding temporality in the form of intentionality towards future repayment. It is not the single human cortex in development that is decisive here so much as the trans-individual formation of collective relations and modes of organizing. In this early form of accounting technology, we can also postulate its role in generating a grammar of difference between an organizational inside (the debtor) and outside (the creditor). It is an emergent distinction already implied by the mark on the clay tablet that signifies both the otherness of the transaction partner and also temporality as deferral of repayment to a future. The technology therefore governs and produces relations between two parties through time. This simple material manifestation of organized reciprocity to manage an uncertain future reflects the "technological rooting of all relations to time" (Stiegler, 1998). The multiple temporalities of acts of organizing, including accounts, can therefore be plausibly understood and analysed in terms of how scripts (algorithms) and material technologies encode specific forms of retention (memory) and protention (projection).

To summarize, there could be no history, no experience, and no organization without the "trace" that is at the centre of the profound mystery by which temporality, technology, and humanity have co-emerged. Even when we move away from the onto-biological level of the argument, the trace remains significant to the temporality of organizing. In the remainder of this chapter, we view this relationship between traces and temporality in a more concrete way through the lens of a practice field—risk management—which is concerned very broadly with making the future traceable.

Making the Future Traceable

Specific practices of prognostication and prediction when considered concretely are enormously varied. Human beings have always looked to the future, for example to understand, anticipate, and predict the weather for agricultural purposes or, as anthropology teaches us, for salvation, meaning, and purpose. Indeed, history is replete with examples of organized futurologies, such as the mythological projections of traces in the natural world as portents for events in the human world of politics. Today we would regard this mythologizing and its signification as mere superstition, but such signs were often embedded in highly developed practices of prognostication. For example, the popular saying "red sky at night, shepherd's delight" is something we learn as children, yet it reflects practices of "traceifying" transient natural phenomena as signs of things to come. In this way, traces became assembled inductively into bodies of folk-knowledge, accounts to live by, which were highly imperfect judged by today's standards of science yet acquired status as a legitimate "trace of" for a specific community practice of prognostication. Such observation-based traces and clues about the future have become increasingly organized and scientized and are now embodied in disciplines like meteorology and volcanology. Indeed, it is through such sciences that "traces of . . ." futures are generated and become datafied within elaborate and rationalized apparatuses of anticipation, prediction and forecasting, representing, and controlling. Hence, traces are not just the ground upon which histories are built but, even while they do this, they can also operate as clues and signs of possible futures and become the basis for organized enquiry and the "taming of chance" (Bernstein, 1996).

At first glance, the very idea of a "trace of the future" seems contradictory. Traces are residues of past events. Yet, any initial puzzlement disappears when we distinguish between the temporality of trace production, the materiality of traces as marks and inscriptions, and their practice-relative semiotics. As elaborated in Chapter 2, in this book we adopt a processual understanding of the trace, not as an entity in and of itself but as the outcome of traceification in which something, anything, can be marked and constructed as a "trace of. . ." a phenomenon of interest. Traces considered as bare marks reflect and register past actions; they endure beyond their point of creation either by intention or by accident in the archaeological case. But traces are always also relational, they are "traces of . . .". What they are traces of, what they reference and point to, what they are signs of, are functions of the practices of tracking and tracing within which their meaning co-develops. Considered semiotically, traces are signs whose reference and temporality are never fixed and permanent but are open to specification and change. Hence it is through traceification that things can be made into traces of the future, acquiring their temporal orientation from the collective expectations that mobilize their production and from the devices that enable that production. There is therefore nothing unusual about collecting and processing "traces of the future". Furthermore, such generated traces often do not point to the future in a singular way, and the nature of their traceification may vary according to the practice context and need for legitimacy.[5] Hence, futurity is a contingent, constructed, and often contested orientation, especially so for the practices of future-organizing, which are commonly described as "risk management" in which specific risks are both defined as objects and made traceable via indicators—the "risk accounts" we live by.

[5] See, for example, Rindova and Martins (2022), who analyse the variability of strategic imagination and projections in terms of characteristics of plausibility and desirability. Different temporal encodings of traces may coexist as a function of different potential interests and objectives within organizations.

Risk is relational (Boholm and Corvellec, 2011) in the sense of being a "risk to X", where X is something that is valued and where we often have to decide how much risk to X is tolerable and how much we value X relative to another value Y (Jarzabkowski et al., 2025, p. 128). This idea of something valued being at risk implicates temporal depth by which X can be temporally remote (e.g. the well-being of future generations as compared with Y; e.g. maintaining my current lifestyle). Hence, which traces of the future to track and how to act prospectively to mitigate them as risks can be highly contentious, for societies and organizations. Furthermore, traces of remote futures can also be easily "discounted", both literally and technically via the mechanics of applying a discount rate to future possible cash flows associated with risk crystallization (e.g. costs of future clean-up of hazardous waste; Doganova, 2024). So there is always a question as to which traces of the future become institutionalized in the organization of traceability. This problem of how to anchor the future in the present is partly one of risk object construction.

From Traces to Risk Objects

Hilgartner's (1992) theory of risk objects as sources of harm points to how they are selected and constructed from many possible objects within socio-technical networks. These networks of distributed and connected actors support the attribution of causal links between such risk objects and the harms associated with them. Taking the system of automobile travel as one such network, the dominant conceptualization of a risk object had been "driver error" as the source of accidents. This changed following Ralph Nader's campaign in the 1970s against General Motors' Corvair and its accident experience. Until Nader's activism, crashes were conceptualized as events that were external to the industry and were risks that could be addressed by better driver education. Nader, a critic and safety campaigner, refused to accept this prevailing explanatory trope and sought actively to change it by elucidating many design flaws of the Corvair as unrecognized risk objects. He was ultimately successful in problematizing the dominant causal account of the harmful outcome, in part by bringing to the fore and traceifying the "second collision" phenomenon by which a driver collides with the inside of the vehicle.

Hilgartner shows how Nader was able to assemble networks of support for this new conception of the cause of excessive crash site injury, thereby establishing a new and persuasive causal link between the defects of design and excessive harm to human car occupants in the event of a crash. But like any scientific endeavour facing a burden of proof, the claims about defective design were initially ill-formed and contested, being based on ad hoc observations (traces) by

Nader himself and niche expert investigative communities. Over time, these early traces, hints, and suspicions came to be accepted and assembled as data in the larger automobile network, and the source of harm came to be recognized as a risk object (i.e. causally related to a harmful outcome), demanding the regulation of manufacture. This process of "emplacing" a new risk object—design defects—in new apparatuses of data production and regulation eventuated in it being ultimately "dis-emplaced" by design modifications. The case suggests that risk objects often begin life as disputed traces, anomalies, weak signals, and puzzles (see Chapter 2) about existing accounts of causality. Critical actors, scientific communities, and others must build support for new accounts of risk, often under difficult conditions. The risk object crystallizes in a socio-technical sense as a combination of newly attributed causal connectivity or linkage to the harm and new forms of network connectivity that make that causality credible and actionable.[6]

The notion of the weak signal of harm is relevant to risk object formation, being the idea of an encounter with something anomalous or puzzling, a trace that could suggest possible future harm. Yet, what is the "weakness" of the weak signal? Following Hilgartner, we might say that it implies that the strength of the causal relation linking the signal to some future undesirable harm is indisputable to some but not sufficiently established within a relevant socio-technical network. In other words, rather than thinking of weakness as an objective or inherent property of the trace as a signal, we can conceptualize it in terms of the consensus that surrounds its articulation.

From this point of view, risk object construction can be seen as the work of progressively transforming weak signals into strong ones, thereby translating them into data. Risk objects in Hilgartner's analysis begin as weak in this sense, although they may be strong for specific advocates (like Nader himself) and specialists. Where a weak signal points to remote future harm, present benefits may conspire to keep the signal weak until, as we are experiencing in the case of climate change, the signals are no longer weak and the resulting harms are increasingly present. Nevertheless, many people still smoke knowing risks of cancer, and we still consume excess sugar knowing the risks of ill-health because present gratification dominates the imagination of future harm. So, even where a risk object is firmly established as a strong causal signal of harm, other values may dominate action, and regulation may not change behaviour. The general point is that the weakness or strength of a signal is an institutional and cultural

[6] Latour's (1987) analysis of science in action draws out this co-dependency by initially inverting the commonsense idea that credible causal claims must precede their acceptance in a network; rather, he argues that it is the credibility of experts that enables connectivity to acquire causal status. This may be too strong an inversion, but it supports Hilgartner's specific arguments about risk objects.

feature of risk object construction and its embeddedness or otherwise in systems of management, regulation, and wider social habits.

The weakness of weak signals of future harm is also often a function of temporal proximity. Causal relations between risk object and harm are often contested and denied, not least when the harm is temporally remote from the risk object and causality must be established by complex bodies of science. It is also now widely, but still not universally, accepted that fossil fuel consumption is at the heart of climate change, but it has taken decades to embed this relationship in apparatuses for monitoring, despite the initial warnings from many scientists. As I write these words, that project of embedding is becoming more fragile. The politics of risk object construction is therefore a politics of causality, connectivity, and temporal depth that implicates the credibility and power of different experts and voices. The causality and temporality of risk objects therefore involve both epistemic and political struggles, especially when the "harm" itself is temporally remote (e.g. deforestation), presently invisible (e.g. risks from background radiation from radon), or threatening to lifestyle (mobile phone usage, driving cars).

Within this politics of the connectivity supporting risk objects, indicators of distant future harms tend to have weaker traction and signalling power for action in the present. Hence, temporal horizons can be a source of struggle as different groups seek to dramatize and make the future present or absent via preferred indicators (Reinecke and Lawrence, 2023). To repeat: the weakness or strength of any signal or trace of risk is a function of its wider acceptance, including by scientists if relevant, and the institutionalization of the risk object that it signifies. It follows that the traceification dynamics at the origination of risk objects are also political, value-laden, and potentially distributive of harms. Risk object construction involves a "contest for the future" (Beckert and Suckert, 2021, p. 11) in which "short termism" is a form of continuing failure of temporal depth (Alexander, 2023, p. 20). From this point of view, accounts are important technologies by which distant future events can be translated into/connected with the situated temporal structures of practice, thereby "pulling" the future into the present (Hernes and Schultz, 2020). At the centre of these contests over risk object construction is the politics of the indicators that make risk traceable.

Risk Objects and Indicators

The socio-technical networks that connect diverse elements in the construction of risk objects necessarily include ways of accounting for them. Hence the formation of indicators and the emergence of risk objects go hand in hand, since it is the former that encapsulate and represent the causal relations underpinning the latter. In other words, the traceification of risks and their accounting indicators co-develop. Without being anchored in credible metrics for tracking and measuring, a risk object lacks a determinate basis for intervening to manage it. And both risk objects and their indicators encode variation in the temporal depth of the connectivity between object and future harm. Hence, risk indicators are the contingent outcomes and expressions of the often hidden politics of temporal depth suggested in the previous section of this chapter. They are value-laden accounting metrics that are technical in their form and appearance.

Lead Indicators

Classic organization-focused studies of risk have identified many of the processes, practices, and cultural antecedents of accidents and disasters. Notably, Turner's (1976) inductive analysis concludes that accidents are not sudden, and that their temporality is not that of a punctuated present, although they may be experienced in that way. Rather, he argues that disasters are preceded by what he calls an "incubation" period in which their conditions accrete and the opportunities for prevention are missed. He draws attention to the early warning signals, such as compliance violations, defective operator training, and the rationalization of operating anomalies, which are risk objects in Hilgartner's sense and are often poorly understood and accounted for. Vaughan's (1996, 2005) analyses of NASA argues similarly that disasters arise from deviant practices that become normalized by key actors. These organization-focused explanations of failure have become widely accepted by scholars, and have also come to be understood broadly by practitioners as issues of organization "culture". Furthermore, the pathology of missed early warnings and failures of foresight have generated attention both to cultural reform and to the design of information systems that transform traces as "weak signals" of possible harms in the future into actionable metrics, which might inform early preventative interventions. Central to these efforts is the construction of what have come to be known as "lead" indicators to track a risk object.

This design of lead risk indicators depends on establishing clarity about the risk object itself. The core idea is to identify and track activities or things that are causally linked to an undesirable outcome and to set a "tolerance" level for indicator-enabled observable variability of their relevant features. Good design in these terms means that an individual or organization is equipped with "evidentially sufficient observability" in the form of indicators that enable intervention to prevent the primary risk from crystallizing, or at least reduce its likelihood and impact. It is the causal and temporal properties of a risk object that are the basis for designing its indicator. Yet this design process, while simple in principle, is also complex in practice. The greater the temporal (and spatial) distance between traces of the putative risk object and its associated harmful outcomes, then the potentially less determinate and convincing is any claimed relationship with the dependent primary risk. Hence, risk objects and the construction of their indicators face the same design challenges. Indeed, the credibility of the indicator is core to credible and stable risk object formation.

Beasley et al. (2010) discuss the example of a restaurant whose sales depend on consumer discretionary income. Accepting this causal relation, changes in GDP can be regarded as a lead indicator/risk object for disposable income and hence for variation in restaurant sales. Acting on changes in GDP and forecasts of economic growth in lean times (e.g. by lowering prices or offering special deals) could mitigate this risk to some degree. Yet this apparently simple case generates complications. GDP may be a less reliable predictor than local economic conditions; and competitor reactive behaviour may be significant. In other words, the causal relation, though a priori plausible, is too remote and unspecific, rendering this risk object and its lead indicator problematic. However, this may just be a temporary issue. Advances in digital technologies and the datafication of customer habits are generating new possibilities for building multifactor lead indicators with more granular predictive capability (e.g. Kretschmann, 2020; Ibrahim et al., 2021).

Both Hilgartner (1992) and Latour (1987) remind us that the "facts" of causality as connection must be negotiated, that is, built from traces, inscribed in tracking practices, and narrated by practitioner networks. Furthermore, the burden of proof in the causal chain linking risk object and harm, even where big data and related analytics have been used, will be a function of values and overall risk tolerance. For example, organizations that place a high value on safety and on the avoidance of negative outcomes will invest extensively in the development of lead indicators and use them for highly pre-emptive and anticipatory forms of control and intervention (Aykut, Demortain and Benbouzid, 2019). Here the strict demonstration of causality may be overridden by precautionary values, even to the point where some risky activities are simply discontinued ("exit"). In settings such as air traffic control, a paradigm case where high reliability is the dominant value, the security and safety of passengers and crew are the primary risk to be managed by the system. Specifically, to avoid mid-air and on-ground collision between aircraft, clear rules of separation exist for pilots, which are enforced and monitored in real time by air traffic controllers. The rules are highly conservative—a breach of them does not mean that an accident is imminent, but it is treated as if it were. Aircraft separation is therefore technically a lead indicator that tracks the risk object—aircraft proximity—very conservatively to minimize the causal link to harm. Tolerance of a breach of these rules, even though this does not mean that aircraft are in immediate danger of collision, is low to near zero. Loss of separation so defined is also a performance indicator for controllers, who are judged by how they manage their region of airspace. Hence the primary risk to be avoided—collision—is translated into a less consequential proxy (i.e. breach of separation as a compliance risk), while nevertheless making it consequential and culturally significant in terms of zero tolerance and remedial action responses.

Air traffic control is an example of a "high reliability" setting in which future harmful events are managed by creating "safe" proxy traces for them. Rules of separation are digitally encoded into air traffic control maps that track aircraft in real time (Vaughan, 2005, 2021). In this way, the very concept of the primary risk to avoid shifts from aircraft collision to the lead indicator/risk object, which becomes a proxy for primary risk around which management activity is organized. In turn, this shift generates management attention to a new series of potential risk objects further down the causal chain, such as controller capacity to manage airspace and enforce separation. While risk objects and their lead indicators always stand in a temporally and causally antecedent relation to primary risks, there can be fluidity in how the primary risk to be avoided/managed is defined and organized. Relations and connections between risk objects and primary risks can be therefore constructed in causal chains that bring the possible harmful future into a less harmful routine present.

Staff capability and training in general, not just that of air traffic controllers, is an area where the need for lead indicators of performance risk has been recognized in many settings. Despite the case of the Corsair vehicle design defects discussed by Hilgartner, many cases of failure and accidents do in fact point to operator error, which in turn may be causally linked not only to defective competence, training, and supervision, but also to more personal factors. Thus, as training quality and intensity have come to be accepted generally by organizations as causally related to organizational performance, they are tracked by metrics that acquire the status of lead indicators of primary operational risks. Indeed, as the case of the senior managers regime in financial services discussed in Chapter 6 suggests, training data and processes frame a risk object associated with a harm and are thereby placed in a new temporalized relation to risks to organizational performance. In general, lead indicators are specific temporal constructions to enable risk traceability. The examples of customer complaints and value at risk modelling provide further colour to the arguments so far.

Complaints

Consider the case of complaints in the setting of a financial services organization like a wealth manager that provides investment advice to its clients. Complaints about investment performance and the advice given are in themselves undesirable events to be avoided where possible. But organizations accept that there will always be some level of complaints and create processes to manage them. Let us assume that a complaint is registered as a trace of dissatisfaction. This is normally "captured" as narrative in a complaints management system, which then produces complaints data and accounts (in a complaints dashboard). These complaints will be investigated and either upheld or not upheld by the organization. When not upheld, a client may seek further redress with a regulator—in the United Kingdom this is called an "ombudsman"—or even in a court of law. In short, there is a kind of mini-traceability complex for complaint handling.

A complaint can be conceptualized as an undesirable event and therefore as a dependent variable pointing to the need for root cause analysis with the aim of associating it with a risk object. Taking the complaint as a primary risk or harm to be avoided in the sense of indicating client dissatisfaction, possible risk objects and their lead indicators could be: the quality and intensity of training for advisers on a specific product and/or the clarity of communication with the client. Another lead indicator of possible future client detriment could involve metrics for tracking the quality of the oversight and supervision of financial advisers (commonly known as "spans of control"). From this point of view, the complaint data itself is framed as a "lagged" indicator (i.e. an undesirable adverse event that has happened). Its temporal orientation is primarily retrospective, and the analytical task is to determine its specific causes/risk objects and also, if such specific causes prove to be systemic, to use them to design "lead" indicators, such as for the quality of training and supervision noted earlier.

Complaint "data" can also itself be constructed as a future-oriented leading indicator when taken in aggregate form. Changes in the historic frequency of complaints in the form of spikes may indicate future risks to the business, such as loss of brand and customer loyalty, leading to decline. Or it may indicate that the business may be overheating and expanding too rapidly. Such "overselling" may generate business strain in the future. In short, the complaint, as an event that seems so simple and obvious, can itself be constructed as a risk object and leading indicator of harm. It depends on the encoding of its temporal orientation. Lead indicators are based on the traceification of complaints data and their encoding as signs that organize risk prospectively (Hardy et al., 2020). Indeed, changing patterns of complaints data can now be combined analytically with other sources of data inside and outside of the organization to generate a risk profile for the franchise value of the organization, and as a lead indicator of possible share price deterioration. While complaints may be perceived as negative events, provided they remain at acceptable levels they may also be regarded as the price of risk-taking to create overall economic value. This is undoubtedly the case for investment management, the entire point of which is to take risk with a view to gain.

Value at Risk (VAR) Modelling

Risk objects and their lead indicators can be statistical constructs. Value at risk measures for an investment portfolio are based on historical data, the application of finance theory, and related statistical techniques. While VAR has been much debated and is controversial (Danielsson, 2002), the value that is "at risk" is, unsurprisingly, the investment portfolio's economic value. The related risk object and source of harm to that value is a loss that exceeds acceptable limits. Those limits are modelled as the expected probability of the maximum level of loss from various scenarios over various time horizons (temporal depth), given the nature of the assets and relevant economic variables. The VAR measure is in this sense a "lead" indicator of portfolio risk that can be tracked over time and monitored with a view to understanding whether and how the portfolio is becoming riskier or not, as defined by its modelled variance. Such VAR monitoring may lead to changes in portfolio construction. Its modelling is future-oriented and predictive in a conditional way but, as with all risk management, reality can always produce low probability "tail-event" losses. For all their assumption-laden imperfections, measures like VAR make portfolio financial risk in principle trackable, and financial regulators insist that models are auditable and subject to regular critique and challenge by oversight bodies.

Reliance on models such as VAR has drawn critical attention to other related risks, such as model mis-specification, measurement error, and data quality that are usually classed as operational, and all with their own potential risk objects. In the 2008 financial crisis, we also learned of the destabilizing and amplifying effects when all market actors use the same risk-management model (Danielsson et al., 2012). In general, we can say that these measurement devices, as they have emerged from the discipline of financial economics, aim at the "taming of chance" (Bernstein, 1996) and at bringing the uncertain future into the present for management. In this respect, prospective temporality is their defining orientation, notwithstanding their dependence on historical data.

In this section, we have made more explicit the co-formation of risk objects and their traceification in the lead indicators that enable them to be tracked and managed. The design of such indicators is inherently challenging—their linkages to future harm become less determinate and more controversial as their temporal depth is extended. For this reason, "proxies for harm" are often evident in precautionary settings, such as air traffic control. However, the temporality of risk is not confined to the specificities of a risk object and its indicators. As we zoom out from the specifics of lead indicator design, we see, as noted in the example of VAR, that they also express general "temporal orientations" that are more institutional in nature.

Risk and Temporal Orientation

Based on the synthesis of a large body of work, Hardy et al. (2020) argue that there are *three* core temporal orientations for organizing the management and regulation of risk. First, they show that standards and goals provide prescriptive frameworks for techniques of managing risks *prospectively*, that is, identifying and constructing risks as objects of concern capable of being tracked, assessed, measured, and mitigated consistent with a risk appetite or tolerance (see also Hood et al., 1999). Standards can also be set for crisis reaction capabilities via plans and for designing resilience into existing critical processes. These frameworking, planning, and tracking activities may be supported by scenarios and modelling, like VAR, which are also prospective in intent, even if they build on past experience (Flyverbom and Garsten, 2021). In short, many practices, frameworks, and standards organize risk prospectively with a view to managing both the likelihood of event crystallization and also its impact via the development of reactive capability. This prospective orientation for risk management enables organizations in theory to be prepared for the future (Esposito, 2024). It is also characterized by increasing tracking and monitoring of identified risks via risk indicators to ensure that they are "under control" and within tolerance. Prospectively oriented risk-management discourses and ideas are also a powerful source of institutionalization as frameworks and protocols become widely diffused scripts of best practice.

As we discussed in relation to risk indicators and risk objects, an important source of institutional variation in the prospective mode of organizing risk is that of temporal horizon or *temporal depth* (Reinecke and Lawrence, 2023). For example, nuclear energy companies need to plan for ensuring available engineering expertise many years ahead. This potential non-availability is a critical risk over the long term but is usually non-urgent. It is a primary risk with a long lead time for management, which is advantageous, but for which it is difficult to construct compelling indicators (e.g. enrolment data for physics and engineering degrees could be traces of the risk of expertise shortages). Thus, attention to this risk and others like it ("not urgent but critical") may be overridden and even may be invisible to management and politicians who are focused on the near term, especially immediate cost considerations. Yet it is well known that failure to plan and invest significantly damages the future capabilities of businesses and societies. For example, the United Kingdom is known to face periodic water shortages as summers become manifestly hotter, but investment in additional reservoir capacity has lagged this phenomenon. Similarly, the Macondo Gulf of Mexico disaster for BP demonstrated that managing shorter time horizon financial risks by constraining maintenance expenditure incubated a longer temporal horizon risk, which eventually crystallized. Hence, the prospective mode of risk organizing, and its related construction of risk objects (e.g. insufficient reservoir capacity) to valued goods (adequate water supply), may involve temporal trade-offs and an organizational politics of temporal depth biased to the near term. The question for accounting systems design and regulation is to what extent can such future costs be estimated and recognized as liabilities in the present, thus making them difficult to ignore.

Accounting for the past and accounting for the future have always existed side by side. So called historical-cost accounting was never for this reason solely retrospective and was pervaded by estimations of the future (e.g. of remaining lives of assets or of contingent liabilities). What is commonly called the "going concern" assumption is normally understood as a projection of twelve months after the balance sheet date of the financial statements in which an entity is expected to continue in existence. This temporal horizon, though short, has generated reporting risks for accounts preparers and their auditors. Financial reporting and auditing are also increasingly under pressure to extend this temporal horizon, driven by corporate failures shortly after the publication of accounts. In the United Kingdom, there is now a requirement for a "viability" statement that projects a longer time horizon for reporting—three to five years. Existing data about liquidity, customer diversity, balance sheet strength, and much more must be traceified to enable "viability" as a new risk to be created, tracked, and explicitly reported. This is much like a "prospectus" approach to the financial statements. Indeed, via their accounting for viability, organizations are unwillingly becoming "promissory organizations" (Pollock and Williams, 2010) for their shareholders. With the increased use of "fair values" in the measurement of assets and liabilities, underpinned conceptually by valuation techniques based on estimated expected future cash flows, this prospective and prospectus-like nature of financial statements is more apparent than ever. Furthermore, pressure to fully cost economic activities in the present leads to the potential recognition of liabilities that may not crystallize for many years, such as nuclear plant decommissioning costs (Johnson, 1994). As Reinecke and Lawrence (2023) suggest, nearer temporal horizons and their temporal structuring tend to have greater institutional stability and attention than those which are more remote. This partially explains the difficulty of achieving the same kind of consensus for sustainability accounting as for financial accounting. The so-called "double materiality" debate is therefore also a politics of temporal depth (Barker and Mayer, 2025) in which the limits of prospective risk organizing are at stake (Rindova and Martins, 2022).

Prospective risk organizing stands in contrast to what Hardy et al. (2020) call the *real time* organization of risk that in essence involves reaction to events and risk crystallization as it unfolds. Crystallization or materialization of risks can range from small deviations in operational routines and expected risk tolerances, such as a spike in customer complaints that must be managed, to more serious issues, such as a material shift in the risk profile of an organization following the loss of a major customer, or the 2020 pandemic, which caused millions of deaths and generated immediate liquidity problems for many businesses. In these non-routine "hot" situations, risk organizing acquires a heightened orientation to the present, to real-time actions to deal with immediate issues depending on their degree of urgency (e.g. flooding). However, transitioning and pivoting from a predominantly prospective style of risk management and its "cool" forms of risk traceability to real-time crisis management is known to be a significant challenge for organizations and states (Mikes and Power, 2020; Sanasi and Ghezzi, 2024). It requires swift recognition that the operating environment has changed and a capability to execute rapid "switching" to high-tempo working with temporal horizon compression and operating demands for real-time information flow. It follows that preparedness for such switching is likely to be unevenly distributed, and this was evident in March 2020 as countries entered lockdown at different times, with material consequences.

What we normally call resilience involves the investment in capabilities to make smooth transitions from "normal" prospective risk management to "abnormal" real-time responses, from low-tempo to high-tempo modes of working, and to shorter time frames. But we know a number of things about such transitions. First, they are in principle difficult to "prepare" for, because crisis planning has an element of fantasy (Clarke, 1999; McConnell and Drennan, 2006). Second, there is often delay for a wide variety of reasons, not least collective and individual denial. Third, conventional forms of oversight and traceability are often suspended as resources are drawn into response activity, and action dominates the creation of traces of the future. In essence, there can be a loss of traceability in transition since it can be a low priority. Fourth, new prospective risks may be generated, leading to the need to manage hybrid temporal orientations. The onset of the pandemic in 2020, discussed in Chapter 6, provides a good, if controversial, example of the transition in the dominant temporal-orientation. It suggests that stable traceability complexes are primarily constructed for normal, prospective risk processing, which allows for some ongoing normally expected risk crystallization. The temporal orientation of their practice elements may shorten dramatically at times of crisis (e.g. daily/hourly liquidity reporting displaces monthly budget monitoring).

Hardy et al. (2021), like Hood et al. (2001), identify a range of practices orientated to *retrospective* analysis—feedback in systems-theoretic language—including enforcement in the face of defective practice. The production of major reports and inquiries in retrospective mode is intended to lead not only to the attribution of responsibility and blame, but also to the generation of memory and learning, for example in the recognition of emergent or new risks that had been overlooked or minimized. For instance, it can be argued that until the collapse of the Maxwell empire in 1991 (Stiles and Taylor, 1993), the notion of the "dominant CEO" was not well established as a possible source of harm to organizations, employees, and pensioners, as compared with the frame of entrepreneur and creator of value. The retrospective orientation often takes on an investigative and discovery-oriented character, the findings of which construct or sharpen the focus of prospective risk-management practices, traceifying new sources of risk, such as CEO-generated toxic corporate culture. However, retrospection is not restricted to major public enquiries following a discrete event. It is also itself a feature of routine oversight practices, as discussed in Chapter 5. For example, so-called "third line of defence" internal audits may routinely investigate prospective risk-organizing practices in order to determine whether they are working as prescribed and, if not, will seek to identify root causes of defective practice and report to management, with recommendations for change. Thus, the retrospective mode of risk organizing can vary from spectacular, high-profile investigations and public enquiries to private, internal reviews and incremental adjustments to practice.

These three temporal orientations for organizing risk are not mutually exclusive. Some retrospection is part of the oversight embedded in the prospective mode. In many large organizations there is always ongoing analysis and evaluation of incidents and events to understand why they happened, to learn, and to incrementally adjust prospective risk management. In short, non-material risks and their proxies crystallize all the time and stimulate investigation of root causes and remediation. Layers of monitoring build a normal form of retrospective risk organizing into the prospective mode—there is no dramatic transition. The situation is different when major events are subject to public investigation and enquiry. Usually initiated in the wake of high-profile disasters and scandals, such as corporate collapse and systemic health care failures, investigations look back forensically and seek to discover what was done, why, and whether it was reasonable. To do this, such enquiries collect evidence in the form of witness representations and also revisit available traces of actions, such as minutes, memos, emails, and internal and external reports, in order to construct a retrospective account and diagnosis of the failure event and its causes. The different traces, when examined as a whole, may signify something new, such as defective practice in need of reform or a new source of harm in need of explicit and managerial attention. Thus, in the wake of the 2008 financial crisis, toxic "organizational culture"—long investigated by scholars—came to be understood as a source of harm by a wider network of regulators and politicians and as a new risk object requiring explicit traceification and tracking (Palermo et al., 2017).

If we return once again to the example of flight protocol checklists discussed in Chapter 3, we see a mix of the three temporal orientations. The checklist is part of a safety apparatus for *prospective* risk management. It is also part of real-time risk management as pilots conduct their checks. And it is also retrospective because the tick is a trace that endures for oversight, audit, and investigative purposes. In this way, the checklist also makes a risk-management process traceable and governable. As reasonable as this may seem, the epistemic and practical priority of the prospective orientation also embodies "prospective retrospection" as a risk to the risk-management practitioner. And this in turn suggests that in many settings, prospective risk management can involve the continuous creation of traces of practice, in part to stand up to possible retrospective scrutiny, especially where the experience of failure is recent. This also applies to the real-time orientation where actors and organizations can be held to account retrospectively for the reasonableness of their actions in unfolding situations of risk crystallization, for example, for reacting too slowly to events.

These reflections on the power of anticipated retrospection point to what we might broadly call an "audit society" effect when future-oriented practices of prospective risk management become constituted to be retrospectively defendable in terms of providing audit trails of decisions and actions. Standards, frameworks, and protocols for tracking risks become more elaborated and intense, and the prospective mode of risk organizing becomes interwoven with the potential for future retrospection, in the form of an audit, public enquiry, or other kind of evaluation (especially if failure is "expected" as part of policy experimentation). It is not just that risk as contingent future outcome is fictional and must be scripted to become real and mobilizing for organizational actors. It is also that risk must be made traceable in the present to support the *future possibility of retrospection*. Temporal orientations are intermingled, and this mix is always specific to the context.

At the extreme, prospective risk-management protocols and practices may operate within cultures of blame (Hood, 2002), leading to "timid" organizations (Hunt, 2003) that amplify audit trails for risk management (Power, 2021a). Organizational actors will pay considerable attention to the manner in which risk management is represented and accounted for in order to manage the risk of being blamed (see Pidgeon et al., 2003; Rothstein et al., 2006). This defensive anticipation of retrospection is only one possible reaction pathway among many, but it is a powerful source of *riskification*.

Riskification and Traceability

The singular event of risk crystallization as an actuality means that it no longer has the temporal modality of risk, of a prospective yet-to-occur event. If we accept this, it means that risks in the sense of possible future harms can never by definition be real in the ordinary sense of that term, even when great danger is imagined. They only have reality when they can be traced, datafied, represented, and tracked (monitored) in risk-management apparatuses (Power, 2013, 2014, 2016). It follows that the unreal, imaginary nature of prospective risk (Beckert, 2013) is given specific form as an object of attention and practice via modes of representation, which take many material forms, including models, maps, and metrics of many kinds. These representations and calculations of risk, like all accounts, may be partial, incomplete, or biased. Minor risks may be overrepresented at the expense of more consequential ones, and we are often retrospectively disappointed by faulty accounting for risk. The practice of risk management is therefore dense with devices and scripts that aim at traceifying the future and bringing it into the present. For example, risk maps are not neutral representations of risk but are aggregative accounts that visualize the risk profile of an organization for the purpose of understanding and tracking its directionality (Jorgensen and Jordan, 2016). Similarly, accounting regulations bring obligations to pay in the future into the accounting present as liabilities that can define a financial risk profile. But the future is not always so easily tamed and represented. In addition to outright failure, there can be uncertainty about when and how to "recognize" possible futures in the present because of a combination of measurement uncertainty, temporal remoteness (Johnson, 1994), and hard trade-offs.[7]

There is a long technical tradition that conceptualizes risk assessment as the use of data-informed calculative techniques in order to anticipate and even predict risk as the likelihood of harmful events and outcomes (Royal Society, 1992). The more extensive the data availability, frequency, and quality, then the better the capability of extrapolation to determine the probability of relevant future occurrences (Power, 2007; Demortain, 2023). This widely accept "scientific" model of risk assessment has been an important knowledge base for the governance of risk by scientists, regulators, and organizations, not least where risk is known to be highly consequential, such as in the chemical industry (Hardy and Maguire, 2016). Furthermore, there have been extensive debates about the claimed neutrality of assessment as compared with management that involved values and decisions about risk tolerance. Science and values were to be kept apart, but this distinction could not be sustained (Jasanoff, 1987). It became apparent that risk and risk management are not simply technical solutions to the puzzle of the future. They are also cultural and political scripts in their own right, especially evident in the development of a more abstract and process-based model of risk management within the heartland of regulatory

[7] The materialization of one risk may signify new risks and other possible future events. Risks are often related to each other in causal chains and there are usually many trade-offs to consider in which management of one risk may generate another. For example, as is well known, improvements in health care that lower mortality risk can generate funding risk for pension systems. Similarly, electric car usage to manage carbon emissions risk can generate risks for lithium-producing countries and communities (Karacan and Kayacan, 2024).

science (Demortain, 2016). This model expanded from the mid-1990s onwards, generating scripts in the form of highly diffused templates and protocols for organizing risk in many fields. This general expansion of risk management is visible in the reframing of corporate governance in the United Kingdom and elsewhere (see FRC, 2014). It is as if there can be no proper governance that is not at the same time the governance of risks in all their variety, including the risk of defective or malign leadership. Indeed, in recent years, UK regulators have pressed independent directors to challenge management more as part of mitigating this risk, a challenge function that must be evidenced (i.e. made traceable) in board meeting minutes. This apparent general expansion of the reach of risk and its management to "tame the future" represents a cultural shift by which organizational and societal operations came to be understood and explicitly and managed in terms of risk as a category or "master-script". This is "riskification" (Hardy and Maguire, 2016).[8]

Riskification not only is the generation of new risk objects but also can be imagined as the scripting of risk-management templates into existing organizational processes, a scripting process that intensifies in the wake of errors, accidents, and disasters and leads to a potential risk management of everything (Power, 2004a). Riskification is also associated with a reactive swing to more precautionary and risk-averse approaches to an activity where potential harm is magnified in relation to benefits, even to the point of risk avoidance—especially when the general public and children are considered to be in some sense "at risk" (Munro, 2004, 2010). For example, it has been shown that there has been a decline in school trips and external activities for children, due in part to the demands of explicit risk assessments, which disincentivize teachers (Rothstein et al., 2006). While riskification is often generated by events, it should not automatically be correlated with an increase in risk in a seemingly objective sense and thereby understood as a rational functional response to a more dangerous world. Rather, the spread of riskification involves the re-coding of many operations and their purposes in terms of the master script of risk and related management ideas and processes.[9] At the same time, riskification is not merely the expansion of the word "risk" as a label, although the power of linguistic changes should not be underestimated as engines of change in their own right (Hacking, 2002; McCloskey, 2016). It is also associated with the emergence of "risk-based"

[8] Riskification cuts across Knight's (1921) famous analytic distinction between risk and uncertainty. It references the process by which Knightean uncertainties become framed as risks to be managed. Luhmann (1993) has a similar nominalist thesis when he claims that risk implies a decision space about the future, whereas uncertainty does not. Hence, when we use the term "risk" in this book it must be taken in the riskified sense of encompassing uncertainties in their classical sense. Indeed, much of what we currently call risk management is, in strictly Knightean terms, uncertainty management in situations of thin data (Power, 2007).

[9] See, for example, Burgess and Horii (2012) on rituals of risk in the context of mask-wearing practice in Japan.

narratives of regulation, control, and oversight. The riskification of practices not only involves reframing them and rationalizing their functions as forms of risk processing and tracking, but also makes them observable and auditable for oversight purposes (Power, 2007, 2016). In short, riskification intensifies audit trails and is a continuation of audit society (Power, 2007).

The Risk-Based Traceablity Complex

Riskification also suggests the possibility of a more explicitly risk-based understanding of traceability complexes. Thus, risks to quality in the sense of the inauthenticity of goods are mitigated by labelling and tracking. In the specific setting of food and drugs, risks to quality are managed by analysing ingredients and tracking them from point of harvest/manufacture. And risks to the quality of financial reporting and regulatory compliance are in theory addressed by auditing and monitoring practices. Risks of crime, financial insecurity, and ill-health are managed in part, for example, by tracking people, money, and viruses. Risks to the creation of new forms of knowledge, in the sense of error and mistakes, can be mitigated by making processes of experiment and testing traceable and subject to peer review and replication. In short, the value-purposes of traceability, as discussed in Chapter 1, can be re-conceptualized as "values at risk", and the entire model of a traceability complex in Figure 2.1 can be reframed and explicitly riskified. As Figure 7.1 indicates, in addition to risk-based framings of purpose, traces of harmful futures become risk objects, are datafied, tracked, and accounted for.[10] This riskified conceptualization of the traceability complex suggests how the organization of risk and of traceability are interdependent. And given the fictional nature of risk such that it must be scripted (Power, 2016), riskification is likely to increase the production of traces of the future and related processes.

Archaeologies of the Future

The riskification of practices has become widely naturalized as a meta-script of performance that not only makes explicit an orientation to future possible harms to performance but also, in many cases, amplifies attention to them. Hence, a

[10] The conceptual architecture of Figure 7.1 has a topological resemblance to prior studies. For example, the Committee of Sponsoring Organizations COSO (2004) articulates the building blocks for a cybernetic model of risk governance in terms of: objectives (value-purposes); risk identification and risk measurement (trace production), risk monitoring (tracking), reporting, and feedback (accounts) (see Knechel, 2007). Hood et al. (1999, 2001) also extend cybernetic thinking to construct a similar framework for comparing what they call "risk regulation regimes" (RRRs).

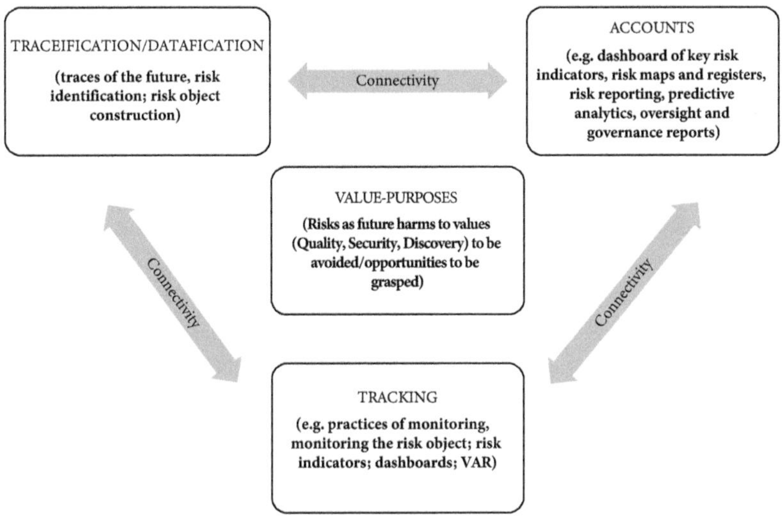

Figure 7.1 Organizing risk as a traceability complex.

sub-set of the accounts we live by have, in a riskified sense, a flavour of fear, precaution, and blame avoidance. Yet riskification as risk bureaucracy in this sense, while still relevant, is also transformed in the digital age. Digitalization not only has generated extensive datasets, making possible advanced analyses of risk by both practitioners and scholars, but also has animated long-standing dreams of algorithmically based prediction and behavioural control, especially, as discussed in Chapter 6, for its potential to enhance "anticipatory" and "preventative" forms of governance (Henman, 2020; Flyverbom and Garsten, 2021). For example, the risk assessment of hazardous chemicals is now dependent on modelling techniques based on data expansion via digitization and is transforming toxicology into a predictive science (Demortain, 2023). Furthermore, multiple practices of prognostication and forecasting have been re-energized by capacities to process heterogeneous digital traces and to explore the predictive potential of the patterns they reveal. This is the promise of big data (Bhimani and Willcocks, 2014). And financial risk-analysis techniques, like value at risk (VAR), discussed earlier in this chapter, can be understood generally as the "discovery" of patterns in historic data that can be made to point to the future. VAR is a form of accounting and statistical projectification in which more or less likely financial futures for collections of assets can be brought into the present for decision-making purposes. Similarly, life insurance is a centuries-old field of practice, with its foundations in the emerging availability of historic data about the incidence of mortality, to which have been added "leading" factors such as age, location, smoking habits, and so on. Life insurance began with, and depended on, the ability to traceify aspects of lifestyle and organize them into actuarial datasets, which could move practice beyond mere gambling on lives (Alborn, 2009). Advances in digital technologies and data availability now enable ever more finely tuned calculations of risk in insurance practices and many other applications of financial and insurential economics.

In addition to these developments, the digitization of all manner of texts, from annual reports to newspapers and much else, has also created the conditions of possibility for variants of "sentiment" analysis in many fields of practice, such as banking (Nyman et al., 2021), and in the detection of optimism bias in corporate board meeting papers.[11] Patterns in collective sentiment are an emerging form of risk object that can be causally related to undesired outcomes, such as poor economic performance or customer switching. In this way, the behavioural traces of the individual consumers become transformed into the digitized wisdom of the crowds (Surowiecki, 2005), which yields large-scale accounts, new objects for tracking, and predictive narratives of the future. Developments in machine learning are accelerating these trends even as the words of this chapter are being crafted (by this human author). The scale and implications of these changes, not least for both the management and generation of risks, are much debated in 2025—they are multiple, complex, and ongoing.

How might we characterize these changes that are consequential for how we think of risk, traceability, the future, and much else? A digitally neutral analogy may help. Traditional archaeologists excavate sites to unearth material traces of the past with a view to generating new historical data and insights. Novel digitally-enabled analytical practices are much like archaeology. However, instead of directly seeking to understand the past, digitization and the explosion of methods for data production and analysis can be understood as *archaeologies of the future*. The present is increasingly littered with digital residues, raw materials that can be made into traces of the future to be excavated and brought to light and which can be generative of novel accounts to live by. Three themes that are indicative of these archaeologies and their implications are considered in the remainder of this chapter: traceability as a risk object; the uncertain future of uncertainty; and the future of human projection.

Traceability as a Risk Object

In Chapter 1 it was argued that while traceability can be understood as a meta-value that mobilizes a wide variety of practices, nevertheless there is also a counter-politics in which it is constructed as a risk object causally related to a

[11] For example, see https://www.boardintelligence.com/ (accessed 8 January 2025).

harm to something that is valued. More specifically, algorithmically driven practices of tracking people via extracted data for a range of surveillance purposes are claimed to threaten values of privacy (Veliz, 2023), governance (Ziewitz, 2016), and democracy (Zuboff, 2019). The general point is that the digital enhancement of tracking capabilities and the organizational appetite for data represent points of contestation about the balance of risks and benefits that are difficult to disentangle (Alaimo and Kallinikos, 2024). Arguments to bring back people into the governance of automated processes are being articulated in parallel with dreams of granular prediction and other benefits associated with the availability of big data (Puranam, 2025). Controversies about insurability and the rise of AI applications in policing are a focus for these conflicts. How can we make sense of them?

These developments suggest that traceability is both a risk object and a value at risk. The digital age, broadly speaking, has been characterized by a dramatic expansion of what in this book we refer to as "trace*ability*" (i.e. the ability of machines to capture/produce traces of human behaviour in digital form). Traceability in this sense is a risk object, generating both enormous new opportunities and benefits but also placing other values at risk. Indeed, traceability in the second evidentiary sense developed in Chapter 1 as the forms of connectivity that make human observation and oversight possible is now "at risk". As discussed in Chapter 6 in the case of auditing algorithms, this is not only due to lags in institutional development and reaction, or ambiguity about precisely what should be the focus of oversight (i.e. audit scope). It also has to do with a sense that algorithms, especially those associated with machine-learning applications, are somehow beyond human oversight and comprehension (Amodei, 2025).

The distinction between the two senses of traceability—as trace generation and as oversight capability—also corresponds to an emerging differentiation in fields of practice, their expertise, and their main temporal orientation (Farrell and Fourcade, 2023). Traceability in the form of oversight practice tends to be populated by regulators, lawyers, accountants, risk managers, auditors, and evaluators in leading roles. They are agents of governance, riskification, and traceification in the sense of creatively utilizing existing forms of data within risk-management frameworks and encouraging their elaboration as traces of an uncertain future to be managed and mitigated. They invest in producing audit trails as evidence of good practice, a logic that is predominantly retrospective even when it informs prospective risk organizing. In contrast, practices of trace generation and analysis tend to be populated by chief information officers, data scientists, elite programmers, security specialists, and more recently, AI specialists. They are immersed in digital technologies and are driven by the imagination of the data-driven organization and what digital data as a critical resource can provide. They or their operatives will be engaged in extensive datafication, not least to generate proprietorial intelligence about the future. The audit trail for the work of these groups is either a specific application or lacking in direct relevance.

This contrast is stylized, but it references an emerging shift in the mode of riskification and traceability generated by digital advances, not least AI, and the rise of tracking capacity. From this point of view, some of the concerns being raised about the governability of algorithms and platforms may have their origins in the status insecurity of incumbent occupational groups. The future has become a jurisdiction over which there is now intense professional competition, and it appears that the data scientist is set to become its pre-eminent archaeologist. Such a systemic shift in expertise and its cognitive orientations in turn has implications for how the future is imagined.

The Uncertain Future of Uncertainty

It has become a cliché to say that the only constant in life is uncertainty and change. And yet the centuries-long project to "tame chance", (Bernstein, 1996; Hacking, 1990), which began to take shape with the emergence of statistics, has had the reduction of uncertainty and increased controllability of the future firmly in its sights (Esposito, 2011, 2024). It was in the context of this long-standing ambition that Knight (1921) developed his famous distinction between uncertainty and risk, reminding scholars and practitioners of the unknowability of the former and the limited scope of the latter. Beck's (1992) risk society thesis, and the sociology of risk more generally, cuts across Knight's distinction and advances what could be described as a "macro-riskification" thesis in which the risk object to be identified had shifted from nature as external fate of mankind, to human activities and their undesirable side effects. As I write in what is now called the Anthropocene age, there is growing evidence that "nature", including that of humans, is at risk. Beck's related motif of "manufactured risk" was also developed with implications for the individual in risk society; she must confront both the risk, in the loose sense of uncertainty in general, generated by this man-created reality, and also the weakness of institutions, like the welfare state, to absorb and redistribute it on her behalf. Risk society therefore posits an unravelling of the collective guarantees and security of post–World War II Western liberal democracies, leading to the involuntary individuation of responsibility.

Beck was far-sighted: forty years after his seminal work, this burden of the uncertain future for individuals is being partly self-managed via a multiplicity of devices and prosthetics to monitor health, wealth, and well-being. As we discuss in Chapter 8, individuals in 2025 are engaged in personalized trace production and self-tracking in ever more elaborate ways. This self-riskification is arguably the inevitable telos of the neoliberal project to transfer risk from state and organizations to humans, equipping newly individualized subjects with the means to track and manage their personal financial, health, and social risks (O'Malley, 2012). As the state retreats, retail insurance and financial markets blossom. The expectations of security and the seeming delivery of it to many in the developed world by a new form of "regulatory capitalism" (Levi-Faur, 2005) immunized individuals and states, at least temporarily, from the existential threats of climate, pandemic, wars, and growing inequality. Yet, this wave of riskification also generated false security (Kornberger, 2013), and expectations had already begun to unravel before the 2008 financial crisis, which resulted in the prolonged and ongoing period of reaction against the failure of institutions and experts that we now call populism. In addition, as a counterweight to the collective belief in the manageability of risk, a new accent on resilience in the face of uncertainty began to emerge at all levels—individual, organization, and state.

The post–World War II dream of global security and uncertainty management via trade and cultural integration has faltered, if not disintegrated, at the time of writing the words in this book. Outsourcing efficiencies and supply chain management, as emblems of this dream, have come to be reimagined through the lens of national resilience as risky forms of dependency and a weakening of sovereignty. A progressive retreat from global connectivity, symptomized by the UK 2016 Brexit referendum result, is correlated with the rise of nationalism and populism, in which the failures of neoliberalism have mutated into varieties of illiberalism (Davies, 2021) via the emergence of tropes such as "enemies of the people", who might be judges in courts of law or academics or journalists or refugees. Further seismic shifts have also given uncertainty a new salience for Western-style democracies: the insistent reality of climate change as extreme weather is no longer deniable (although it is in fact denied); the ongoing rise of China as a "successful" society; the 2020 pandemic that threatened societies at their very core; and the 2022 Russian invasion of Ukraine. It has therefore come to be recognized that existing ways of life for developed countries and democracies, including cheap fossil fuel energy, have no inherent logic of continuation as a superior model of social ordering. It is in the context of these uncertainties that the category of "geopolitical risk" has made its way onto the corporate agenda, rivalling even cybersecurity and AI-related issues.

In the face of these uncertainty-amplifying trends, which seem, at least superficially, to be correlated with the rise of mental health issues for younger generations in the West and declining birthrates in developed economies, there are also ambitions to reboot the project of taming chance. For many digital transformation projects within the ambit of what Zuboff (2019) calls "surveillance capitalism", the implicit imaginary is to know everything about everyone and everything, and thereby to eliminate risk and uncertainty, at least for large tech corporations. At the same time as this imaginary is taking shape, the idea and practice of risk management is also changing. It is shifting from the conception of an identifiable, organizationally specific, and regulatable risk "object" that is causally connected in a more or less singular way to a specific harm to the organization, to being a form of systemic knowledge defined by a complex array of correlations between data sources, many of which are beyond conventional organizational boundaries (Demortain, 2023). This kind of predictive "accounting" based on the aggregative analysis of risk factors has been under development for many years, for example in the context of understanding the behavioural drivers of fraud and misconduct in organizations (Greve et al., 2010). Now the digital means exist to realize and further elaborate such holistic models of behavioural risk. Digital traces of human actions for profiling and surveillance not only support the imagination of possible futures for organizations and markets but also provide the basis for bringing them about, by securing the future and protecting it from many sources of uncertainty.

What are the implications of these broad developments for understanding traceability as riskification and its prospective temporal orientation? On the one hand, the "big data" agenda seems to represent the end of traceability as oversight, as argued in Chapter 6. It references an "archaeology of the future", in which vast numbers of traces of past human and non-human actions can be reassembled into accounts of risk using statistical analysis. From this point of view, data analytics can be understood as a new field for excavating or "mining" the digital landscape of the past in order to make the future somehow observable, and is therefore continuous with traditions of calculative risk assessment, like VAR. Yet, as Zuboff notes more generally, these developments are also imaginaries of de-riskification, uncertainty elimination, and of controlling the future via intensified tracking of the present. Temporal depth is being potentially eroded because the future is becoming contained in the data-crowded moving horizon of the present. Digitalization may be manifestly contributing to a culture of speed (Tomlinson, 2007; Wajcman, 2020), but this is becoming conjoined with a culture of the permanently immediate. The trace is transformed from an anomalistic, tension-ridden, projective human encounter with uncertainty into the homogenized echo of multiple events. It is no longer that which "precedes" data and which implicates history. Because everything can now become data—there is no difference between the digital trace and data that makes a difference. It follows that datafication is a process that, almost by definition, erases the temporal tension of the trace, understood as "deferral" (which we can also read as code for existential uncertainty), in favour of data as identity (certainty). This means that, in aspiration, digital data is becoming that which aims to stand outside of time, a point we develop further in Chapter 9 when we discuss digital positivism.

The ideas of the data-driven organization, and of platformization as a process, also reflect an implicit aspiration to efface temporality in two ways, first by eliminating the uncertainty that resides in the difference between organization and environment, and second by maximizing the expulsion of the humans whose judgement and Knightean orientation to an uncertain future can be displaced by the automated production of a perpetual present. In this automatic society, Stiegler's co-productive alliance of human projection and technology shrinks to a potential vanishing point (Matringe and Power, 2024).

Such a vision of the logic of the data-driven organization is certainly dystopian and overstated for rhetorical effect, but it has some interesting theoretical implications. Many scholars have argued in different ways that formal organizations arose as "solutions" to problems of uncertainty. Whether these solutions are framed as transaction cost reduction, optimal principal-agent contracting, or survival by institutional isomorphism, they share an aspiration to somehow manage uncertainty. Indeed, organization theory and practice have their foundations in this basic problematic and its variants (Lounsbury and Gehman, 2024). Yet, the if the deep teleology of the data-driven organization is the elimination of uncertainty, then the conventional organization is not just becoming de-centred in Alaimo and Kallinikos's (2024) sense, but it is also characterized as the best means to confront and manage uncertainty. The Coaseian theory of why firms exist is thereby turned on its head (Pistor, 2020) and there would be no need for accounting other than to enable data architectures to monitor themselves. Put even more melodramatically perhaps, the evacuation of humans also evacuates account-giving and account-ability in Garfinkel's sense, leaving only operational monitoring.

One can quickly see that such a trajectory and the logic of its development are riddled with contradictions. Where, for example, would the behavioural data come from if humans are expelled from workplaces? So we are very far from being in this postulated world that has eliminated both uncertainty and therefore time itself. But the purpose of the preceding arguments, and indeed of this entire book, is that of a thought experiment to draw out the features of a socio-technical logic whose telos and dream is the elimination of uncertainty. As Douglas and Wildavsky (1982) argue, orientations to uncertainty are coextensive with particular forms of social and temporal ordering. Hence, the expansion of digital trace production and the corresponding contraction of traceability as human observability posit a world of unfettered trace production and datafication without oversight, the flattening of governance, and the shortening of audit trails postulated in Chapter 4. This is a telos that must fail, as all totalizing dreams do eventually, but its logic has effects, especially on the projective capacity of accounts we live by.

The Future of Human Projection

Knight famously reserved uncertainty as a space for human invention and entrepreneurship beyond rational calculation, for forms of projection that situate the inspired human actor in history and tradition. The logics of platformization and surveillance capitalism run counter to this conception, in which past and future become compressed into the ever-renewable data horizon of the present. The past as indiscriminate data reservoir is no long a source of cultural transmission and learning in the face of uncertainty. The logic of platformization is in this sense post-hermeneutic in that the weight of "tradition" is being displaced by what we might call the "weight of a datafied future in the present". This uncertainty-eliminating logic of platformization matters especially to forms of projection, and their affective character, which are the accounts we live by. Such projection has been defined as the "raw expression of movement and growth, an inherent mobility in which things are coming into being, and doing so in the company of other beings, all of which beckon organization" (deVaujany et al., 2023, p. 2). This statement captures nicely the sense in which projection is far from being cool automated prediction and control, but is an energy and affectivity with a temporal orientation to an uncertain future.

While much has been written about the spatial reach of accounts and the capacity of inscriptions to act "at a distance", their projective character and temporal reach are equally significant (cf. Quattrone, 2015; Chua et al., 2024). Matringe and Power (2024) draw on Stiegler's thinking to compare the projective logic of medieval merchants' double-entry bookkeeping (DEB) with that of contemporary forms of blockchain. While both are transaction recording systems, they encode contrasting conceptions of history, projection, and the place of the human actor in time. Medieval DEB operated in a turbulent world, as merchants combined risks of transacting and metaphysical uncertainties with elaborate social controls. They were able to do this because DEB was embedded in traditions of behaviour and was connected to, and depended on, wider social systems of projection, such as the church and family. DEB at that time was just one element of economic projectification in the face of Knightean uncertainty. In contrast, the logic of blockchain is that of the impersonal, anonymous transaction, displaced from time and space, in which the postulated immutability of transaction history is fixed in a permanent present. While there is animation by an anarchistic dream of disintermediation, such a stripping down of transactions leaves little room for human projection. As trustless systems, blockchains aim, at least in theory, to evacuate the risks associated with the human itself.

The contrast proposed by Matringe and Power (2024) is highly stylized and programmatic. Even for blockchain, the human and projective become visible at times of stress (DuPont, 2017). Yet, their analysis provides a further theoretical perspective for comparing what we have called tracking-led accounts and accounts-led tracking in terms of their respective logics of projection. Tracking-led accounts correspond to the blockchain model described earlier. All that is required is connection to the object to be tracked and observed, which, once completed, fulfils the entirety of its accounting. The tracking is the end. Accounts-led tracking corresponds to the DEB model in which accounting is situated within collective human projects of uncertainty management, and tracking is a means for the giving of accounts. Put another, more dramatic way: in the former, the human is object (to be tracked); in the latter, it is subject (account-giver and receiver). These are very different logics of accounting to live by, with very different temporal characteristics and projective potentials. In short, the rise of tracking-led accounts corresponds to a systemic decline of human projective capability. We develop this claim further in the next chapter.

Conclusions

This chapter addresses the multifaceted temporal characteristics of traceability. Risk-management thinking and practice have been used to bring out the deeply intertwined nature of traceability and temporality at different levels—from questions of ontology to risk indicator design. We began with onto-biology, drawing on Stiegler's analysis of the role of the trace in the evolution of human brains. Pre-human encounters with crude ready-to-hand technologies, like flints, co-evolved with human capacities for projection and intentionality. We then extended this co-developmental thinking to theories of organizing and time, arguing that scripts (Chapter 5) are technologies that generate the temporal structures and rhythms of organizations and thereby encode diverse orientations to the future and the past. In short, the argument follows existing scholarship to propose that organizing and temporalizing cannot be thought of independently and in isolation from each other.

The chapter argues that the organization of risk is one of the many "faces" of traceability. It is a face from which we can read the contingent temporal character of traceability as organized practice, and the deep epistemic and cultural affinities between traces, memory, and history. We addressed the seemingly paradoxical notion of "trace of the future", a paradox that disappears when we consider traceification and the manner in which data, things, people, and processes can be framed and encoded as risks. Drawing on Hilgartner's theory of "risk objects", we considered the design of risk indicators for such objects and how they implicate a politics of temporal depth, triggered by problems of temporally distant but serious harms.

Finally, the notion of an "archaeology of the future" was coined to characterize a possible developmental trajectory of risk management and traceability in an era of big data and AI. Advances in digitalization have not only shifted the technical landscape of risk management but also generated new risk objects. For critics of machine learning and advocates of privacy, traceability as the production of traces has become a risk object itself, while traceability as oversight has become weaker. Following Zuboff's provocation, it is proposed that the telos of platformization is the elimination of uncertainty and, by implication, human projective capability. In this sense, the economy of digital traces is both "overlit" and also crowded with a perpetual present. This has implications for the accounts that humans live by and their possibilities for imagining futures, both good and bad.

Chapter 7 Summative Propositions

The following propositions express the entanglement of traceability, temporality, and projection via the lens of risk management:

1. **The trace is inherently temporal in nature. It is always both memory and projection.**
2. **The scripted nature of organizations encodes their temporal structure and orientation as a source of their continuity and stability.**
3. **The traceification of risk objects in the form of lead indicators enables imagined harmful futures to be tracked and accounted for in the present.**
4. **Temporal depth is a critical and controversial aspect of the construction of risk objects and the design of their lead risk indicators.**
5. **Traceability complexes organize risk and combine prospective, present, and retrospective temporal orientations.**
6. **Riskification is a cultural "macro-script" of organizing by which activities and practices are framed explicitly in risk terms. Riskfication generates precautionary attitudes to risk.**
7. **Traceability can be both a value at risk and also a source of harm (risk object).**
8. **Digital "archaeologies of the future" aim at the elimination of uncertainty and place human capacities for projection at risk.**

8
Self-Tracking Selves and Pervasive Performing

Overview

This book introduced its agenda to explore the changing intersections between traceability, accounting, and performance with a vignette about a marathon runner using a smart watch for self-monitoring. In this chapter we turn our attention directly to the humans who are entangled in traceability complexes, who engage in various modes of self-observation, and who are simultaneously producers and consumers of traces. We ask whether and how tracking practices are formative of a certain kind of performing subject or self, as has been argued for accounting and quantification more generally. We also ask whether tracking itself generates human dispositions to trace and track activities, thereby constructing selves that value traceability and which orient their activities around the performance accounts that tracking produces. These questions demand a change in the orientation of our enquiry into traceability evident in previous chapters, from the complexes that connect traces, data, and accounts, to the analysis of how humans are attached to and enact tracking practices, of themselves and others. And the larger question that hangs in the background is whether and how digital technologies are implicated in reformatting the human and "making up" a new kind of "traceable" self.

The argument begins, as other chapters do, at a general level by reviewing relational theories of self and self-formation. While there is a diversity of such theories, they share a de-centring of traditional, Cartesian-inspired conceptions of self. Furthermore, this de-centring process challenges all dualisms of self and nature, and of body and machine, arguing that such distinctions and relations are historical *outcomes*, are always provisional, and are often ideological in nature. Relational theories position selves as contingent nodal points in networks of things and people, in which technologies, including documentary technologies like accounting, play formative roles (cf. Stiegler, as discussed in Chapters 2 and 4). Having established this general conception, the argument turns to the role of quantification practices in the formation of selves, and revisits strands of thinking from critical accounting studies, as discussed in Chapter 3, and recent work on the "quantified self". While this material is well-trodden ground, it enables an

Economy of Traces. Michael Power, Oxford University Press. © Oxford University Press (2026).
DOI: 10.1093/9780197681527.003.0008

important further conceptual and theoretical move, which has already been prefigured, namely to re-centre traceability and tracking as mobilizing values for the quantification of performance and as critical features of the relational dynamics of self-formation. An important quality of these dynamics is the "pull" of practices for tracking performance (cf. Chapter 2), and how they may be productive of dispositions and orientations that become "naturalized".

These arguments lay the ground for a series of reflections on the formative impact of traceability on the relational dynamics of self. It is not the intention of this chapter simply to repeat claims about the general risks of digital technology to humans and societies, which have been covered to some degree in Chapter 7, although there is inevitably reference to such critical arguments. Rather, the purpose is to continue the analysis of traceability, tracking, and accounting by making more explicit their implications for self-formation under conditions of expanded digital trace production.

Relational theories of the self teach us that the unity of personhood has always been mythical and plural, but the potential now exists for multiple digitally supported identities grounded in many forms of accounting, including self-tracking. While no specific practice may be formatively decisive, their volume and range suggest that for humans, individually and collectively, tracking has become valued in itself and we/they increasingly curate our/themselves to be "trace-ability-ready". To illustrate this point, three out of many possible formative pathways are considered: the self as produced "profile"; the self as a source of feedback; and the self-tracking self. This discussion reveals how there is no monolithic "digital-self" story to be told and that there are many continuities between the role of older documentary processes and their digital correlates. It also reminds us of the need to understand the specific nature of the devices and the intensities of human engagement that enable tracing and tracking practices.

It is proposed that digitalization in its broadest sense has not only enabled individual humans to trace and track—and have tracked—many aspects of their lives, from health to sociality to employability, but has also greatly expanded the applicability of the category of "performance" well beyond the boundaries of formal organizations and into the "personal" sphere. Humans are increasingly habituated to tracking and tracing many aspects of themselves over time and space, and all manner of apps and wearable devices provide new capacities for doing so. The very idea of "performance" and the cultural imperative for individuals, organizations, and states to perform implies a need for monitoring (i.e. tracking and accounting) and action as continuous corrective intervention and curation. In essence, the expansion of tracing and tracking in the digital age presupposes, and is generating, populations of humans readily disposed to forms of self-accounting. In relation to a growing range of activities, they are now compelled to ask: "How am I doing?" Furthermore, the chapter argues that the balance of constituents making up relational webs with formative power for selves may be shifting from "thick" mediated encounters with other humans towards the "thin" mediation of prosthetic technologies for self-accounting.

The Relational Self

The nature of self, mind, and identity has puzzled philosophers, sociologists, psychologists, scientists, and others for centuries (Callero, 2003). The Cartesian metaphysics of a singular self—understood as a self that already knows itself before it "looks out" on, and engages with, the world—has been an object of extensive critique from the late nineteenth century onwards. Philosophers as different as Wittgenstein, Peirce, and Heidegger, along with many others, share a view that we are fundamentally and primarily thrown into worlds of practice and action within which we must navigate and orient ourselves. Embodied human actors define themselves by the practices in which they are embedded and which they shape, rather than by a prior consciousness and intentionality. Shakespeare, Freud, Nietzsche, and others have also shattered the notion of the self-transparent self and pointed to the darker grounds of motive in personal biography. In short, these different counter-Cartesian reactions propose a more fluid and processual conception of self. The self has a history and is co-formed not only with other selves in cultural contexts but also in relation to the multiple technologies through which communication and action occur (cf. Foucault, 1977; Stiegler, 2016). Hence, we must think of selfhood as an outcome of socio-material and cultural processes and not as some kind of ineffable and private interiority (Butler, 2005; Douglas, 1992, p. 215).

Notwithstanding the compelling and established nature of these critiques, Platonic-Cartesian notions of interiority and mind-body dualism have proven to be remarkably durable. This is because they underwrite an important institutional and metaphysical myth for many (but not all) societies, namely that of the singular intentional and deliberative self that can be held to be free and responsible for its actions. The durability of this myth is partly anchored in language and the dominant subject-predicate separation in many cultures, but it is evident also in organizational sociology and in the efforts by scholars to provide accounts of personhood understood as "agency", which are a mix of both structural and deliberative-reflective factors. Debates about the nature of this mix are extensive, disputed, and most likely essentially contestable. However, between the extremes of selves as contingent, historical epiphenomena of their social and institutional environments and as free deliberative agents consciously and reflectively shaping those environments, there is at least an agreed conceptual space for debate and analysis. This is the space in which explicitly *relational theories* of self and personhood have been developed. In general, such theories propose that selfhood as a property of humans can and must be analysed in terms of the relations through which it is constituted and can, in turn, shape. Or, as Abbott (1995, p. 863) puts it, "actors are to be explained not assumed".

At the outset of reviewing this general relationalist perspective, we immediately encounter a terminological impasse: "person", "agent", "actor", "individual", "subject", "I", and "self" are all adjacent but differently nuanced concepts in English that seek to characterize, even provisionally, an object of analysis. A full history of the formation of these different concepts would be too much of a detour, and the Cartesian myth hangs over them all. Although sociological and economic analysis has tended to gravitate towards the notion of agency, here we will use the term "self" to characterize properties of the more or less psychologically continuous, linguistically capable, and socially competent embodied human being (Parfitt, 1984). This is no doubt arbitrary, but it will do as shorthand. In broad terms, from the relational point of view, this notion of self is not given but is a continuous formative achievement within a web not just of human others as co-producers of sociality, but also of non-human artefacts and technologies.

These sensibilities about selfhood vary considerably in their specific conceptions of "relationality" and in the strength of their de-centring of the self. For example, Bourdieu is realist about relations in the sense that selves understood as bundles of dispositions are formed primarily from class structures and social position. His notion of *habitus* can be understood as the total of acquired dispositions formed over an individual life-history as it moves through fields (Butler, 1999). Hence, one's position in the division of labour makes a certain kind of disposition (e.g. "aesthetic disposition") possible (Bourdieu, 2010, p. 47). In contrast, for Foucault, who often made explicitly anti-structuralist statements, relational ontology consists of specific and multiple "apparatuses" of control for bodies and persons. Selves are constituted by engagement in, and governance by, material "systems of intense registration" (Foucault, 1977, p. 188; Raffnsøe, Mennicken, and Miller, 2019). Hence, while Bourdieu and Foucault share a rejection of neo-Cartesianism and the myth of the autonomous self, and are both relational theorists in the sense outlined previously, nevertheless they are committed to different ontologies of the relation and thereby emphasize different formative pathways (Callewaert, 2006; Cronin, 1996).

Relational theories of the self also vary in the strength of their anti-Cartesianism. At one extreme, there are efforts to retain and reconstruct the coherent, reflective, intentional self as an enduring core of selfhood and as something that enters into, and is to some degree formed by, different relations with other selves, things, and ideas. Role theories have some of this flavour. At the other extreme are more radical relational theories that dissolve the self into the flux of relations, maintaining that there is nothing more to the self than relations and their dynamics, rooted in a processual ontology (Bencherki et al., 2024). From this point of view, there are no unitary selves, only multiple "dividuals" defined as forms of selfhood that emerge from "relations of division and connection, relations not of sameness but of self-similarity" (Day and Lury, 2016, p. 61). Relational dynamics are conceptualized primarily as processes of "dividuation", of multiple self-formation in which the "edges of a person cannot easily be stablised or secured" (Day and Lury, 2016, pp. 61–62). Such multiple, dividuated selves need not be sequential in time; they may even exist simultaneously across multiple relations. Clearly, the singular, intentional actor—an important myth in law and ethics—is fundamentally challenged by relational theories that point towards dividuation, rather than individuation, as the natural condition of the self.[1] Yet a dividuated view of the self has precedents in the radical empiricism of Hume (1955) and Parfit (1971), as well as affinities with Buddhist thinking (Giles, 1993).

If the self is to be understood in broad terms as a bundle of shifting relationalities, then there remain questions about their specificity and how they work to build the stable categories and classifications through which selfhood is formed. Indeed, classification and relationality are co-dependent (Strathern, 1995, p. 14), and the work of Ian Hacking (2002) is helpful in reinforcing this point. As discussed in Chapter 5, he builds on the basic relational imaginary of the self to argue that language and its evolving web of categories, and hence acts of communication, must also be understood as "technologies" that co-develop with conceptions of self. He argues persuasively that we come, to varying degrees, to react to and be shaped by language and the categories that are attributed to us or which we attribute to ourselves. For Hacking, new categories can "make up people", but this formative process, which he calls "dynamic nominalism", is far from deterministic and plays out empirically in many different ways. Where horses and atoms are indifferent to being labelled as such, the same is not true for the human beings, who react in many different ways to how they are described. Some labels and categories have strong formative and recursive effects on the self and on collective practices of self-description. For Hacking, this is especially evident in the emergence of new categories of mental disorders, which take hold not only in medical practices but also as forms of self-labelling and "scripting" of conduct, supported by apparatuses of knowledge production. In effect, language is the ultimate relational technology. As the later work of Wittgenstein suggests, we live and constitute ourselves as selves within its boundaries, albeit that these boundaries are fluid and open. Haraway (quoted in Gane, 2006, p. 147) pushes

[1] Even institutional theories that are not explicitly processual position what they call "actorhood" as a cultural attribution inscribed in texts (Meyer and Jepperson, 2000; Hwang and Colyvas, 2020).

this position even further to argue that categories and concepts are the fictions through which we actively constitute ourselves and our worlds. They are the products of continuous semiotic work to build relations and organize connectivities (Chapter 3). They also constitute and reproduce the building blocks for accounts of the self. Just as we emphasized the processual and relational nature of organizations in Chapter 5 in terms of scripts, so too are selves in a state of formation through the enactment of the scripts they inhabit (Goffman, 1959; Hacking, 2004). Such scripting need not be literally in the form of a material document but, as routines theory shows us, may be inferred from patterns of action and communication. In this way, the agency of the self is an outcome of the agentic power of scripts as communicative technologies and implied grammars as governing algorithms (Bencherki et al., 2024).

A more explicit inversion of the centrality of self is to be found in the ontogenetic and biologically oriented relationalism of Simondon (2020), who seeks to avoid tendencies to prioritize either relations or selves as entities. For Simondon, the self as "individual" is an outcome of long-run processes of individuation from amorphous collectivities. Both individual embodied selves and the collective or group co-develop from, and crystallize out of, a pre-individual reality (Bencherki et al., 2024). As noted in Chapter 4, Stiegler (1998) builds on this to emphasize the role of technology as an important factor in the process of the individuation of selves, in particular for the formation of the human brain, memory, and intentionality as being simultaneously collective (organizational) and individual in nature. To repeat, for Stiegler, technology is not simply pure instrumentality for navigating the world, as he thinks Heidegger and others suggest. Rather, self, group, and technology-enabled memory are co-produced (Matringe and Power, 2024). The self is both outcome and agency, shaping and being shaped by technologies.

In summary, while relational theories of self vary in nuance, scope, and the strength of their anti-Cartesianism, there seems to be a broad consensus that selfhood is the outcome of continuous processes of entification and individuation formed within, emergent from, and dependent on a web of relations to others and to objects, including linguistically infused material technologies. Within this fundamentally co-productionist conception, relational theorists examine the specific dynamics of how persons/selves/actors and organizational forms emerge—biologically, linguistically, and culturally. And if we accept that the primary ontology is that of the relation or web of relations between biological humans and material objects, including technologies, then it follows that, as this web changes, so too do the formative dynamics of the self. Selves are "made up" in the practical, linguistically and technologically rich situations in which they are embedded and whose looping effects they experience. An especially important sub-theme in these relationist analyses of self emphasizes the significance of the human body.

Bodies, Machines, and Cyborgs

Relational theories of the self that emphasize situatedness necessitate analytic attention to the body, to the physical orientations and flows of gestures that act as cues in the ongoing stream of mutual human sense-making but which also blur the boundaries of the self and its biological embodiments (Mol, 2008; Wacquant, 2015). Even in the seemingly simple act of pointing, mind and body cannot be parsed from one another. The use of the "index" finger as a form of bodily indexical competence has attracted considerable analytical attention from scholars such as Wittgenstein, who argue that it represents a uniquely human cultural ability, an ability that comes before all theory, abstraction, dualisms, and generalizations (see also Chapter 2). To extend the "digital" capabilities of the hand, human bodies have developed prosthetics of many different kinds, from agricultural tools to weaponry, and human brains have co-evolved. Hence the formative nature of body-technology linkages in all their variety is far from recent. Yet, it seems likely that the Platonic-Cartesian mind-body dualism and its institutional importance for multiple theologies distracted many thinkers from addressing the relational dynamics of body-technology co-evolution as Stiegler and others have done. Relations between the physical and technical are always seamless and mediated by the evolving human brain. Indeed, the embodied self is now increasingly produced at the interface between computer screens and life, where "bits meet atoms" (Hassan, 2003; Valiaho, 2014).

The reorientation of theories of the self around body-machine connectivities and relationalities has generated a stream of critical studies, not least among which has been the focus on the body for gender studies (Ball, 2005; 2009; Ball et al., 2016; Blanche and Feldman, 2021). Haraway's (2013) notion of the "cyborg" informs some of this work and is used as a political category that rejects sharp distinctions between human and non-human, between nature and society, and between the social and the material. She articulates a pervasive and constitutive concept of cyborg that is not restricted to machine-like components being "built into" human bodies, but references body-technology proximity and mutual formation in general. Pens, pencils, keyboards, watches (non-digital and digital), phones (non-digital and digital), and glasses come to mind. They are not (yet) implants in the specific sense of penetrating the surface of human skin, but for Haraway, the surface of the human body would only be an arbitrary threshold for identifying cyborgization processes. Smart watches and phones may not be literally implanted inside human bodies, but it is not wild to think of them *as if* they are, given evidence of the intensity of their use. From this point of view, biological humans have always been to a greater or lesser extent cyborgs in Haraway's sense in that they are enmeshed in multiple agencies and ontologies (Law and Mol, 1995; Nyberg, 2009).

To conclude, relational theories of the self have incorporated to varying degrees the role of the body, in its corporeal and cultural situatedness, and the related importance of technologies both humble and complex. Much of this work is broadly critical in the sense of seeking to de-naturalize categories of the self and related distinctions, and thereby to reveal the politics of formation by which some aspects of selfhood are validated while others are not. Yet such a broad socio-material agenda for understanding the co-formation of selves can collapse under the weight of its own vision, since the number of possible relationalities that "make up people" and can be traced is potentially vast, if not in principle infinite. Hence, despite this overview, we should also be careful not to overgeneralize. The very idea of relation and connectedness is itself somewhat fluid and perspectival, as we saw in Chapters 3 and 4, and hence relations-based analysis must necessarily make decisions about which specific connections and linkages to highlight for their formative significance. So while a radical dispersion and dividuation of the self into relations is ontologically compelling, some parsimony and focus are needed in order to identify and trace some of the more significant relationalities that create relatively congealed and stable selves. For accounting scholars, the quantification and constitution of performance is one such important region of formation and positions accounting as a technology within the general relational dynamics of self-formation.

Quantification and Self-Formation

Quantification pervades modern life in many forms, so much so that it has come to seem obvious and natural in many settings. This is partly because quantification does not simply measure but is widely understood to constitute the objects to which it is applied. We could not easily imagine blood pressure or Gross Domestic Product (GDP) without quantification, and without the instruments that operationalize quantification and enable the measurement of these and other phenomena. Scholars and policymakers may debate whether quantification has a "tyrannical" hold over modern life or whether it enables accountability and transparency, but its cultural and organizational significance can hardly be doubted (Boyle, 2001; Strathern, 2000b). As we elaborated in Chapter 3, quantification in many fields of human activity is founded on, often invisible, practices of abstraction and reduction in order to create commensurable quanta (Espeland and Stevens, 1998; Mennicken and Espeland, 2019). We know that this abstraction is often political, and always value-laden, involving choices about what is and is not significant. Yet, if deciding what counts as countable and commensurable is a value choice, it is a value choice that is also shaped by technological capacities to quantify phenomena of interest. Advances in digital technologies have greatly expanded the possibilities for the quantification of human behaviour. Digitization in the sense of converting and reducing bodily actions to electronic pulses and the use of binary codes to process such pulses expand the reach of quantification and related forms of classification, and provide the material for "data sciences" (Fourcade and Healy, 2024).

The rise of quantification in a myriad of forms—statistics, social media metrics, and rankings—continues to be extensively documented and analysed (e.g. Rottenburg et al., 2015). For the moment we focus on the role of quantificational practices, and the standards and norms of performance that they embody, in constituting selves. Such a relational conception of self and quantification has more or less defined the critical accounting agenda. Miller and O'Leary's (1987) classic study of standard costing shows how it was formative of "governable persons" in the sense of persons constituting themselves through their orientation to accounts of their performance. Drawing on the work of Foucault, this study (and many that followed it) develops the notion of "subjectification" to show how persons/selves/actors come to govern themselves within webs of relations with other things, ideas, and people. It points to the formation of humans as subjects of a specific kind as they define themselves in relation to quantitative practices that, to varying degrees, also make them trackable within apparatuses of control (Power, 2011a; Power and Miller, 2013). In their organizational roles, human actors orient themselves to accounting representations of their performance that come to seem natural and taken for granted as the way the world is (Miller, 1992). Indeed, the power of accounting in this sense is not to appear coercive but to govern at a distance in that humans "internalize" and even enjoy performance requirements (Foucault, 1977; Miller, 1992; Townley, 1993). A certain kind of accountable and performing self is thereby "made up" by its repeated engagement with accounting practice (Hacking, 2002). This is not to suggest that accounting, or any practices of quantification, are "iron cages" that fully determine selves, even if they are designed with that Taylorist ambition. There are always contingent conditions that may enable or inhibit the way accounting has such effects (Bay, 2018). Rather, we can say that accounting, control, and auditing practices have significant formative potential for human selves as they attend to, are immersed in, and even resist, performance apparatuses and their metrics. The power of accounting, as discussed in Chapter 3, not only is a function of the purposes that mobilize it or the techniques which embody such purposes but also depends on being entangled with the human actors who are necessary to make it a "practice" (Ahrens and Chapman, 2007).

While we can think of financial and managerial accounting practices as specific institutional manifestations of quantification, this should not, as argued in Chapter 1, restrict our view of what counts as accounting. Beyond workplace settings, people increasingly quantify, monitor, and evaluate dimensions of their personal lives, such as their health and educational attainment (Sharon and Zandbergen, 2017; Mennicken and Espeland, 2019). Digital transformations and the rise of social media have significantly increased the scope of such practices via an array of new "accounting" devices for measuring steps, calories, and much more as aspects of personal performance. These developments are encapsulated in the motif of the "quantified self" (Lupton, 2016c), which points beyond formal organizational settings to reference all manner of accounts of the self in terms of fine-tuned metrics. However, we should also be careful not to draw sharp distinctions between organizational and non-organizational settings. They are becoming more digitally entwined; metrics of the self are enabled by organizations and the devices they produce and sell. These developments mark an intensification of the relations between measurement and self-formation. In particular, they expand the idea and scope of "performance" and of accounting and quantification as human beings situate themselves in webs of devices and sensors that trace their actions and aggregate them into metrics of health, reputation, fitness, sociality. As these new calculative "spaces of identity" are generated (Morley and Robins, 1995), the construction of the governable person is no longer restricted to formal organizational settings. Its formative processes have expanded their reach into what might be regarded as the personal or "non-work" sphere and have generated multiple quantifications in which selves are immersed.

The question as to why and how humans enter into formative relations with technologies of quantification has generated a number of different answers. One is that we are drawn to the seeming objectivity and rationality of numbers as a feature of our "scientized" culture (e.g. Drori, 2003). Another points to the power of a single number or ratio and its ability to compress complexity for decision-making purposes (Kurunmäki and Miller, 2013). This may be especially the case for rankings and ratings. Yet another highlights the properties of fairness and transparency, which are valued by contracting parties and for governance in general (Porter, 1996). And there are even studies that emphasize how "false numbers" can be generative of valued relations (see Chapter 3). While all of these and other perspectives on the power of quantification and accounting provide compelling analyses that are not mutually exclusive, in this book we provide a further optic on quantification and self-formation, one that points to a potentially more primitive explanation of the power of numbers. In short, quantification is theorized as a mode of traceability and, in particular, as an enabler of tracking in general. The quantified self is embedded in practices of tracking in which the boundaries between the personal and organizational become fluid.

This perspective is not entirely new; it has been more or less implicit in prior work on, for example, auditing (Power, 1997). As noted in Chapter 3, we tend to think of auditing as a derivative of accounting (i.e. we produce accounts that can then be audited). The theoretical counter-proposition is an inversion of this assumed relationship, namely the idea that it is auditing and the need to make organizations auditable and traceable that shape the accounts that we produce (Power, 1996). Of course, empirically this is an overstatement, but it generates the potential for re-centring the significance of tracking, for which quantification is means rather than end. Lupton's notion of the "quantified self" is consistent with this re-centring, reminding us that we are also, and have become, selves that track our "performance" over time via technologies of quantification. This is not a methodological point about how to study the formation of agency by tracing relations (see also Chapter 9); it is a theoretically substantive point that humans and the devices that support tracking capacities exist in relations of co-formation.

We began this section with a general overview of relational theories of the self. Contrary to myths of unity, we are multiple dividuated selves not as a matter of pathology but as a function of the different relational networks of people and technologies that we inhabit in different places and times. We are made up and make ourselves up, yet the precise dynamics of this process not only are a matter for empirical investigation but also involve theoretical choices about what a "relation" is assumed to be, and value choices about which relations, so defined, are formatively significant. We should not detain the present argument with doctrinal differences between theories, but it is important to repeat that there is no implicit claim that humans are dupes in iron cages when they enter into relations. As Hacking's notion of "making up people" suggests, there is no general thesis about how quantification devices that enable tracking by others and selves are powerfully formative. Rather, there is likely to be considerable empirical variety. Later in this chapter we elaborate some stylized pathways by which multiple selves, or dividuals, and their orientations to representations of performance are shaped. Before this, we need to explore a little more of the psychic investment in, and disposition-formative nature of, human engagement with accounts.

The "Pull" of Accounts

As a working simplification, we can think of dispositions generally as dynamic and affective portfolios of resistance and allure, what we shall call "push" and "pull", in relation to new representations of performance. Dispositions in this sense are not deterministic and allow explicitly for play and flexibility (Crossley, 2013, p. 139) and even scepticism. We "observe" and infer such dispositions imperfectly from dominant patterns of actions by individuals and groups, or what we might call their habits (Camic, 1986, p. 1044). Hence dispositions are not themselves events but capacities revealed in the analysis of events (Ryle, 1949). For Dewey, a disposition to act in specific ways is built up via experience (Dewey, 1922; Turner and Cacciatori, 2016, p. 78), yet it is not merely a mechanical, automated response to cues. Routines theory teaches us that habits and routines allow for agency and learning about how to go on in the "same way" and can be generative (Cohen, 2007; Feldman and Pentland, 2003). Furthermore, dispositions with varying degrees of reflexivity and automaticity may become imprinted in selves at key moments and junctures in social fields (Marquis and Tilcsik, 2013; Cardinale, 2018, 2019). We propose that a disposition for self-tracking, while not mechanical or monolithic, arises in conjunction with technological affordances and wider cultural and field norms about self-improvement and performance (Lupton, 2014).

Push

"Push" can be understood as a label for the disposition(s) to resist new accounts and their data requirements (e.g. doctors' pushback against new appraisal systems; McGivern and Ferlie, 2007). Conflict, resistance, and other more complex reactions arise as reductive accounts of performance jar with established modes of evaluation and work identities (Thornton et al., 2012, ch. 7). In a more explicitly affective sense, push can also be understood as a placeholder for emotional-cognitive complexes (Cohen, 2007; Voronov and Weber, 2016; Lok et al., 2017), including anxiety (Espeland and Sauder, 2016). Forms of push are highly varied and contingent. As Marx (2006) notes when considering different forms of surveillance, how an individual will experience them will be a function of many factors, which include: the technical means; its perceived legitimacy; the setting; the content; perceptions of the violation of privacy; and whether there is intrusion into core areas of intimacy. In the same vein, the push against novel forms of accounting and control has been theorized as weaker when there is participation in the design of new controls (Falk and Kosfeld, 2006). Low push is also argued to reflect "high cultural fit" and continuity (Marti and Gond, 2018; Ansari et al., 2010, p. 78). This cultural fit is known to be weaker and more contested when new performance requirements disrupt, and are discontinuous with, existing patterns of work and self-understanding (Dent, 1991; Townley, 1997). Here there may be pressure for decoupling novel traces from action (Baxter and Clarke, 2013).

There is therefore no general story of push in relation to the introduction of new accounting requirements, and this plurality of reactions and engagements is consistent with the observed variety in studies of self-tracking (Lupton, 2014). Furthermore, as many scholars note, push as resistance to new accountings and efforts at decoupling are relatively rare and often short-lived (Boxenbaum and Jonsson, 2017). Forms of coupling and acquiescence are more frequently observed. One reason for this is that human actors, even as they overtly criticize new arrangements, such as new accounting and control systems or rankings systems, are nevertheless drawn to them. This is pull.

Pull

The notion of "pull" is also a label that simplifies a complex array of processes. But we can suggest some of their dynamics. At a fundamental level, selves are constituted by the pull of what they take as "real". There seems to be a "natural" disposition or compulsion to "externalize" social facts, as Berger and Luckman (1966) have shown. Hence the facticity and naturalness of what counts as performance are produced in settings populated by humans who are exposed to accounts of self that are built from the traceification of their behaviour (Chapter 3). Material prosthetics and devices are important enablers for the repetition of representations, creating "deeper ruts in the road" (Pentland et al., 2011), as discussed in Chapter 4, and stronger dispositions to see such representations, especially numeric ones, as describing an objective reality. Furthermore, we can postulate looping effects (Barnes, 1983) by which accounting techniques, the facticity of performance data, and dispositions to externalize and compare (across space, time, groups, societies, organizations) are mutually reinforcing and endogenous (Dionysiou and Tsoukas, 2013). Pull must therefore be understood temporally, rather than episodically, as a process that accretes and unfolds in specific ways, building on the onto-biological disposition to externalize that Stiegler identifies.

Relatedly, anthroplogists also talk of the "pull of documents" (Riles, 2006, p. 8), and Mathiesen's (1997) notion of a "viewer society" draws attention to pull as a "love of watching". Indeed, an orientation to watching, observing, and studying others constitutes observer fascination with behaviour and bodily functions that can be captured, represented, and made traceable by arrays of accounts and metrics (Lyon, 2006).[2] It is a fascination that also embodies a compulsion for comparison with similar others, both imagined and real, and for the competitive curation and refinement of self and performance over time. Representations acquire formative power when they are constituted as performance accounts that are adjudicated by others and also drive more or less continuous forms of self-adjudication. Thus the so-called "tyrannies" of light (Tsoukas, 1997),

[2] Those who are watched and whose actions are transparent to others may value some degree of privacy and unobservability and will push back (see Bernstein, 2017).

transparency (Strathern, 2000b), and numbers (Boyle, 2001) are also suggestive of a desire to be seen and evaluated by others, which can become a form of addictive self-tyranny. This investment and formative power are augmented by digitally enabled gamification techniques that strengthen affective engagements in quantifying self-performance (Chapman et al., 2021) and related forms of performance visualization in summative dashboards (Ronzani and Gatzweiler, 2022). If there is a form of self-tyranny at work in the gamification of control technologies, what Sherer and Neesham (2023) call their "organized immaturity", then what we call the pull of accounting for self-tracking may also be experienced as fun.

Gamification as a specific mode of pull towards accounts consists in self-reinforcing forms of psychic pleasure associated with externalized representations of performance—the "to do" app being a simple but powerful form of gamified self-accounting (Bergen and Verbeek, 2021). This form of pull is evident in many studies of the motivation for self-tracking (Lupton, 2014, 2016a) and enables us to explain why the coupling of new performance measures happens even when we expect decoupling. As Sauder and Espeland (2009, p. 64) show, rankings have allure and pull despite widespread criticism of their limitations. Leaders who doubt the intellectual substance of rankings as highly reductive representations of complex organizations nevertheless take pride in a good performance in relation to them. Indeed, performance comparability is valued by humans even when they understand that it is based on reductive simplifications (Esposito and Stark, 2019). This is as true for organizations as it is for individuals engaged in intensive self-tracking via quantified measures of their health, wealth, and sociality. Organizational leaders such as CEOs are also drawn to the externalization of their own performance in financial accounting representations, a potentially narcissistically fuelled pull that in some cases drives the manipulation of accounts (Cragun et al., 2020). In general, pull is an affective force generated in the encounter between accounting representations and a self in a continuous process of formation.

Finally, pull—like any disposition—is necessarily relational, collective, and cultural. As noted already, according to Bourdieu, dispositions emerge at the juncture of field-positions and life history. They are both collective—they might be the general dispositions of a group or class that shares a structural position—and also individual, a function of specific life history. In this sense, we can take from Bourdieu the accumulative and historical trajectory of dispositions that correlate with shared conceptions of reality (i.e. forms of objectification). It follows that selves are fundamentally historically produced sets of dispositions, albeit with agentic space to be inventive within the rules of the game. For example, Lupton (2014) refers to the cultures of self-tracking as a form of collective individualism. Individual humans may regard their engagement with and use of personal informatics for self-tracking as a matter of choice, but this choice is also a function of an entire socio-techno apparatus of organizing, producing devices, writing algorithms, and the marketing of self-monitoring. In Stiegler's (2016) terms, this represents a process of *trans-individuation* in which technology, individual, and collective co-emerge (Matringe and Power, 2024). This is also how human bodies transact with the traceability complexes that enable practices of self-tracking. The following extended vignette provides a stylized "process narrative" (Langley, 1999) by way of illustration:

> *The CEO of a private company sends an email to a university business school researcher noting how her published research has helped him to make important changes to management processes. The email is a matter of personal satisfaction for her, but little more. It is not yet even to be considered a trace of something interesting; and it is not yet data to be taken seriously and acted upon. However, subsequently her university is subject to a new performance accounting regime and is required to report on the external impact of its research (Power, 2015). The researcher now recognizes that the email in question could be used as textual evidence for this new accounting requirement. She is deeply sceptical of the process and of the entire idea of accounting for external impact. She believes strongly in curiosity-driven research for its own sake, and knows that the benefits of her work to society flow in many indirect and subtle ways, including teaching, and cannot be encapsulated in something as crude as "impact". Yet she is also "strongly encouraged" by her dean to produce a case study of her research impact based on the email and other pieces of what can now be construed (traceified) as primary evidence.*
>
> *She receives help in preparing an account of her impact from the newly appointed "chief impact officer" and, to her surprise and pleasure, her case study—one of many submitted by her academic colleagues—receives the highest numerical score by external evaluators and contributes to the high ranking for impact of her university. Despite her initial scepticism, she naturally enjoys being congratulated by the dean, who says he shares her misgivings but is also delighted by the university's performance. Indeed, impact is one of the dean's key performance measures and he was personally involved in appointing the new chief impact officer. The dean's office has also developed management information in the form of a dashboard of Key Performance Indicators (KPIs) to keep track of the university's, and therefore also his, performance over time, enabling interventions when defined performance targets are at risk. The dean receives a bonus from the governing body for delivering these KPI-defined outcomes, and the researcher's perceived success in impact becomes part of both formal and informal discussions of her own performance. She is increasingly described by others as an "impactful" researcher and is seen as a source of expertise on how to expand*

the impact of other colleagues' research, supporting the work of the chief impact officer. Via case studies like hers and the overall ranking, research impact as a policy value has acquired organizational facticity in the university and is a high-level KPI for its leadership.

The researcher and those whom she now advises as part of the "impact strategy" of her university not only routinely attend to emails like the one she originally received but also actively seek them from a newly defined class of "users" of their research. She often thinks that the active searching for potential users and their curation as impactees is all a distraction from actually doing good research, but she and others enjoy being recognized as impactful, and emails are valued as legitimate traces of impact. She has become committed to collecting and editing them to be auditable for the impact officer and any possible external inspection. The original email from the private organization that used the research has thereby been transformed ontologically, becoming a "primary" trace of possible impact within an emergent traceability complex that systematically datafies these traces to support the production of a new form of performance accounting. Recently, the researcher has also regularly been checking her Google Scholar and ResearchGate profiles and updating her CV with the latest citation count for her papers. She knows this is silly and it's the quality of her papers that is the most important thing, but "h-scores" were mentioned in passing at a recent career progression meeting, and while there is no suggestion that they will be part of any formal evaluation process, she thinks she should keep an eye on hers and try to find ways to boost her citation count. She also notices that many academics now publicize new papers on social media sites such as Linkedin, often saying how pleased and humbled they are to be able to announce their new publications to the world. She has always dismissed this as pure narcissism and was considering cancelling her account, but now she wonders if she needs to do the same. She received a small one-off bonus from the dean (his was larger) for her impact case study and decided to reward herself with a new Apple watch. Now she regularly uses the apps on this watch to monitor aspects of her fitness and daily activity, but she is also tracking her blood sugar levels and heart rate and is able to plot their variation over time. In addition to LinkedIn, she still has a Facebook profile—she cannot be bothered to delete it—an academic webpage hosted by her university, and separate profiles on Google Scholar, Researchgate, and Web of Science, as well as an old Instagram account. She has just begun to develop her own dashboard for research, teaching, impact, fundraising, and service in order to be better able to monitor her career and manage her public profile. (adapted and extended from Power, 2021a)

The vignette is not itself an empirical case; it is constructed from ad hoc empirical observations to suggest how the "pull" of accounts may unfold over time. The original email and emails like it become subject to both traceification and datafication. At first, it is simply a trace of a communication, not of the research; it is stored and exists for possible future scrutiny in the case of employment disputes or for security purposes. It is a trace relative to this possible purpose but is not yet traceified for impact accounting. In the vignette, the email comes to be seen as a putative evidential trace of research impact, implying a causal relationship between the research and the user, albeit a tenuous one. Indeed, we can say that it becomes a primary trace of impact as a "performance" value. This primary traceification drives subsequent datafication in the sense that such traces come to be systematically organized and an infrastructure emerges for their explicit management. The email becomes desirable impact data for organizational actors as they orient themselves to the new accounting requirement.

The individual researcher depicted in the vignette is already positioned in an academic and cultural milieu with its associated collective dispositions. As Bourdieu reminds us, "knowledge for its own sake" is a specific formation in the history of the division of labour. Yet the vignette also suggests how the new form of performance accounting co-emerges with a shift in the researcher's motivation and sense of self as she begins to accept impact as a value and plays the game. Impact is collectively externalized and qualified as a value in both her university and the field more generally (Hammarfelt et al., 2016). This is not a monolithic or deterministic process, and an initial rejection/push and residual conflict of dispositions may persist, not least because there can be multiple performance values, logics, and accounts in play (Thornton et al., 2005; Kraatz and Block, 2008), all with different degrees of pull and disposition formation. Our researcher may also be engaged with many other technologies for defining and representing performance in her research, health, and sociality and is increasingly responsive to the cultural pressure to take citations seriously. She is therefore progressively dividuated by multiple accounting processes, only one of which involves research impact.[3]

The vignette suggests the contours of a formative process with multiple channels of disciplinary power that produce self-regulating, self-tracking, dividuated selves across a variety of performance dimensions. Humans may be more or less anxious, enthusiastic, and cynical, but nevertheless they may come—as our stylized researcher does—to reorient their behaviour to a greater or lesser extent to new technology-enabled accounts and representations of themselves, including research impact, to the point of enjoying regular engagement with, and interaction with, them. The vignette also points to the phenomenological microfoundations of the institutional power of accounting—microfoundations constituted by the dynamics of traceification, datafication, and performance accounting.

[3] See Burrows (2012) and Chan et al. (2018) on metrics in academic life. See also Biagioli and Lippman (2020) on how metrics generate games and academic fraud.

Humans encounter and come to embrace varieties of primary traces of their performance that are collectively formative of a disposition for self-accounting across many domains of activity, and which blur traditional distinctions between private and public life (Jepperson, 1991, p. 145; Phillips et al., 2004, p. 638).

To summarize the chapter to this point: we began by providing a general overview of relational theories of self-formation. This material is rich, complex, and often contested, so this review was necessarily limited. However, it was sufficient to provide the backdrop to a more specific focus on the role of technologies as part of those relational dynamics and, in particular, on the self-formative implications of quantification and accounting practices in their broadest sense. These relational dynamics of self-formation are then theorized in terms of the generation of dispositions of resistance and attraction—push and pull—to forms of accounting. The vignette of the impactful researcher suggests how specific dispositions also have a cultural or institutional form and co-emerge over time with the elaboration of organizational infrastructures for tracking and accounting (Power, 2015). It is in these varieties of self-tracking that we find the critical link between traceability complexes and the humans that are "plugged in" to them. It also follows from the ontology of relational theorizing that there can be many selves in one human body, understood as bundles of different and not necessarily consistent dispositions and practice-relative orientations. Some of these dispositions may be weakly grounded and easily changed or discarded. Others may be stronger. The vignette was used to draw out some of the underlying dynamics by which both accounting systems and an orientation towards them co-develop. This brings us to one of the core propositions of this chapter, namely *that individuals form themselves and are formed as they are immersed in the webs of traceification, datafication, and accounting that generate the facticity of individual and organizational performance.* While this proposition is digitally neutral in its formulation, it is also helpful to consider more explicitly the implication of digitalization for this model of self-formation.

The "Trace-Enabled" Self: Three Pathways

From the point of view of general relational theories of the self, it is preferable to begin with the assumption that there is nothing special in principle about digital technologies and processes of digitalization broadly understood. They are technologies like any other, embodied in machines that have been widely discussed by historians of science and technology, and which enter into relations with their human operators and users. Furthermore, the relational constitution of the self in relation to technologies of tracking, as discussed earlier, is not uniquely a feature of digitalization. Documents such as diaries, lists, and files of many kinds have all been studied for their formative potential, as Foucault and Hacking show us, to recursively shape how humans think of themselves (Hull, 2012a, 2012b; Vermeer, 2022; Bergen and Verbeek, 2021). Nevertheless, against such an assumption of continuity, it is widely accepted that there is something new in the sheer immersive intensity of digital technologies and their implications for traceability and self-formation. In what follows we highlight three, among many possible, vectors or pathways of self-formation in which this intensity is evident: reputation and profile formation; evaluation and feedback; and self-tracking.

From Reputation to Profile

The explosion of traces generated by users on social media platforms led originally to extensive investment by marketing agencies in developing composite user profiles by interweaving traces of online and offline sociability (Cardon, 2020). The early aspiration was to understand how social media traces could produce socio-metrically constituted actors as digital counterparts of a person, thereby generating new ways for persons to see themselves and to strategize their relations and reputation within networks (for an economics perspective, see Mayer, 2009). Yet, as Cardon notes, this ambition to measure and monetize the reputation of a social media user failed because it was metrically too ambitious. The project was beset by many familiar accounting problems, such as measurement uncertainty, the impossibility of standardizing metrics, the difficulty of interpreting complex indicators of social relationships, and the strategic gaming of reputation scores. In short, ad hoc traces of popularity could not be made into robust measures of reputation.

This failed aspiration nevertheless created and left behind an infrastructure for digital tracking. Instead of trying to construct, measure, and represent an elusive quality like reputation in an index, more or less the same traces of behaviour came to be used for predictive and profiling purposes. Recommender platforms, which have received a considerable amount of scholarly attention, typify the formative processes at stake (Seaver, 2019). Digital traces of behaviour, such as choices and clicks regarding music, restaurants, or partners, are processed by algorithms and are used to produce higher-order patterns and "data objects" based on statistical associations. It is now well known that the music suggested to me by a popular music platform is based on associations between my choices and the set of choices of others that overlap with mine. As Alaimo and Kallinikos (2020) and others show, this algorithmic production of preferences is based only on statistical associations and inferred probabilities between the choice patterns of many consumers. In doing this, the algorithm effectively generates a digital profile of me as an ongoing hypothesis based on choice histories. The crucial point of self-formation is that these trace-based hypotheses are then re-presented to human users who react to confirm or disconfirm them. In the face of these reactions, the algorithm revises and refines its hypothesized user profile and its tastes, prompting and suggesting new choices (Newlands, 2021; Alaimo and Kallinikos, 2020).

Many readers will be familiar with platforms that do this—Spotify, YouTube, Tinder, Amazon, and many others. As we know from online retailers such as Amazon, we are told that people who "bought X also bought Y", and on platforms such as Spotify and Apple, suggestions of music and products seem clever and based on personal knowledge. Yet they are not clever in the sense of possessing "genuine" knowledge of individual tastes. Traces are extracted from platform interfaces with human users (Caliskan, 2021; Cohen, 2019). Patterns and accounts of self are produced behind the backs of human actors who, in some cases, are re-fed with algorithmically composed representations of their preferences. In this way, recommender algorithms process "relationalities" from a mass of digital traces of choices and also generate formative relations between humans and their statistically hypothesized selves. Where these statistically grounded relations cluster for a specific platform user, then one can talk of a trace-enabled digital self that is formative to the degree to which it is recursively reconfirmed and stabilized by further actions (clicks). This preference formation and curation are often experienced as benign and enjoyable, for example by reconnecting individuals easily to the music of their past and its associations.[4]

Recommender platforms are a specific example of how digitization has given rise to new "biographical ontologies" in which selves enter into multiple relations with their digitally mediated selves (Alaimo and Kallinikos, 2019). The increasingly dividuated self and its "data doubles" are mutually formative and potentially converge around finely calibrated digital representations of tastes, sociality, and many other dimensions of human life. While humans may not be fully determined by these doubles as multiple online identities, they are a new and growing ingredient of the relational formation in which humans affectively encounter themselves in data (Ruckenstein, 2014). In the age-old human-technology dialectic, humans now confront richly textured versions of themselves as profiles, which are assemblages of primary digital traces of their actions. Forms of intimacy and interiority are also amenable to being traced and profiled in this way. In short, relationality as the historical engine of self-formation is itself mutating under conditions of digitization as new forms of self and sociality are being constructed (Stiegler, 2016; Fourcade and Johns, 2020). It

[4] Varoufakis (2023) positions this experience of pleasure as a defining feature of what he calls "technofeudalism", in which platforms and their technologies replace competitive markets. There are echoes of Foucault in this thesis.

follows from a broad conception of relationality that algorithms, as programmed rules, can be understood as having formative agency in just the same way that the law and accounting systems do. They have a "programmed intentionality" that creates circuits of behavioural observation (tracking) of the self by the self.

According to Rouvroy and Berns (2013), algorithms displace and radicalize the forms of neoliberal subjectivization that have animated accounting analyses of governable selves discussed earlier in this chapter. The profiles or data doubles that are constructed from digital traces can now bypass circuits of reflexivity and internalization. They are also created in a manner that can be detached from the individual self, and that can be used by others to trace and track that self, for profit, security, or quality purposes, regardless of their relationship with, and knowledge of, their profile. For example, such profiles can be deployed in an anticipatory and preventative manner, informing risk-based governance programmes, insurance strategies, and credit rating (Henman, 2020; Millo et al., 2024). Algorithmically generated profiles can also in principle be created and governed in the name of specific "risky" individuals for the security purposes of the state as well as commercial interests in insurability profiles (Egbert and Esposito, 2024). In effect, the traceability of the person for security purposes is enabled by algorithms that produce a digital profile from their behavioural traces. Yet, while this creates possibilities for tracking the digitalized self, the formative question always remains, and is always, empirically open: How does a digitally enabled profile re-enter the web of relations in which selves are formed? This is equivalent to Hacking's question regarding the formative power of classifications, and the empirical extent to which the nature of the specific profile is reinforced by individual humans via feedback mechanisms.

In all these developments of profiles, there may seem to be a tension between a "real" and a digitally produced self, often resting on unstated assumptions of the de-humanizing effects of technology. This residual essentialism of the human is understandable. Yet, most relational theories discussed previously provide an insistent reminder to avoid any backdoor route for a Cartesian ontology of a true self, to which technology is being somehow "applied". Hence, some critical analyses of algorithms resemble earlier studies of the effects of quantification when they focus on the power of the code to abstract and quantify in a way which "hollows out meaning" and is severed from some notion of genuine human experience, the human "lifeworld" as some would call it. Algorithms are argued to be post-social organizing processes (Barad, 2003), which constitute a machinic habitus (Airoldi, 2021) of an automated society (Stiegler, 2016). Nevertheless, even if we renounce any residual romantic Cartesianism, there can be little doubt that the scale by which individual behaviour can be captured as a trace and subject to the algorithmic production of a profile is a development in our age that potentially creates both risks to privacy as we have come to know it, and also granular forms of discrimination and exclusion, for example in medical insurance, which are well-documented (Kordzadeh and Ghasemaghaei, 2022). And, as discussed in Chapter 6, there is emerging interest in the auditing of algorithms to detect these new and pervasive forms of granular discrimination in digital profiling (Sandvig et al., 2014).

Notwithstanding these many critical voices on behalf of the human, relational theorizing suggests that the unity of self and human experience, what we mean by it, and its phenomenology, are all up for grabs in a digitally mediated world. We are, and only ever have been, multiple dividuated selves and relationally constituted "profiles". This is not to rule out all critical positioning in relation to technologies, but rather to admit that if we are relationally shaped, fluid and distributed selves as a matter of ontology, there are still ethical questions to be asked about the kinds of relations that should matter to our self-formation and how to control them. Later in this chapter we reflect more on this *ethics of self-formation* and the role of the accounts we live by, where we discuss the choice between "thin" and "thick" relationalities of self. The point here is that however we formulate this task, the notion of the "real" person at risk can only ever be a placeholder for further analysis. Conversely, we cannot automatically assume that digital profiles or doubles produced from traces are also "unreal". Since Berger and Luckman (1966), we know that the reality of both our worlds and our notions of self are subject to conditions of continuous construction and maintenance. Indeed, the profiling and tracking of people did not begin with digitization. It has a history based in many diverse forms of organized curiosity about individuals in their roles as merchants, artists, scholars, and much else. Still, it must also be admitted that the trace-enabled production and processing of digital profiles as accounts of self have emerged as extraordinary sources of reality construction, which build on our human fascination with how we are perceived.

The Self as Feedback Machine

In the previous sub-section it was argued that digital technologies have intensified "profilization" as a source of self-formation. A closely related formative vector is the expanded potential for evaluation to take the form of "feedback" as information generated by humans as "users" in traceability complexes. At the time of writing this book, it has become almost impossible to visit hospitals and restaurants, to use airlines and taxis, to stay in hotels and apartments, and to have goods delivered without receiving online requests for feedback and to rate one's experience. Having blood taken, ordering a takeaway meal online, checking in luggage at the airport, and a multiplicity of other activities of daily lives have been constructed as "experiences" that can be captured digitally in user-generated ratings and which provide data about performance for platform organizations and many others. "How did we do today?" has become a common question, and a brief response often triggers requests to complete a fuller questionnaire. In short, all manner of systems exist to capture and constitute primary traces of our experience and to aggregate them into performance data for analysis and intervention. Questionnaires and polls that seek to understand consumer satisfaction and citizen attitudes have a long history, but digitalization supercharges the ability to track feedback and to use it to construct higher-level data on, for example, consumer sentiment. Such practices are supported by a long-standing consensus that customer experience is a significant lead risk indicator (see Chapter 7) of brand loyalty and retention. This means that the granular traceification of customer satisfaction is important for platforms that bring buyers and sellers together, such as Airbnb, Tripadvisor, Booking.com, and many others.

In these settings, evaluation as feedback on individuals and companies may also flow in multiple directions, as Kornberger et al. (2017) show in their study of eBay. Customers and suppliers evaluate and provide feedback on each other in what they call "evaluative infrastructures". The former who provide feedback may find themselves also subject to feedback as "good" hotel guests, taxi passengers, and even academic reviewers. There can be potential rewards, discounts, and other bespoke offers attached to such evaluations. Digital technologies therefore enable human users to be both raters and rated at the same time. They are also "pulled" further into these practices by what scholars now call "gamification" in which the process of providing feedback is designed to be enjoyable in and of itself, and there can be rewards in the form of tokens and discounts that can be used as currency within the platform. Hence, these evaluative infrastructures generate multilateral forms of evaluation, auditing, and rating, creating practices in which each may observe the other in tight networks of feedback, and towards which each may feel some level of compulsion or pull.

The feedback form as a survey instrument is not especially novel and predates the rise of digital platforms. It is part of a family of checklist devices and lists discussed in Chapter 4, which have a long history. Survey-generated ratings all existed prior to the rapid expansion of their automation. So it might be argued that the phenomenon of feedback is simply the digital augmentation of pre-existing analog paper-based systems of evaluation. However, the expansion, explosion even, of possibilities for near continuous feedback also suggests something qualitatively different. For example, it has been argued normatively that these developments represent the democratizing power of digital technologies insofar as individuals as purchasers of goods and services are being enfranchised as evaluators, and as everyday auditors with "voice", via surveys and ratings (Jeacle and Carter, 2011; Scott and Orlikowski, 2012). It is as if auditing has been de-professionalized, disintermediated, and popularized; everyone can now audit and evaluate (Jeacle and Carter, 2022). There is of course variation in practice. In some cases, feedback is publicly shared and available to other customers as a resource for their decision-making. Often it is aggregated into ranking and rating systems that acquire performative power irrespective of the response rates on which they are based. And user feedback can also be imagined as a form of data-driven de-centring, as discussed in Chapter 4, in which organizations do not just *have* customers but exist where customers leave traces as feedback. In place of audit society pressures to turn organizations "inside-out", the organization encapsulates more of its environmental "outside".

This explosion of feedback presupposes and shapes users as subjects who both evaluate in a certain way, and are subjects who generate data for platforms and their clients to process for more aggregated accounts of performance. Hence there is a formative potential at stake in terms of what we might call an "evaluative disposition" to provide feedback. To say this is to build on Woolgar's (1990) observation about the agentic power of accounting systems to "configure" good users. Such configuration is an uneven process at best. First, we know, doubtless from our own experience, that individuals often do not comply with requests for feedback (although enough do so to make the process worthwhile and statistically meaningful for platforms). Indeed, the expansion of multiple requests for feedback may diminish response rates in general, although there may be also systemic effects on non-respondents. I am configured as a user in general even when I choose not to provide feedback in any specific instance. Second, it could be argued that feedback bears little relation to what we commonly historically understand as audit or evaluation. Digitally enabled feedback by design encourages snap coded judgements (even though some versions employ text boxes for narrative and the giving of reasons). What is valued is not the individual view in any deliberative depth but the immediate opinions and the statistical patterns they afford. If our repeated and intrusive exposure to requests for feedback can be said to be formative of an evaluative disposition, it is one in which the technology enables and encourages snap judgements. Feedback is at best "reductive evaluation" and has become almost costless to request from users and buyers. It is also a further manifestation of governance "flattening", discussed in Chapter 6. Feedback is now a technology-enabled flattening and impoverishment of costly deliberation and is an exemplar of the accounts we live by in the digital age.

These developments suggest that digitally enabled feedback systems represent the intensified economization of experience. In other words, human users of platforms are valued not only for direct economic exchange purposes but also, as Zuboff reminds us, for generating economic value in the form of "surveillance assets" via the traces they produce, intentionally or otherwise. Explicit systems for feedback and ratings have proliferated and have become a part of everyday life; a simple economic transaction is often accompanied by a request for feedback not just about the product itself but about the experience. Punctuality, courtesy, communications, and many other experiential attributes of a transaction, in addition to successful execution—attributes that sociologists since Polanyi have highlighted in relational analyses of markets and economies—can now themselves be economized and subject to forms of near-continuous accounting that construct and represent them as objects of value to be tracked (as lead indicators; Chapter 7). As the capability, the traceability, to track, say, goods from factory to home has become digitized and more granular, the point of delivery becomes an important feature of the "goods" themselves, as well as a basis for the evaluation of delivery workers and other selves involved in supply chains. In short, the ontology of goods and services, and of transactions, is decentred to encompass explicitly traceable and economically valuable relations with users/buyers. The experiential reception of goods and services had always been a target for marketing specialists; now it is a product in itself. And the self that gives feedback is constituted as an economic agent-user of the platform.

Platform People and Self-Tracking

The multidirectionality of feedback discussed in the preceding suggests that the ultimate or master "user" is the platform itself, the machine to which multiple human bodies are attached and which provide the feedback for system regulation and control purposes. On this view, to configure the user in Woolgar's sense is also to configure humans as a good economic actors and as good feedback machines and as mini-platforms, a theoretical inversion that evokes by analogy the world depicted in the film *The Matrix*. This "inverse theorizing" of the notion of platform is directly relevant to relational theories of the self. As a thought experiment, albeit an extreme one, it can be proposed that human selves are constituted as platform-like cyborgs or "platform people" (i.e. they are the dividuated nodal points for multiple applications and trace production via buying, selling, feedback, and profiling). Dividuated platform selves in this sense are the conditions of possibility for platforms to function; to continue the analogy with the film, they are its energy source. Furthermore, as discussed earlier in this chapter, there is evidence that humans are drawn or pulled towards these evaluative infrastructures and their machineries of feedback and ratings. Selves are shaped to a greater or lesser extent by a desire to be visible and to be rated, although we should not overstate the strength or hegemony of the formative role of these feedback mechanisms. Indeed, empirically there is likely to be a crowding and fragmentation effect in which the formative power of any single one is diminished. Nevertheless, it can be proposed that there is a digitally enabled web of practices, what we might call a kind of *evaluative habitus*, in which a single human being is dividuated as a rater of others and is rated by others across many different activities. If it is reasonable to propose this idea of "platform personhood" as a placeholder for this mix of mutually reinforcing orientations towards both the giving and receiving of feedback, one important further elaboration is needed: the phenomenon of self-tracking.

It is a short step from being rated by others to rating oneself. Indeed, similar digital affordances underpin the rating of products and services and self-rating, which is especially evident in the development of biosensors and how they underpin the forms of self-tracking (Nafus, 2016). There now exist all manner of devices that can be attached to bodies and which provide a means for detailed monitoring, tracking, and tracing of activities, such as running and walking, and their biochemical impacts, such as calories burned and much else besides. To this digitally enabled quantification of bodily functions must be added the "vanity metrics" on social media websites and other measures of sociality in the form of hits and likes, as well as the tracking of many forms of performance, from savings and investments, to the research citations of the impactful researcher in our vignette. All of these things set in motion practices not only to curate individual performance in quantified terms but also simultaneously to constitute accounts of the self as performing well or badly according to an ethic of self-responsibility (Lupton and Smith, 2018). Such practices of curation form and reinforce a disposition that might be called "data hunger" (Fourcade and Johns, 2020) as a feature of "metric culture" (Ajana, 2018), namely a desire for "quantified" representations of self (Swan, 2012, 2013; Lupton, 2016c) and the presumed potential for control that they bring. A further development of this curation of numeric representations of the self takes the form of app-supported "dashboards" of multiple metrics, trends, and visualizations. They constitute personalizable accounting statements that can be continually monitored, much as a formal organization would do. Indeed, as organizations become de-centred by data (see Chapter 4), so too do people as they track multiple dimensions of their performance.

Foucault's (1988) work on "technologies of the self" reminds us that practices of self-formation and advice on conduct reach back centuries to ancient Greece. He explores the history of notions of "knowing oneself" and the more elusive Socratic idea of "care of the self". He argues that the former anticipates not only the Cartesian epistemology of the self discussed earlier in this chapter, but also religious projects of asceticism, self-denial, and orientation to others. Foucault's problem was how to understand "care of the self" as practice, and this remains a pertinent issue in the setting of digitally enabled technologies (e.g. Aycock, 1995), especially self-tracking. When experience itself can be registered and tracked as the "performance" of a dividuated self to be rated and improved, the distinction between "knowing thyself" and "caring for thyself" becomes a distinction between Cartesian introspection/meditation, and an ethical project of the self and its relatedness to others and codes of conduct. Technology-supercharged capacities for self-knowledge via tracking devices may be accounting mechanisms that are antithetical to any "care of the self" as an ethical disposition, depending on whether they generate thick or thin relationalities of self (i.e. accounts for self-knowing without caring). Hence we must come back to what is at stake in traceability complexes for the accounts we live by and that somehow frame the selves we become, relate to, and care about (Vollmer, 2007).

The Accounts We Live by Revisited

In the previous section we considered three related pathways or vectors by which the generation of digital traces of bodily actions are recursively formative of selves defined by a disposition to self-track: profile generation, feedback-enablement, and self-tracking. Each pathway is slightly different, populated by different devices and underpinned by algorithms in different ways. Profiles arise in part from logics of security, perhaps most obviously in instances of state control (e.g. Egbert, 2019; Aho and Duffield, 2020). They also emerge from projects of economic security, such as credit rating (Millo et al., 2024) and recommender platforms that economize users. Yet, the recursive reinforcement of constructed profiles as "data doubles" is never deterministic, as Hacking (2002) has demonstrated for the categories that make people up. Profiles may become embedded in institutional categories with organizing power (e.g. motor insurance), or they may be transient and fluid as the context of their emergence changes (e.g. social media). Profiles emerge from traces of behaviour, which may or may not be extracted with consent, and in turn they enable tracing and tracking of the human attached to the profile. For the feedback pathway, selves as users are theorized in a more active and explicitly consensual way, choosing to provide or withhold feedback. Yet emerging mechanisms for rating raters and gamification are systemically significant and draw human users into the digitally enabled feedback culture. In turn, this drives the formation of an evaluative disposition of a certain kind in which experience and feelings can be registered and made visible. In the self-tracking pathway, this evaluative disposition turns in on itself as digital technologies and a range of devices enable the quantification and tracking of all manner of bodily activities. Now the dividuated self becomes the human correlate of the de-centred organization (see Chapter 4).

These three pathways for self-formation in the digital age are not proposed to be unique or mutually exclusive; they are a snapshot. We should be cautious about generalizing; technologies, including accounting technologies, have never been monolithic determinants of the human or what we call the social. Reflexive relations to new technologies are always evident and we should be wary of all-embracing claims about the perils of automation, although they may be compelling in some cases. Furthermore, it would be theoretically contradictory to emphasize the fluidity of self, on the one hand, while arguing for a new essence of the human generated in the digital age, on the other. So the rise of digital technologies for self-tracking is best regarded as a field in which new relationalities with distinctive formative potentials are emerging (Neff and Nafus, 2016).

With this modesty duly noted, digital technologies also force us to confront the big question as to whether new kinds of people, more cyborg-like, are being created from the human entanglements in traceabilty complexes suggested by the three pathways. We are now in a position to track not only parcels, aircraft, and our children but also calorific intake, pulse rate, steps, personal net asset value, distance walked, and much else. We can build our own personal regimes for monitoring others and ourselves; and the vignette of the impactful researcher suggests that the life and career of a social scientist is lived more by reference to specific constructions of performance and transparency than it ever was. We can make ourselves traceable—indeed we often desire this—in ever greater detail. And we can therefore build multiple "accounts" of ourselves to ourselves—the accounts we live by—in a way that previous generations never could. If it is true that organizational actors do in some way feel "pulled" by accounting representations of performance, which become social facts to which they orient behaviour, then how much more likely is this when they are also engaged in multiple practices of self-tracking beyond the formal workplace?

Here, finally, is the telos of our journey from relational theories of the self, from general ontology to an economized self, constituted by profiling, feedback, and self-tracking. That these practices are forms of accounting with formative and generative potential for selves is uncontroversial and is consistent with earlier studies of the role of accounting. Accounts can take many specific technical and institutional forms and purposes, but they commonly consist of trace-based representations of an activity of interest, primarily for a party with an interest. Yet these three practice clusters or pathways also suggest that there are some systematic shifts in the very idea and practice of accounting that have already been hinted at in prior chapters. To conclude, we now theorize this shift in the accounts that we live by in terms of three mutually reinforcing transformational themes: *tracking as value*; *organized interiority*; and *pervasive performing.*

Tracking as Value

In Chapter 1 it was postulated that traceability is a value or logic that is increasingly visible and which can be mapped in terms of three broad sub-logics of quality, security, and discovery. Yet, as previous chapters have argued, tracking in the basic sense of being able to identify and follow objects and people through space and time underwrites the operationalization of these values. In our digital world, the capability for such tracking has greatly expanded, as have the potential objects, which can now be digitally marked and made "trackable". Indeed, as studies of self-tracking and the quantified self reveal, the objects of tracking are not only the ontologically secure furniture of our daily experiences, such as motor vehicles, products, and people. They also include a growing array of qualitative objects of concern, such as health and sociality, which can now be constructed as objects, precisely quantified, and tracked across time. In short, traceability as a value is in a process of becoming predominantly realized in practices of tracking, which in turn constitute an expanding world of trackable things.

This ongoing shift towards, and salience of, tracking as a logic of organizing is not only technological in nature. It is not simply a product of technical affordances. Rather, it represents an intensification and valorization of ambitions that have a longer history than the digital age. It represents a socio-materially formed disposition that has primitive roots as early humans negotiated and operated to survive in demanding and hostile natural environments but which has, over time, acquired some epistemological dignity within biopolitical projects to know and study human populations. It also originates in, and continues today as, an epistemology of security, of knowing the location of enemies of the state and, as we continue to observe, constructing such enemies in the process. Tracking as surveillance and observation is deeply embedded in many practice fields but is becoming less implicit and more visible as a value, not least in multiple forms of self-tracking accounts.

In Chapter 1 we developed a working distinction between accounts-led tracking and tracking-led accounts. The idea behind the former is that the tracking of transactions in an audit trail is a means to a larger accounting purpose, such as accountability for economic and/or social performance. With tracking-led accounts, tracking becomes valued not as a forensic record of the past but as a generative-orientation to possible futures, both organizational and personal. Much of what we would call self-tracking is a form of tracking-led accounts production, and the paradigm is the personal dashboard that tells me not just how I have done, but which necessarily situates the self in a world of performance that demands projection in the form of future improvement. Relatedly, the temporal rhythms or speed of tracking-led accounts and their dashboards have increased the electronic organization of time (Erickson and Wajcman, 2022; Rosa, 2010). In effect, tracking-led accounting for personal performance is "always on" and close to hand via the mobile phone.

The proposition, already stated in Chapter 1, is that a systematic shift is taking place, away from the relevance of accounts-led tracking to tracking-led accounts. While the latter is far from being a fully automated social order (Stiegler, 2016; Fourcade and Johns, 2020), it is likely that digitalization is changing relational webs of self-constitution and sense-making by expanding the portfolio of accounts through which a more porous organizationality is constituted (Chapter 5) and through which new human orientations and dispositions are generated. Furthermore, whatever the precise mechanics of disposition formation, the accumulation and multiplication of orientations to ratings and metrics in personal life potentially define a shift in the relational constitution of selves, from a mix in which physical proximity to and interaction with other humans play a central role (cf. Garfinkel, as discussed in Chapter 1) to one in which possibilities for continuous tracking of the human body are becoming more salient (Lupton, 2016a; Esposito and Stark, 2019). Accounting began with tracking using traces on clay tablets, and from these beginnings have emerged elaborate architectures of accountability and obligation. In the digital age, accounting is becoming tracking once more, not only as a prosthetic to human memory but also as a register of performance. Tracking could not become this value or logic with such strong organizing power if humans were not somehow pulled towards it as a form of primordial accounting.

Organized Interiority

Accounting derives its meaning and purpose from the production of representations that mediate, connect, and construct entities (Miller and Power, 2013). Yet this relationality can take many different institutional forms, sometimes as explicit accountability relations between agencies that, either legally or by expectation, are obligated to give an account of themselves. Such accounts are never complete or perfect—quite the opposite—yet they play a role in constituting the "organizationality" of organizations and in underwriting institutional attributions of actorhood and responsibility to them (Butler, 2005; Bromley and Sharkey, 2017). To say that organizations are impossible without accounting is not a claim about choosing US GAAP for external reporting or the role of balanced scorecards in management decision-making. Rather, at this level of ontological argument, accounting is understood as the general capability of an organization to represent and memorize itself, and thereby to persist over time and space (see Chapter 5). For example, financial accounting is a form of accounting by which organizations have a distinctive kind of institutional life both in, and constitutive of, capital markets.

These highly institutionalized forms of accounting hardly seem relevant to the idea of the accounts that humans live by, yet they are. Garfinkel's interactive and relational approach to the reproduction of social order was discussed in Chapter 1 with the intention of not only broadening the notion of accounting but also grounding it in human interaction. Garfinkel wanted to understand how our continually sustained social reality works. This was his ethnomethodological project, namely to document how, in our encounters with others, and our processing of cues and traces, including bodily movements and facial expressions as well as speech in specific settings, we make up forms of mutual accounting over space and time. Much of this micro-accounting is what today is called "sense-making". It often remains tacit and unstated and generates sufficient mutual understanding for coordination and semi-consensual continuation of interaction (Vollmer, 2019). Accounts in the sense of explicit reasons emerge when such mutuality and implicit consensus are disturbed. As noted in Chapter 5, for Garfinkel and those he influenced, documents and records were also important elements of this ongoing construction of social and organizational worlds (Garfinkel, 1967; Smith, 2001). Imperfect and humble forms of record keeping support the accounts by which organizations and their human members generate distinctive relational orders in and across work settings. Formal and abstract practices of accounting become progressively layered onto these primary orders and begin to acquire normative autonomy and an expertise-base that aspires to disconnect itself from the organizational everyday. Yet, these more visible accounts, which seem to make the organization legible to itself, also depend on the invisible relational orders of the humans and scripts that support them.

Understanding this relational embeddedness of organizing has been one of the most significant research themes in organization studies and economic sociology over several decades, and the co-development of organizationality and accounting has been an important strand of this work. For example, studies have shown that organizational accounts do not only presuppose an organizational entity but can be powerful practices for generating new kinds of entity and new organizationalities that align with their accounts (Hopwood, 1983; Hines, 1988). Hence it is almost true by definition to say that accounts and organizations co-develop. This co-development is not always smooth or consensual—quite the opposite. To a greater or lesser extent, human members of organizations pay attention to, are changed by, react to, and resist new accounting forms, not least those which reflect new conceptions of organizations as economic entities, especially but not exclusively evident in programmes of reform in the public sector (d'Astros and Morales, 2024).

The many studies of what we call the "push" and "pull" of accounts remain implicitly wedded to the formal organization as their frame of reference. With few exceptions, the relevant human self in these studies is characterized as a worker, a manager, a supplier—in short, an "organizational" actor-category of some kind. What we might imperfectly call the extra-organizational or "private" conditions that might impact the push or pull of organizational accounts is relatively unstudied, with the exception of critical accounting studies of gender and race (e.g. Annisette, 2017). Hence, analysis of the accounts we live by seem to have been restricted in scope to the human experience of accounting in the workplace.

The dualism of organizational and private life, which has enabled the former to be a discrete field of study, has been progressively eroded not only theoretically by many critical scholars but also empirically by the emergence of platforms as new organizational forms, discussed in Chapter 6. Not only are humans attached in many different ways and intensities to platforms spanning what we might traditionally describe as work and leisure, but forms of accounting have also become disengaged from traditionally bounded hierarchical pathways (Kornberger et al., 2017), a disengagement that has spawned waves of experimentation and exchange between the notionally private and public levels. Information is understood to flow in more lateral and multilateral ways to and from humans who can be thought of as both inside and outside an organization. The explosion of micro-practices of self-monitoring and tracking discussed in this chapter symptomize this blurring of the personal and the organizational, the private and the public. As Day and Lury (2016) argue, such distinctions are challenged and reworked by the growth of biosensing technologies. The boundaries of the public and private, the organization and its environment, machine and nature are being deconstructed in the very design of sensing devices (Nafus, 2016) and notions of "interiority", "privacy", and "intimacy" are no longer secure reference points. Indeed, it is argued that a new "politics of interiority" (Ball, 2005) is emerging from the final break with the Cartesian myth and the recognition that interiority is not a given but a stake in a struggle with machines and their controllers. These sensibilities are also entangled with a reactive explosion of interest in privacy, in the right not to be known, and in exposing practices of data misuse (Veliz, 2023).

Such an emergent politics of interiority is necessarily also a politics of the explosive expansion of self-accounting. As self-tracking practices transform more aspects of our lives into a performance to be monitored, the distinction between public and private becomes meaningless. It is ironic that, in a period when many corporations are engaged in extensive programmes under the umbrella of ESG to value their employees, to invest in their welfare, and in some sense to recognize their humanity in discourses of happiness and well-being, many of the same human employees are also engaged in multiple and parallel self-tracking practices. We might even say that as organizations are becoming more human, at least in attribution and aspiration, humans are becoming more like organizations, via the intensity of their investments in self-tracking. So we need to re-theorize the very nature of the pull of tracking-led accounts in the digital age. We need to move beyond a conception of *singular* disposition formation in relation to a *singular* accounting practice towards a conception of a far more crowded but complimentary portfolio of orientations to different accounts that may vary in their content as *tokens*, but which represent a *type* of accounting that exerts a common and complimentary pull, namely the pull of self-tracking as a value or logic, rather than its specific form. The hypothesis is that while we may be dividuated by a plurality of digital entanglements and their implications for the dynamic constitution of selves with cyborg-like features, humans also have a general disposition in the sense of a pull towards what these entanglements have in common, namely tracking. The logic of tracking as such is the source of the pull, no matter how seemingly weird or private its objects and concerns, and humans are embedded in its multiple tokens in the digital age. But what is the source of this unbounding of accounting and the multiplication of tracking-led accounts? The answer has something to do with the manner in which the very idea of "performance" itself has also expanded and transformed.

Pervasive Performing

To locate any activity under the category of performance is a cultural act, expressive of a certain kind of social order in which the activity is made visible to others and becomes an object of evaluation against some form of standard. Hence we can say that the notion of performance is always inherently normative; it implies the potential, if not the actuality, for intervention and reform (Nafus, 2016, p. xvii; Leonardi and Treem, 2020). The category of performance also necessarily implicates selves who perform, selves that we might call social and organizational actors and who operate on the various "stages" that define scripts for appropriate performance (Goffman, 1959). Indeed, the notion of performance has evolved beyond its theatrical metaphor to become almost self-evident to the extent that humans, at least in some parts of some societies, concern themselves with the performance of nations, organizations, and themselves. Performance norms are all around us and the question of "how am I doing?" has become existential. Yet, this expansion in performance as an object, the potential performance of everything, has not evolved in a technical vacuum. It has emerged in conjunction with the changing technical means, the accounting and statistical practices, which play a critical role in constituting performance and transforming it into an object capable of being captured, traceified, and tracked over time. Indeed, performance must be understood as essentially, if not always explicitly, in its pure formality as a time series that supports the comparison between past and present and which can be narrated as an "account". Hence, the self-tracking self also projects itself as an externalized time series of traces, connected by memorizing devices and metrics and assembled into narratives of self and organization.

The onset and expansion of digital technologies has undoubtedly transformed the means of registering and tracking performance, making it more efficient from a record-keeping perspective. But there has also been an expansion of the scope and range of performance as an object; more activities can be constituted as discrete performances to be evaluated by metrics in every area of life (Strathern, 2000a; Shore and Wright, 2018, p. 15). The effects of this postulated expansion of the logic of performance are especially evident in self-tracking practices. For example, it has been suggested that the digital multiplication and increased granularity of vectors of personal performance are generating new and extreme forms of neoliberal individualization, which reinforce ideals of self-managing an entire life (Lupton, 2014).

Ideals about how selves should perform are not new. It is the elaboration and expanded scope of performance in the digital age that is new. Performance is relational in its grammar: "A performs B for C" even if A and C are the same human. Yet the expansion of performance objects also marks a shift in the mix of relationalities that constitute self, and therefore a shift in the mix of the accounts we live by, from a grounding in the hermeneutics of interactive sense-making to that of device-mediated individually focused dashboards of metrics. This shift has been underway for many years and subject to extensive analysis and critique by scholars of new media. Yet in self-tracking metrics, and the individualism of performance that they engender, it finds its paradigmatic form. Notwithstanding critical discourses about addiction and control associated with social media, online gambling, gaming, and other digitally accelerated activities, there is also an ongoing shift in the ontology of relationalities that constitute selves, from networks of dialogic humans and things to monad-like domains populated by multiple vectors of performance. While performance objects have always implicated practices of tracking, digitization enables them to be increasingly tightly coupled, not least because the distinction between performing and gaming, between public work and private pleasure, is breaking down (Whitson, 2013). Practices of self-accounting have always existed, but they now assume ever greater significance as a mode of trace*ability* (i.e. an ability for selves to track themselves and be tracked by others). "Smart" devices act as the technological conditions of possibility for the expansion of performance, including the optimal management of time as a kind of meta-performance (Hassan, 2003; Erickson and Wajcman, 2022), and thereby underpin the systemic shift in the mix of relationalities that constitute selves from other humans towards the devices through which performance can be experienced and enjoyed. This can be theorized as a shift from *thick* to *thin* relationalities of self.

The mutually formative nature of the technology-human nexus is already well understood by historians and sociologists of technology. And if one is fully relational about both technology, digital or otherwise, and about the self, then neither can have an essence and each must be situated in their social and cultural dynamic. Furthermore, new technologies, from the printing press to the automobile, and from the radio to the television, have always engendered criticism about their risks to the human soul. Digital technologies seem to be no different in this respect, although the speed, scale, and precision of their effects add something to the critical discourse. Yet, without overstating the case, it is proposed that tracking as a value is generating an ongoing shift in the portfolio of relations that make up people. Humans have always developed reputations in social settings, have been givers and receivers of evaluations, and have sought to manage their lives and conduct. But the digital apparatuses for doing this have undoubtedly changed the scope and scale of possibilities for each of these practices. While digital technologies cannot entirely de-situate the human, notwithstanding the unfolding promise of machine learning, it seems that we must also re-theorize the very notion of the "situatedness" of practices to take account of these new formative conjunctions between relationally constituted dividuals and the designed agency of the machines that produce traces of the self (Murray, Rhymer, and Sirmon, 2020).

To summarize: it is proposed that the accounts we live by and through which selves are constituted are subject to (at least) three co-related and mutually reinforcing transformations that expand with the avalanche of digital data. First, tracking has become an explicit organizing value or logic to which humans are drawn, towards which they form dispositions and from which they derive pleasure and security, as well as performance anxieties. Second, the specific manifestations of this logic are multiple, meaning that humans form themselves across plural relationalities, not in a singular binary manner. Accounts are therefore unbounded in that digitization enables and represents many different vectors of performance that render conventional distinctions between work and leisure, public and private, work and home, at best fluid, if not analytically redundant. It is not that accounting as experienced in the workplace spills over to the "private" sphere, but rather that there is an alignment of performance-tracking clusters that transcend and dissolve such distinctions. The experienced plurality of these performance-tracking clusters in turn reinforces the general disposition or pull of tracking as a value. Third, there has been a dramatic expansion in the very idea of performance itself, which now encompasses new objects and concerns embedded in profiling, in feedback as a form of evaluation, and in practices of self-tracking enabled by biosensors, wearables, and other devices. And at the centre of this new world of pervasive performance sits the personalized dashboard.

Conclusions

It is far from new to suggest that the human self is not an essence. Indeed, the word "self" is a more a label or placeholder for questions about relations, rather than being a referent for a kind of entity. These many questions motivate and pervade the arts and the humanities in general. Furthermore, as noted in this chapter already, the notion of self competes with many other labels with overlapping but different nuances, appealing to different intellectual webs and social scientific traditions as well as to different models of the person and the nature of the human condition. Try as hard as we might to resist them, we are beings who make distinctions in language—between self and other, mind and body, society and nature, and many others. The terms of these distinctions are being continually reworked. They can be historicized, politicized, and deconstructed in many different ways but often re-emerge in new forms. Even when they are fictions, lacking in origin and grounding as post-structuralist theories tell us, it seems as if we cannot write coherently about anything without such distinctions and cannot do without their manifestation in scripts to organize core aspects of our collective life (e.g. to write laws, collect taxes, be good "performing" workers, and so on). Given all this, theories of the self are fraught with the risk that they are muddled simplifications from the outset. They are also beset by a fundamental tension between theoretical sensibilities that entirely de-centre the self into a multiplicity of specific relations—"dividuation"—and those which somehow try to preserve or presuppose a stable core as coherent subject that "enters into" different relations.

Notwithstanding these analytical tensions, in this chapter it has been proposed, albeit at a considerable level of abstraction, that there is some consensus about the relational formation of the selfhood of human beings, understood minimally as a collection of orientations and dispositions. In this sense, it might be said that we are all relational theorists of the self (and organizations) now. The key issue, which defines the concerns of this book, is the nature of the formative relationalities between accounts and selves and how this portfolio of relationalities may be shifting in the digital age. Drawing upon examples of profiling, feedback, and self-tracking, it has been argued that the human self is increasingly and formatively orientated or pulled towards tracking as a value, is entangled in a plurality of tracking practices and the variable pull of their accounts, and experiences an expanding reconfiguration of activities under the category of performance. In short, this chapter proposes that tracking is a value with multiple manifestations through which performance is defined and represented in accounts. These are the tracking-led accounts and their dashboards that we increasingly live by.

There may or may not be a radically new kind of person or self under construction in the more recent years of the digital age, but some cultural effects of the contemporary economy of trace-enabled tracking are evident. First, while the ubiquity of digitally enabled feedback may lead to survey fatigue and lose momentum, it also points towards the "look at me!" society (Lyon, 2018) generated by a technical capability for conceptions of performance to move well beyond the fluid boundaries of formal organizations. The human self has always sought to have its story, its account, heard. Now the means exist for the proliferation of accounts on an almost unimaginable scale. Second, we must always keep in mind the two-sided nature of the digital trace-enabled self. On the one hand, as has been argued in this chapter, this involves at least the pull and increased orientation of the self to digitally produced traces as representations of its performance. Whether this process is fully recursive and formative is an empirical issue, but there is little doubt that "dashboards" of various kinds are prominent features of human self-accounting—academic readers need look no further than their Google Scholar profiles. On the other hand, the underlying traces of self-tracking activity, the keyboard strokes, the biosensing, GPS location data, and the like, can be co-opted by organizations as valuable assets for profit and risk management. They may be utilized by organizations to track employees and create behavioural visibility, or by states for a variety of social control and security purposes. Hence, it is impossible to discuss self-tracking practices and shifts in the relational constitution of the self, without recognizing that the accounts we live by are both outputs from, and inputs into, powerful organizations.

Chapter 8 Summative Propositions

The following propositions point to the self-formative nature of accounts under conditions of advanced digitalization:

1. **Relational theories share a broad anti-Cartesian consensus but vary in terms of the strength of their de-centring of the self.**
2. **Selves are constituted to varying degrees by relations to technologies of quantification in general and accounts in particular.**
3. **Individuals form themselves and are formed as they are immersed in the webs of traceification, datafication, and accounting that generate the facticity of individual and organizational performance.**
4. **Accounts are formative of self by virtue of the pull of their representations through which the self encounters and intervenes in its "data double".**

5. **Three critical vectors of digital trace-enabled self-formation are: profile construction and curation; the self as feedback machine; self-tracking and the data-double.**
6. **As the self generates a disposition towards tracking, the latter is increasingly valued as an end rather than as a means.**
7. **Selves are formed in relation to multiple accounts that blur boundaries between organizational and private life.**
8. **Digital trace production for self-tracking has expanded the reach of performance as a normative category demanding monitoring and improvement.**

9
Platform Science, Digital Positivism, and "Accountics"

Overview

When it comes to tracking people, viruses, and carbon and to tracing chemicals in foodstuffs, the air, and the sea, the natural sciences play a critical role in investigation and testing. Indeed, for the many traceability complexes whose primary purpose is to ensure the quality and safety of food, or the security of the public via the forensic analysis of crime scenes, scientific practice is central. Yet, relatively little has been said so far about *discovery* as a value-purpose or logic of traceability in its own right. Hence, in this chapter we address how traceability is implicated in the generation of new knowledge and the implications of this for the accounts we live by. To recap a point made in Chapter 1, our framing of discovery as a "logic" is very different from Popper's notion. Rather than being a *methodological* logic of conjecture and refutation, it points to the socio-material organization of traceability in the production of new knowledge.

The objective of this chapter is to explore whether the postulated shifts in the accounting and governance mix towards tracking, as discussed in earlier chapters, are in any way reflected in shifts in science and knowledge production. The thesis is that a related shift is becoming evident in the trajectory of the social sciences in the form of "digital positivism", which can be understood as an epistemological variant of traceification. We might put the shift in a stylized way as follows: in the old economy of traces of the audit society, public scientific practice primarily was required to be more transparent and accountable (Power, 1994a). This generated a societal demand for demonstrating the impact of science and, in so doing, most likely shifted some research agendas towards impactful and more easily fundable activities. Under conditions of the new economy of traces—we reference this loosely as "surveillance capitalism"—these effects intensify and radicalize, not only with the advent of research rankings, but also by transformations in the empirical basis of science towards a positivism of digitally produced data.

We begin with a brief review of positivism and its critics, derived from the history and sociology of science. In particular, counter-positivistic theories of scientific practice are reviewed, drawing on Rheinberger's (2011) thesis about

Economy of Traces. Michael Power, Oxford University Press. © Oxford University Press (2026).
DOI: 10.1093/9780197681527.003.0009

"data-driven" research in the life sciences and Knorr Cetina's (1999) study of high energy physics (HEP). The latter develops the notion of "epistemic culture" to characterize the extensive human and technological machinery of "big science". It is proposed that both these cases, while different, are manifestations of what we can call "platform science". When we turn to the social sciences, it is evident that, while philosophical positivism may be dead, "digital positivism", as the machine-based traceification of empirical phenomena, is on the rise and is closing the "distance" between scientific and managerial practices, both of which increasingly share the epistemic orientation of the data sciences. As digital traces about more aspects of human behaviour can be "datafied", they constitute both an expansion and a radical behaviourist intensification of the empirical domain of social science.

The idea that forms of social scientific knowing about organizations and managerial forms of governance and control are increasingly convergent and symbiotic is not entirely new. Foucault (1970 [1966]) argues that what he calls the sciences of the human have their origins in projects of control. Indeed, from some of his writings, he evidently regarded the social sciences as always in some sense "post-human" in nature. Furthermore, there has long been a schism within the social sciences between reductive, large data sample approaches amenable to an array of statistical techniques, and more contextual, case-oriented analyses of human practice, such as ethnographies. Digital transformations of social phenomena are not the source of this schism and its periodic *Methodenstreit*, but they have raised its stakes as more areas of social life become amenable to datafication. While many researchers welcome this augmentation of research capacity, it is also argued that these same developments reconfigure and potentially homogenize conceptions of the empirical, and narrow the scope of theorizing (cf. Anderson, 2008).

The general discussion of digital positivism and social science then moves to the field of accounting, an academic discipline that is a variable combination of both practitioner pedagogy (e.g. rules for the construction of accounts) and the social science of the production and effects of accounting numbers on markets, organizations, and individuals. In this chapter, the notion of "accountics" is borrowed and repurposed to characterize a convergent hybrid of these practice-facing and science-facing aspects of accounting, a convergence due to their increasingly common orientation to, and entanglements with, data science. The hypothesized rise of accountics as a practice-research complex is argued to have potentially significant implications, both for the conduct of research and for the accounts we live by. The argument is not that some innocent and pure independence of social scientific research is being displaced by the rise of digital data and advances in machine learning. Rather, we use the imagined category of "accountics" to suggest an emergent trajectory for the social sciences. The analysis of digital positivism provides a useful critical optic on this trajectory.

The construct of accountics also suggests that the accounts we live by are becoming increasingly tight combinations of operational tracking and performance monitoring, both for individuals and organizations, and this is consistent with the speculative arguments for "platform people" in Chapter 8. Hence, a shift in conception of the empirical in social science correlates with a shift in the nature of experience itself. Finally, the chapter suggests elements of a counter-science to "accountics" in the form of a critical traceology, of which this book is a preliminary exemplar.

Traceability and Science

In Chapter 2, it was argued that the production of empirical knowledge has its foundation in the traces of the world revealed to humans in direct experience and then progressively mediated by instruments and the highly organized practices of science. Hence, we postulated that the broad purpose motivating the systematic production and processing of such traces could be understood as one of "discovery" in the broad sense of generating new facts, theories, inventions, technologies, and their applications for benefit (or harm). Discovery is a logic that mobilizes scientific practice, understood in general terms as organized collective work to produce and process the primary empirical matter—the traces—from which new associations and theories can be developed and tested.

It is difficult to imagine science in its empirical form without the idea of a natural world that is somehow independent of our theorizing and which constrains what we can say about it. Indeed, notwithstanding extensive mediation by instrumentation, we find it hard to think of scientific practice in the absence of such an empirical referent. The production of traces and their datafication generate this primary empirical referent as the "exteriority" of the world to which science is oriented. Yet, even if this broad view of the conduct of the practices we call "science" can be agreed, there has historically been disagreement about the status of these traces and their referentiality. One view is known as "positivism", which, as we argue in this chapter, is not just a philosophical position but becomes relevant to understanding the dynamics of the economy of traces and the accounts we live by.

Positivism and Its Critics

Early conceptualizations of traces as "input"—the primary stuff upon which empirical knowledge is constructed—are varied. For Hume, such traces are what he calls "impressions" (Hume, 1955). For Kant, they are a manifold of sense-data requiring organization by the human mind into experience (Kant, 1978 [1787]).

For Husserl (1970, p. 9), despite its evident technical success, there is a "crisis" of science, namely its positivistic self-understanding that "decapitates" the philosophy on which it stands. And for Peirce, much influenced by Kant, traces are the varied indices that connect cognition to a world and are the essential specific components of experience from which humans can generate universals (Peirce, 1957). These and other philosophers provide different but overlapping accounts of traces, understood as that which is "given" to us in experience and which ground the limits of the empirical. In particular, phenomenology as a project has endeavoured to pay close analytical attention to this elusive givenness of experience and its experiential structure, which permits us to operate in a spatio-temporal world, making sense of both it and ourselves (Zahavi, 2018). Notwithstanding the differences between all these philosophical accounts, it is as if any system of knowledge requires points of reference that are beyond question, beyond interpretation, and which somehow underwrite the "exterior" character of the world that its produced knowledge can be "about". To be empirical is, by definition, to pay close, systematic attention to the force of this exteriority.

Variants of "positivism" are more radical and reductive versions of empirical sensitivities. The concept of positivism has a complex history coinciding with the origins of philosophy of science as a discrete field of systematic study, origins often attributed to the reflections of Ernst Mach on his own scientific endeavours (Ray, 2017). Versions of positivism range from strong ontological claims about the foundations of all knowledge in sense-data, to weaker claims about the nature of proper method. These different versions share an anti-metaphysical orientation and are "demarcationist" in intention, that is, they seek to distinguish sharply between proper science and non-science (or nonsense). Philosophers like Carnap went further to develop positivistic programmes for language itself modelled on mathematics, and Ayer (1952) famously popularized the so-called verificationist theory of meaning, namely that an expression is only meaningful to the degree to which it is verifiable in experience. This view suggests that meaning is determined by the traceability of terms to sense-experience as a form of what we might call a "meaningfulness-audit". This latter form of positivism controversially rendered statements about art, religion, and many other fields of human activity literally meaningless. In general, positivism is anchored in the view that traces or data are all there is, and can be taken as "raw" and "given" for the purposes of science.

As the field of philosophy of science developed, strong versions of this positivist programme began to falter for many reasons. In particular, it became more evident that it was difficult, if not impossible, to distinguish between the conventional (value-based) and non-conventional (factual based) aspects of scientific practice (Feyerabend, 1968). Furthermore, the positivist foundational conceptual apparatus of "experience", "sensation", and "fact" was argued to be both metaphysical and semiotically imprecise, much as was argued for the notion of "trace" in Chapter 2. Philosophers like Sellars (1963) argued against what he called the "myth of the given", which had animated various schools of positivism, and this critique coincided with a revaluation of the pragmatist theories of science articulated by Peirce, Dewey, and James. No longer to be understood as a muddled form of positivism, pragmatism emerged as a coherent anti-foundationalist and naturalistic philosophy. Knowledge was to be understood as holistic, habitual, and grounded in practical contexts of experience, reasoning, and action (Rorty, 1980). This post-positivist turn in philosophy of science did not deny the origins of knowledge in our contact with a world that is prior to any conceptualization of it, but it disputed the coherence of the positivist analysis of the nature of that contact as somehow unmediated, thereby ignoring the deeply conventional, collective, and material aspects of knowledge production.

The truth of empiricism, which becomes distorted by positivism, is that there is a world that constrains what we can say about it and do within it. We cannot easily do without this notion of a world that is different from and exterior to our desires and actions, even in the case of the sciences of social life. So if it is wrong to think that data about the world are simply given as self-evidently meaningful, there is nevertheless something that resists our practical and cognitive efforts and which gives science and many other practices their purpose in seeking to reveal and discover this nature, and whose resistant quality is a benchmark for exteriority and objectivity. Positivism as a philosophical position gives a too simple and definitive account of this exteriority. As we see in the next section of this chapter, more critical accounts lead away from the idea of a primitive given and towards the individual and collective organization of human practices. Indeed, that which is supposedly "given" (i.e. data) ends up as more complex, mediated, fragile, and elusive than commonly imagined. It is very far from being a fixed and ready-made resource (Alaimo and Kallinikos, 2024, ch. 5).

It must be recognized that the notion of positivism is used in many different ways, often loosely and pejoratively in disputes about the status of social sciences. Furthermore, to be against positivism as it is often framed is not to be against careful data collection and analysis; it is not to let "anything go" in scientific practice. Rather, positivism is best understood as a *meta-view* of science and knowledge production, a meta-view that is often implicit and presumed in the conduct of many disciplines and which underpins the operating assumption that the "data" of those disciplines provide *atheoretical* and unmediated contact with reality. While this meta-view was the target of post-positivists like Quine, Feyerabend, and Sellars, many natural and social science practitioners are also reflective enough to know that the traces that count for them as data are often mediated by instruments, are theory-laden, and are "proxies" for reality. Yet, knowing this, they work even harder at interpreting what they "observe", and do not give up on it as data.

Nevertheless, we should be cautious about the claim that positivism as a meta-view of knowledge and positivism as a practical commitment to data-collection practice are two entirely different levels of reflection. The question for the science-traceability nexus is how a meta-view might influence first-order practice. Can what we understand as the world become "positivized" so that our sense of the empirical is exhausted by, and restricted to, data as the given? In such an imagined case, positivism is no longer a meta-view of science that is mistaken. It "becomes" true because the practice is dependent on digitally constituted data. In other words, a version of philosophical positivism that the world as data is simply given and the practice of science become convergent because they share the same digital ontology of the empirical. Before we can develop this convergence thesis further, we need to review reactions to positivism, especially relational theories of knowledge production.

Science in Its Context

Post-positivist critique within philosophy supported a renewal of the history and sociology of science. Sociology and history were no longer limited to studying the behaviour and biography of scientists but began to address core epistemological issues in science and the production of knowledge. Foundational work, such as Shapin and Shaffer's (2011) study of Hobbes and Boyle, set the tone for close attention to how the logic of discovery in Popper's formal sense is embedded in, and abstracted from, the rich *context* of science and to the implications of this for how we might rethink the social foundations of epistemology. Instrumentation and laboratories came into view as important socio-material and epistemologically-loaded settings for experimentation that had been black-boxed by more traditional philosophies of science. There was an intense research focus on the practice of scientific research, not to undermine the authority of science but to reveal the strategies for establishing the *credibility* of scientific claims. Indeed, in the work of Latour, Callon, and others, the relation between credibility and truth is provocatively inverted: science is not credible because it produces true statements, but rather truth emerges from the production of credibility. From this point of view, philosophies of science that provide formal reconstructions of its method (e.g. Hempel, 1968) are also abstractions from practice. For a new generation of historians and sociologists, the cultural prominence of science was something to be explained rather than implicitly assumed. Furthermore, with this practice-turn in science studies, it became possible to focus on the infrastructural organization of science as networks of human actors and machines engaged in scientific work and animated broadly by programmes aiming at discovery, not as a timeless logic of method but as the contingent organization of credible practice.

The intellectual terrain of this emergent field of science studies combining history, sociology, and philosophy is complex and characterized by its own internal controversies about the role of so-called "social" factors in the production of scientific knowledge. Latour and colleagues articulate an explicitly relational sociology of science in which the role of the analyst who wishes to account for the production of scientific truth is to trace the critical relations that connect different actors and contribute to the stabilization of knowledge. For this brand of analysis, the task is not primarily to trace scientific claims back to their origination in sense-data or to the methods of positivism, but to understand how scientific facts emerge from an array of material objects and inscriptions that connect different actors within and beyond scientific practice. The approach highlights the agentic power of both humans and things, between which acts of translation and allegiances contribute to (temporarily) stable networks for generating general forms of knowledge (Latour, 1987, 1999). And like Hilgartner's theory of risk objects, discussed in Chapter 7, as knowledge claims become accepted, the supporting network of actors traced by the analyst-sociologist—the socio-material infrastructure—disappears from view and only the science "itself" as "rational" activity is left, recorded in accounts of scientific findings.

Latour's approach to science has been controversial for several reasons, not least because of the role he provides for non-human actors in networks and how they are ascribed with the intentionality normally reserved for humans. These and other issues, such as the label of Actor-Network Theory (ANT) as a shorthand for this work, need not detain us. Latour's primary methodological and ontological vision is that the networks that support scientific practice are in principle traceable and can be made visible in analytical accounts that enable us to understand how science produces its distinctive kind of truth over time. It is also because science practice is constituted by relations, documents, and scripts, like organizations in Chapter 5, that tracing them is possible. Such secondary accounts of science are "risky", says Latour, meaning that they are open to rebuttal, but there is no "social" substrate upon which science is grounded, as the so-called "strong" programme of sociology of science has appeared to maintain (Barnes, 2013; Bloor, 1991). Rather, as we saw when discussing theories of self in Chapter 8, there are only relations connecting a multiplicity of so-called "actants". Making science traceable in Latour's sense involves recovering and revealing critical dynamic connections, especially what he calls the "circulating reference", between things, inscriptions, and people, and showing how, once a network has formed and stabilizes, it becomes, like Star's notion of infrastructure, invisible, leaving only "facts" that seem natural.

Traceability as a methodological principle for analysing knowledge production has an ontological side. Latour's anthropological view of science also requires that networks are defined by a prior population of durable traces. These traces may be varied and idiosyncratic, such as formal documents, photographs, newspaper articles, speeches, minutes of meetings, and all manner of durable remnants of persons, things, and actions within and beyond the spatial confines of the laboratory. They are material features of the world and so it is not too fanciful to describe Latour's relationism as being a form of "liberal positivism" insofar as all manner of things can feature as "given" referents in a network. For the purpose of tracing the network of knowledge production, the analyst must be initially agnostic about what counts as a relevant trace that could feature in an explanation of the production of scientific credibility. As the subtitle of *Science in Action* suggests, such an analyst must "follow" engineers and scientists through society; tracking them is a methodological imperative. The overriding project is to make the network of scientific knowledge production traceable and visible beyond the official story of its production, including sanitized accounts of its rational methodology. Latour's conceptual language for understanding scientific practice is strategic in its connotations, using terms like "mobilization", "enrolment", and "alliance-building". The very possibility of facts that can be true or false are the hard-won outcomes of network building by scientists themselves, including their work to efface and make the network invisible so that the production of knowledge appears in a specific light (e.g. as a discovery). Historically, public demonstrations of science have also played an important role in network expansion and knowledge stabilization (e.g. Shapin and Schaffer, 2011). The job of the analyst is to re-trace and recover this network-building work and thereby to open the "black box" of science. It is perhaps a fine point but, for Latour, this is not a "social" theory of science since the very notion of the social is itself made up from the activities of actors to connect their immediate localities to others (Latour, 2005).

In conclusion, we can say that Latour's relational theory of science is motivated by traceability as a method of discovery, but this is the "discovery" of the network of relations that enable scientific work to count as producing discoveries. Traceability is methodologically important to this specific way of doing the sociology of science and knowledge. It follows that traces of the real, in the sense of what is produced and counts as data within a network, are also critical resources and an ontological presumption, for *both* the scientist *and* the network analysis of science. From this point of view, as Latour insists, there is no great difference in principle between the work of the scientist in building connections and that of the Latourian analyst seeking to understand and account for that connection-building activity. Both are in the game of producing traces and building relations to support their respective claims to know something. The scientist wants to know about the world. The Latourian scholar wants to know about how the scientist's claims to know about the world are produced.

Platform Science

In the spirit of Latour's analysis, Rheinberger's (2011) study of the life sciences argues that scientific practices are increasingly "trace-generating experimental environments" (p. 240). He points to such trace production as the "shadowy end of knowledge-making" prior to ordering into datasets, the analysis of patterns, and the production of facts. However, he also argues that, in the context of the life sciences, this trace-data-fact-production process, which can be understood as a scientific form of traceabilty complex, is changing its nature as the imperatives of experimental tracking "force" nature to generate traces of itself. Furthermore, in the digital age this imperative has been radicalized. Traces no longer have any primitive epistemological status but are generated and pooled as "datasets", and as resources for modelling and pattern analysis. This digital datafication of experimental science means that data has become a "resource rather than a result" (p. 346), a resource that is increasingly self-referential: "The data, mediators between traces and technophenomena, have proliferated and created a world of their own" (p. 346). This datafication of science has two important and related consequences. First, it leads to a reconstruction of the very meaning of the empirical, which we discuss later in this chapter. Second, it suggests that science increasingly has the properties of a "platform" in which scientists are its users.

The platform-like character of science is even more evident in a setting such as high energy physics (HEP). In her classic study of the organized context of HEP, Knorr Cetina (1999) identifies a world of "signs and secondary appearance". Here the objects of science only reveal themselves via expensive detectors for very short periods of time and must somehow be captured as traces for further work. The detector itself, which produces the traces, becomes a focus for enquiry and investigation to identify and interpret distortions. As Knorr Cetina puts it, "In these experiments the universe of signs and traces is overlaid by a universe of simulations and distortions of signs and traces" (p. 49). The traces of nature are produced with enormous background noise; they do not speak for themselves, but their signification is a matter for further productive work. Instrumentation in this setting is subject to numerous specific distortions, not least among which are known as "ghost" or false traces, which are also the focus of considerable experimental and interpretative work. In such a world, the commonsense idea of "measurement" that implies autonomous, definitive calibration of independently observable and representable phenomena is hardly meaningful. To use the terms introduced in Chapter 1, the status of these traces as data, the very possibility of their datafication, hangs in the balance. Unlike Rheinberger's (2011) thesis about the trajectory of datafication in the life sciences, experimental traces in HEP are often not yet mature enough to become pooled as data. But like Rheinberger, Knorr Cetina suggests that HEP processes signs and traces in which the empirical world as we commonly understand it is experientially remote.

Knorr Cetina argues and demonstrates that the world of HEP is a self-enclosed system or context with a distinctive "epistemic culture", to be understood as a machinery of knowing and related practices of processing experimentally generated traces. The very meaning and nature of the empirical and therefore of "data" are internal to these epistemic cultures that comprise: "specific constructions of the referent, particular ontologies of instruments, and different social machines" (p. 3). While tracing is a method for the Latourian relational analyst of science as discussed earlier, for both Rheinberger and Knorr Cetina his position is too pluralistic and liberal in conception to shed enough light on specific modes of trace production and their shadowy referentiality in machineries of knowing (p. 9). These machineries are a form of traceability complex linking traceification, datafication, experimental tracking, and knowledge production. Moreover, specific "epistemic subjects" (as the procurers of knowledge) are derivatives of its machineries; scientists are "enfolded in construction machineries" that are themselves constructed (p. 11). This user construction echoes the discussion of platformization in Chapter 6 and the general proposition that systems and apparatuses "make up" and "construct" their users (Barad, 2007; see also Millo et al., 2024, on machine learning).

It is proposed that HEP is a case of what we might call "platform science". Indeed, the traces of sub-atomic particles discussed by Knorr Cetina and what has come to be called the "digital exhaust" of human behaviour have much in common as features of platformization (see Chapter 6). Both require highly specialized apparatuses for capturing and processing that which is fleeting. Both forms of trace are embedded in, and are constructs of, the practices that work on them and subject them to further analytic processes that filter out noise and produce something regarded as knowledge—new "particles" or patterns in the economy with predictive and therefore economic value. And both settings for platformization demonstrate how the exteriority of their worlds of interest—sub-atomic processes and human behaviour—becomes internalized and re-constituted in a way that produces highly specific ways of being empirical, eroding the distinction between trace and data. Yet there is also an important organizational difference between these manifestations of platformization. HEP is more or less contained in elaborate, if very expensive, laboratories. Indeed, it is only possible in such restricted settings. In contrast, the industrial harvesting of traces by digital technologies is becoming pervasive and, as noted elsewhere in this book, many scholars are fully embarked on the task of understanding this new digital order and its implications for all aspects of our lives.

This brief and selective excursion into the philosophy and sociology of science underscores how the very idea of the empirical and our cognitive grasp of it is neither as simple nor as singular as the positivistic viewpoint would suggest. Traces of nature, and their datafication and signification as knowledge, must be understood as highly mediated by specific machineries of knowing and modes of discovery that are generative of the natures that they investigate. Even the world of HEP, which seems epistemologically closed in on itself and almost phantasmagoric in nature, is a node within, and dependent on, a larger web of conventions, concepts, theories, and instruments and thereby subject to "spiralling of nested feedback systems" (Arbib and Hesse, 1986, p. 9). There is therefore no simple, one-off experimental "confrontation" between the world and reality. There is only the "mangle" of practice (Pickering, 1993), which is increasingly underpinned by digital data.

As previously suggested, Knorr Cetina's conception of epistemic culture has affinities with the idea of "traceability complex". Both concepts reference bundles of material practices and machines for trace production and use, and the forms of connectivity that enable them. For any practice machinery, there must be a form of trace construction/collection by which actions can be made to refer to, be about, and be connected to, a world of interest that is, notionally at least, independent of it. As already emphasized in this chapter, the difference between what we think and do, and a world that is often resistant to us, is fundamental to our notion of the "empirical", even though philosophical accounts of this resistance and the pushing back of the world can vary. We refer to this resistance generally as the "exteriority" of the world as experienced by all kinds of practitioners, including HEP scientists, accountants, risk managers, and many others. These worlds overlap and share more or less material and linguistic structure. So, even when it seems otherwise, the world of HEP is not hermetically sealed off from that of accounting. Yet the manner in which their respective forms of exteriority are manifest in the things that count as traces is enormously varied—from the bad weather that destroys our crops to the invoices that make an economic transaction durable in space and time, to the data pools that inform life science experiments, to the ghostly traces that interfere with HEP experiments.

Traceability as Method and Practice

Knorr Cetina's emphasis on the need for more specificity in the analysis of epistemic machineries also prompts a broader discussion of the tension between relational theories of knowledge production for which traceability is a *method* of analysis, and traceability as a feature of specific *practices* oriented to quality, security, and discovery. This tension is best demonstrated with an example. Let us assume that a published scientific outcome in behavioural psychology is being challenged by several researchers who are unable to replicate the results. Notwithstanding the difficulties in the idea of replication itself (Collins, 1992), a forensic audit of the underlying data is conducted and there is evidence that some of the data has been falsified. In short, there is a prima facie case for academic misconduct, with implications for retractions and much else. Events like this have had an impact on the future conduct of science and journal policies. Researchers are increasingly required to be more transparent about both their methods and any underlying data, and for reputational reasons they are also strongly motivated to do so. In short, the quality, in the sense of the basic veracity, of science has been put in question, and scientists must generate what is in effect an *audit trail* (Chapter 2) connecting their results to their primary source data in such a way that it is legible to an independent evaluator. This is a trail that connects "texts to things" (Latour, 1987, p. 64). Scientific discovery must be made traceable by scientists themselves in order to demonstrate its quality. Existing and new research processes will need to be traceified to enable this traceability of discoveries, understood as a mode of accountability. A form of tracking as quality assurance is becoming a prominent feature of epistemic cultures, alongside research ethics and laboratory safety protocols. Hence, the practice of science is increasingly being required to be traceable in order to be accepted as legitimate.

Relational theories of science, such as Latour's, do not have their sights set directly on this problem of scientific accountability and potential fraud in science, despite an emphasis on understanding how credibility is constructed. The main interest is in how traces of various kinds—not only those that might become datafied—contribute to and are assembled in networks to support knowledge production. Such knowledge may prove to be fraudulently generated, but this is a less prominent concern in his work than the general network model of credible science creation, of discovery.[1] It is an open empirical question as to whether the traces used by the analyst to understand the forward building of knowledge will be the same as those used forensically by a potential data auditor to verify that "good" science has taken place.

This tension between traceability as *method* for analysing the production of science as discovery and traceability as a *practice* of checking the quality of science is a tension between the observational modes of Latour's analyst and, say, a data auditor. On the one hand, it is unlikely that the audit trail of traces used by an auditor will correspond exactly to the traces of a Latourian analyst engaged

[1] However, science studies scholars are highly motivated to analyse the production of fraudulent science since many of the processes of interest will be potentially more visible in post-fraud documents and enquiries. They are also committed to the principle of symmetry by which true and false knowledge creation must be studied in the same way.

in building risky accounts of how, in a specific setting, scientific production of new facts—discovery—happens. On the other hand, it is also unlikely that they will have nothing in common, especially in the digital age. After all, as noted in Chapter 2, Latour's notion of the "circulating reference" of inscriptions has many affinities with, and helps us to theorize, the notion of an audit trail that might be used by an auditor of science. And, we can only speculate, based on similar comments, that it is most likely that Latour himself would have expressed the issue as follows: "my analyst who checks and connects inscriptions is very like your auditor, and your auditor is very like my analyst i.e. a good relational theorist who produces risky accounts. Why do you want to make so much of this distinction between traceability as method and practice, and to draw sharp lines between analysts, auditors and scientists themselves?"

One could of course imagine these different roles in one hybrid individual, the reflective manager-scholar perhaps, but equally they can be distributed across different agencies working to different protocols and time scales. The tension, if such exists, is therefore an empirical question. And if we return briefly to Knorr Cetina's study, it seems most likely that the HEP scientist will be the least positivistic in orientation about the traces produced by her experiments. Datafication in this setting is hard interpretive work. In contrast, both the Latourian analyst and the quality auditor need, above all, durable traces to make scientific practice traceable for their respective purposes. This positivistic aspect of the trace becomes especially significant as we next consider the social sciences in general and accounting in particular.

To summarize the argument of this section: We began by reviewing different positivist theories of science, how they conceptualize traces as given, and the role of verifiability in thinking about "data". Then we explored reactions to positivism that argue for more relational and co-dependent conceptions of data, theory, and instrumentation. There is no unmediated, primitive connection to the world, and even the very idea of sense-data is constructed. Latour's distinctive relational approach expands the relevant ontology of science to include all manner of human and non-human agencies, especially documents, involved in its production. For him and his followers, it is the production of credibility that underpins the production of scientific facts. Knorr Cetina builds on this relational conception of science and its work in the setting of HEP but argues for the specificity of machineries of knowledge production, which have been conceptualized as having platform-like qualities on which different "apps" may run: experiments, quality control, training, ethical clearance, and so on. Throughout the discussion of HEP, the notion of the trace and conceptions of traceability are implicated in scientific activity, not only as a general method of analysis qua Latour but also, according to Rheinberger (2011, p. 346), as "primary entities which populate our infra-worlds of knowledge" orientated ultimately to the production of knowledge, or what we call "discovery". Traceability is therefore implicated in knowledge production in several different ways: via instrument-mediated traces or encounters with the world that may or may not have a grounding in sense-data; via the construction of such traces as data that can enter into postulated causal relations supporting modes of scientific inference and the production of explanatory accounts; and via the variety of quality control and auditing processes that increasingly characterize the accountability of scientific practice and connect it to the values of quality and security. Traceability is therefore always multifaceted. It is both analytic method in Latour's sense, a method to discover the nature of scientific discovery, and also practice in which scientists produce and use traces to generate new associations (accounts), and in which auditors (most likely other scientists) check the quality of their discoveries.

Digital Positivism and Social Science

Debates about the nature of what have come to be called "social" sciences have a long and complex history. From time to time, these debates have crystallized in the form of *Methodstreite*, or disputes about proper method, and there has been some visible polarization of views (Adorno, 1976; Lepenies, 1988). Put simply, and a little crudely, on the one side are those who argue that social science can and should adopt as far as possible the methods and discipline of the natural sciences, as they understand them. On the other side are those who argue that social science deals with the activities not of atoms or particles but of human beings engaged in making sense of the world and whose actions and behaviour reference systems of meaning. Social science must therefore have its own method for understanding meaning-saturated contexts and adopt interpretative approaches that draw from disciplines of textual interpretation—hermeneutics and its variants—rather than the natural sciences, whose real methods are in any case poorly understood.

This polarization, by which strong forms of positivism sought to demarcate meaningful "proper" science from nonsense, is closely related to what C. P. Snow has called two cultures (1998). This not only is a meta-debate conducted by philosophers but also is manifest in the conduct of social science itself. At the level of research practice, the debate is often about the relative merits of quantitative and qualitative methods, and of large data versus small case studies, involving detailed arguments and intense disputes about robustness, replicability, and generalizability (Pratt et al., 2020). A version of demarcationism has therefore taken shape in a number of social sciences and is most usually attributed to economics and the use of quantitative methods for investigating social and economic phenomena. The implicit positivistic view is that there is only one way to do social science, grounded in "hard" data as variables and using statistical modelling and econometric analysis to generate meaningful and defendable associations between these variables. These views on method have generated an institutional tension in the organization of social scientific knowledge between the perceived cultural priority of the quantifying social sciences so-called, and qualitative research practice grounded in close contextual situated observation and interpretation. Notwithstanding the frequent celebration of "inter-disciplinarity", this divide persists in the academy, not only as an implicit issue of method, but also as a form of tribal partisanship.[2] Quantitative social research is variously accused of being: not as scientific or robust as it imagines; guilty of "physics envy"; and based on a misunderstanding of the nature of the natural sciences. Ultimately some of these arguments at the level of method are motivated by concerns about the perceived intellectual dominance of quantitative research and the apparent refusal by some of its practitioners to accept that there are other ways of doing social science.

These debates, or some version of them, will be familiar to many academic readers. However, our intention is not to take sides or to clarify their contours in more detail and with greater nuance, although it is most likely that the debates have become falsely polarized by mutual misunderstandings and confusions. Rather, they provide a pre-text to our focus on how digital technologies are generating a distinctive form of digital positivism of the trace that is impacting the idea and practice of social science.

Digital Postivism

Mirowski's (2002) historical analysis of the rise of modern economics argues that it grew from post-war elements of operational research, the mathematics of game theory, and cybernetic thinking. These elements constituted what he calls the underlying "machine dream" of economics and related disciplines. He argues that economics emerged as a post-human "cyborg science" that had the ambition to evacuate human behaviour from its conceptual framework. This ambition was diluted somewhat by the behavioural turn in the 1980s (e.g. Thaler, 2016). Whatever the merits of Mirowski's analysis, the material conditions for empirical economics to realize this trajectory have come about in the expanded ability to capture traces of human activity in digital form by machines (Hayles, 2008; Zuboff, 2015, p. 81; Evangelista, 2019). It is proposed that the datafication of these traces is not simply an expansion of research capability

[2] The tension is, in an important sense, asymmetric. It is mainly an object of commentary and critique by qualitative researchers who are driven to look for new and explicit models of "robustness" (e.g. Gioia et al., 2013).

but also generates new operational conceptions of the "empirical", just as Knorr Cetina and Rheinberger show in the cases of particle physics and life science, respectively.

Debates about what it is to do empirical social research and changes in the sites of knowledge production have a longer history than the recent explosion of digital data production (Adkins and Lury, 2009). For example, Savage and Burrows (2007) identify a crisis for sociology arising from the fact that increasing amounts of relevant data are being produced outside of universities via surveys and other instruments (an argument made before the explosion of "big data"). They argue that sociologists are losing any claim to superior social knowledge production. In other words, outsiders are doing the tracing of social phenomena. Latour, as noted earlier in this chapter, is adamant that this claim to a special kind of "sociological" knowledge of the social is mythical; the empirical is a composition of relational traces produced by all kinds of actors, and the professional sociologist has no epistemic privilege. Such reflections on the changing nature and status of social scientific empiricism direct our attention to the broader machineries and infrastructures of knowing in the digital age, to the forms of platformization in which traces are mass produced, and to how the datafication of such traces spans both social science and managerial control. In effect, we must consider the nature and effects of digital positivism.

In the first section of this chapter, we discussed the nature of positivism as a specialist philosophical or meta-view of science and empirical investigation. Positivism is opposed to the idea that anything is hidden; the surface of things is all there is, and data is that which supports meaningful statements of facts. While these claims have become easy to challenge and problematize, as Rheinberger (2011) notes for the life sciences, digitalization is generating a new kind of substantive positivism of the trace. This is not the positivism of Humean impressions or sense data, as Mach and those who followed him argued, but is a direct result of traceification practices enabled by digital technologies themselves and their role in redefining the nature and boundary of the empirical. Digital positivism is machine-enabled, with much broader reach than the complex instrumentation of HEP and other specialist laboratories. It is implicated in reshaping how humans experience social life (see Chapter 8). And, in common with older versions of positivism, that which is not captured digitally as a trace, and which cannot become data, is therefore "not-given". Hence, digitalization inherently generates a division between that which is digitally enabled, visible, and meaningful, and that which is non-digital, non-visible, and meaningless—a division that is also found in control systems for workers (Newlands, 2021). In short, digital positivism is not so much an emerging feature of social scientific practice, but a pervasive force of transformation in the phenomena of interest, which extends both to managerial practices of control as well as to the social sciences. As noted at various junctures in this book, a differentiating nuance of the "trace" as compared to the idea of data is that it points to an absence. Traces are always "traces of . . ." and this remains true even when we consider digital traces that have been "scraped" or which represent the "exhaust" of human behaviour. Digital positivism erodes this nuance—they become one and the same. The trace and its organized datafication are all there is; there is no absence, nothing is hidden, and context itself is only meaningful in digital form.

It must be emphasized that the digital production of traces and their datafication are largely seen as a great opportunity for social scientists and a source of scientific innovation with enormous potential benefit, not least in medicine. Many researchers of society are also excited about the methodological innovations and opportunities that it makes possible as new regions of human activity become amenable to granular data formation and related analysis (Grimes et al., 2023). Furthermore, the distinction between qualitative and quantitative research is being eroded as texts, conversations, organizational routines, and many forms of behaviour can be captured in digital form, thereby changing the scale, scope, and methods of social inquiry. Corpus linguistics and the analysis of word frequency, co-location, and many other analytical categories are not only made more efficient under conditions of digitization but also give rise to a new and powerful granularity in the production of knowledge. Von Brocke et al. (2021) see these developments as heralding a new future for the process science of organizations. Organizational routines now increasingly generate digital traces that are in principle rich data sources for the analysis of such routines, obviating the need for embedded observational tracing and laborious mapping of actions over time.

More generally, organization studies are turning to advanced algorithmic methods, such as machine learning, which are being imagined as useful supplements to theorizing (Leavitt et al., 2020) and as resources for simulation studies. The underlying argument is that artificial intelligence will generate, rather than replace, demand for higher-level critical skills (Larson et al., 2024). Among other innovations have been netnographies (i.e. online ethnographies for studying computer-mediated interactions; Kozinets, 2012) and, familiar to many readers, the use of Zoom and related applications to conduct and transcribe interviews, which was especially advantageous to qualitative researchers during the pandemic. It therefore seems entirely logical that, as the world organizes itself around digital technologies, social scientific methods respond and seek to be adequate to the study of this changing world. From this point of view, the explosion of data in digital form simply augments empirically oriented social science by expanding datasets as resources for enquiry. The use of heterogeneous data was once the province of the skilled social scientist investigating the nature of social structure, but big data analysis has greatly enhanced the ability to find significant structuring patterns (Hannigan, 2015).

This expanded scope of digital data is favourable to quantitative researchers as "data sciences" in various forms become central to the conduct of the social as well as the natural sciences. For many researchers, their research was always defined and limited by the availability of datasets of various kinds; building such datasets "by hand" was regarded as worthy but hard work. So digitization has greatly expanded the availability of the "dataset" in the form of off-the-shelf data packages and has made significant incursions into the territory of qualitative research, as noted previously. And empirical phenomena, as the objects of social scientists' interests, are increasingly constituted (i.e. digitalized) by these digital datasets. For example, as discussed in Chapter 8, the classification of different "social groups" is no longer solely the product of careful observational work and innovation by sociologists, but is also revealed inductively by algorithm-driven analyses of digital data. This results in "dividuation" in which multiple human identities and groupings can be derived. While such data-driven identity pluralism is in fact philosophically consistent with debunking the myth of the unitary Cartesian self, it also potentially makes the reflective human actor increasingly redundant in social research (Ruppert, Law, and Savage, 2013, p. 29). Furthermore, digitally supported simulations are becoming compelling modes of analysis because the situations being simulated are themselves saturated by digital technologies. We might put this provocatively by suggesting that there is a digitally driven convergence between simulation and reality as all manner of activities are understood in terms of their digital traces. This points to the ubiquitous digital traceification of modern life.

The circuits by which the social sciences have emerged from, and are connected to, the world of their applications have taken many different forms across time and space (Foucault, 1970 [1966]; Lepenies, 1988). Yet we may be entering a phase when these circuits become tighter, narrower, and more pervasive as they become grounded in common data architectures and methods that define the limits of the empirical and therefore the possibility of what, in Foucault's (1980) terms, it is possible to say: "It is a question of what governs statements, and the way in which they govern each other so as to constitute a set of propositions which are scientifically acceptable" (p. 112). In such a world governed by digital data, which is by no means yet fully an actuality, the very conditions of possibility for the old disputes about method in the social sciences—so-called *Methodenstreite*—no longer exist. All forms of knowledge production participate in digitally mediated data, leading not only to the de-centring of organizations, as discussed in Chapter 3 (see Alaimo and Kallinikos, 2024), but also to the accelerating de-centring of knowledge production from its conventional sites. A tight fit between the conduct of social science and the social world itself has long been an implicit aspiration of the more control-oriented parts of academic fields, such as operational research, management, accounting, finance and economics, and of course cybernetics itself. Now the conditions of digital positivism make these aspirations possible with the consequence that many regions of qualitative field research have become amenable to the methods usually reserved for the analysis of a limited range of datasets. The rise of digital positivism also has implications for organization theory (Bechky and Davis, 2024).

The Data-Driven End of Theory

We can think of theorization as a fundamental process of conceptual reflection and imaginative "sorting out" in the face of phenomena and events that seem puzzling (Swedberg, 2014, p. 8). The nature of this puzzlement can vary a great deal. It can arise from a striking and specific empirical anomaly. It might arise from an intuition about what we take for granted, forcing the question, "how did we get here?" Or it might just arise from unsettlement in communities of enquiry leading to experimentation with new ways of looking at a world of interest (Reed and Zald, 2014). In short, the impulse to theorize is a critical feature not just of science but of human experience itself, even if the nature of such theorizing is varied and even contested. Theorizing can also be something we hardly notice. As stated in Chapter 2, practical accounting is simultaneously practical and theoretical via its abstract classifications. Yet theory can also be an activity in its own right. It organizes and sets up empirical enquiry not only in terms of developing precise testable hypotheses of the "If . . . then" kind, but also by the generation of general models and conceptualizations of mechanisms and processes (Cornelissen, 2017). Theory is always in this sense critical even if it is not "critical theory", as this is normally understood by sociologists. Theories can also be taken to be "explanatory" on their own terms when their models of the world have sufficient correspondence to how things are. Game theories and related simulations have much of this quality. And some theories have been shown to be performative to a greater or lesser degree as their abstractions become validated by human behaviour (Marti and Gond, 2018).

Stiegler's (2016) concerns for the "proletarianization of theory" in the digital age, and the question of risks to theory and reflection, are shared by many others. For Bechky and Davis (2024), the industrialized production of papers in journals and the use of machine learning in the conduct of research threaten the nature of theory work in organization studies. They call for a reassertion of craft and community in the conduct of research. Similarly, Cornelissen et al. (2024) explore the prospects for organization theory given the rise in use of large language models (LLMs), which seem likely to replace many kinds of data analytics, especially in scientific and medical fields, where synthesis and pattern formation greatly augment practitioner diagnostic capability. Yet they argue that, notwithstanding these benefits, LLMs are not "meta-representational" in the sense of allowing for human reflection and creating new connections. The theoretical outputs of LLMs are stale, predictable extensions of existing literatures that are unable to blend ideas in the surprising ways associated with advances in organizational theorizing. While it is claimed that LLMs can get close and be useful as theoretical heuristics (Grimes et al., 2023), Cornelissen et al. challenge this augmentative argument and suggest that the use of LLMs in social science may reconfigure and displace scholarship in subtle ways, leading to a levelling-out of theory work and a kind of epistemological capture: "algorithmic models drive and limit the range of what we understand phenomena to be, and what in turn we can theoretically say about them, at the expense of what else we might otherwise theorize about organizations and organizational life" (p. 11).

This theoretical impoverishment and epistemic narrowing are in Stiegler's sights when he talks of proletarianization. It is arguably also an effect of the "digital undertow" (Orlikowski and Scott, 2023) by which powerful citation systems like Google Scholar exert a drag on the conduct of research (Bechky and Davis, 2024). Indeed, we can postulate that the "flattening" process in the setting of organizational governance also extends to the social sciences. Digital positivism manifests itself as progress and augmentation but gradually undermines theoretical work, potentially reducing the social scientist to an auditor or facilitating operator of the LLM, a hollowing-out of expertise that we also see in non-academic settings (Millo et al., 2024). And yet, theorizing in general begins with a critical attitude to the world of appearances. It is a disposition, both individual and collective like any other, which involves standing back and bracketing that world in order to understand its history and conditions of genesis. It is the very opposite of positivism.

"Digital positivism" is a trajectory and not yet a fully determined reality. An agenda for a *critical traceology*—to be outlined later in this chapter—would be committed to understanding the gains and losses of digital positivism in different fields and determining whether we are on the way towards a fully "post-social" social science or not (Knorr Cetina, 2001). Without discounting the many advantages and benefits of the digital revolution for how we can know nature and society, digital positivism embodies the risk of all positivisms, namely an erosion of the hermeneutic tension between data and analysis/interpretation, and a reduction of theory-building to hypothesized patterns in datasets, which might even be delegated to smart machines.

In conclusion, we have outlined what might be at stake for the social sciences when both object and method are pervaded by digital technologies and take digitally harvested data by commercial organizations to be exhaustive of the relevant empirical domain. Is the practice of social science itself becoming an epiphenomenon of the economy of traces as an infrastructure for organizing trace production for discovery, a "platformized social science" that runs plug-and-play applications?[3] Or have we suffered under the illusion of the autonomy of research from other developments in society for too long, and digital positivism is simply its necessary corrective? We address these general questions by considering the specific field of accounting research and its transformations, and invite the reader to take this case as being symptomatic of more general changes in social sciences.

Accounting Becomes a Social Science: A Brief History

Accounting is considered by many to be a practical art and therefore not research-worthy. Indeed, accounting has always struggled to establish its standing within the social sciences of the leading global universities. The reasons for this struggle are various, in part reflecting national differences in the cultural positioning of university education (e.g. Power, 2004b). In general, accounting practice developed its own pedagogy in the form of the techniques and skills necessary to be a professional accountant. The mechanics of double-entry book-keeping were an important part of this pedagogy to support and prepare students for professional practice. Grounded in assumptions about the skilled judgements of its practitioners, accounting practice could be said to be "what accountants did". In other words, while accounting itself can be said to be thousands of years old, as old as writing (see Chapter 3), it was not an especially self-reflective discipline until well into the twentieth century. An early practice text on auditing by Dicksee (1919) was organized by industry sector, suggesting that accounting did not yet have the equivalent of an overarching jurisprudence in law as a meta-level of enquiry into principles and fundamentals. In Abbott's (1988) terms, it lacked a grounding in abstract knowledge.

Yet if accounting was defined as what accountants did, universities themselves did not refrain from teaching it. Indeed, they helped to reproduce the professional field, remaining closely aligned to, even if not identical with, professional examination systems introduced by accounting associations. For example, at the London School of Economics (LSE) in the early twentieth century, accounting

[3] Digitization has enabled new research practices, such as that of "search" using an engine or platform provided by organizations like Google. This development is not without its critics: "as humanists, we need to pay much better attention to the epistemological implications of search, an entirely new and already dominant form of inquiry, a form with its own rules, and with its own notable blind spots both in design and use" (Rosenberg, 2013, p. 35); See also Bechky and Davis (2024).

teaching was explicitly vocational (Dahrendorf, 1995, pp. 205, 419). Elsewhere in Europe, business education and the teaching of economics had opened up at the end of the nineteenth century, giving rise to different traditions of business economics that slowly had implications for accounting teaching and research. As Napier (1996a, 1996b) notes, with the exception of LSE, England lacked a strong business economics orientation compared to, say, Scotland and the Netherlands, where closer ties and exchanges developed between the accountancy professions and the academy.[4]

Differences in relations between the academy and the emerging accountancy professions reflect variations in higher education institutions themselves. At one end of a spectrum are those elite research institutions with a loose relationship to the world of accounting practice and the professions. If they teach accounting at all, it is infused with the social sciences, not least economics and, more recently, finance. At the other end are those who position themselves as part of the professional field itself, servicing the industry for professional qualifications. Yet in both cases, the teaching of accounting (and finance) has become big business and a significant revenue stream for universities. Accounting students expect, and pay for, an education that will confer career advantages. Even the elite research universities cannot deviate too far from these expectations for both undergraduate and masters teaching. What has come to be called "research-led" teaching in accounting remains somewhat constrained by these expectations.

While early forms of accounting pedagogy were largely technical and uncritical in their approach, this was not true for some of the practitioners and teachers who began to worry about foundations and principles from the 1930s onwards. For example, there were debates and concerns about the nature of "income" and "cost" (Parker and Harcourt, 1969), as well as growing collective awareness of inconsistencies in accounting practice, often triggered by scandals in which accounting had somehow failed. For many years, these individual and collective reflections were mainly what is today called "normative" in nature (i.e. they developed models and conceptualizations aimed at what accounting *should be*). As Ball and Brown (1968) famously note, these approaches had an abstracted sense of what was going on in practice, and they lacked any systematic empirical enquiry *into* practice. In parallel with, and influenced by this critical-normative thinking, the policy level of the accounting profession was slowly developing an abstract knowledge base involving the explicitization and codification of the rules of practice. In the United States, accounting principles were articulated and informed the writing of standards that became ever more

[4] Among the first chairs of accounting in England was a Nobel-winning economist at Cambridge, Richard Stone, with an interest in National Accounts and little connection with the accounting profession.

specific and elaborated over time (Solomons, 1983). Authorities also sought to generate conceptual frameworks that could serve as a jurisprudential foundation for accounting (Macve, 2015). This was something that its creators imagined would ensure the consistency of financial accounting standards, as the ability to compare companies was assumed to be important for capital markets. Financial accounting was moving beyond its history as a practical "craft" to develop an abstract knowledge base, a development in which universities and researchers, as well as regulators, were key actors.

The Data Revolution in Empirical Research

While the normative-jurisprudential strand of critical thinking about accounting practice was taking shape, another important development occurred in the 1960s that fundamentally changed the nature of accounting research, namely the quantitative transformation of social sciences in general, and especially economics and finance. This transformation was enabled by the availability of data that accelerated the possibilities for statistically grounded empirical research. Ball and Brown (1968) was a seminal paper in this respect, which cut through normative assumptions about how accounting works to pose the question of its role as a source of information for price formation in capital markets. The question of whether the concept of income was meaningful or not was replaced by the study of its production and effects. This paper therefore established an "externalist" view of accounting practice as an object of study that took hold in the United States, the United Kingdom, and gradually elsewhere.[5] From the 1960s onwards, in the elite universities, the field of academic accounting began to shift as accounting professors trained in economics looked beyond the normative agenda of what accounting should be and initiated studies of the impact of accounting numbers on capital markets and management behaviour. Described as a "revolution" in accounting thought (Beaver, 1981), this empirical turn was also a turn towards the methods of economics, not in the sense of a European business economics tradition focused on the whole enterprise, but as the basis for investigating the qualities of accounting as *information* for capital market participants and contracting parties. Over time these methods, including game-theoretic analytical methods and advances in contracting theory, were also applied to the "internal" accounting of organizations, including costing and performance measurement. In short, accounting research emerged as a sub-region

[5] This paper also challenged assumptions about the usefulness of published accounts in price formation by suggesting that market prices already embody, and are "efficient" with respect to, these accounts and other sources of information prior to publication.

of economics in general and financial economics more specifically, a shift that corresponded to the transformation of business economics into finance (Whitley, 1986; Power, 2012). Today much research in accounting and finance, though distinct in many ways, draws from the same intellectual well. Accounting practice became a phenomenon or object whose production and effects were to be studied using the methods of the economic sciences: if accounting was not itself a social science, the study of it could be. From the early 1980s, practical accounting and its pedagogy begin to part company from research, generating a perceived gap between the two.

The empirical turn in accounting research was not only a methodological shift. The so-called revolution in accounting thought was also driven by advances in computerization and the availability of datasets, for example of daily stock price movements and corporate governance variables. Large volumes of public data were placed within relatively easy reach of researchers, and university departments of accounting began to invest heavily in all manner of packages to support empirical accounting research. At the same time, PhD programmes in accounting grew, and students were trained in econometric techniques in order to be able to utilize these resources and to investigate patterns and theories involving accounting numbers as variables. This avalanche of data and its growing availability generated strong "positivistic" sensibilities about the scientific credentials of accounting research. At the extreme, the meaning of accounting numbers and the possibility of better forms of accounting came to be regarded as value-laden distractions from the business of discovering patterns in accounting-related datasets—datasets that increasingly defined the boundaries of the empirical world of accounting research.[6]

Critical Reactions

At the same time as the data- and methods-driven empirical accounting research was expanding from North America, another very different development was occurring in the United Kingdom (Cooper and Hopper, 1990). With the growth of business education in the 1970s and the creation of business schools to teach lucrative MBA students, there was a need to recruit faculty to service this demand (McKinlay and Starkey, 1998). In contrast to the US academic accounting field, it was possible for sociology-trained academics to be hired by accounting and management departments, and this initiated a vibrant stream of what might be broadly called critical management studies, including within accounting (Spicer

[6] Within the elite universities, rich case studies remained an important basis for pedagogy even as research gravitated to large data analysis, generating a dualism of skill sets that leading academics were able to master.

and Alvesson, 2024). Building on a behavioural turn in accounting research, and drawing on the thought of Marx, Weber, Habermas, Foucault, and many others, as well as using ethnographic and discourse analytic methods, a more critical approach to accounting and organizational research emerged (Tomkins and Groves, 1983). Notwithstanding some ambiguity about the very meaning of "critical", this broad wave of work became part of the academic accounting field with its own research journals.[7] As with economics-based research, accounting practice was treated as social scientific object without presuming its normative self-understanding. However, the critical project was broadly aimed at understanding and explaining the implications of accounting for organizational control, managerial processes, and aspects of wider society, rather than just capital markets and their information needs (Power, 2021b). A further contrast was that this body of research drew heavily on the qualitative research traditions that emphasize close engagement with fields of practice and with the understandings and perceptions of humans in their situational context. Empirical methodologies of the field still had data in their sights, but less as a "dataset" of standardized points and more as experientially derived traces resulting from degrees of immersion in fields of accounting practice. In short, the canvas for these so-called critical approaches was large, ranging from macro-political economies of accounting emphasizing the power and ideology of the profession and the devices of accounting, to close attention to accounting practice as a local process that is made and continually remade (Chapman et al., 2009).

Convergent Positivisms

This brief history of the emergence of accounting research is highly stylized and could be further nuanced.[8] Indeed, major developments in the internal accounting of organizations, innovations in scorecards, and the rise of non-financial leading indicators have been important sources of change and expansion in accounts production (see Chapters 1 and 7). But the purpose of this stylized history of the accounting research field is to focus on the so-called "gap" between researchers and practitioners (e.g. Laughlin, 2011). Such a postulated gap is itself complex, and we should not take it necessarily at face value. Indeed, it has many faces. It is a gap that gives rise to antagonism episodically when practitioners—the large firms—complain about the lack of "relevance" of academic research,

[7] It should be noted that Ball and Brown (1968) was highly critical in substance at the time of its publication. Hence, we should resist equating critical/non-critical with qualitative/quantitative, although this equation is often made.

[8] Auditing research followed its own path with a focus on the auditor judgement process and drawing on the methods of cognitive psychology. See Power (2003).

and such episodes are more prevalent in some cultural environments than others (Hopwood, 2007). So it should not be overstated, even as it is rhetorically asserted. Here we frame the notion of a "gap" epistemologically to signal the historically different orientations of academics to practice, a difference we can characterize provisionally as "externalist" and "internalist". The empirical revolution in accounting described in the preceding can be thought of as the rise of an external "academic" orientation to accounting as an object of study. While this framing of the gap can be challenged for being too simplistic (accounting academics have been key members of policy bodies and the rise of fair value accounting reflects in part the introduction of financial theory into accounting practice) it will serve our purpose, which is to explore what happens to these two orientations under conditions of social science digitalization, and to understand the nature of digital positivism in the accounting research setting.

In simple terms, the avalanche of data made possible by the capture of digital traces of actions and activities from both organizational and so-called private settings is expanding the universe of possible datasets for investigation using quantitative methods. Taking just one example, survey techniques have become cheaper and easier through the use of digital platforms such as "SurveyMonkey". The study of practice settings and the sense-making and meaning formation of human practitioners had, until these developments, and despite the use of surveys and questionnaires, been seen as too subjective and almost "unknowable" for more quantitatively oriented accounting research, or as something requiring the painstaking collection of textual data. But with rapidly expanded capability to capture and process traces of the world digitally, idiosyncratic, subjective, and intimate features of our behaviour are becoming digitally readable. To put the point more generally, research approaches where hermeneutic sensibilities and so-called "softer" immersive methods of enquiry have been pre-eminent find themselves vulnerable to this explosion of digitally generated traces of human behaviour, and at best become reduced to heuristics. Hence, traceability as the ability to generate traces of things and events that might otherwise be transient is transforming knowledge production in the social sciences in general and in accounting research in particular. The world is both seen and experienced through a "digital prism". It is more transparent in one sense, but also less so as phenomena become their digital traces (Flyverbom, 2022). More specifically, we can postulate a nascent re-convergence between practice and academia, if not in topics, then at least in terms of the production of data and the methods of its analysis.

Advances in digitization are closing the historical gap between accounting in organizations and the social science of that accounting, a proximity of method driven by the rise of "data science" methods in both academic research and business strategy and planning.[9] This dual biography of data is hardly new. For example, an early database used by accounting researchers was *Compustat*, which was developed by Standard & Poor and began life in the early 1960s. As both capital markets and computing technology developed, such data apparatuses were commercially motivated responses to demands for credit and investment intelligence. Databases like *Compustat* also became a necessary if not sufficient condition for the empirical revolution in accounting.[10]

The wide diffusion of data-analytic methods has the potential to converge the methodological skill sets associated with the internal and external perspectives on accounting. Analytical techniques utilizing digitized data, both financial and non-financial, have become important for organizations, not least for understanding and tracking customer acquisition and retention processes, and for supply-chain logistics and management. Sources of capital-market-related data have also evolved well beyond *Compustat*, opening up new research possibilities and agendas. Sensing both existential threat and opportunity, many university accounting departments have rebranded teaching programmes to signal their pedagogic commitment to data science in one way or another. In short, we can hypothesize that there is a digitally enabled convergence between accounting practice and the social science of that practice at the level of utilizing similar analytical techniques and data sources. Notwithstanding proprietorial sensitivities about data as a commercially valuable asset, both accounting practitioners and researchers now feel the compulsion to embrace very similar apparatuses for the analysis of data. This is not a trivial observation; from the sociology of science we know that methods are not innocent applications but shape conceptions of reality and of what counts as an empirical domain capable of being investigated and known (Savage, 2013).

One small but indicative example of this postulated digital convergence was visible in a call for papers for a 2023 conference on "Emerging Technologies in Accounting and Financial Economics", which stated that it was to be held jointly by the accounting group, the finance group, and the FinTech Initiative at Cornell, Johnson College of Business, in the United States.[11] What is especially interesting here is the menu of topics and, in particular, the themes of unstructured data and machine learning. Submissions were invited to consider the significance of these techniques for "audit *practice*, the finance *industry* and for academic *research*"

[9] Arguably this has also taken place in finance as an operational science in which the methods of financial economics are used, for example, for valuation and portfolio management.

[10] Competitor databases were developed, and their classification biases and errors were much discussed (Ulbricht and Weiner, 2005).

[11] See 2023 Conference on Emerging Technologies in Accounting and Financial Economics (CETAFE), https://business.cornell.edu/centers/fintech/news-and-insights/ (accessed 9 September 2024).

(emphases added). This call for papers in 2022 for a 2023 event is in many respects entirely unremarkable and similar to many others. Yet the very same digital technologies and related sources of data are being envisioned explicitly as impacting both the practice and the research of that practice, and the ambition is to bring them into dialogue with one another. This is emblematic of the implicit normative power of digital positivism in constituting both a practical accounting object domain and also accounting research method to be applied to that domain. It is proposed that this *convergent digital positivism* is generating a new accounting knowledge hybrid that is neither just external nor internal, neither purely research nor practice. We call this hybrid "accountics".

The Rise of Accountics

In the infancy of the digital age, Lyotard (1984) wrote an essay on the "condition" of knowledge where he argued that the new "informatic" sciences are replacing truth with values of performativity and impact. Specifically he suggested that social science is becoming "operational" and "computational" in nature. This was prescient. Here we repurpose the notion of accountics to capture the sense in which academic accounting is also becoming an operational and informatic science. The idea of "accountics" was originally used to refer to the idea of a "mathematical science of accounting values" (Sprague, 1922; McMillan, 1998; Suzuki, 2007). It was grounded in dreams of computation that are now being realized in "algorithmic culture" (Dourish, 2016; Glaser et al., 2021). In effect, accountics provides an instructive example of the broader changes in knowledge production anticipated by Lyotard. The thesis is that accounting practice and research are becoming operationally oriented and convergent by virtue of the digital data climate in which they are both conducted. In one sense, this is unsurprising; one would expect accounting practice to be responsive in this way to new technologies. Yet, the idea of accountics also points to an important effect of this responsiveness, namely a levelling out of the internal-practice/external-academia distinction as it has existed at least in one form or another for many decades. Accountics refers to much more than just the entanglement and symbiosis of accounting practice and research but to a convergence in which historical tensions and perceived gaps are being erased.

What is today fashionably called "data analytics" has a long history, not least within statistics, operational research, and the management sciences. It is also a form of knowledge production and implicit reality construction in and of itself. Reality for research purposes is conceptualized in ways that are coextensive with data availability for analysis, data that is a product of the choices underlying the datafication of traces (Alaimo and Kallinikos, 2024). Hence, the data-driven organization (Chapter 5) and data-driven social science draw from the same general precepts, training, and positivist epistemology and are convergent in their orientations, skills, and the problematizations—mainly operational problematics rather than truth—that they develop for investigation, even where they may seem to be driven by curiosity alone. The so-called academia-practice gap is, if not disappearing, becoming less pronounced. While there has always been a flow of academics between universities and business, and the aforementioned gap has been less evident in MBA-focused business schools, the growth of digital data literacy is likely to accelerate the blurring of accounting academia and its practice.

Accountics as an emerging research-practice hybrid is more than just a response to the automation and mechanization of accounting practices. If we imagine financial accounting as a model of accounting in general, its stability consists in the organization of numerical economic data into categories that have become highly institutionalized. While financial reporting has evolved and refined these categories over time, the basic elements of income statement and balance sheet have remained stable. This is because accounting in this setting has been organized "from above" in a manner intended to enable comparability. The historical power of this model has been to reduce economic activity to institutionalized representations of performance.[12] In contrast, the data analytic foundations of what we call "accountics" suggest a different accounting dynamic, namely one in which patterns and categorizations emerge from the analysis of data rather than being presupposed. In this mode, accounting is to be understood not only as an elaborate record of performance, but also as the *discovery* of relationships that may be commercially valuable for their predictive properties. The engine of accounting in this mode is not an internal audit trail that is available for use by auditors, but one of many boundary-spanning algorithms that pose new challenges of auditability and are prima facie invisible (see Chapters 5 and 6). Historically, accounting practice has had a firm foothold in the past, upon which dreams of prediction have been constructed (future economic performance, bankruptcy, etc.). In contrast, the data analytic foundations of "accountics" point more explicitly to the future; it is a distinctive regime of truth in Foucault's sense, which has been many decades in formation but which accelerates under conditions of advanced digitalization. Individual academic accounting researchers are beginning to operate within an industrialized system of knowledge production in which the digital dataset shapes what it is possible to problematize, to say, and to think. This is troubling because there is evidence

[12] Famously, it was argued several decades ago that internal accounting and control were too heavily influenced by external reporting categories and had lost their relevance. Internal accounting therefore needed to reinvent itself and focus on drivers of value (Johnson and Kaplan, 1987).

that organizations which rely heavily on the data sciences tend to produce only incremental innovations; those which combine this with more qualitative managerial styles are riskier but also more innovative overall (Allen and McDonald, 2025). For the same reasons, there is a case for the potential of methodological pluralism in research as a counterpoint to convergent monotheistic research cultures.

The concept of accountics references this ongoing convergence between data science and accounting, in research, pedagogy, and practice. It is perhaps too strong to say that this relationship has been inverted and that digital data now "rule" accounting as social science (Alaimo and Kallinikos, 2024), but it is reasonable to suggest that there is a trajectory of change with momentum. Accountics is therefore like a field of force, an "undertow" (Orlikowski and Scott, 2023), in which the forms of accounting practice that validate the role of expert judgement and skilled interpretation, and the critical orientations in social science noted earlier, are being transformed by the imaginary of data sciences and their promise of the algorithm-driven discovery of impact and sources of future value.

Accountics and the Accounts We Live By

At this point in the chapter, we have progressed through discussions of positivism, to relational theories of big science, to the social sciences and digital positivism, and now to the history of accounting research and the postulated emergence of accountics as a science-research hybrid. The general thesis and provocation are this: the phenomena that the social sciences address, namely human behaviour, are increasingly constituted as traces in digital form that in subtle ways change the nature of research practice. Through these ongoing transformations, the "social" sciences are also reconnecting to their originating constitution as projects of control (Foucault, 1970 [1966]; Ruppert et al., 2013). In the case of accounting, where there were gaps and tensions generated by vibrant research communities operating independently from the practices of accounting, there is now a trajectory of symbiosis. Data science is not in this sense just a body of techniques for analysis but is also a value-system through which both research and practice are being reimagined as data-driven. But what does this mean for the overall concern with traceability and the accounts we live by?

Elsewhere in this book it has been proposed that the mix between tracking-led accounting and accounts-led tracking is shifting towards the former. While it would be too strong to suggest that the rise of data-analytic methods in accounting research is a driver of this shift, accountics and tracking-led accounts have a mutually reinforcing affinity. Tracking, as discussed in previous chapters, is dependent on primary traceification that is positivistic in nature insofar as it generates traces as durable marks of objects. Advances in digital technologies have also greatly extended the reach of traceification to an "internet of things" and thereby have accelerated tracking capability. Hence, digital positivism is the foundation of both accountics and tracking-led accounts production.

The human "giving of accounts" has always been intertwined with, and partially dependent on, forms of tracking. Hence accountics has always been latent in both research and practice since the empirical turn in the social sciences in the 1960s. Yet the rise of data science is challenging the collective identities and expertise of both researchers and accounting practitioners. It is likely that professional accountants will find the advent of digital positivism more disconcerting; theirs was always a soft positivism of numbers that left space for reflection and a market for interpretations (Gill, 2009). In the world of accountics, there is still human interpretation and judgement involved in algorithmic design and the determination of what counts as data, but these are the invisible judgements of largely unaccountable data experts. Accountics, like all forms of positivisms, is like an operational science that does not provide an account of itself; it is permeated by implicit and unwritten claims that digital data is all there is to reality and to the accounts we live by. And if we push this further, we might even suggest that its constitutive principle is this: "*to be is to be traceable*".

To conclude: a concept of "accountics" has been proposed that is intended as an exemplar of trends in social science more generally, namely that they are becoming increasingly symbiotic with the expansion of digital traces that support organizational control architectures (Chapter 4). In other words, drawing on Lyotard's insights, it is hypothesized that if we could develop a relational analysis of the social sciences over time, we would find increasing connectivity with organizational control systems mediated by data analytic practices. In addition, machine-learning programmes, as emergent non-human "users" of data science, straddle and reduce the divide between science and control, and hybridize the value-purposes or logics of discovery and security. Accountics symptomizes this trajectory of convergent forms of positivism that reconstruct the nature of the empirical world. At the extreme, just as big science becomes platformized and dislocated from nature, accountics becomes dislocated from accountability—both hierarchical and lateral—when the tracking and processing of traces have no determinate purpose or external referent. It becomes more like play, experiment, search, and activity just to see what might be "there", much as market traders are known to trade simply to find out how the market will react (Willman et al., 2006). While we may hope for the augmentation of public accountability by digitization (Raisch and Krakowski, 2021), accountics marks a shift towards, and expansion of, private self-generative forms of operational accountability (Kornberger et al., 2017).

The postulated rise of what we call accountics marks a critical underlying shift in the nature of the accounts we live by and therefore of the kinds of performance we track. It also represents a potential symbiotic transformation of accounting research into a cyborg-science that is: operations-impact orientated; dataset bounded; de-moralized (i.e. morality-neutral) while being value-laden; post-human (i.e. human motivation is an operational category); anti-intellectual (little space for reflective theorizing); and self-legitimating as a platform social science. With accountics, a traceological theorization of accounting reaches its limits in which both the world and accountability are data-driven.

Towards a Critical Traceology of Accounting

The prospect of digital positivism and the growth of operationalism in the social sciences—of which "accountics" is symptomatic—is in many respects an old problem in new clothing, reaching back to many earlier critiques of technology. For example, Marcuse (1986) identified what he called "one-dimensional thinking" as a result of the rise of positivism as the scientific organization of society. Horkheimer and Adorno (1972) distinguished between traditional and critical theories in which only the latter could break the grip of this positivism. And Habermas (1977) famously draws attention to the impact of technical progress on possibilities for practical and political reflection. Notwithstanding ambiguities in the manner in which these thinkers frame positivism, technology, and technical reason, their sensibilities remain relevant in the digital age, and are echoed in Zuboff's critique of surveillance capitalism. Fourcade and Johns (2020) argue that in the twenty-first century, social struggle is already platformized, and an operationally grounded positivism is produced by the normative elevation of data sciences over and above their augmentative advantages. This new and expanding economy of traces overflows traditional distinctions between organizational control and science, and fuels a form of digital positivism that, though not yet monolithic, has the potential to redefine both the nature of the empirical world, perhaps even behind the backs of researchers, and human experience itself. These tendencies in effect relocate the sources of meaning in social science from historically and spatially situated groups of human subjects to the aggregate patterns revealed by the analysis of large volumes of datafied traces.

Without doubt, digital positivism has an entirely benign methodological side, but it becomes problematic when it exhausts the meaning of the empirical, and when its effect is to proscribe human reflection on the nature of traces and its own conditions of emergence. Positivistic presumptions of the given close off entire swathes of enquiry, such as histories of traceification and datafication, and favour certain kinds of social investigation over others,. In response, there are counter discourses in the form of what Stiegler (2016) calls, following in the footsteps of the Frankfurt School, a "critical traceology". Such critical traceologies are already implicit in a growing body of studies of digitalization effects on organizations. They necessarily include the descriptive comparative mapping of traceability complexes, which we discuss in Chapter 10 as a form of "traceography". Here, we focus on two defining themes and problems for a critical traceology: datafication and cyborgization.

Datafication

Axiomatic for a counter position to digital positivism is an understanding of "datafication" (and traceification) as a process and of data as having a complex history of formation (Chapter 2). Indeed, the very idea of data, of the given, is much less clear-cut than positivism suggests. For example, Rosenberg's (2013) compelling analysis focuses on the history of the word "data" and related debates about its usage, which reach back to the eighteenth century. It is a word that expands in usage and is transformed rhetorically with the computer revolution:

> [F]rom the beginning, data was a rhetorical concept. Data means—and has meant for a very long time—that which is given prior to argument. As a consequence, the meaning of data must always shift with argumentative strategy and context—and with the history of both. The rise of modern economics and empirical natural science created new conditions of argument and new assumptions about facts and evidence. (Rosenberg, 2013, p. 36)

Commenting on Poovey (1998), Rosenberg also notes that many scholars have taken data to be somehow "before" and a precondition for the articulation of facts. However, while facts can be true or false, false data is still data and can circulate and have effects. So the idea of data as the given is both a necessary myth to underwrite empirical methods—we investigate nature and society "as if" there is data that is given—and also a concept with no essence:

> Even today, when we speak of data, we make no assumptions at all about veracity. Electronic data, like the data of the early modern period, is given. It may be that the data we collect and transmit has no relation to truth or reality whatsoever beyond the reality that data helps us to construct. This fact is essential to our current usage. It was no less so in the early modern period; but in our age

> of communication, it is this rhetorical aspect of the term "data" that has made it indispensable. (Rosenberg, 2013, p. 37)

Rosenberg's arguments are an implicit critical traceology. They point to the need to understand and analyse the reality-constituting functions of specific constructions of data-status, digital or otherwise. Alaimo and Kallinikos (2024) also challenge the self-evidence and taken-for-grantedness of digital data in order to analyse how the electronic capture of a raw click is an outcome of subtle and understudied formative processes. They transform "data-making" into an area of enquiry in its own right, thus challenging the seeming "hardness" of digital data and its positivistic self-understanding. They argue that digital data encodes reality in specific ways, with formative implications for meaning, cognition, communication, and therefore politics. Central to their analysis is the understanding of data "hardness" or facticity as an outcome rather than a given. This analysis confronts positivism with the formative processes that make its illusions of data fixity and stability possible in the first place. If data is now the fundamental building block of organizational and social life, then the terms of theory and critique must also evolve to understand it (Alaimo and Kallinikos, 2020).

From the point of view of these and other studies, digital positivism, like all positivisms, represents a programme to eliminate tensions in the concepts of data, to abstract from its context of production and use, and to frame it as somehow prior to any mediation, semantic or instrumental. For these reasons, as argued in Chapter 2, the notion of the trace is an attractive corrective for several reasons. As evident in the life sciences and HEP cases discussed earlier in this chapter, it retains tension by referencing the mediated nature of the encounter between knowledge practices and an empirical world that both comes before and is produced by data. In short, the notion of trace is central to the agenda of a critical traceology of this "infra-knowledge" production (Rheinberger, 2011). It helps to sustain a focus on the tensions between data and an empirical world of interest, tensions that are lost and effaced under conditions of digital positivism and the convergence of social control and scientific practice that it underwrites.

Cyborgization

A second and related constitutive theme of critical traceology has been foreshadowed in Chapter 8, namely the study of "cyborgization" processes and machine-human interfaces at both the point of trace creation and their continued use in tracking practices. Under the banner of a "material turn" there is a large body of scholarship that takes these interfaces as its primary focus, long before the explosion of digital datafication. Indeed, humans have always been cyborg-like from the moment they began to use tools and weapons for hunting, and as their brains co-evolved with technologies (Stiegler, 1998). We have conceptualized cyborgization more narrowly in terms of the processes by which humans are increasingly "plugged in" to machines. In this chapter, the thesis of a convergent digital positivism suggests that social science in general is not just becoming a cyborg science, as Lyotard and Mirowski suggest, but also requires for its operational analytics that humans are increasingly plugged into machines that can extract traces of behaviour and datafy them. In short, social science becomes increasingly dependent for its *content* on cyborgization processes. This is how digital positivism is more than a philosophical position about the status of data but something that is actively being performed.

To summarize: the postulated convergence in which digital positivism erases tensions between worlds of academia and practice, between contemplation and control, involves not just the operational framing of social knowledge in Lyotard's sense, but also its world of reference. The notion of accountics has been proposed as a symptomizing hybrid in which research and operations converge and in which the motivational and hierarchical basis for thinking about accountability is weakened. The rise of accountics is suggestive of how the relational nets of the social sciences are shifting in a manner that is symbiotic with the constitution of selves discussed in Chapter 8. Processes of datafication and cyborgization mediate this symbiosis. Hence, self-tracking and accountics have a common source in digital positivism. While it has been well known for decades that accounting has reality-generating properties to varying degrees (see Chapter 3), the notion of accountics suggests an inversion of this model and a need to understand more about how the reality-constituting effects of digital positivism shape accounting. In the concluding chapter we return to the implications of this thesis for "the accounts we live by" and hence for the lives that we lead in the so-called post-social world.

Conclusions

This chapter approaches traceability from the point of view of knowledge production. Organized scientific practices can be conceptualized as traceability complexes of a distinctive epistemic kind that convert traces into new bodies of knowledge. In this process, which realizes the value-purpose of "discovery" (Chapter 1), experiments produce traces that must somehow be turned into accepted data supporting risky scientific accounts and the articulation of new facts. But what are the implications of this focus on the various entanglements of science and traceability for the accounts we live by?

We came at this question circuitously by beginning with a general discussion of traces and positivism, followed by a review of critiques of positivism within relational theories of science and knowledge production. Studies by Knorr Cetina and Rheinberger were used to suggest that the notion of big science is productive of its own distinctive and somewhat self-referential empirical reality, a benchmark of being "platformized". Indeed, this is literally true in the case of particle accelerators where physicists must book "beam time" for their applications. The life sciences and HEP cases were used to indicate more general developments in what we call "digital positivism", and the chapter explores the implications for the social sciences in general. At the heart of the argument is the polemical notion of "accountics", which is repurposed from its original usage to exemplify a practice-research hybrid, a data-centric operational discipline in which managerial and research interests are convergent. This idea of accountics is not yet fully realized, but it points to a trajectory in which digital data acquires positivistic status as that which is given for research, without reflection on its own conditions of production and inherent value-biases. The thesis is that when such digital positivism permeates both the ontology of social facts (data) and the methodology of the social sciences (analytics), the "scientific" study of society and organizations by researchers becomes increasingly symbiotic with their processes of self-constitution and internal control by digital processes. So while the expansion of digital traces is rightly celebrated for augmenting the reach of robust social science into new areas, digital positivism is its constant shadow, representing a potentially monolithic re-engineering of what it is to do social research. At the extreme, the social scientist is reduced to the role of impact-auditor. A "critical traceology" is proposed that addresses the phenomenon of digital positivism by unpicking two core areas of its reproduction—datafication and cyborgization—where critical work is already far advanced.

Chapter 9 Summative Propositions

The following propositions point to digital positivism as a societal trajectory and as a source of convergence between social science and managerial control:

1. **Traceability is a distinctive social epistemology, a mode of knowing people, processes, and things; discovery as the production of new knowledge is one general value-purpose or logic of traceability that is typically evident in science.**
2. **Within relational theories of science, traceability is a method for analysing the production of knowledge within networks.**

3. **"Platformized" science is characterized by scientist-machine hybrids that produce mediated traces of the world for datafication and fact-building.**
4. **Strong philosophical positivism is the idea that data provide unmediated contact with an empirical domain.**
5. **Digital positivism is a version of strong positivism in which digital data operationally define the nature of an empirical domain and thereby influence research agendas.**
6. **The idea of "accountics" is symptomatic of developments in the social sciences and is postulated as an accounting research-practice hybrid that is based on increasingly overlapping data sources and methodologies.**
7. **Critical traceologies address the mechanisms and processes by which digital positivism reproduces itself, and include a focus especially on datafication and cyborgization.**

10

The Accounts We Live By

Tracking in the Trace-Age

Overview

We live in accounts and they live through us. They are the multiple narrations, theories, representations, and calculations in which we immerse ourselves. They are formed in encounters with others and organize us, even as we think we organize them. Sometimes they have the objectivity and aura of science, sometimes they affect and move us, and sometimes they are expressions of our hopes and plans. Accounts can be highly technical, on the one hand, yet also rich in symbolic meaning, on the other. They can be the preserve of experts as well as the glue of everyday human interaction. They connect us to our past, assemble histories for use in the present, and project possible futures. In doing so, they may justify, minimize, or forget forms of violence and injustice. And yet, while these accounts that we live by are undoubtedly a complex mix of value, expectation, and technique, they are also undergoing a shift that is subtle and systemic. This book locates the sources of this shift in the changing nature of traceification in the digital age.

In this summative chapter, we begin by revisiting the motif of the "accounts we live by" before providing a sequential overview of each chapter and outlining how their different arguments contribute to a traceological theorization of accounting that illuminates the postulated systemic shift towards digitally enabled tracking. It then turns to reflect critically on whether we now live in a digitally supercharged audit society—audit society 2.0, perhaps—or whether what has come to be called surveillance capitalism and its variants, to be discussed further in this chapter, represent a new and qualitatively different "trace-age".[1] Comparing and contrasting these claims shines further light on the inherent tension and intertwined duality of traceability for evidentiary oversight purposes, on the one hand, and for object generation and tracking, on the other. The chapter then offers some closing reflections on the economy of traces as a portfolio of cross-cutting traceability complexes. What is at stake normatively in all this are collective and individual choices about whether the mediated

[1] I am grateful to Caroline Muller for this suggestion.

Economy of Traces. Michael Power, Oxford University Press. © Oxford University Press (2026).
DOI: 10.1093/9780197681527.003.0010

relationalities that generate the accounts we live by are to be primarily "thick" or "thin", whether expansive and humanized, or reductive and machine-mediated.

The Accounts We Live By

The original idea for this book was to develop an explicit phenomenological theory of accounting. The intention was to explore how accounting is a technology whose quality of "appearing", both orally and in inscribed form, is an important feature of human experience, both in everyday and formal organizational settings. Furthermore, the plan was to ground this approach in an understanding of the traces that underpin accounting and determine its quality of manifestation. In the concept of the trace could be found the necessary building blocks of a critical accounting phenomenology, including indexicality, facticity, and temporality. While many accounting studies have drawn attention to the partial, interested, and cultural nature of accounts, and how they shape human agency to various degrees, they nevertheless fall short of delivering a systematic phenomenology that could reveal how accounting produces a distinctive texture of experience and operates as a medium of sense-making (Sandberg and Tsoukas, 2020).

Several scholars have provided elements for, and pointers towards, such a project (e.g. Vollmer, 2019; Chua et al., 2024). Furthermore, Busco and Quattrone's (2015) study of visualization and the revelatory and processual nature of accounting are important steps in this direction. In addition, early work on the auratic power of accounting (Gallhofer and Haslam, 1991), drawing on the political aesthetics of Walter Benjamin, points to the affective-agency of technologies like accounting. Indeed, Benjamin invites us "to sense the lingering qualities of materialities looking back at us" (Napolitano, 2015), and how they may connect to repressed and uncomfortable histories. The implication is that the traces that underpin accounts not only are bearers of reference to the past but also have an affective power which enables history or specific histories to "look back" at an observer. This auratic power of the trace can also be normalizing in its effects, generating facticity as a property of how things appear to be features of an objective reality. Even so, many of the accounting forms that we live by, and around which humans orient themselves, have fissures and cracks through which alternative accounts seek expression and which, for both the anthropologist and critical accountant, are their latent subject matter.

For all these pointers, a critical phenomenological project of the kind originally envisaged was bound to be inherently problematic, largely because it sought to analyse the experience of accounting in abstraction from its sociomaterial context. Despite the attraction of the metaphysics of absence and ethics in both Derrida and Levinas, and in critical anthropologies, it was theoretically fruitful to focus less on the trace as a mode of appearing and, following Peirce, more on it as an outcome of semiotic and technical work to encode features of human *practice*. Indeed, post-phenomenological studies, which draw attention to the technology-mediated nature of experience, suggest the necessity of such a practice turn in the approach to traces (Verbeek, 2011). Once this shift in focus away from pure phenomenology towards a more practice-relative conceptualization of the trace is taken, it is only a further short step towards the idea of *traceification* as practice and as an engine of the traceability complexes that underpin human accounts production (Rheinberger, 2011).

Notwithstanding this abandonment of a systematic phenomenology of accounting, conceptual residues of it are scattered throughout the arguments of this book. One such residue is the notion of the "accounts we live by" itself. At an early stage in their studies, accounting students are introduced to the information view of accounting, namely the idea that if accounting has any use at all, then it is to support decision-making, usually, but not always, in investment settings. Taken at face value, this seems an entirely reasonable and natural orientation, perhaps even commonsensical. Yet studies have shown that this decision-theoretic conceptualization of accounting has a distinctive history of formation and was to some extent invented to underwrite its purposefulness and rationality (Young, 2006; March, 1987; Hopwood, 1983). When accounting is studied in socio-material settings, the information view of accounting has been shown to be either mythical or at best qualified in its applicability. And given this looseness of fit between accounting and actual decision-making, studies have also revealed the symbolic, cultural, and rhetorical features of even the most seemingly economically rational accounting statements. So while a full phenomenology of accounting may be out of reach, this does not mean that the rich variations in the relations between accounting and human experience cannot be studied—far from it. For Garfinkel, as noted in Chapter 1, and also for anthropologists like Douglas (1986) and Strathern (1995), such relations are self-evident and a core object of study. In this book, at various junctures, we have also followed Latour's (2013) anthropology of modern life to position accounting beyond its specialist manifestations as a fundamental "mode of existence". Accounting is not something apart and for experts only; in all its material forms it is a pervasive feature of the orders we construct to make life bearable. We therefore seem to have no choice but to live by accounts in all their different technical and material forms—financial statements, social media, rankings, self-tracking metrics, and so on—where living is taken to signal that technologies, including digital technologies, and humans exist in continuous relations of co-formation (Stiegler, 2016). Distinctions between the everyday and the organizational, the private and the public, play and work are no longer adequate to grasp the exchanges and interactions that shape both accounting practices and human experience.

The motif of the "accounts we live by" matters more than ever in 2025, as I write these concluding words. Societies around the world are faced with significant challenges about how to live, in the existential sense of how to survive. In general, this requires new accounts to emerge in symbiosis with new ways of living together, both with each other and also with rapidly evolving AI. To do this, we need to remake accounts in a more fundamental way than the curation of disclosures in annual reports, or even by controlling social media. Theoretically, the question as to which is first—new ways of living collectively or new accounts—cannot be definitively answered and depends on the granularity of the analytic and temporal lens. But in the long run the two are strongly correlated, and new accounting forms in their widest sense of action-oriented interpretations are needed, whether they come before or after the changes in living that they represent. Accounting is an ongoing process of world-making, and there are choices to be made about what kind of world that should be, not least because of the looming post-democratic Anthropocene (Bebbington et al., 2020; Bebbington et al., 2024). And, given the core proposition in this book that traceification and accounting are deeply intertwined, it follows that we must somehow decide which traces matter as the matter of accounting. As we saw in Chapter 2, Borgmann (1999) argues that traces as signs face in two directions—towards persons and towards the things of the world. Yet this primary connectivity, and the accounting that goes with it, is becoming lost as traces, via advanced datafication, become a self-referential world of signs. Somehow, relations both to persons and the world, not least the natural world in crisis, must be recovered.

The accounts we live by are never complete and fully formed. There is no immaculate representation, no complete interpretation. They must be organized and composed from practices of trace accumulation that congeal into data and can be expressed as facts (Rheinberger, 2011). Individual and organizational accounts are the outcomes of trace-enabled tracking practices, mobilized according to different traceability value-purposes or logics. It is from the production of traces in all their variety, from passing facial expressions that are remembered, to durable and mobile records, that collective sense-making efforts by humans condense into accounts of greater or lesser durability, greater or lesser idiosyncracy or standardization. Such accounts are always historical in nature, artefacts of representation that continuously develop in response to events and pressures of many different kinds, not least pressures from new methods of digital tracking that reveal and create new accounting objects (Hopwood, 1983).

At the outset, this book has adopted a liberal and pluralistic conception of accounting because the scope, reach, and variety of accounts is increasing under conditions of digitization and expanded domains of performance. Is such breadth conceptually coherent? Personal dashboards containing metrics of physical prowess are certainly different from the retrospective investigatory reports by regulatory bodies. Yet they are both accounts that we live by and which shape us to varying degrees. The former encourages self-curation and self-improvement, which may or may not depend on contact with other humans. The latter concerns the manner in which societies can generate collective reflection and learning from disruptive events. The former individualizes, the latter collectivizes, at least in principle, even where specific individuals are blamed. The former is generative and prospective, promising a better self. The latter is retrospective and forensic. In short, if these are different accounts by which we live, then they also implicate different social and temporal orders and organizational forms that may conflict with one another. With multiple accounts, the prospects for richness and mutuality undoubtedly exist—a republic of accounts—but so does the potential for conflict, both between and within humans. As Chapter 8 suggested, we live in, and are constituted by, a matrix of different accounts and their performance imperatives, pulling in many directions. And to this image of plurality, we must also add the accounts that struggle to be heard, for which there may be possible traces but which are too fleeting and transient to be datafied, and therefore lack the political organization and resources to assemble them. These shadow counter-accounts in waiting are the subject matter of critical analysts working in accounting, anthropology, and many other fields. As Hopwood (1983) put it elliptically over forty years ago, accounting is always becoming "what it is not".

This book aims at a *traceological theorization of accounts*, which connects traceability and accounting more explicitly than hitherto, and to "bring traces back in" as a corrective to theories of accounting that have been dominated by information economics, on the one hand, and sociologies of quantification, on the other. This theoretical endeavour has been developed from "above" and "below". From "above", the notion of a traceability complex is proposed as a proto-unit of analysis and a frame for the mutually formative general components that organize specific forms of the traceification-accounts nexus. From "below", the chapters of this book, which we now summarize, have developed a number of the specific themes that are at stake in the empirical manifestation of traceability complexes. The resulting theory of accounting helps to explain how and why tracking is an expanding "mode of existence".

Summary of the Chapters

Chapter 1 provides a general introduction to traceability, arguing for its systemic significance as an organizing logic according to three broad values or ends: quality, security, and discovery, and highlighting its essential duality.

On the one hand, traceability is a capacity to *generate* traces (i.e. to traceify and constitute objects), a capacity that has dramatically increased in scope in the digital age. On the other hand, it points to the *evidentiary* nature of such generated traces and their use for tracking (first-order observation) and oversight (second-order observation) purposes. The chapter also introduces and defends a broad conception of accounting, encompassing diverse forms of narration, numeric representation, and summation that organize and mediate human relations; these are the many accounts we live by and which are undergoing systemic change. It is proposed that traceability and accounting are intertwined and pervasive, but not hegemonic.

Chapter 2 builds on Chapter 1 by considering the elusive notion of the trace. The argument converges on the philosophy of Peirce in viewing the trace as any object, inscription, document, process, thing, electrical pulse, datum that is generated, constructed, and attributed with status as a "trace of" and as a signifier of a primary object of interest *relative to a practice*. On this view, a trace is the outcome of *traceification* as a process, and tracking is the trace-enabled practice by which an observer is connected to, and can act upon, as well as account for, an object. Tracking practices vary in terms of the connectivity enabled by their "observational reach" across space and time. Relatedly, it is argued that accounts are always empirically varied combinations of tracking and oversight. The core thesis is that there is a change in this mix towards what we call *tracking-led accounts* and away from *accounts-led tracking*. Chapter 2 concludes by proposing a conceptual architecture consisting of: purposes (value-purposes or logics); traceification and datafication; tracking; and accounts production. These are the mutually formative elements of a *traceability complex*. This is a template that allows for considerable empirical variety, as we argue in Chapter 6.

Chapter 3 begins by reviewing theories of accounting that emphasize their calculative and quantitative properties, and their power of abstraction and economization. The "inscriptivist turn" in accounting theory provides the point of departure for a traceological approach that places the audit trail at its centre and that inverts the traditional conceptual priority of accounting over auditing. Audit trails are evidentiary "infrastructures of traceability" (Power, 2019) whose event boundaries are defined by the primary traceification of objects of interest for tracking and accounting. Chapter 4 extends the analysis of audit trails, arguing that they are paradigmatic modes of connectivity which are evident in many settings. Such trails are connective structures that are co-produced by the very tracking practices they host, and which generate the facticity of the values that mobilize them. It is proposed that, under conditions of advanced digitization, audit trails are becoming less densely populated by discrete human agencies exercising oversight and interpretative functions, and this reflects the shift from accounts-led tracking to tracking-led accounts. Drawing on the examples of blockchains and machine learning, the chapter concludes by highlighting the paradox of audit trail connectivity: as digital connectivity increases work process efficiencies, the audit trail as a basis for discrete human oversight decreases in depth to the point of disappearing entirely.

Chapter 5 develops this theme of oversight to focus more explicitly on the relationship between traceability and governance. The argument begins by reviewing scholarship on the role of documents and scripts in constituting organizations and organizing. It is proposed that there can be no complex organizing without the minimal scripting that enables self-observation across time and space. Furthermore, scripts, which may or may not take documental form, prescribe "acts of organizing", including the accounts that represent and entify organizations. Drawing on the discussion of audit trails and connectivity, the chapter then revisits conventional debates about organizational oversight as "layers" or "chains" of connected agencies and their observational practices. It is proposed that traceability, in one form or other, has come to define the nature of governance and regulation within and across organizations. This proposition is re-enforced in Chapter 6, which draws upon several cases for illustrative purposes, including anti-money-laundering regulation and trans-organizational supply-chain governance. Using the traceability complex template as a basis for their comparative analysis, governance and regulation are conceptualized as second-order modes of observation or oversight that are becoming de-layered under conditions of plaformization. In particular, debates about auditing by, and of, algorithms are revisited to address the broader question of the opacity of algorithms and their implications for traceability and oversight. As audit trails contain fewer discrete human agencies (Chapter 4), the governance mix may become more efficient, but it also potentially reduces governance to a series of operational apps, even to the point of losing traceability as human-led oversight entirely.

Chapter 7 extends the general thesis about the shift in the nature of governance by explicitly addressing the temporality of traceability across three levels of analysis. First, the scripted nature of organizations discussed in Chapter 5 encodes temporal structure and orientation as a source of their continuity and stability. Furthermore, as Chapter 2 has argued, a trace is also only a trace relative to a practice and can be made to signify anything of interest, including possible futures. Practices of prognostication based on traces have long and varied histories, from the sciences of meteorology to strategic and financial planning, to valuation in general, and to big data and sentiment analysis. Second, traceification processes enable imagined harmful futures to be tracked and accounted for in the present, using "leading" indicators based on their causes (risk objects). However, "temporal depth" is always a critical and controversial aspect of risk-indicator design. Connections between present action and future harm can be suppressed and denied, as is evident in the history of debates about climate change and smoking. Third, borrowing from Zuboff and others, it is argued that a growing variety of digital "archaeologies of the future" aim at the elimination of uncertainty in many areas of human practice. The chapter concludes by suggesting that, notwithstanding their many benefits, fundamental human capacities for projection and the imagination of possible futures are at risk from digital technologies that absorb both past and future into a continuous present.

Chapter 8 addresses the implications of this posited risk to projective capacity for selves and performance. The argument begins with an overview of relational theories of the self that, broadly understood, share an anti-Cartesian consensus but vary in terms of how far they "de-centre" the self. The chapter revisits and deepens claims about the relations between traceification, accounting, and self-formation, and two streams of research are brought into conversation with one another: studies of how accounting and quantification construct governable subjects, and analyses of the power of self-tracking and the formation of the "quantified self". In both streams, accounts are formative by virtue of the "pull" of their representations through which the self-encounters and seeks to improve itself. Via digitized prosthetics for self-monitoring and self-accounting, enabled by social media and a myriad of applications, the boundary between the organizational and notionally private sphere has become fluid. The chapter addresses three critical vectors of digital trace-enabled self-formation: profile construction and curation; the self as platform and social media-enabled feedback machine; and the self-tracking self that pursues its "data double". These three themes also reveal the expanded and expanding reach of "performance" as a normative category demanding monitoring and improvement across time. A conspicuous feature of these developments is that tracking seems to become valued as an end in itself. Yet, there remains a politics of traceability generated by a tension between the desire for visibility and feedback (i.e. to know "how am I doing?"), and counter-values emphasizing privacy, intimacy, and interiority, which promote trace erasure and the right to be forgotten. Overall, the chapter argues that the postulated shift towards tracking-led accounts is correlated with the growth of formative processes that de-centre and dividuate the self.

The intention of Chapter 9 is to explore the implications of "digital positivism" for the social sciences. understood as sources of the accounts we live by. The argument begins by discussing a strong form of philosophical positivism, namely the idea that "data" provide unmediated contact with an empirical domain, and then considers how this view has been subject to extensive and compelling critique. Studies of the life sciences and high energy physics provide powerful post-positivist accounts of science by focusing on the significance of datafication as a process of trace conversion. While strong philosophical positivism may be discredited, a positivism of digital data is emerging that increasingly redefines the nature of researchable empirically reality, and which becomes a resource rather than an outcome of investigation. Taking the field of contemporary accounting research as a proxy for such trends in social science, it is also proposed that research methods and modes of organizational control are increasingly symbiotic. While this is not a new idea—Foucault locates the origins of the human sciences in projects of control—it points to the expansion of a "post-hermeneutic data positivism" in social science in which the trace is no longer a site of interpretative work. The implications for the future of social science are symptomized by the manner in which accounting is giving way to an economized hybrid of accounting research–accounting practice, with overlapping data sources and methodologies. We label this new hybrid "accountics", and it is the social scientific correlate of tracking-led accounts. The chapter concludes by proposing a critical traceology that might address the mechanisms, including datafication and cyborgization, by which digital positivism reproduces itself.

Elements of a Traceological Theory of Accounting

Each of the different chapters summarized in the preceding conducts a "dive" into a feature of traceability and explores how it may be changing in the face of digitalization. In doing so, the chapters provide the conceptual building blocks for a traceological theory of accounting, which are summarized in stylized form in the left-hand column of Table 10.1. For each building block, individual chapters have discussed their tensions and how they shape the accounts we live by. These tensions are presented in the right-hand column of the table. Hence, Table 10.1 shows that: traceability is constituted by a tension between its evidentiary and generative features; traceification can enable both accounts-led tracking and tracking-led accounts; audit trails and digital algorithms are contrasting modes of connectivity; organizations embody competing forces for both hierarchy and de-centring; oversight can consist of dense or thin layers of agencies; temporal orientations can be a mix of the retrospective and prospective; the self-formative properties of accounts can be disciplinary or dividuating; and societal models of knowledge production combine expert human judgement and data-driven patterning.

The thesis of the book, that there has been a shift in the nature of the accounts we live by, can now be explicitly and schematically stated in terms of Table 10.1 as a broad shift from left to right in the second column. This in turn can be broken down into sub-shifts and changes within the various different elements. Table 10.1 is therefore a stylized summary or map of the different arguments of the book and how they reinforce each other. While this postulated shift is not intended to suggest a wholesale move from one "side" to the other, we also conceptualize it paradigmatically at the bottom of Table 10.1 as a shift from audit society to surveillance capitalism (Power, 2022). *Ceteris paribus*

Table 10.1 Elements of a Traceological Theory of Accounting

Building Blocks (Chapters)	The Mix of "Accounts We Live By"		
Traceability duality (1)	Evidentiary (auditability)	⟺	Generativity (new objects)
Role of traceification (2)	Accounts-led tracking	⟺	Tracking-led accounts
Mode of connectivity (3, 4)	Audit trail for oversight	⟺	Algorithms for tracking
Organizational control model (5)	Hierarchical, bounded	⟺	De-centred, unbounded
Oversight structure and values (6)	Dense, multilayered	⟺	Thin, flat (operational)
Temporal emphasis (7)	Retrospective	⟺	Prospective
Self-formative dynamics (8)	Disciplinary (cf. Foucault)	⟺	Dividuating (cf. Stiegler)
Model of knowledge production (9)	Expert judgement	⟺	Platformization
Stylized motif (10)	Audit society	⟺	Surveillance capitalism

accounts within the former paradigm are products of traceability complexes for: auditability, tracking as a means, hierarchical control, multiple oversight layers, retrospection and discipline, and expert knowledge production. Accounts under conditions of surveillance capitalism are, by contrast: generative of their objects, tracking-led, based on algorithmic forms of connectivity, unbounded in their scope, operationally focused, future-oriented, dividuating in self-formation, and platformized.

This traceological theorization of accounting draws attention to the combinations of attributes that exist in tension and fluidity with one another and which provide some dynamic explanatory potential. While the theory lacks a fully developed mechanism for the shift in the accounts we live by, it has the merit of directing empirical research to where these mechanisms are likely to be found. For example, investigations could focus on settings in which auditability and the audit trail are changing or declining in the face of machine-learning; or, relatedly, it could analyse how and why oversight layers are becoming thinner and flatter; or there could be studies of whether and how tracking is driving the "dashboardization" of the accounts we live by, and even becoming an end in itself because of the generative, prospective benefits it confers. In addition, while the theory has been motivated by a sense of how accounting is changing in the digital age, the conceptual apparatus and lexicon in Table 10.1 is in itself digitally agnostic and could be used for historical analysis. In short, the theory defines a space of enquiry into the changing nature of the traceification-accounting relationship.

Finally, Table 10.1 uses "audit society" and "surveillance capitalism" as convenient labels for its stylized duality. This is fine as far as it goes, but it presupposes and simplifies the answer to an important question, namely, whether the shift in the accounts we live by towards intensified tracking can be better characterized as an acceleration and radicalization of audit society tendencies—Audit Society 2.0—or whether the motif of surveillance capitalism provides a superior explanatory theory.

The Oversight Explosion: Audit Society 1.0

The audit society thesis sought to explain the observed expansion of performance accounting in public services in the United Kingdom and many other countries. It attributed this expansion to the mobilization of a number of myths that jointly constituted what came to be widely understood as the "new public management" (NPM). These myths or values were broadly *neoliberal* in nature, meaning that they promoted the primacy of the market, transparency, efficiency, and responsibility (Bromley and Powell, 2012, p. 498; Hood, 1995).

New forms of accounting for, and audit of, performance expanded rapidly as the mechanisms for operationalizing and realizing these myths (Meyer, 1986; Miller and Rose, 1990; Power, 1997, p. 96; Bromley and Sharkey, 2017), leading to the increased cultural and economic significance of accounting practitioners and their expertise in codifying performance (Meyer and Rowan, 1977, p. 347; Suddaby, Cooper, and Greenwood, 2007).

Initially, the NPM and the audit society were widely criticized for their unintended consequences. It was argued that organizations and service providers were distracted from their primary purpose by an explosion of performance indicators that generated incentives for gaming them (Hood, 1995; Bevan and Hood, 2006). It was also argued that new performance regimes were demoralizing. The "intrinsic" motivation of public-sector professionals was being crowded out by the "extrinsic" language of accounting (Strathern, 2000b, p. 314; Frey and Jegen, 2001; Falk and Kosfeld, 2006) and its "economization" of public services (Strathern, 1997; Guter Sandu and Mennicken, 2022). In other words, it was claimed that the NPM led to value-subversion, understood as "[t]he tendency to emphasize methods rather than goals [which] is an important source of disorientation in all organizations" (Selznick, 1957, p. 12; Cooper, 2001; Kraatz and Block, 2008; Kraatz et al., 2010, p. 1522; Kraatz and Flores, 2015).

Yet for all these critical observations of its effects and consequences, there was not widespread rejection and resistance to NPM and the new forms of performance accounting that it promoted (Hood et al., 1998). Specific reactions to new accounting requirements were varied, but the coupling of new accounting requirements was more evident than decoupling (Espeland and Sauder, 2007; Sauder and Espeland, 2009; Kraatz et al., 2010). In part, this was because the opportunities and capabilities for resistance were weak and the costs of prolonged decoupling were most likely quite high. But there was also another dynamic in play in which new accounting practices acquired operational autonomy and came to be "prized for their own sake" (Selznick, 1957, p. 17). This process has been described as "means-ends decoupling" (Bromley and Powell, 2012, p. 498) and is relevant to the analysis in this book of the rise of tracking-led accounts. It proposes that, rather than resistance in the form of strategies for decoupling accounting from the everyday practices of service delivery (Meyer and Rowan, 1977; Zajac and Westphal, 2004), there was a highly rationalized implementation of performance accounting, in which organizational power shifted to the accounting system. This means-end decoupling helps to explain how audit society effects reproduced and expanded despite criticism.

The self-generative nature of the audit society also reveals how the expanded forms of performance accounting and auditing are not simply neutral practices of observation but also change agents. In the name of transparency and accountability, they are the means by which organizations turn themselves "inside out" to make themselves observable, auditable, and legitimate. The engine of the audit society is therefore a "logic of auditability" (Power, 1996) that is operationalized in the audit trail, as discussed in Chapter 2. This theorization of the microfoundational engine of the audit society (Felin, Foss, and Ployhart, 2015; Barney and Felin, 2013; Power, 2021a) also implicates an agenda that is much wider than the NPM and the expansion of performance measurement in public organizations. Indeed, it is much broader than conventional accounting and auditing; it references the "increasing emphasis on monitoring and *tracking* organizational activities" (Bromley and Powell, 2012, p. 484, emphasis added). Traceability as a value and tracing and tracking as forms of practice were always central to the dynamics of the audit society and expressive of its logic of auditability. The reach of this logic is much wider than the scope of the original audit society thesis.

Audit society developments in the 1980s and 1990s were not devoid of digital technologies, far from it. Indeed, the accounting requirements of the NPM demanded investments in costly new information systems and internal process design. There was much innovation at this time in developing integrated information architectures. Yet, as a broad view, digital innovation at this time was a means to make existing organizational practices more efficient, to convert and digitize paper documents and systems. It had not yet entered the "phases" of intense personalization and datafication described by Kolb (2008), and it did not yet have the kind of radical reorganizing power that has come to be associated with the notion of digitalization (Leonardi and Treem, 2020; Puranam, 2025). In this sense, notwithstanding technology applications, the audit society and the mechanism of the audit trail were essentially documental in nature, even when progressively modified and streamlined by technology.

The audit society was not a surveillance society (Power, 1997, pp. 128–134). Auditing and performance indicators were powerful change agents, but they were limited in their observational basis for knowing about individuals as organizational participants, and in forming them into subjects oriented to accounts. The tracking of transactions and people was driven mainly by performance accounting demands in specific organizational settings. In the audit society, tracking as first-order observation was a kind of surveillance that generated self-surveillance for control purposes, but it was limited to the sphere of performance accounting, even when set in motion by ideals of efficiency and transparency. A parallel world of surveillance practices was also in motion at the time of these changes in the 1980s and 1990s and was an object of extensive scholarship leading inter alia to the founding of critical journals such as *Surveillance & Society* (e.g. Lyon, 1994, 2001).

These two worlds of critique—accounting and surveillance studies—addressed similar societal tendencies and shared similar theoretical reference points, such as Foucault's notion of the panopticon. Yet they had little to do with each other. If the audit society thesis was framed in a largely technology-neutral manner, this was not the case for surveillance research. Studies of societal policing (Marx, 1988) accelerated as a response to the proliferation of a huge variety electronic devices for observation and monitoring (Marx, 2002). Surveillance technology and practice could not be discussed apart from each other. Many years before the advent of blockchains, AI, platforms, social media, and facial recognition software, there were critical debates about CCTV, DNA testing, and ID cards. Scholars of managerial accounting addressed these developments in studies of information technology and the evolution of systems, such as Enterprise Resource Planning, which provide both financial and non-financial data. But these changes were primarily framed in terms of management control rather than the concept of surveillance. Tracing financial transactions, building them into meaningful reports, and auditing them seemed to have little to do with the granular tracking of people and things. The audit society was focused primarily on the quality of organizational performance and the role of accounting and audit as catalysts for change. It touched on security and surveillance practices only as they impacted the quality of organizational control environments.

Finally, the audit society thesis was premised on a number of dualisms that have become more questionable than ever in the "trace-age". These dualisms include the working distinctions between: organizations and their institutional environments (Meyer, 1986); work and non-work or private life; principals and their accountable agents; the measurable/visible and the unmeasurable/invisible; and, as discussed previously, accounting and surveillance. All these dualisms have become problematic and non-descriptive in the face of new modes of tracking and traceability that challenge traditional conceptions of organizational boundaries (see Chapter 5). If the audit society was characterized by an audit and oversight explosion, operationalized by accountants and other evaluators, it seems that the new economy of traces is one in which data-driven practices of surveillance are driving a tracking explosion. So does the concept of audit society still have any theoretical and empirical viability? To address this question we need to consider further the idea of surveillance capitalism.

The Tracking Explosion: The Rise of Surveillance Capitalism

There have always been critiques of technology and its de-humanizing de-skilling aspects, from the automation of looms to motor cars, televisions, mobile phones, and much else besides. In one sense, critical commentary about the effects of digital technologies follows a similar pattern in which the balance of gains (e.g. efficiency and new capabilities) and losses (e.g. loss of control, opacity) are continuing matters of dispute. One line of critical enquiry extends long established concerns with the de-skilling effects of technology as labour is replaced. Indeed, it is argued that workplaces are undergoing a form of digital pre-automation in preparation for fuller human labour replacement (Vertesi et al., 2021). If the human actors in organizations can be made more machine-like in their work processes, this smooths the way for more intense automation. In addition, it is argued that digitally enabled monitoring of labour in the so-called gig economy is emblematic of post-human practice (Kellogg et al, 2020; Newlands, 2021). Thus, digitization in the form of datafication has expanded the possibilities for granular "behavioural visibility" of both workers and citizens. Traces of worker activity that had hitherto remained invisible can now be organized and analysed for performance-evaluation purposes (Leonardi and Treem, 2020; Flyverbom, 2021; McDaid et al., 2023). This is similar in principle to the tracking of citizens for political-control purposes. As noted in Chapter 1, in the German Democratic Republic (GDR), which collapsed in 1989, the regime invested in creating documentary traces of lives in great detail, a venture that required an army of spies, enrolling a large proportion of the population. These observers—often friends and family—generated a deluge of files that documented movements and connections. The official objective was to assess risks to the state, but in substance this was an auto-expanding form of organized paranoia. Traceability became dedicated to the detailed observation and documentation of the most intimate aspects of human life.[2] These files, which were cumbersome and difficult to shred when the regime fell in 1989, have given way to their digital successors, and in many states the security purpose of traceability is the same. The dream to know the population, which began with the rise of statistics (Hacking, 1990), has undoubtedly been supercharged by digital technology, heralding ambitions for control and governance by algorithmic means (Stiegler, 2016; Jaser and Tourish, 2024; Stark and Pais, 2021).

Corporate control and state surveillance capacities are grounded in very similar digital technologies and their algorithmic underpinnings. It is this that motivates Zuboff's diagnosis of what she calls "surveillance capitalism" (Ball, 2019). In essence, she argues that the giant tech organizations, and Google in particular, engage in covert practices of surveillance and data extraction from users of their internet services. For Zuboff, this means that Google and other platform-based organizations have become a form of truth-engine for knowing everything about the people who connect to them. As noted in Chapter 8, all such digitally mediated interactions are a source of user-created traces that may

[2] For a sense of this, see the 2006 film *Das Leben der Anderen* (The Lives of Others) directed by Florian Henckel von Donnersmarck.

have economic value. Such traces can be datafied and analysed to yield potentially predictive insights, not least in the form of lead indicators of customer retention. These traces are sources of valuable knowledge that potentially obviate market uncertainties about product demand, for example by enabling precisely targeted advertising. Hence, Zuboff's theoretical language, and the very notion of surveillance capitalism itself, already aligns the project of securing market power with that of authoritarian state power in which the tracking of people is pre-eminent.

The critical thrust of Zuboff's analysis concerns the impact of processes of trace extraction on humans, namely "psychic numbing", and the threat this poses for civic participation and democracy. This appears to be a different and bleaker conception of subject-formation than the panopticon metaphor made famous by Bentham's dictum that "the more we are watched, the better we behave", and developed by Foucault and the many accounting studies influenced by his work. For these analyses, the freedom of a self-regulating subject is constituted by the experience of the disciplinary power of performance-measurement systems. Such subjects orient themselves to the "gaze" of such systems and, as argued in Chapter 4, they can be pulled towards, and entangled with, their representations as they come to define a particular kind of common sense about performance. For Zuboff, the fortunes of the self under conditions of surveillance capitalism are different from this "governmentality" thesis that allows for a matrix of freedom-power. In her view, the self is somehow neutralized by the invisible extraction of traces of human activity. There is no pull or compulsion to forms of accounting, because the surveillance technology operates behind their backs. They have themselves no cognitive or affective relation to any specific "accounting" representation of what they are, but are nevertheless accounted for by a control system that extracts traces of bodily movements, keystrokes, eye movements, clicks, and paces—and constructs them for profit.

Zuboff's notion of "surveillance capitalism" is a label for a form of order in which trace-production generates a new asset class, "surveillance assets", which must be tracked for security purposes—political, economic, and epistemic (Cohen, 2019; Whitcomb, 2020). As noted at the end of Chapter 9, her thesis can be read as a continuation of the critical-theoretical analysis of technology evident in the work of the Frankfurt School. Their *neo-Marxist* view of the falsity of the apparent consent of populations to the prevailing capitalist order resembles Zuboff's claims for the psychic numbing of populations by big tech, where even the pretense of consent is absent. Thinkers like Marcuse (1964) and Habermas (1977) would recognize the contours of her surveillance capitalism arguments and its post-human, post-democratic dystopianism, notwithstanding dramatic shifts in the nature of technology since the 1970s. However, because the primary focus of Zuboff's concern is corporate power and data extraction, her thesis is less focused on the wider forms of self-accounting and self-tracking enabled by an array of portable digital technologies and the wider effects of platformization. As noted in Chapter 6, Kornberger et al. (2017) demonstrate how platforms correspond to infrastructures in which multiple evaluations can flow in many directions between users, a situation of multidirectional surveillance of all by all, which is not well described by the idea of panopticon (Brivot and Gendron, 2011). Furthermore, surveillance capitalism in this wider sense is not only extractive of data assets but also generative of new forms of performing and observability. This platformization of human relationality (Chapter 8) is also formative of more dividuated and data-driven humans enmeshed in multiple matrices of performance accounting. There is no singular "governing" link between the self and accounts.

While there are some continuities between the old and new economy of traces, between audit society and surveillance capitalism, the latter inverts and radicalizes many features of the former. State and governance structures are becoming platformized and de-centred; and dreams of hierarchical control via performance measure design are giving way to data-driven production and the multiplication of performance categories "from below". Furthermore, engines of social change are to be found as much in the home-based laptop as in the workplace, domains that are also increasingly indistinct. And as argued in Chapter 6, the nature of audit practice seems to be losing its cultural authority in a sea of control-related apps. The central fault line between conceptions of audit society and of surveillance capitalism, which has surfaced repeatedly in this book, concerns the relationship between oversight and tracking.

Oversight and Tracking: An Essential Tension

To recap previous claims: traceability practices embody two intertwined dynamics that represent different aspects of observation/surveillance (Chapter 1). The first is the evidentiary or forensic dynamic that underpins audit trails and enables oversight. The second is the generative or constitutive dynamic by which new objects can be constituted, observed, and tracked. These two dynamics correspond to the two faces of traces and traceification, which are not mutually exclusive. Rather, any traceability practice and its accounting are necessarily an oversight-tracking hybrid or mix reflecting their mutual dependence; oversight and governance depend on the observability that tracking provides; tracking as observability requires some minimal degree of oversight and self-observation of its operational efficacy. Oversight without tracking capability is blind; tracking without oversight is out of control.

Beyond these mutual dependencies, the dynamics of oversight and tracking also exist in tension with each other because they emphasize these different aspects of traceability, aspects that underpin stylized differences between audit society and surveillance capitalism. For example, as Chapter 4 argued, digital technologies in principle enhance oversight as observability by enabling audit trails to be more complete, by enhancing informational and data connectivity, and by creating new possibilities for a certain style of governance, not least in supply chains. Yet technology also makes the audit trail potentially redundant when goals of traceability can be achieved by directly tracking and observing things and people. In this sense, tracking and oversight converge and become one and the same; there is a loss or dilution of the relatively independent forms of agency that oversee and stand "outside" as potential critic.

What is at stake here is subtle: oversight is not surveillance, even though, considered from the point of view of technology, it often looks like it. Rather, it has been argued that oversight, for all its imperfections, mobilizes human accounts that have the potential for interpretation, critique, and the performance of accountability. In contrast, surveillance aims at observational control, producing accounts in the form of risk profiles and control dashboards in which performance and objects can be tracked across space and time. In reality, traceability complexes do not divide neatly between these two stylized dynamics or logics of oversight and tracking, since they are always found in combination. For example, innovations in supply-chain management involve both product tracking and oversight/accounting practices mobilized by sustainability values.

Theoretically there is no question of deciding definitively between the oversight emphasis of "audit society" and the tracking emphasis of "surveillance capitalism". They point to different dynamics of traceability, but they are also always both in play and intertwined under conditions of digitalization. However, while their precise relation in any specific setting is an empirical question, the thesis of this book is that the logic of tracking, and the primacy it gives to surveillance, is becoming the dominant partner in this hybrid. In other words, the oversight-tracking mix is undergoing a systemic shift with consequences not only for the accounts we live by but also for the organizations we work in. This also explains the shift in direction and intensity of the politics of traceability, from audit society concerns with the side effects of performance measurement, to the need to govern algorithms, protect privacy, and mitigate opacity in an economy of traces in which tracking is expanding.

Tracking is a fundamental practice-type for human communities; structured oversight and governance emerge in more complex environments. The need to hunt animals for food, and to detect their tracks and signs, reach back to the dawn of mankind. And the creation of tracks and trails in the physical landscape, either by habit or by intention, undoubtedly provided the foundations for trade, as noted in Chapter 4. Whereas traceability as governance emerges from more complex geographically dispersed forms of social organization that generate impersonal trust relations (Shapiro, 1987), tracking as action-oriented observation is more primordial in nature. Nevertheless, as Zuboff and many other scholars and commentators demonstrate, the digital transformation of tracking is enabling control practices with a scale and reach that even theorists like Foucault could not have imagined. Societies are grappling with how to generate meaningful oversight of these capabilities for the digital extraction and datafication of all manner of aspects of human life, personal and organizational. The economy of traces seems to be all-pervasive.[3]

Developments in algorithmic-based management and AI raise the stakes for human oversight. Studies show how the relationship between humans and machine-learning technologies can be very varied, not simply dominating and de-skilling but potentially also empowering as "tools", "teammates", and "templates". Much depends on the organizational designs within which technologies are situated (Puranam, 2025). However, the prospect that such technologies also become decision-making "black boxes" beyond human interpretation preoccupies many scholars and practitioners. Amodei (2025), the CEO of Anthropic, argues that this issue is urgent and proposes the development of "mechanistic interpretability" to enable models to be legible to humans. Such legibility is tantamount to a form of traceability-enabled human oversight that involves being able to track the circuits or steps in a model's "thinking". Such interpretative oversight is at risk as AI becomes more organic and emergent in its properties, where traces are its food and tracking itself is opaque.

Overall, it is probably not productive to argue about whether the rise of digitally enabled tracking is really "audit society 2.0" or not. Today there is more monitoring as observation in general, and more watching and tracking. Some of this began with audit society developments, some did not. We can theorize thresholds of continuity and discontinuity in a number of ways, but the fortunes of the logic of the audit trail are indicative and symptomatic. The audit society, and neoliberalism more generally, expanded the scope of this logic in the face of pressures to make performance legible and trackable for distant evaluators, whether managers or auditors. Digital technologies were in play at this time, but were relatively subservient to functional concerns with efficiency and

[3] I recently came across a trade advertisement offering digital technology to monitor "team attendance". The sales pitch stated: "easily track team attendance via QR-Code, Slack, Facial Recognition or via Mobile or Desktop". The supporting narrative urges the purchaser of this product to "empower your employees to manage their own time". Readers may or may not find this example chilling and disturbing, and it may stimulate different theoretical reflections. It reads potentially as digitally enabled Taylorism and it promises "omniopticonic" possibilities in which all can see the performance of all.

the speed and accuracy of information processing. As in accounting, scholars of information systems started to write critically about these developments, seeing in them more agentic potential and fundamental change than was immediately evident (i.e. shaping organizations and the individuals within them, projecting rationalistic images that could not be realized; Ciborra, 2000). There were also fears for democracy and for the occlusion of different values in the face of financialization. The audit society was therefore an oversight explosion that was argued to threaten democratic forms of accountability because it shaped the language of accountability in expert terms. Audit trails, and the forms of oversight and governance that they supported, were part of the problem.

Looking back at the height of the audit society as an empirical phenomenon and its deep association with a neoliberal turn in public policy, there is some irony.[4] However crude the instruments of performance transparency and tracing were, and whatever their second-order effects, the datafication of everything and the rise of AI are moving the economy of traces well beyond neoliberalism towards a technocratic and potentially illiberal form of black-boxing, with even more profound implications for democratic values.

Economy of Traceability Complexes

In Chapter 1 the economy of traces was conceptualized as enabling infrastructure for the expansion of traceability practices in a wide variety of contexts. It was argued that such practices could be understood as manifestations of a template, the traceability "complex". This template was defined in Chapter 2 in terms of four interrelated practice elements: value-purposes of quality, security, and discovery; practices of trace production and datafication; specific practices of tracing and tracking that utilize and reproduce forms of connectivity; and multiple and varied practices of accounts production that realize and revalidate the mobilizing purpose of the complex. These elements constitute a stylized model of traceability "from above" derived from reflection on specific practices of tracing and traceability (see Figure 2.2 in Chapter 2). The traceability complex idea is not intended to be perfectly descriptive, but it is framed at a sufficient level of abstraction to suggest both a widespread form of institutional ordering and a model that enables different regulatory and organizational manifestations of traceability to be compared (see Chapter 6).

[4] The notion of audit society has always been ambiguous, being both epochal in its connotations (characterizing the neoliberal "period") and also theoretical by referencing a self-amplifying mechanism of social ordering. This ambiguity begins to matter less under conditions of surveillance capitalism in which both epoch and mechanism are superseded.

We should not overstate the coherence, power, or hegemony of identifiable traceability complexes in action. They can be, and usually are, fragmented and incomplete. They are bounded by critical issues of injustice, non-compliance, and even problems of violence that make them weak or disconnected. They may give rise to the "wrong" accounting (Chapter 6). Accounts of risk may be based on traces of the future that restrict temporal depth (Chapter 7). And humans often have sufficient agency to resist the dividuating pull of traces of performance (Chapter 8). Furthermore, traceability is not an all-powerful cultural value and principle of social ordering. Counter-traceability movements and discourses exist in abundance. For example, there is continuous debate about rights to privacy in areas such as medical records and identity cards in the United Kingdom (Whitley and Hossain, 2008). New regulations, such as GDPR 2018, seek to enshrine a right to be forgotten by which organizations are subject to stringent controls about the kinds of data that they can hold on existing and past employees as well as customers. Traceability is also an ambivalent value within insurance markets. Insurers seek to fine-tune their risk exposure but, if there is too much specific and granular knowledge of, say, individual medical risk, it paradoxically undermines the risk pooling concept. In general, empirical instances of traceability complexes are value-ambivalent, on the knife edge between quality and security, between democratic and totalitarian operationalization, and between liberalism and what some commentators refer to as "neo-illiberalism" (Davies, 2021), which Zuboff implies in her notion of "surveillance capitalism". Furthermore, perceptions of failure, inefficiency, non-neutrality, exploitation, and intrusion implicate a more or less continuous politics of traceability.

The economy traces can be theorized as the totality of overlapping traceability complexes. A traceography to map this totality would be a Herculean task and would necessitate tracing relations between internally complex traceability complexes. Figure 1.1 in Chapter 1 does not begin to constitute such a map, but it does suggest that the economy of traces should be understood as an ecology of traceability complexes characterized by intertwined logics of quality, security, and discovery; concerned with tracing and tracking people, processes, and things; and utilizing an array of devices and practices. The expanded production of digital traces provides the raw material for AI, which in turn expands its capacity to process, learn, and self-programme. As this happens, there is a prospect of opacity of both tracking—what is being observed and how?—and oversight—how can humans understand and interpret advanced algorithmic models whose outputs are surprising? At the extreme, an AI-driven economy of traces will no longer need to produce accounts for human consumption and self-formation. Traceability complexes, if they exist at all, will be just one part of algorithmic circuitry among others. AI may even reconstitute oversight functions and hierarchies within itself while remaining opaque to human understanding. We have not reached this point, but the postulated shift in the mix of oversight and tracking is suggestive of a trajectory that requires that we somehow re-centre human interpretability. And this means that our imperfect, value-laden, and often biased forms of human oversight practices based on traceability should not be allowed to drift into non-existence because of their alleged inefficiency.

Conclusions

Whatever the many flaws of reductive forms of accounting and auditing in the audit society, they were grounded in aspirational social narratives of mutual obligation, of the reasonable expectation that we need to give an account of ourselves, as organizations and individuals. Principal-agent theories articulated this organized mutuality in terms of contracts for which accounts enabled monitoring. Taking a broader view of this contractualism, accounting expressed, at least in imagination, a social order based on a promise of the redeemability of its claims. Reductive forms of accounting in the audit society may have seemed distorted and interest-laden to critics, but the imagined social order that they presupposed embodied well-intended and reasonable values of democratic governance and accountability.

This potential for accounts to be vehicles for sustaining values that matter, notwithstanding the inevitability of measurement difficulties, was overlooked by early critical accounting literature that was hostile to reductive quantification. Its important focus on understanding the cultural power of accounts may have led to an initial underestimation of their "value-infusive" potential (Selznick, 1957). However, recognition of this potential has been growing since the early social audits of the 1970s, leading to experiments with alternative and critical "counter-accounts" (Gallhofer et al., 2006; Vinnari and Laine, 2017) and even some normalization.

Such a revaluation of audit society becomes possible in part because of the contrast, developed in this concluding chapter, with the post-humanist tendencies of the algorithmic trace-age. Giving an account of oneself is mutating towards an emphasis on what we call "tracking-led" observational accounts, whether of ourselves by ourselves or by others, for which accountability is not the tyranny of performance management but a precarious value at the heart of human struggles to govern technology. Tracking is becoming post-accountability accounting, whose primary implicit purpose is security. It follows that traceability complexes and their accounts are the hinges on which values of accountability, democracy, privacy, and sustainability may turn towards variants of authoritarianism. As Zuboff (2022) puts it, surveillance capitalism is what happens when "democracy stands down". The shift in the mix of accounts we live by from accounts-led tracking to tracking-led accounts is one mechanism of this standing down, but it is gradual and distributed rather than sudden and focused, and it is a shift accompanied by justifiable hope in the benefits of digital technologies, many of which are evident. But there is nothing clear-cut here. Any political economy of traceability must grapple with the potentially seamless and subtle transitions that digital technologies can make between very different value positions. To say this is to agree that in the twenty-first century, social conflict is "platformized" (Fourcade and Johns, 2020), which we take here to mean that it is played out within traceability complexes and manifests itself in the accounts we both do and don't live by. In this new economy of traces there is more accounting about more things. But it is profoundly "under-lit" in the sense of moving beyond human legibility and governance. This book, with its traceological perspective on accounting, is a modest and imperfect attempt to understand and theorize the dynamics of these changes in terms of the rise of tracking as a mode of both accounting and existence that has a trajectory (Latour, 2013).

Finally, at the heart of the economy of traces is the "trace" itself as a constitutive-evidential product of traceification that is distinct from data. We turn to it in conclusion to restate what is ultimately at stake in the economy of traces and to invoke Levinas's ethics of alterity. As difficult as it may be, there are choices to be made about the accounts we live by, collectively and personally. The traces we use to build the heterogeneous accounts that pervade our lives can lead to dead sources of narcissistic self-fascination and engines of surveillance, built on thin relationalities with machines and their inner workings. Or they can be generative of risky and rich encounters with critical alterities, with the thick and uncertain relationalities to co-workers, community, and eco-systems, in human-centric organizations and their enabling technologies. This is not a matter of mystical theology or metaphysics; it is a question of designing the traceability-accounting nexus to enable human and environmental flourishing in this economy of traces.

References

Abbott, A. (1988) *The system of professions: An essay on the division of expert labor.* Chicago: University of Chicago Press.

Abbott, A. (1995) 'Things of boundaries'. *Social Research*, 62(4), pp. 857–882.

Abbott, A. (2005) 'Linked ecologies: States and universities as environments for professions'. *Sociological Theory*, 23(3), pp. 245–274.

Accounting Tools. (2018) 'Audit trail'. https://www.accountingtools.com/articles/2017/5/7/audit-trail?rq=audit%20trail (accessed 17 January 2019).

Acemoglu, D. (2025) 'AI's biggest secret'. *Prospect Magazine*, July, pp. 13–17.

Adkins, L., and Lury, C. (2009) 'Introduction: What is the empirical?' *European Journal of Social Theory*, 12(1), pp. 5–20.

Adorno, T. W. (ed.) (1976) *The positivist dispute in German sociology.* Translated by G. Adey, and D. Frisby. London: Heinemann.

Aho, B., and Duffield, R. (2020) 'Beyond surveillance capitalism: Privacy, regulation and big data in Europe and China'. *Economy and Society*, 49(2), pp. 187–212.

Ahrens, T., and Chapman, C. S. (2007) 'Management accounting as practice'. *Accounting, Organizations and Society*, 32(1–2), pp. 1–27.

Ahrne, G., and Brunsson, N. (2008) *Meta-organizations.* Cheltenham: Edward Elgar Publishing.

Airoldi, M. (2021) *Machine habitus: Toward a sociology of algorithms.* New York: John Wiley & Sons.

Ajana, B. (ed.) (2018) *Metric culture: Ontologies of self-tracking practices.* Bingley: Emerald Group Publishing.

Alaimo, C., and Kallinikos, J. (2017) 'Computing the everyday: Social media as data platforms'. *The Information Society*, 33(4), pp. 175–191.

Alaimo, C., and Kallinikos, J. (2019) 'Social media and the infrastructuring of sociality'. In Kornberger, M., Bowker, G., Pollock, N., Miller, P., Mennicken, A., Nucho, J. R., and Elyachar, J. (eds.), *Thinking infrastructures.* Research in the sociology of organizations. Bingley: Emerald Group Publishing, pp. 289–306.

Alaimo, C., and Kallinikos, J. (2020) 'Managing by data: Algorithmic categories and organizing'. *Organization Studies*, 42(9), pp. 1385–1407.

Alaimo, C., and Kallinikos, J. (2022) 'Organizations decentered: Data objects, technology and knowledge'. *Organization Science*, 33(1), pp. 19–37.

Alaimo, C., and Kallinikos, J. (2024) *Data rules: Reinventing the market economy.* Cambridge, MA: MIT Press.

Alborn, T. L. (2009) *Regulated lives: Life insurance and British society, 1800–1914.* Toronto: University of Toronto Press.

Alexander, C. (2023) 'Writing failure: Knowledge production, temporalities, ethics, and traces'. *Journal of the Royal Anthropological Institute*, 29(S1), pp. 8–30.

Allcott, H., and Gentzkow, M. (2017) 'Social media and fake news in the 2016 election'. *Journal of Economic Perspectives*, 31(2), pp. 211–236.

Allen, R. T., and McDonald, R. M. (2025) 'Methodological pluralism and innovation in data-driven organizations'. *Administrative Science Quarterly*, 70(2), pp. 403–443.

Amodei, D. (2025) 'The urgency of interpretability'. https://www.darioamodei.com/post/the-urgency-of-interpretability.

Anagnostopoulos, I. (2018) 'Fintech and regtech: Impact on regulators and banks'. *Journal of Economics and Business*, 100, pp. 7–25.

Ananny, M., and Crawford, K. (2018) 'Seeing without knowing: Limitations of the transparency ideal and its application to algorithmic accountability'. *New Media & Society*, 20(3), pp. 973–989.

Anderson, C. (2008) 'The end of theory: The data deluge makes the scientific method obsolete'. *Wired Magazine* 16(07). https://www.wired.com/2008/06/pb-theory/.

Andrejevic, M. (2013) *Infoglut: How too much information is changing the way we think and know*. New York: Routledge.

Angwin, D., and Vaara, E. (2005) 'Connectivity in merging organizations: Beyond traditional cultural perspectives'. *Organization Studies*, 26(10), pp. 1445–1453.

Annisette, M. (2017) 'Discourse of the professions: The making, normalizing and taming of Ontario's "foreign-trained accountant"'. *Accounting, Organizations and Society*, 60, pp. 37–61.

Ansari, S. M., Fiss, P. C., and Zajac, E. J. (2010) 'Made to fit: How practices vary as they diffuse'. *Academy of Management Review*, 35(1), pp. 67–92.

Anthony, C. (2021) 'When knowledge work and analytical technologies collide: The practices and consequences of black boxing algorithmic technologies'. *Administrative Science Quarterly*, 66(4), pp. 1173–1212.

Arbib, M. A., and Hesse, M. B. (1986) *The construction of reality*. Cambridge: Cambridge University Press.

Arjaliès, D.-L., Casa Nova, S., Gendron, Y., Lehman, C. R., Navarro Pérez, P. A., Resende de Lima, J. P., Stoner, G., and Vera-Colina, M. A. (2021) 'Breaking boundaries: (Counter) accounts during the pandemic: Letters for future generations'. *Journal of the Royal Anthropological Institute*, 29(S1), pp. 8–30.

Aronson, J. (2007) *Genetic witness: Science, law, and controversy in the making of DNA profiling*. New Brunswick: Rutgers University Press.

Ashcraft, K. L., Kuhn, T. R., and Cooren, F. (2009) 'Constitutional amendments: "Materializing" organizational communication'. *Academy of Management Annals*, 3(1), pp. 1–64.

Astley, W. G., and Zammuto, R. F. (1992) 'Organization science, managers, and language games'. *Organization Science*, 3(4), pp. 443–460.

Aycock, A. (1995) '"Technologies of the self": Foucault and internet discourse'. *Journal of Computer-Mediated Communication*, 1(2). https://doi.org/10.1111/j.1083-6101.1995.tb00328.x.

Ayer, A. J. (1952) *Language, truth and logic*. London: Dover Publications.

Aykut, S., Demortain, D., and Benbouzid, B. (2019) 'The politics of anticipatory expertise: Plurality and contestation of futures knowledge in governance—Introduction to the special issue'. *Science & Technology Studies*, 32(4), pp. 2–12.

Ayres, I., and Braithwaite, J. (1992) *Responsive regulation: Transcending the deregulation debate*. Oxford: Oxford University Press.

Bach, J. (2020) 'Merit, morality, and market'. In Stark, D. (ed.), *The performance complex: Competition and competitions in social life*. Oxford: Oxford University Press, pp. 228–240.

Bailey, D. E., Faraj, S., Hinds, P. J., Leonardi, P. M., and von Krogh, G. (2022) 'We are all theorists of technology now: A relational perspective on emerging technology and organizing'. *Organization Science*, 33(1), pp. 1–18.

Baldwin, R., Cave, M., and Lodge, M. (2011) *Understanding regulation: Theory, strategy, and practice*. Oxford: Oxford University Press.

Ball, K. (2005) 'Organization, surveillance and the body: Towards a politics of resistance'. *Organization*, 12(1), pp. 89–108.

Ball, K. (2009) 'Exposure: Exploring the subject of surveillance'. *Information, Communication & Society*, 12(5), pp. 639–657.

Ball, K. (2019) 'Review of Zuboff's "The Age of Surveillance Capitalism"'. *Surveillance & Society*, 17(1/2), pp. 252–256.

Ball, K., Di Domenico, M., and Nunan, D. (2016) 'Big data surveillance and the body-subject'. *Body & Society*, 22(2), pp. 58–81.
Ball, R. (2001) 'Infrastructure requirements for an economically efficient system of public financial reporting and disclosure'. *Brookings-Wharton Papers on Financial Services*, 2001(1), pp. 127–169.
Ball, R., and Brown, P. (1968) 'An empirical evaluation of accounting income numbers'. *Journal of Accounting Research*, 6(2), pp. 159–178.
Bandy, J. (2021) 'Problematic machine behavior: A systematic literature review of algorithm audits'. *Proceedings of the ACM on Human-Computer Interaction*, 5(CSCW1), pp. 1–34.
Bansal, P., Reinecke, J., Suddaby, R., and Langley, A. (2022) 'Temporal work: The strategic organization of time'. *Strategic Organization*, 20(1), pp. 6–19.
Barad, K. (2003) 'Posthumanist performativity: Toward an understanding of how matter comes to matter'. *Signs: Journal of Women in Culture and Society*, 28(3), pp. 801–831.
Barad, K. (2007) *Meeting the universe halfway: Quantum physics and the entanglement of matter and meaning*. Durham, NC: Duke University Press.
Barker, R., and Mayer, C. (2025, December) 'Seeing double corporate reporting through the materiality lenses of both investors and nature'. *Accounting Forum*, 49(2), pp. 259–289.
Barnes, B. (1983) 'Social life as bootstrapped induction'. *Sociology*, 17(4), pp. 524–545.
Barnes, B. (2013) *Scientific knowledge and sociological theory*. London: Routledge.
Barney, J., and Felin, T. (2013) 'What are microfoundations?' *The Academy of Management Perspectives*, 27(2), pp. 138–155.
Baxter, J., and Clarke, J. (2013) 'Farewell to the tick box inspector? Ofsted and the changing regime of school inspection in England'. *Oxford Review of Education*, 39(5), pp. 702–718.
Bay, C. (2018) 'Makeover accounting: Investigating the meaning-making practices of financial accounts'. *Accounting, Organizations and Society*, 64, pp. 44–54.
Beasley, M. S., Branson, B. C., and Hancock, B. V. (2010) *Developing key risk indicators to strengthen enterprise risk management*. Raleigh: ERM Initiative at North Carolina State University and the Committee of Sponsoring Organizations of the Treadway Commission.
Beaver, W. (1981) *Financial reporting: An accounting revolution*. Engelwood Cliffs: Prentice Hall.
Bebbington, J., Blasiak, R., Larrinaga, C., Russell, S., Sobkowiak, M., Jouffray, J. B., and Österblom, H. (2024) 'Shaping nature outcomes in corporate settings'. *Philosophical Transactions of the Royal Society B*, 379(1903), https://doi.org/10.1098/rstb.2022.0325, pp. 1–8.
Bebbington, J., Österblom, H., Crona, B., Jouffray, J. B., Larrinaga, C., Russell, S., and Scholtens, B. (2020) 'Accounting and accountability in the Anthropocene'. *Accounting, Auditing & Accountability Journal*, 33(1), pp. 152–177.
Bechky, B. A., and Davis, G. F. (2024) 'Resisting the algorithmic management of science: Craft and community after generative AI'. *Administrative Science Quarterly*, 70(1), pp. 1–22.
Beck, U. (1992) *Risk society: Towards a new modernity*. London: SAGE Publications.
Beckert, J. (2013) 'Imagined futures: Fictional expectations in the economy'. *Theory and Society*, 42, pp. 219–240.
Beckert, J. (2021) 'The firm as an engine of imagination: Organizational prospection and the making of economic futures'. *Organization Theory*, 2(2), pp. 1–21.
Beckert, J., and Suckert, L. (2021) 'The future as a social fact. The analysis of perceptions of the future in sociology'. *Poetics*, 84, https://doi.org/10.1016/j.poetic.2020.101499.
Bellanova, R., and De Goede, M. (2022) 'The algorithmic regulation of security: An infrastructural perspective'. *Regulation & Governance*, 16(1), pp. 102–118.
Bencherki, N., Brummans, B. H. J. M., and Vézy, C. (2024) 'Agency without agents: Affective forces, communicative events, and organizational becomings'. *Organization Studies*, 45(9), pp. 1349–1372.
Bergen, J. P., and Verbeek, P. P. (2021) 'To-do is to be: Foucault, Levinas, and technologically mediated subjectivation'. *Philosophy & Technology*, 34(2), pp. 325–348.

Berger, P. L., and Luckmann, T. (1966) *The social construction of reality: A treatise in the sociology of knowledge*. New York: First Anchor.

Bernstein, A. (2017) 'Agency in state agencies'. In Enfield, N. J., and Kockelman, P. (eds.), *Distributed agency*. Oxford: Oxford University Press, pp. 41–47.

Bernstein, E. (2017) 'Making transparency transparent: The evolution of observation in management theory'. *Academy of Management Annals*, 11(1), pp. 217–266.

Bernstein, E. S. (2012) 'The transparency paradox: A role for privacy in organizational learning and operational control'. *Administrative Science Quarterly*, 57(2), pp. 181–216.

Bernstein, P. L. (1996) *Against the gods: The remarkable story of risk*. New York: John Wiley & Sons.

Besharov, M. L., and Khurana, R. (2015) 'Leading amidst competing technical and institutional demands: Revisiting Selnick's conception of leadership'. In Kraatz, M. (ed.), *Institutions and ideals: Philip Selznick's legacy for organizational studies*. Bingley: Emerald Group Publishing, pp. 53–88.

Bevan, G., and Hood, C. (2006) 'What's measured is what matters: Targets and gaming in the English public health care system'. *Public Administration*, 84, pp. 517–538.

Bhimani, A. (2015) 'Exploring big data's strategic consequences'. *Journal of Information Technology*, 30(1), pp. 66–69.

Bhimani, A., and Bromwich, M. (2009) 'Management accounting in a digital and global economy: The interface of strategy, technology, and cost information'. In Chapman, C., Cooper, D., and Miller, P. (eds.), *Accounting, organizations and institutions*. Oxford: Oxford University Press, pp. 85–111.

Bhimani, A., and Willcocks, L. (2014) 'Digitisation, 'big data' and the transformation of accounting information'. *Accounting and Business Research*, 44(4), pp. 469–490.

Biagioli, M., and Lippman, A. (eds.) (2020) *Gaming the metrics: Misconduct and manipulation in academic research*. Cambridge, MA: MIT Press.

Birch, K., and Muniesa, F. (eds.) (2020) *Assetization: Turning things into assets in technoscientific capitalism*. Cambridge, MA: MIT Press.

Birhane, A., Steed, R., Ojewale, V., Vecchione, B., and Raji, I. D. (2024) 'AI auditing: The broken bus on the road to AI accountability'. *IEEE Conference on Secure and Trustworthy Machine Learning (SaTML)* (pp. 612–643). Institute of Electrical and Electronics Engineers, https://www.ieee.org/.

Black, J. (2002) 'Regulatory conversations'. *Journal of Law and Society*, 29(1), pp.163–196.

Black, D. E., Christensen, T. E., Ciesielski, J. T., and Whipple, B. C. (2021) 'Non-GAAP earnings: A consistency and comparability crisis?' *Contemporary Accounting Research*, 38(3), pp. 1712–1747.

Blanche, C., and Feldman, M. S. (2021) 'Bodies and routine dynamics'. In Feldman, M., Pentland, B. T., D'Adderio, L., Dittrich, K., Rerup, C., and Seidl, D. (eds.), *The Cambridge handbook of routine dynamics*. Cambridge: Cambridge University Press, pp. 343–356.

Bloor, D. (1991) *Knowledge and social imagery*. Chicago: University of Chicago Press.

Boellstorff, T. (2016) 'For whom the ontology turns: Theorizing the digital real'. *Current Anthropology*, 57(4), pp. 387–407.

Bogard, W. (2006) 'Welcome to the society of control: The simulation of surveillance revisited'. In Haggerty, K. D., and Ericson, R. V. (eds.), *The new politics of surveillance and visibility*. Toronto: University of Toronto Press, pp. 55–78.

Boholm, Å., and Corvellec, H. (2011) 'A relational theory of risk'. *Journal of Risk Research*, 14(2), pp. 175–190.

Boltanski, L., and Thévenot, L. (2006) *On justification: Economies of worth*. Princeton: Princeton University Press.

Borgmann, A. (1999) *Holding on to reality: The nature of information at the turn of the millennium*. Chicago: University of Chicago Press.

Bottausci, C., Robson, K., and Dambrin, C. (2024) 'Technological mediation, mediating morality and moral imaginaries of design: Performance measurement systems in the pharmaceutical industry'. *Accounting, Organizations and Society*, 112, https://doi.org/10.1016/j.aos.2023.101535.

Bourdieu, P. (2010) *Distinction: A social critique of the judgement of taste*. Translated by R. Nice (1984). London and New York: Routledge.

Boxenbaum, E., and Jonsson, S. (2017) 'Isomorphism, diffusion and decoupling: Concept evolution and theoretical challenges'. In Greenwood, R., Oliver, C., Lawrence, T., and Meyer, R. (eds.), *The Sage handbook of organizational institutionalism*. Thousand Oaks, CA: Sage, pp. 79–104.

Bowker, G. C., Elyachar, J., Kornberger, M., Mennicken, A., Miller, P., Nucho, J. R., and Pollock, N. (2019) 'Introduction to thinking infrastructures'. In Kornberger, M., Bowker, G. C., Elyachar, J., Mennicken, A., Miller, P., Nucho, J. R., and Pollock, N. (eds.), *Thinking infrastructures*. Bingley: Emerald Publishing, pp. 1–13.

Boyle, D. (2001) *Tyranny of numbers*. London: Flamingo Press.

Boyle, D. (2020) *Tickbox*. London: Hachette.

Brickey, K. F. (2003) 'From Enron to WorldCom and beyond: Life and crime after Sarbanes-Oxley'. *Washington University Law Quarterly*, 81(2), pp. 357–402.

Brivot, M., and Gendron, Y. (2011) 'Beyond panopticism: On the ramifications of surveillance in a contemporary professional setting'. *Accounting, Organizations and Society*, 36(3), pp. 135–155.

Bromley, P., and Powell, W. (2012) 'From smoke and mirrors to walking the talk: Decoupling in the contemporary world'. *The Academy of Management Annals*, 6, pp. 483–530.

Bromley, P., and Sharkey, A. (2017) 'Casting call: The expanding nature of actorhood in US firms, 1960–2010'. *Accounting, Organizations and Society*, 59, pp. 3–20.

Brown, J. (2009) 'Democracy, sustainability and dialogic accounting technologies: Taking pluralism seriously'. *Critical Perspectives on Accounting*, 20(3), pp. 313–342.

Buchanan, I. (2015) 'Assemblage theory and its discontents'. *Deleuze Studies*, 9(3), pp. 382–392.

Buchdahl, G. (1969) *Metaphysics and the philosophy of science*. Oxford: Blackwell.

Bueno, N., Bernaz, N., Holly, G. and Martin-Ortega, O. (2024) 'The EU Directive on Corporate Sustainability Due Diligence (CSDDD): The final political compromise'. *Business and Human Rights Journal*, 9, pp. 294–300.

Bukh, P. N., Larsen, H. T., and Mouritsen, J. (2001) 'Constructing intellectual capital statements'. *Scandinavian Journal of Management*, 17(1), pp. 87–108.

Burchell, S., Clubb, C., Hopwood, A., Hughes, J., and Nahapiet, J. (1980) 'The roles of accounting in organizations and society'. *Accounting, Organizations and Society*, 5(1), pp. 5–27.

Burchell, S., Clubb, C. and Hopwood, A. G. (1985) 'Accounting in its social context: towards a history of value added in the United Kingdom.' *Accounting, Organizations and Society*, 10(4), pp. 381–413.

Burgess, A., and Horii, M. (2012) 'Risk, ritual and health responsibilisation: Japan's "safety blanket" of surgical face mask-wearing'. *Sociology of Health & Illness*, 34(8), pp. 1184–1198.

Burrell, J. (2016) 'How the machine "thinks": Understanding opacity in machine learning algorithms'. *Big Data & Society*, 3(1), https://doi.org/10.1177/2053951715622512.

Burrell, J., and Fourcade, M. (2021) 'The society of algorithms'. *Annual Review of Sociology*, 47, pp. 213–237.

Burrows, R. (2012) 'Living with the h-index? Metric assemblages in the contemporary academy'. *The Sociological Review*, 60(2), pp. 355–372.

Busco, C., Consolandi, C., Eccles, R. G., and Sofra, E. (2020) 'A preliminary analysis of SASB reporting: Disclosure topics, financial relevance, and the financial intensity of ESG materiality'. *Journal of Applied Corporate Finance*, 32(2), pp. 117–125.

Busco, C., and Quattrone, P. (2015) 'Exploring how the balanced scorecard engages and unfolds: Articulating the visual power of accounting inscriptions'. *Contemporary Accounting Research*, 32(3), pp. 1236–1262.

Busco, C., and Quattrone, P. (2018) 'Performing business and social innovation through accounting inscriptions: An introduction'. *Accounting, Organizations and Society*, 67, pp. 15–19.

Busuioc, M. (2021) 'Accountable artificial intelligence: Holding algorithms to account'. *Public Administration Review*, 81(5), pp. 825–836.

Butler, J. (1999) 'Performativity's social magic'. In Shusterman, R. (ed.), *Bourdieu: A critical reader*. Oxford: Blackwell Publishers, pp. 113–128.

Butler, J. (2005) *Giving an account of oneself*. New York: Fordham University Press.

Caliskan, K. (2020) 'Data money: The socio-technical infrastructure of cryptocurrency blockchains'. *Economy and Society*, 49(4), pp. 540–561.

Caliskan, K. (2021) 'Platform works as stack economization: Cryptocurrency markets and exchanges in perspective'. *Sociologica*, 14(3), pp. 115–142.

Caliskan, K. (2023) *Data money: Inside cryptocurrencies, their communities, markets, and blockchains*. New York: Columbia University Press.

Callero, P. L. (2003) 'The sociology of the self'. *Annual Review of Sociology*, 29(1), pp. 115–133.

Callewaert, S. (2006) 'Bourdieu, critic of Foucault: The case of empirical social science against double-game-philosophy'. *Theory, Culture & Society*, 23(6), pp. 73–98.

Callon, M. (1984) 'Some elements of a sociology of translation: Domestication of the scallops and the fishermen of St Brieuc Bay'. *The Sociological Review*, 32(1 Suppl), pp. 196–233.

Callon, M. (1998) 'Introduction: The embeddedness of economic markets in economics'. *The Sociological Review*, 46(S1), pp. 1–57.

Campbell, D. W., and Shang, R. (2022) 'Tone at the bottom: Measuring corporate misconduct risk from the text of employee reviews'. *Management Science*, 68(9), pp. 7034–7053.

Camic, C. (1986) 'The matter of habit'. *American Journal of Sociology*, 91(5), pp. 1039–1087.

Canavari, M., Centonze, R., Hingley, M., and Spadoni, R. (2010) 'Traceability as part of competitive strategy in the fruit supply chain'. *British Food Journal*, 112(2), pp. 171–186.

Cardinale, I. (2018) 'Beyond constraining and enabling: Towards new microfoundations for institutional theory'. *Academy of Management Review*, 43(1), pp. 132–155.

Cardinale, I. (2019) 'On action, embeddedness, and institutional change'. *Academy of Management Review*, 44(3), pp. 673–676.

Cardon, D. (2020) 'What are digital reputation measures worth?' In Stark, D. (ed.), *The performance complex: Competition and competitions in social life*. Oxford: Oxford University Press, pp. 208–227.

Carruthers, B. G., and Espeland, W. N. (1991) 'Accounting for rationality: Double-entry bookkeeping and the rhetoric of economic rationality'. *American Journal of Sociology*, 97(1), pp. 31–69.

Casilli, A., and Posada, J. (2019) 'The platformization of labor and society'. In Graham, M., and Dutton, W. H. (eds.), *Society and the internet: How networks of information and communication are changing our lives*. Oxford: Oxford University Press, pp. 293–306.

CGMA. (2016) *Business analytics and decision making: The human dimension*. Chartered Global Management Accountants. https://www.aicpa-cima.com/resources/download/business-analytics-and-decision-making-the-human-dimension.

Chalmers, D., Fisch, C., Matthews, R., Quinn, W., and Recker, J. (2022) 'Beyond the bubble: Will NFTs and digital proof of ownership empower creative industry entrepreneurs?' *Journal of Business Venturing Insights*, 17, https://doi.org/10.1016/j.jbvi.2022.e00309.

Chan, J., Johns, F., and Moses, L. B. (2018) 'Academic metrics and positioning strategies'. In Ajana, B. (ed.), *Metric culture*. Leeds: Emerald Publishing, pp. 177–195. https://doi.org/10.1108/978-1-78743-289-520181010.

Chapman, C., Chua, W. F., and Fiedler, T. (2021) 'Seduction as control: Gamification at Foursquare'. *Management Accounting Research*, 53, https://doi.org/10.1016/j.mar.2021.100765.

Chapman, C. S., Cooper, D. J., and Miller, P. (2009) 'Linking accounting, organizations, and institutions'. In Chapman, C. S., Cooper, D. J., and Miller, P. (eds.), *Accounting, organizations and institutions*. Oxford: Oxford University Press, pp. 1–29.

Charlebois, S., Latif, N., Ilahi, I., Sarker, B., Music, J., and Vezeau, J. (2024) 'Digital traceability in agri-food supply chains: A comparative analysis of OECD member countries'. *Foods*, 13(1075), https://doi.org/10.3390/foods13071075.

Chenhall, R. H., Hall, M., and Smith, D. (2017) 'The expressive role of performance measurement systems: A field study of a mental health development project'. *Accounting, Organizations and Society*, 63, pp. 60–75.

Chia, R. (1994) 'The concept of decision: A deconstructive analysis'. *Journal of Management Studies*, 31(6), pp. 781–806.

Christensen, L. T., and Cornelissen, J. (2015) 'Organizational transparency as myth and metaphor'. *European Journal of Social Theory*, 18(2), pp. 132–149.

Chua, W. F., Fiedler, T., and Boedker, C. (2024) 'Projecting, infrastructuring and calculating: From an in vitro to an in vivo carbon market'. *Accounting, Organizations and Society*, 112, https://doi.org/10.1016/j.aos.2024.101549.

Ciborra, C. (2000) *From control to drift: The dynamics of corporate information infrastructures*. New York: Oxford University Press.

Ciborra, C. U. (1996) 'The platform organization: Recombining strategies, structures, and surprises'. *Organization Science*, 7(2), pp. 103–118.

Clark, A. (2025) 'Extending minds with generative AI'. *Nature Communications*, 16 (4627), https://doi.org/10.1038/s41467-025-59906-9.

Clarke, L. (1999) *Mission improbable: Using fantasy documents to tame disaster*. Chicago: University of Chicago Press.

Clemens, E. S. (2007) 'Toward a historicized sociology: Theorizing events, processes, and emergence'. *Annual Review of Sociology*, 33(1), pp. 527–549.

Coffee, J. C., Jr. (2006) *Gatekeepers: The professions and corporate governance*. Oxford: Oxford University Press.

Cohen, J. E. (2019) 'Review of Zuboff's "The Age of Surveillance Capitalism"'. *Surveillance & Society*, 17(1–2), pp. 240–245.

Cohen, M. D. (2007) 'Reading Dewey: Reflections on the study of routine'. *Organization Studies*, 28(5), pp. 773–786.

Coles, S. A. (2001) *Suspect identities: A history of fingerprinting and criminal identification*. Cambridge, MA: Harvard University Press.

Collins, H. (1992) *Changing order: Replication and induction in scientific practice*. Chicago: University of Chicago Press.

Comeau-Vallée, M., and Langley, A. (2020) 'The interplay of inter-and intraprofessional boundary work in multidisciplinary teams'. *Organization Studies*, 41(12), pp. 1649–1672.

Committee of Sponsoring Organizations of the Treadway Commission (COSO). (2004) *Enterprise risk management: Integrated framework*. https://www.coso.org (accessed 6 December 2024).

Comunello, F., Martire, F., and Sabetta, L. (2022) 'Toward a sociology of traces'. In Comunello, F., Martire, F., and Sabetta, L. (eds.), *What people leave behind: Marks, traces, footprints and their relevance to knowledge society*. Cham: Springer, pp. 1–18.

Comunello, F., Martire, F., and Sabetta, L. (2024) 'Brushing society against the grain: Digital footprints, scraps, non-human acts, crumbs, and other traces'. *American Behavioral Scientist*, 68(5), pp. 623–639.

Conlon, T., Corbet, S., and Hu, Y. (2023) 'The collapse of the FTX exchange: The end of cryptocurrency's age of innocence'. *The British Accounting Review*, https://doi.org/10.1016/j.bar.2023.101277.

Constantiou, I. D., and Kallinikos, J. (2015) 'New games, new rules: Big data and the changing context of strategy'. *Journal of Information Technology*, 30(1), pp. 44–57.

Cooper, A. (2001) 'The state of mind we're in: Social anxiety, governance and the audit society'. *Psychoanalytic Studies*, 3(3–4), pp. 349–362.

Cooper, D. J., and Hopper, T. (Eds.) (1990) *Critical accounts: Reorientating accounting research*. Basingstoke: Macmillan International Higher Education.

Cooper, R. (2015) 'Organization/disorganization'. In Parker, M., and Burrell, G. (eds.), *For Robert Cooper*. London: Routledge, pp. 79–115.

Cooren, F. (2004) 'Textual agency: How texts do things in organizational settings'. *Organization*, 11(3), pp. 373–393.

Cornelissen, J. (2017) 'Editor's comments: Developing propositions, a process model, or a typology? Addressing the challenges of writing theory without a boilerplate'. *Academy of Management Review*, 42(1), pp. 1–9.

Cornelissen, J., Höllerer, M. A., Boxenbaum, E., Faraj, S., and Gehman, J. (2024) 'Large language models and the future of organization theory'. *Organization Theory*, 5(1), https://doi.org/10.1177/26317877241239056.

Cornelissen, J. P. (2004) *Corporate communication: A guide to theory and practice*. London: Sage.

Cornelissen, J. P., Durand, R., Fiss, P. C., Lammers, J. C., and Vaara, E. (2015) Putting communication front and center in institutional theory and analysis. *Academy of Management Review*, 40(1), pp. 10–27.

Corvellec, H., Ek, R., Zapata, P., and Campos, M. J. Z. (2018) 'Acting on distances: A topology of accounting inscriptions'. *Accounting, Organizations and Society*, 67, pp. 56–65.

Cowen, D. (2010) 'A geography of logistics: Market authority and the security of supply chains'. *Annals of the Association of American Geographers*, 100(3), pp. 600–620.

Cragun, O. R., Olsen, K. J., and Wright, P. M. (2020) 'Making CEO narcissism research great: A review and meta-analysis of CEO narcissism'. *Journal of Management*, 46(6), pp. 908–936.

Cronin, C. (1996) 'Bourdieu and Foucault on power and modernity'. *Philosophy & Social Criticism*, 22(6), pp. 55–85.

Crossley, N. (2013) 'Habit and habitus'. *Body & Society*, 19(2–3), pp. 136–161.

Crvelin, D., and Löhlein, L. (2022) 'Commensuration by form: Lists and accounting in collective action networks'. *Accounting, Organizations and Society*, 100, https://doi.org/10.1016/j.aos.2021.101333.

D'Adderio, L. (2008) 'The performativity of routines: Theorising the influence of artefacts and distributed agencies on routines dynamics'. *Research Policy*, 37(5), pp. 769–789.

D'Adderio, L. (2011) 'Artifacts at the centre of routines: Performing the material turn in routines theory'. *Journal of Institutional Economics*, 7(2), pp. 197–230.

D'Adderio, L., Glaser, V., and Pollock, N. (2019) 'Performing theories, transforming organizations: A reply to Marti and Gond'. *Academy of Management Review*, 44(3), pp. 676–679.

Dahrendorf, R. (1995) *LSE: A history of the London School of Economics and Political Science 1895–1995*. Oxford: Oxford University Press.

Dambrin, C., and Robson, K. (2011) 'Tracing performance in the pharmaceutical industry: Ambivalence, opacity and the performativity of flawed measures'. *Accounting, Organizations and Society*, 36(7), pp. 428–455.

Danielsson, J. (2002) 'The emperor has no clothes: Limits to risk modelling'. *Journal of Banking & Finance*, 26(7), pp. 1273–1296.

Danielsson, J., Shin, H. S., and Zigrand, J. P. (2012) 'Endogenous extreme events and the dual role of prices'. *Annual Review of Economics*, 4(1), pp. 111–129.

Daston, L. (2022) *Rules: A short history of what we live by*. Princeton: Princeton University Press.

d'Astros, C. D., and Morales, J. (2024) 'The silent resistance: An ethnographic study of the use of silence to resist accounting and managerialization'. *Critical Perspectives on Accounting*, 99, https://doi.org/10.1016/j.cpa.2023.102648.
Davies, H., and Zhivitskaya, M. (2018) 'Three lines of defence: A robust organising framework, or just lines in the sand?' *Global Policy*, 9, pp. 34–42.
Davies, W. (2021) 'The revenge of sovereignty on government? The release of neoliberal politics from economics post-2008'. *Theory, Culture & Society*, 38(6), pp. 95–118.
Day, S., and Lury, C. (2016) 'Biosensing: tracking persons'. In Nafus, D. (ed.), *Quantified: Biosensing technologies in everyday life*. Cambridge, MA: MIT Press, pp. 43–66.
De Certeau, M. (1988) *The Writing of History*. Translated by T. Conley. New York: Columbia University Press.
De Vaujany, F. X., Holt, R., and Grandazzi, A. (Eds.)(2023) 'Organization as time: Power and emancipation in the happening of management'. In De Vaujany, F. X., Holt, R., and Grandazzi, A. (eds.), *Organization as time: Technology, power and politics*, Cambridge: Cambridge University Press, pp. 1–10.
Dean, M. M. (2009) *Governmentality: Power and rule in modern society*. London: Sage Publications.
Deken, F., Carlile, P. R., Berends, H., and Lauche, K. (2016) 'Generating novelty through interdependent routines: A process model of routine work'. *Organization Science*, 27(3), pp. 659–677.
Demortain, D. (2016) 'The work of making risk frameworks'. In Power, M. (ed.), *Riskwork: Essays on the organizational life of risk management*. Oxford: Oxford University Press, pp. 26–49.
Demortain, D. (2023) 'The digitalisation of risk assessment: Fulfilling the promises of prediction?' In Le Coze, J.-C., and Antonsen, S. (eds.), *Safety in the digital age: Sociotechnical perspectives on algorithms and machine learning*. Cham: Springer Nature, pp. 11–19.
Dent, J. F. (1991) 'Accounting and organizational cultures: A field study of the emergence of a new organizational reality'. *Accounting, Organizations and Society*, 16(8), pp. 705–732.
Derrida, J. (1982) 'Différance'. In Derrida, J. (ed.), *Margins of philosophy*. Translated, with additional notes, by Alan Bass. Chicago: University of Chicago Press, pp. 1–27.
Dewey, J. (1922) *Human nature and conduct: An introduction to social psychology*. New York: Holt.
Diakopoulos, N. (2020) 'Accountability, transparency, and algorithms'. In Dubber, M. D., Pasquale, F., and Das, S. (eds.), *The Oxford handbook of ethics of AI*. Oxford: Oxford University Press, pp. 197–210.
Dicksee, L. R. (1919) *Auditing: A practical manual for auditors*. London: Gee & Co.
Dionysiou, D. D., and Tsoukas, H. (2013) 'Understanding the (re)creation of routines from within: A symbolic interactionist perspective'. *Academy of Management Review*, 38(2), pp. 181–205.
Djelic, M.-L., and Sahlin-Andersson, K. (2006) 'Introduction: A world of governance: The rise of transnational regulation'. In Djelic, M.-L., and Sahlin-Andersson, K. (eds.), *Transnational governance: Institutional dynamics of regulation*. Cambridge: Cambridge University Press, pp. 1–28.
Dock, V. T., Guy, D. M., and Williams, D. Z. (1974) 'Integrating the computer in the classroom: An approach in auditing'. *The Accounting Review*, 49(1), pp. 149–153.
Doganova, L. (2024) *Discounting the future: The ascendancy of a political technology*. Princeton: Princeton University Press.
Donia, J., 2025. 'Algorithmic accountabilities and health systems: A review and sociomaterial approach'. *Big Data & Society*, 12(2), https://doi.org/10.1177/20539517251334099.
Doorey, D. J. (2011) 'The transparent supply chain: From resistance to implementation at Nike and Levi-Strauss'. *Journal of Business Ethics*, 103, pp. 587–603.
Douglas, M. (1986) *How institutions think*. London: Routledge.

Douglas, M. (1992) 'Thought style exemplified: The idea of the self'. In Douglas, M. (ed.), *Risk and blame: Essays in cultural theory*. London: Routledge, pp. 211–234.

Douglas, M., and Wildavsky, A. (1982) *Risk and culture: An essay on the selection of technical and environmental dangers*. Berkeley: University of California Press.

Dourish, P. (2001, September) 'Process descriptions as organisational accounting devices: The dual use of workflow technologies'. *Group'01 Proceedings of the 2001 ACM International Conference on Supporting Group Work*, pp. 52–60, https://doi.org/10.1145/500286.500297.

Dourish, P. (2016) 'Algorithms and their others: Algorithmic culture in context'. *Big Data & Society*, 3(2), pp. 205–216.

DRCF. (2022) *Auditing algorithms: The existing landscape, role of regulator and future outlook*. https://www.gov.uk/government/publications/findings-from-the-drcf-algorithmic-processing-workstream-spring-2022/auditing-algorithms-the-existing-landscape-role-of-regulators-and-future-outlook.

Drori, G. S., and Meyer, J. W. (2006) 'Global scientization: An environment for expanded organization'. In Drori, G. S., Meyer, J. W., and Hwang, H. (eds.), *Globalization and organization: World society and organizational change*. Oxford: Oxford University Press, pp. 50–68.

Drori, G. S., Meyer, J. W., Ramirez, F. O., and Schofer, E. (2003) *Science in the modern world polity: Institutionalization and globalization*. Stanford, CA: Stanford University Press.

DuPont, Q. (2017) 'Experiments in algorithmic governance: A history and ethnography of "The DAO," a failed decentralized autonomous organization'. In Campbell-Verduyn, M. (ed.), *Bitcoin and beyond: Cryptocurrencies, blockchains, and global governance*. London: Routledge, pp. 157–177.

DuPont, Q. (2024) 'A progressive Web3: From social coproduction to digital polycentric governance'. In DuPont, Q., Kavanagh, D., and Dylan-Ennis, P. (eds.), *Defining Web3: A guide to the new cultural economy*. Leeds: Emerald Publishing, pp. 57–74. https://doi.org/10.1108/S0733-558X20240000089005.

Durkheim, E. (1982) 'What is a social fact?' In Lukes, S. (ed.), *Durkheim: The rules of sociological method*. London: Palgrave, pp. 50–59.

Economist. (2007) 'Five years under the thumb'. *The Economist*, July, https://www.economist.com/briefing/2007/07/26/five-years-under-the-thumb.

Edelman, L., Uggen, C. and Erlanger, H. (1999) 'The endogeneity of legal regulation: Grievance procedures as rational myth'. *American Journal of Sociology*, 105(2), pp. 406–454.

Edelman, L. B. (1990) 'Legal environments and organizational governance: The expansion of due process in the American workplace'. *American Journal of Sociology*, 95(6), pp. 1401–1440.

Edelman, L. B. (2016) *Working law*. Chicago: University of Chicago Press.

Edelman, L. B., Fuller, S.R., and Mara-Drita, I. (2001) 'Diversity rhetoric and the managerialization of law'. *American Journal of Sociology*, 106(6), pp. 1589–1641.

Edmonds, J. (2024) *How to think about algorithms*. Cambridge: Cambridge University Press.

Egbert, S. (2019) 'Predictive policing and the platformization of police work'. *Surveillance & Society*, 17(1–2), pp. 83–88.

Egbert, S., and Esposito, E. (2024) 'Algorithmic crime prevention: From abstract police to precision policing', *Policing and Society*, 34(6), pp. 521–534.

Eisenman, M., and Frenkel, M. (2021) 'Remembering materiality: A material–relational approach to organizational memory'. *Organization Theory*, 2(3), https://doi.org/10.1177/26317877211029666.

Elkins, J. (1995) 'Marks, traces, "traits," contours, "orli," and "splendores": Nonsemiotic elements in pictures'. *Critical Inquiry*, 21(4), pp. 822–860.

Elliott, C. (2014) *Elliott Review into the integrity and assurance of food supply networks: Final report: A national food crime prevention framework*. London: Department for Environment, Food & Rural Affairs Food Standards Agency. https://www.gov.uk/government/publications/elliott-review-into-the-integrity-and-assurance-of-food-supply-networks-final-report.

Elyachar, J. (2017) 'Upending infrastructure in times of revolt'. In Enfield, N. J., and Kockelman, P. (eds.), *Distributed agency*. Oxford: Oxford University Press, pp. 49–55.

Emirbayer, M., and Mische, A. (1998) 'What is agency?' *American Journal of Sociology*, 103(4), pp. 962–1023.

Enfield, N. J. (2017) 'Distribution of agency'. In Enfield, N. J., and Kockelman, P. (eds.), *Distributed agency*. Oxford: Oxford University Press, pp. 9–14.

Erickson, I., and Wajcman, J. (2022) 'Optimizing temporal capital: How big tech imagines time as auditable'. *American Behavioral Scientist*, 67(14), pp. 1755–1770. doi:10.1177/00027642221127243.

Ericson, R. V., and Haggerty, K. D. (eds.). (2006) *The new politics of surveillance and visibility*. Toronto: University of Toronto Press.

Espeland, W., and Sauder, M. (2007) 'Rankings and reactivity: How public measures recreate social worlds'. *American Journal of Sociology*, 113(1), pp. 1–30.

Espeland, W., and Stevens, M. (1998) 'Commensuration as a social process'. *Annual Review of Sociology*, 24, pp. 312–343.

Espeland, W. N., and Hirsch, P. M. (1990) 'Ownership changes, accounting practice and the redefinition of the corporation'. *Accounting, Organizations and Society*, 15(1–2), pp. 77–96.

Espeland, W. N., and Sauder, M. (2016) *Engines of anxiety: Academic rankings, reputation, and accountability*. New York: Russell Sage Foundation.

Esposito, E. (2011) *The future of futures: The time of money in financing and society*. Cheltenham: Edward Elgar Publishing.

Esposito, E. (2024) 'Can we use the open future? Preparedness and innovation in times of self-generated uncertainty'. *European Journal of Social Theory*, 27(2), pp. 209–224.

Esposito, E., and Stark, D. (2019) 'What's observed in a rating? Rankings as orientation in the face of uncertainty'. *Theory, Culture & Society*, 36(4), pp. 3–26.

Evangelista, R. (2019) 'Review of Zuboff's "The Age of Surveillance Capitalism"'. *Surveillance & Society*, 17(1–2), pp. 246–251.

Ezzamel, M. (2012) *Accounting and order*. London: Routledge.

Ezzamel, M., and Hoskin, K. (2002) 'Retheorizing accounting, writing and money with evidence from Mesopotamia and ancient Egypt'. *Critical Perspectives on Accounting*, 13(3), pp. 333–367.

Falk, A., and Kosfeld, M. (2006) 'The hidden costs of control'. *The American Economic Review*, 96(5), pp. 1611–1630.

Farrell, H., and Fourcade, M. (2023) 'The moral economy of high-tech modernism'. *Dædalus*, 152(1), pp. 225–235.

Fauré, B., Brummans, B. H., Giroux, H. and Taylor, J. R. (2010) 'The calculation of business, or the business of calculation? Accounting as organizing through everyday communication'. *Human Relations*, 63(8), pp. 1249–1273.

Favarel-Garrigues, G., Godefroy, T. and Lascoumes, P. (2011) 'Reluctant partners? Banks in the fight against money laundering and terrorism financing in France'. *Security Dialogue*, 42(2), pp. 179–196.

Feldman, M. S. (2000) 'Organizational routines as a source of continuous change'. *Organization Science*, 11(6), pp. 611–629.

Feldman, M. S., and Pentland, B. T. (2003) 'Reconceptualizing organizational routines as a source of flexibility and change'. *Administrative Science Quarterly*, 48(1), pp. 94–118.

Felin, T., Foss, N. J., and Ployhart, R. E. (2015) 'The microfoundations movement in strategy and organization theory'. *The Academy of Management Annals*, 9(1), pp. 575–632.

Ferraris, M. (2012) *Documentality: Why it is necessary to leave traces*. New York: Fordham University Press.

Feyerabend, P. K. (1968) 'How to be a good empiricist: A plea for tolerance in matters epistemological'. In Nidditch, P. H. (ed.), *The philosophy of science*. Oxford: Oxford University Press, pp. 12–39.

Flaherty, M. G. (2011) *The textures of time: Agency and temporal experience.* Philadelphia: Temple University Press.

Flyverbom, M. (2015) 'Sunlight in cyberspace? On transparency as a form of ordering'. *European Journal of Social Theory*, 18(2), pp. 168–184.

Flyverbom, M. (2022) 'Overlit: Digital architectures of visibility'. *Organization Theory*, 3(July–September), pp. 1–16.

Flyverbom, M., and Garsten, C. (2021) 'Anticipation and organization: Seeing, knowing and governing futures'. *Organization Theory*, 2(3), https://doi.org/10.1177/26317877211020325.

Foucault, M. (1970 [1966]) *The order of things: An archaeology of the human sciences.* Translated by A. M. Sheridan. London: Tavistock.

Foucault, M. (1977 [1975]) *Discipline and punish.* Translated by A. M. Sheridan. London: Allen Lane.

Foucault, M. (1980) 'Truth and power'. In *Power/Knowledge.* Bury St Edmunds: Harvester Press, pp. 109–133.

Foucault, M. (1988) 'Technologies of the self'. In *Technologies of the self: A seminar with Michel Foucault.* London: Tavistock.

Foucault, M. (2008) *The birth of biopolitics: Lectures at the Collège de France, 1978–1979.* Edited by Arnold I. Davidson, translated by Graham Burchell. London: Palgrave.

Fourcade, M. (2012) 'The vile and the noble: On the relation between natural and social classifications in the French wine world'. *The Sociological Quarterly*, 53(4), pp. 524–545.

Fourcade, M., and Healy, K. (2024) *The ordinal society.* Cambridge, MA: Harvard University Press.

Fourcade, M., and Johns, F. (2020) 'Loops, ladders and links: The recursivity of social and machine learning'. *Theory and Society*, 49(5), pp. 803–832.

Francis, J. R. (1994) 'Auditing, hermeneutics, and subjectivity'. *Accounting, Organizations and Society*, 19(3), pp. 235–269.

Frankopan, P. (2015) *The silk roads: A new history of the world.* London: Bloomsbury Publishing.

FRC. (2014) *The UK corporate governance code.* London: Financial Reporting Council.

Frenken, K., and Fuenfschilling, L. (2021) 'The rise of online platforms and the triumph of the corporation'. *Sociologica*, 14(3), pp. 101–113.

Freud, S. (1900) *The interpretation of dreams.* Leipzig and Vienna: Franz Deuticke.

Frey, B., and Jegen, R. (2001) 'Motivation crowding theory'. *Journal of Economic Surveys*, 15(1), pp. 589–611.

Friedland, R. (2017) 'The value of institutional logics'. In Krücken, G., Mazza, C., Meyer, R., and Walgenbach, P. (eds.), *New themes in institutional analysis: Topics and issues from european research.* Cheltenham: Edward Elgar, pp. 12–50.

Friedland, R., and Alford, R. (1991) 'Bringing society back in: Symbols, practices and contradictions'. In Powell, W. W., and DiMaggio, P. J. (eds.), *The new institutionalism in organizational analysis.* Chicago: University of Chicago Press, pp. 232–263.

Fullagar, R., and Matheson, C. (2014) 'Stone tool usewear and residue analysis'. In Smith, C. (eds.), *Encyclopedia of global archaeology.* New York: Springer. https://doi.org/10.1007/978-1-4419-0465-2_842.

Funder, A. (2002) *Stasiland: Stories from behind the Berlin Wall.* London: Granta Books.

Gadamer, H. G. (2013) *Truth and method.* London: Bloomsbury Academic.

Gallhofer, S., and Haslam, J. (1991) 'The aura of accounting in the context of a crisis: Germany and the First World War'. *Accounting, Organizations and Society*, 16(5–6), pp. 487–520.

Gallhofer, S., Haslam, J., Monk, E., and Roberts, C. (2006) 'The emancipatory potential of online reporting: The case of counter accounting'. *Accounting, Auditing & Accountability Journal*, 19(5), pp. 681–718. https://doi.org/10.1108/09513570610689668.

Galloway, A. R. (2022) 'Golden age of analog'. *Critical Inquiry*, 48(2), pp. 211–232.

Gane, N. (2006) 'When we have never been human, what is to be done? Interview with Donna Haraway'. *Theory, Culture & Society*, 23(7–8), pp. 135–158.

Garfinkel, H. (1984a [1967]) 'What is ethnomethodology?' In Garfinkel, H. (ed.), *Studies in ethnomethodology*. Cambridge: Polity, pp. 1–34.

Garfinkel, H. (1984b [1967]) '"Good" organizational reasons for "bad" clinical records'. In Garfinkel, H. (ed.), *Studies in ethnomethodology*. Cambridge: Polity, pp. 186–207.

Garud, R., and Gehman, J. (2019) 'Performativity: Not a destination but an ongoing journey'. *Academy of Management Review*, 44(3), pp. 679–684.

Gawande, A. (2010) *The checklist manifesto: How to get things right*. London: Profile Books.

Gellert, R. (2022) 'Comparing definitions of data and information in data protection law and machine learning: A useful way forward to meaningfully regulate algorithms?' *Regulation & Governance*, 16(1), pp. 156–176.

Giddens, A. (1999) 'Elements of the theory of structuration'. In *The constitution of society: Outline of the theory of structuration*. Berkeley: University of California Press, pp. 1–40.

Giles, J. (1993) 'The no-self theory: Hume, Buddhism, and personal identity'. *Philosophy East and West*, 43(2), pp. 175–200.

Gill, M. (2009) *Accountants' truth: Knowledge and ethics in the financial world*. Oxford: Oxford University Press.

Gioia, D. A., Corley, K. G., and Hamilton, A. L. (2013) 'Seeking qualitative rigor in inductive research: Notes on the Gioia methodology'. *Organizational Research Methods*, 16(1), pp. 15–31.

Giraudeau, M. (2012a) 'Remembering the future: Entrepreneurship guidebooks in the US, from meditation to method (1945–1975)'. *Foucault Studies*, 13, pp. 40–66.

Giraudeau, M. (2012b) 'Imagining (the future) business: How to make firms with plans?' In Quattrone, P., Thrift, N., McLean, C., and Puyou, F.-R. (eds.), *Imagining organizations: Performative imagery in business and beyond*. London: Routledge, pp. 213–229.

Gitelman, L. (ed.). (2013) *Raw data is an oxymoron*. Cambridge, MA: MIT Press.

Gkeredakis, M., Lifshitz-Assaf, H., and Barrett, M. (2021) 'Crisis as opportunity, disruption and exposure: Exploring emergent responses to crisis through digital technology'. *Information and Organization*, 31(1), https://doi.org/10.1016/j.infoandorg.2021.100344.

Glaser, V. L., Pollock, N., and D'Adderio, L. (2021) 'The biography of an algorithm: Performing algorithmic technologies in organizations'. *Organization Theory*, 2(2), https://doi.org/10.1177/26317877211004609.

Goffman, E. (1959) *The presentation of self in everyday life*. New York: Knopf Doubleday Publishing Group.

Gomez-Barris, M., and Gray, H. (2010) 'Toward a sociology of traces'. In Gray, M., and Gomez-Barris, M. (eds.), *Toward a sociology of traces*. Minneapolis: University of Minnesota Press, pp. 1–16.

Goodhart, D. (2017) *The road to somewhere: The populist revolt and the future of politics*. Oxford: Oxford University Press.

Goodman, B.W. (2016, December) 'A step towards accountable algorithms?: Algorithmic discrimination and the European Union general data protection'. *29th Conference on Neural Information Processing Systems*, https://dblp.org/db/conf/nips/nips2016.html.

Goody, J. (1986) *The logic of writing and the organization of society*. Cambridge: Cambridge University Press.

Gordon, R. J. (2003) *Hi-tech innovation and productivity growth: Does supply create its own demand?* National Bureau of Economic Research. https://www.nber.org/papers/w9437 (accessed 7 December 2024).

Gray, G., and Silbey, S. (2014) 'Governing inside the organization: Interpreting regulation and compliance'. *American Journal of Sociology*, 120(1), pp. 96–145.

Greve, H. R., Palmer, D., and Pozner, J. E. (2010) 'Organizations gone wild: The causes, processes, and consequences of organizational misconduct'. *Academy of Management Annals*, 4(1), pp. 53–107.

Grimes, M., Von Krogh, G., Feuerriegel, S., Rink, F., and Gruber, M. (2023) 'From scarcity to abundance: Scholars and scholarship in an age of generative artificial intelligence'. *Academy of Management Journal*, 66(6), pp. 1617–1624.
Gritsenko, D., and Wood, M. (2022) 'Algorithmic governance: A modes of governance approach'. *Regulation & Governance*, 16(1), pp. 45–62.
Grote, G., Parker, S. K., and Crowston, K. (2024) 'Taming artificial intelligence: A theory of control-acountability alignment among AI developers and users'. *Academy of Management Review*, https://doi.org/10.5465/amr.2023.0117.
Guénin-Paracini, H., Malsch, B., and Paillé, A. M. (2014) 'Fear and risk in the audit process'. *Accounting, Organizations and Society*, 39(4), pp. 264–288.
Guter-Sandu, A., and Mennicken, A. (2022) 'Quantification = economization? Numbers, ratings and rankings in the prison service of England and Wales'. In Mennicken, A., and Salais, R. (eds.), *The new politics of numbers: Utopia, evidence and democracy*. London: Palgrave Macmillan, pp. 307–336.
Haack, P., and Schoeneborn, D. (2015) 'Is decoupling becoming decoupled from institutional theory? A commentary on Wijen'. *Academy of Management Review*, 40(2), pp. 307–310.
Habermas, J. (1977) 'Technical progress and the social life-world'. In Habermas, J. (ed.), *Toward a rational society*. London: Heinemann.
Habermas, J. (1979) *Communication and the evolution of society*. Translated by T. McCarthy. London: Heinemann Educational.
Habermas, J. (2015) *Knowledge and human interests*. New York: John Wiley & Sons.
Hacking, I. (1982) 'Biopower and the avalanche of printed numbers'. *Humanities in Society*, 5(3–4), pp. 279–295.
Hacking, I. (1990) *The taming of chance*. Cambridge: Cambridge University Press.
Hacking, I. (2002) 'Making up people'. In Hacking, I. (ed.), *Historical ontology*. Cambridge, MA: Harvard University Press, pp. 99–114.
Hacking, I. (2004) 'Between Michel Foucault and Erving Goffman: Between discourse in the abstract and face-to-face interaction'. *Economy and Society*, 33(3), pp. 277–302.
Hafermalz, E., and Riemer, K. (2020) 'Interpersonal connectivity work: Being there with and for geographically distant others'. *Organization Studies*, 41(12), pp. 1627–1648. https://doi.org/10.1177/0170840620973664.
Haldane, A. G., and May, R. M. (2011) 'Systemic risk in banking ecosystems'. *Nature*, 469(7330), pp. 351–355.
Halliday, T., and Carruthers, B. (2009) *Bankrupt: Global lawmaking and systemic financial crisis*. Stanford, CA: Stanford University Press.
Hammarfelt, B. M. S., Rijcke, S. D., and Rushforth, A. D. (2016) 'Quantified academic selves: The gamification of science through social networking services'. *Information Research: An International Electronic Journal*, 21(2), p. n2, https://informationr.net/.
Hannigan, T. (2015) 'Close encounters of the conceptual kind: Disambiguating social structure from text'. *Big Data & Society*, 2(2), pp. 1–6.
Hansen, H. K., and Flyverbom, M. (2015) 'The politics of transparency and the calibration of knowledge in the digital age'. *Organization*, 22(6), pp. 872–889.
Haraway, D. (2013) *Simians, cyborgs, and women: The reinvention of nature*. London: Routledge.
Hardy, C., and Maguire, S. (2016) 'Organizing risk: Discourse, power, and "riskification"'. *Academy of Management Review*, 41(1), pp. 80–108.
Hardy, C., Maguire, S., Power, M., and Tsoukas, H. (2020) 'Organizing risk: Organization and management theory for the risk society'. *Academy of Management Annals*, 14(2), pp. 1032–1066.
Hassan, R. (2003) 'The MIT Media Lab: Techno dream factory or alienation as a way of life?' *Media, Culture & Society*, 25(1), pp. 87–106.
Haugeland, J. (1981) 'Analog and analog'. *Philosophical Topics*, 12(1), pp. 213–225.

Hayles, N. K. (2008) *How we became posthuman: Virtual bodies in cybernetics, literature, and informatics*. Chicago: University of Chicago Press.
Hedberg, L. M., and Lounsbury, M. (2021) 'Not just small potatoes: Cultural entrepreneurship in the moralizing of markets'. *Organization Science*, 32(2), pp. 433–454.
Heidegger, M. (2013) *The question concerning technology and other essays*. New York: Harper Perennial Modern Thought.
Heimstädt, M., and Dobusch, L. (2020) 'Transparency and accountability: Causal, critical and constructive perspectives'. *Organization Theory*, 1(4), pp. 1–11.
Hempel, C. (1968) 'Explanation in science and history'. In Nidditch, P. H. (ed.), *The philosophy of science*. Oxford: Oxford University Press, pp. 54–79.
Henman, P. (2020) 'Governing by algorithms and algorithmic governmentality: Towards machinic judgement'. In Schuilenburg, M., and Peeters, R. (eds.) *The Algorithmic Society*. London: Routledge, pp. 19–34.
Hernes, T. (2014) *A process theory of organization*. Oxford: Oxford University Press.
Hernes, T. (2022) *Organizations and time*. Oxford: Oxford University Press.
Hernes, T., and Schultz, M. (2020) 'Translating the distant into the present: How actors address distant past and future events through situated activity'. *Organization Theory*, 1(1), https://doi.org/10.1177/2631787719900999.
Hesse, M. (1995) 'Habermas and the force of dialectical argument'. *History of European Ideas*, 21(3), pp. 367–378.
Hilgartner, S. (1992) 'The social construction of risk objects: Or, how to pry open networks of risk'. In Short, J. F., and Clarke, L. B. (eds.), *Organizations, uncertainties, and risk*. Boulder, CO: Westview Press, pp. 39–53.
Hines, R. D. (1988) 'Financial accounting: In communicating reality, we construct reality'. *Accounting, Organizations and Society*, 13(3), pp. 251–261.
Hinings, C. R., Logue, D., and Zietsma, C. (2017) 'Fields, institutional infrastructure and governance'. In Greenwood, R., Oliver, C., Lawrence, T., and Meyer, R. (eds.), *The Sage handbook of organizational institutionalism*. Thousand Oaks, CA: Sage, pp. 216–245.
Holt, R., and Sandberg, J. (2011) 'Phenomenology and organization theory'. In Tsoukas, H., and Chia, R. (eds.), *Philosophy and organization theory*. Cheltenham: Emerald Group Publishing, pp. 215–249.
Hood, C. (1995) 'The "new public management" in the 1980s: Variations on a theme'. *Accounting, Organizations and Society*, 20(2–3), pp. 93–109.
Hood, C. (2002) 'The risk game and the blame game'. *Government and Opposition*, 37(1), pp. 15–37.
Hood, C., and Heald, D. (eds.). (2006) *Transparency: The key to better governance?* (Vol. 135). Oxford: Oxford University Press for The British Academy.
Hood, C., James, O., Jones, G., Scott, C., and Travers, T. (1998) 'Regulation inside government: Where new public management meets the audit explosion'. *Public Money and Management*, 18(2), pp. 61–68.
Hood, C., Rothstein, H., and Baldwin, R. (2001) *The government of risk: Understanding risk regulation regimes*. Oxford: Oxford University Press.
Hood, C., Rothstein, H., Spackman, M., Rees, W. J., and Baldwin, R. (1999) 'Explaining risk regulation regimes: Exploring the "minimal feasible response" hypothesis'. *Health, Risk & Society*, 1(2), pp. 151–166.
Hopwood, A. G. (1983) 'On trying to study accounting in the contexts in which it operates'. *Accounting, Organizations and Society*, 8(2–3), pp. 287–305.
Hopwood, A. G. (1992) 'Accounting calculation and the shifting sphere of the economic'. *European Accounting Review*, 1(1), pp. 125–143.
Hopwood, A. G. (2007) 'Whither accounting research?' *The Accounting Review*, 82(5), pp. 1365–1374.
Hopwood, A. G., and Miller, P. (eds.). (1994) *Accounting as social and institutional practice* (Vol. 24). Cambridge: Cambridge University Press.

Horkheimer, M., and Adorno, T. W. (2002 [1972]) *Dialectic of enlightenment*. Edited by G. Noerr, translated by E. Jephcott. Stanford, CA: Stanford University Press.

Horvath, A. (2023) 'Organizational supererogation and the transformation of nonprofit accountability'. *American Journal of Sociology*, 128(4), pp. 1031–1076.

House of Commons Business, Energy and Industrial Strategy and Work and Pensions Committees. (2018) *Carillion: Second joint report from the Business, Energy and Industrial Strategy and Work and Pensions Committees of Session 2017–19*. HC 769. London: House of Commons. Published 16 May 2018.

Howlett, P., and Morgan, M. S. (eds.). (2010) *How well do facts travel?: The dissemination of reliable knowledge*. Cambridge: Cambridge University Press.

Huang, J. Y. (2015) 'Effectiveness of US anti-money laundering regulations and HSBC case study'. *Journal of Money Laundering Control*, 18(4), pp. 525–532.

Hudson, W. D. (ed.). (1969) *Is-ought question*. London: Palgrave Macmillan.

Huising, R., and Silbey, S. S. (2021) 'Accountability infrastructures: Pragmatic compliance inside organizations'. *Regulation & Governance*, 15, pp. S40–S62.

Hull, M. S. (2012a) 'Documents and bureaucracy'. *Annual Review of Anthropology*, 41, pp. 251–267.

Hull, M. S. (2012b) Government of paper: The materiality of bureaucracy in urban Pakistan. Berkeley: University of California Press.

Hume, D. (1955 [1748]) *An inquiry concerning human understanding*. Indianapolis, IN: Bobbs-Merrill.

Hunt, B. (2003) *The timid corporation: Why business is terrified of taking risk*. New York: John Wiley & Sons.

Hurley, M., and Adebayo, J. (2016) 'Credit scoring in the era of big data'. *Yale Journal of Law & Technology*, 18, pp. 148–216.

Husserl, E. (1970) *The crisis of the European sciences and transcendental philosophy*. Translated by D. Carr. Evanston, IL: Northwestern University Press.

Hwang, H., and Colyvas, J. (2020) 'Ontology, levels of society, and degrees of generality: Theorizing actors as abstractions in institutional theory'. *Academy of Management Review*, 45(3), pp. 570–595.

Ibrahim, A. E. A., Elamer, A. A., and Ezat, A. N. (2021) 'The convergence of big data and accounting: Innovative research opportunities'. *Technological Forecasting and Social Change*, 173, https://doi.org/10.1016/j.techfore.2021.121171.

Jackson, M. W. (1994) 'Natural and artificial budgets: Accounting for Goethe's economy of nature'. *Science in Context*, 7(3), pp. 409–431.

Jarzabkowski, P., Unger, C., and Meissner, K. (2025) 'Valuing what you risk and risking what you value: Advancing a research agenda for risk studies'. *Organization Studies*, 46(1), pp. 121–139.

Jasanoff, S., and Kim, S. H. (2015) *Dreamscapes of modernity: Sociotechnical imaginaries and the fabrication of power*. Chicago: University of Chicago Press.

Jasanoff, S. S. (1987) 'Contested boundaries in policy-relevant science'. *Social Studies of Science*, 17(2), pp. 195–230.

Jaser, Z., and Tourish, D. (2024) 'Hegemonic surveillance at work: Fabricating the cyberized, totalized and thespianized employee'. *Organization Theory*, 5(1), https://doi.org/10.1177/26317877241235940.

Jeacle, I., and Carter, C. (2011) 'In TripAdvisor we trust: Rankings, calculative regimes and abstract systems'. *Accounting, Organizations and Society*, 36(4–5), pp. 293–309.

Jeacle, I., and Carter, C. (2022) 'Audit society goes viral: The rise of the online auditor'. *Qualitative Research in Accounting & Management*, 19(2), pp. 231–240.

Jeacle, I., and Carter, C. (2023) 'Calorie accounting: The introduction of mandatory calorie labelling on menus in the UK food sector'. *Accounting, Organizations and Society*, 110, https://doi.org/10.1016/j.aos.2023.101468.

Jepperson, R. (1991) 'Institutions, institutional effects, and institutionalism'. In Powell, W. W. and DiMaggio, P. J. (eds.), *The new institutionalism in organizational analysis*. Chicago: University of Chicago Press, pp. 143–163.

Joas, H. (2001) *The genesis of values*. Chicago: University of Chicago Press.

Johnson, T. (1994) *Future events: A conceptual study of their significance for recognition and measurement*. Norwalk, CT: Financial Accounting Standards Board.

Johnson, T. H., and Kaplan, R. S. (1987) *Relevance lost: The rise and fall of management accounting*. Cambridge, MA: Harvard Business Books.

Jordan, S., Mitterhofer, H., and Jørgensen, L. (2018) 'The interdiscursive appeal of risk matrices: Collective symbols, flexibility normalism and the interplay of "risk" and "uncertainty"'. *Accounting, Organizations and Society*, 67, pp. 34–55.

Jørgensen, L., and Jordan, S. (2016) 'Risk mapping: Day-to-day riskwork in inter-organizational project management'. In Power, M. (ed.), *Riskwork: Essays on the organizational life of risk management*. Oxford: Oxford University Press, pp. 50–71.

Joseph, S. (2015) *Positive psychology in practice: Promoting human flourishing in work, health, education, and everyday life*. New York: John Wiley & Sons.

Kaghan, W., and Lounsbury, M. (2006) 'Artifacts, articulation work and institutional residue'. In Rafaeli, A., and Pratt, M. (eds.), *Artifacts and organizations: Beyond mere symbolism*. Mahwah, NJ: Lawrence Erlbaum Associates, pp. 259–278.

Kant, I. (1978 [1787]) *Critique of pure reason*. Translated by N. Kemp-Smith. London: Macmillan.

Kaplinsky, R., and Morris, M. (2000) *A handbook for value chain research* (Vol. 113). Brighton: University of Sussex, Institute of Development Studies.

Karacan, R., and Kayacan, E. Y. (2024) 'How environmentally friendly are electric cars? The relationship between lithium usage and water resources, Chile example'. *Managerial and Decision Economics*, 45, pp. 5346–5358, doi:10.1002/mde.4324.

Kavanagh, D., and Dylan-Ennis, P. (2020) 'Cryptocurrencies and the emergence of blockocracy'. *The Information Society*, 36(5), pp. 290–300.

Kellogg, C. (2009) *Law's trace: From Hegel to Derrida*. London: Routledge.

Kellogg, K. C., Valentine, M. A., and Christin, A. (2020) 'Algorithms at work: The new contested terrain of control'. *Academy of Management Annals*, 14(1), pp. 366–410.

Kilfoyle, E., Richardson, A. J., and MacDonald, L. D. (2013) 'Vernacular accountings: Bridging the cognitive and the social in the analysis of employee-generated accounting systems'. *Accounting, Organizations and Society*, 38(5), pp. 382–396.

Kirsch, D., Moeen, M., and Wadhwani, R. D. (2014) 'Historicism and industry emergence: Industry knowledge from pre-emergence to stylized fact'. In Bucheli, M., and Wadhwani, R. D. (eds.), *Organizations in time: History, theory, methods*. Oxford: Oxford University Press, pp. 217–250.

Kitchen, R. (2022) *The data revolution*. 2nd edition. London: Sage.

Kjellberg, H., Hagberg, J., and Cochoy, F. (2019) 'Enacting a digital market infrastructure in the US grocery retail sector, 1967–2010'. In Kornberger, M., Bowker, G., Pollock, N., Miller, P., Mennicken, A., Randa Nucho, J., and Elyachar, J. (eds.), *Thinking infrastructures: Research in the sociology of organizations* (Vol. 62). Bingley: Emerald Group Publishing, pp. 207–232.

Klamer, A., and McCloskey, D. (1992) 'Accounting as the master metaphor of economics'. *European Accounting Review*, 1(1), pp. 145–160.

Knechel, W. R. (2007) 'The business risk audit: Origins, obstacles and opportunities'. *Accounting, Organizations and Society*, 32(4–5), pp. 383–408.

Knechel, W. R., Thomas, E., and Driskill, M. (2020) 'Understanding financial auditing from a service perspective'. *Accounting, Organizations and Society*, 81, pp. 1–23.

Knight, F. H. (1921) *Risk, uncertainty, and profit*. Boston: Hart, Schaffner & Marx; Houghton Mifflin Company.

Knorr Cetina, K. (1999) *Epistemic cultures: How the sciences make knowledge*. Cambridge, MA: Harvard University Press.

Knorr Cetina, K. (2001) 'Postsocial relations: Theorizing sociality in a postsocial environment'. In Ritzer, G., and Smart, B. (eds.), *Handbook of social theory*. London: Sage, pp. 520–537.

Knudsen, D. R. (2020) 'Elusive boundaries, power relations, and knowledge production: A systematic review of the literature on digitalization in accounting'. *International Journal of Accounting Information Systems*, 36, https://doi.org/10.1016/j.accinf.2019.100441.

Kockelman, P. (2017) 'Gnomic agency'. In Enfield, N. J., and Kockelman, P. (eds.), *Distributed agency*. Oxford: Oxford University Press, pp. 15–23.

Kolb, D. G. (2008) 'Exploring the metaphor of connectivity: Attributes, dimensions and duality'. *Organization Studies*, 29(1), pp. 127–144. https://doi.org/10.1177/0170840607084574.

Kolb, D. G., Caza, A., and Collins, P. D. (2012) 'States of connectivity: New questions and new directions'. *Organization Studies*, 33(2), pp. 267–273. https://doi.org/10.1177/0170840611431653.

Kolb, D. G., Collins, P. D., and Lind, E. A. (2008) 'Requisite connectivity: Finding flow in a not-so-flat world.' *Organizational Dynamics*, 37(2), pp. 181–189.

Kolb, D. G., Dery, K., Huysman, M., and Metiu, A. (2020) 'Connectivity in and around organizations: Waves, tensions and trade-offs'. *organization Studies*, 41(12), pp. 1589–1599. https://doi.org/10.1177/0170840620973666.

Kordzadeh, N., and Ghasemaghaei, M. (2022) 'Algorithmic bias: Review, synthesis, and future research directions'. *European Journal of Information Systems*, 31(3), pp. 388–409.

Kornberger, M. (2013) 'Disciplining the future: On studying the politics of strategy'. *Scandinavian Journal of Management*, 29(1), pp. 104–107.

Kornberger, M., Pflueger, D., and Mouritsen, J. (2017) 'Evaluative infrastructures: Accounting for platform organization'. *Accounting, Organizations and Society*, 60, pp. 79–95.

Kotsantonis, S., and Serafeim, G. (2019) 'Four things no one will tell you about ESG data'. *Journal of Applied Corporate Finance*, 31(2), pp. 50–58.

Kozinets, R. V. (2012) 'Marketing netnography: Prom/ot(ulgat)ing a new research method'. *Journal of Marketing Management*, 28(9–10), pp. 1233–1250.

Kraatz, M., Ventresca, M., and Deng, L. (2010) 'Precarious values and mundane innovations: Enrollment management in American liberal arts colleges'. *Academy of Management Journal*, 53(6), pp. 1521–1545.

Kraatz, M. S., and Block, E. S. (2008) 'Organizational implications of institutional pluralism'. In Greenwood, R., Oliver, C., Suddaby, R., and Sahlin-Andersson, K. (eds.), *The Sage handbook of organizational institutionalism*. London: Sage, pp. 243–275.

Kraatz, M. S., and Flores, R. (2015) 'Reinfusing values'. In Kraatz, M. (ed.), *Institutions and ideals: Philip Selznick's legacy for organizational studies*. Bingley: Emerald Group Publishing, pp. 353–381.

Kretschmann, L. (2020) 'Leading indicators and maritime safety: Predicting future risk with a machine learning approach'. *Journal of Shipping and Trade*, 5, 19, https://doi.org/10.1186/s41072-020-00071-1.

Kucklick, C. (2014) *Die granuläre Gesellschaft: Wie das Digitale unsere Wirklichkeit auflöst*. Berlin: Ullstein eBooks.

Kurum, E. (2023) 'RegTech solutions and AML compliance: What future for financial crime?' *Journal of Financial Crime*, 30(3), pp. 776–794.

Kurunmäki, L., and Miller, P. (2013) 'Calculating failure: The making of a calculative infrastructure for forgiving and forecasting failure'. *Business History*, 55(7), pp. 1100–1118.

La Porte, T. R. (1996) 'High reliability organizations: Unlikely, demanding and at risk'. *Journal of Contingencies and Crisis Management*, 4(2), pp. 60–71.

Lampland, M. (2010) 'False numbers as formalizing practices'. *Social Studies of Science*, 40(3), pp. 377–404.

Landes, D. S. (1984) *Revolution in time: Clocks and the making of the modern world*. Cambridge, MA: Harvard University Press.

Langley, A. (1999) 'Strategies for theorizing from process data'. *Academy of Management Review*, 24(4), pp. 691–710.

Langley, A., Smallman, C., Tsoukas, H., and Van de Ven, A. H. (2013) 'Process studies of change in organization and management: Unveiling temporality, activity, and flow'. *Academy of Management Journal*, 56(1), pp. 1–13.

Lanzolla, G., Lorenz, A., Miron-Spektor, E., Schilling, M., Solinas, G., and Tucci, C. L. (2020) 'Digital transformation: What is new if anything? Emerging patterns and management research'. *Academy of Management Discoveries*, 6(3), pp. 341–350.

Larson, B. Z., Moser, C., Caza, A., Muehlfeld, K., and Colombo, L. A. (2024) 'Critical thinking in the age of generative AI'. *Academy of Management Learning & Education*, 23(3), pp. 373–378.

Latour, B. (1986) 'Visualization and cognition: Thinking with eyes and hands'. In Kuklick, H. (ed.), *Knowledge and society: Studies in the sociology of culture past and present* (Vol. 6). Bingley: JAI Press, pp. 1–40.

Latour, B. (1987) *Science in action: How to follow scientists and engineers through society*. Cambridge, MA: Harvard University Press.

Latour, B. (1999) *Pandora's hope*. Cambridge, MA: Harvard University Press.

Latour, B. (2005) *Reassembling the social*. Oxford: Oxford University Press.

Latour, B. (2013) *An inquiry into modes of existence: An anthropology of the moderns*. Translated by C. Porter. Cambridge, MA: Harvard University Press

Laughlin, R. (2011) 'Accounting research, policy and practice: Worlds together or worlds apart'. In Evans, E., Burritt, R., and Guthrie, J. (eds.), *Bridging the gap between academic accounting research and professional practice*. Sydney: Institute of Chartered Accountants in Australia, pp. 23–30.

Lavie, D., Pollicino, O. and Valletti, T. (2025) 'Certification of business practices and algorithms as a complementary approach to platform regulation'. *Academy of Management Perspectives*, https://doi.org/10.5465/amp.2023.0421.

Law, J., and Mol, A. (1995) 'Notes on materiality and sociality'. *The Sociological Review*, 43(2), pp. 274–294.

Leavitt, K., Schabram, K., Hariharan, P., and Barnes, C. M. (2020) 'Ghost in the machine: On organizational theory in the age of machine learning'. *Academy of Management Review*, 46(4), pp. 750–777, https://doi.org/10.5465/amr.2019.0247.

Leonardi, P. M., and Treem, J. W. (2020) 'Behavioral visibility: A new paradigm for organization studies in the age of digitization, digitalization, and datafication'. *Organization Studies*, 41(12), pp. 1601–1625.

Lepenies, W. (1988) *Between literature and science: The rise of sociology* (Vol. 10). Cambridge: Cambridge University Press.

Levi-Faur, D. (2005) 'The global diffusion of regulatory capitalism'. *Annals of the American Academy of Political and Social Science*, 598(1), pp. 12–32.

Levin, D. M. (1998) 'Tracework: Myself and others in the moral phenomenology of Merleau-Ponty and Levinas'. *International Journal of Philosophical Studies*, 6(3), pp. 345–392.

Levinas, E. (1986) 'The trace of the other'. In Taylor, M. C. (ed.), *Deconstruction in context*. Chicago: University of Chicago Press, pp. 345–359.

Lewis, S., and Boyle, M. (2017) 'The expanding role of traceability in seafood: Tools and key initiatives'. *Journal of Food Science*, 82(S1), pp. A14–A21.

Lezaun, J. (2006) 'Creating a new object of government: Making genetically modified organisms traceable'. *Social Studies of Science*, 36(4), pp. 499–531.

Linck, J. S., Netter, J. M., and Yang, T. (2009) The effects and unintended consequences of the Sarbanes-Oxley Act on the supply and demand for directors. *The Review of Financial Studies*, 22(8), pp. 3287–3328.

Lodge, M., and Mennicken, A. (2019) 'Reflecting on public service regulation by algorithm'. In Yeung, K., and Lodge, M. (eds.), *Algorithmic regulation*. Oxford: Oxford University Press, pp. 176–198.

Lok, J., Creed, W. E. D., DeJordy, R., and Voronov, M. (2017) 'Living institutions: Bringing emotions into organizational institutionalism'. In Greenwood, R., Oliver, C., Lawrence, T.,

and Meyer, R. (eds.), *The Sage handbook of organizational institutionalism*. Thousand Oaks, CA: Sage, pp. 691–620.
Lounsbury, M., and Gehman, J. (2024) 'Introduction: The organization theory landscape'. In *Concise introduction to organization theory*. Cheltenham: Edward Elgar Publishing, pp. 1–28.
Luhmann, N. (1993) *Risk: A sociological theory*. New York: de Gruyter.
Lumineau, F., Wang, W., and Schilke, O. (2021) 'Blockchain governance: A new way of organizing collaborations?' *Organization Science*, 32(2), pp. 500–521.
Lupton, D. (2014, December) 'Self-tracking cultures: Towards a sociology of personal informatics'. In *Proceedings of the 26th Australian computer-human interaction conference on designing futures: The future of design*, pp. 77–86, https://doi.org/10.1145/2686612.2686623.
Lupton, D. (2016a) 'Digital companion species and eating data: Implications for theorising digital data–human assemblages'. *Big Data & Society*, 3(1), https://doi.org/10.1177/2053951715619947.
Lupton, D. (2016b) 'The diverse domains of quantified selves: Self-tracking modes and dataveillance'. *Economy and Society*, 45(1), pp. 101–122.
Lupton, D. (2016c) *The quantified self*. London: John Wiley & Sons.
Lupton, D., and Smith, G. J. D. (2018) '"A much better person": The agential capacities of self-tracking practices'. In Ajana, B. (ed.), *Metric culture*. Leeds: Emerald Publishing, pp. 57–75. https://doi.org/10.1108/978-1-78743-289-520181004.
Lustig, C., and Nardi, B. (2015) 'Algorithmic authority: The case of Bitcoin'. *2015 48th Hawaii international conference on system sciences*, https://www.computer.org/csdl/proceedings/hicss/2015/12OmNyr8Yts, pp. 743–752. IEEE Computer Society.
Lyon, D. (1994) *The electronic eye: The rise of surveillance society*. Minneapolis: University of Minnesota Press.
Lyon, D. (2001) *Surveillance society*. Columbus: McGraw-Hill Education (UK).
Lyon, D. (2006) '9/11, synopticon, and scopophilia: Watching and being watched'. In Ericson, R. V., and Haggerty, K. D. (eds.), *The new politics of surveillance and visibility*. Toronto: University of Toronto Press, pp. 35–54.
Lyon, D. (2018) *The culture of surveillance: Watching as a way of life*. New York: John Wiley & Sons.
Lyotard, J. F. (1984) *The postmodern condition: A report on knowledge* (Vol. 10). Minneapolis: University of Minnesota Press.
MacKenzie, D., Muniesa, F., and Siu, L. (2007) 'Introduction'. In MacKenzie, D., Muniesa, F., and Siu, L. (eds.), *Do economists make markets? On the performativity of economics*. Princeton: Princeton University Press, pp. 1–19.
Macve, R. (2015) *A conceptual framework for financial accounting and reporting: Vision, tool, or threat?* London: Routledge.
Mainelli, M., and Leitch, M. (2017) 'Auditing mutual distributed ledgers (aka blockchains): A foray into distributed governance & forensics,' *Auditing Mutual Distributed Ledgers*- Long Finance, SSRN: https://ssrn.com/abstract=3676198.
Malisic, B., Misic, N., Krco, S., Martinovic, A., Tinaj, S., and Popovic, T. (2023) 'Blockchain adoption in the wine supply chain: A systematic literature review'. *Sustainability*, 15(19), https://doi.org/10.3390/su151914408.
March, J. G. (1987) 'Ambiguity and accounting: The elusive link between information and decision making'. *Accounting, Organizations and Society*, 12(2), pp. 153–168.
March, J. G. (2006) 'Rationality, foolishness, and adaptive intelligence. *Management and Organization Review*, 2(1), pp. 1–30.
Marcuse, H. (1986 [1964]) *One-dimensional man*. London: ARK.
Marquis, C., and Tilcsik, A. (2013) 'Imprinting: Toward a multilevel theory'. *Academy of Management Annals*, 7(1), pp. 195–245.

Marquis, C., Toffel, M. W., and Zhou, Y. (2016) 'Scrutiny, norms, and selective disclosure: A global study of greenwashing'. *Organization Science*, 27(2), pp. 483–504.
Marti, W., and Gond, J.-P. (2018) 'Why do theories become self-fulfilling? Exploring the boundary conditions of performativity'. *Academy of Management Review*, 43(3), pp. 487–508.
Martinez, D. E., Pflueger, D., and Palermo, T. (2022) 'Accounting and the territorialization of markets: A field study of the Colorado cannabis market'. *Accounting, Organizations and Society*, 102, https://doi.org/10.1016/j.aos.2022.101351.
Marx, G. T. (1988) *Undercover: Police surveillance in America*. Berkeley: University of California Press.
Marx, G. T. (2002) 'What's new about the "new surveillance"? Classifying for change and continuity'. *Surveillance & Society*, 1(1), pp. 9–29.
Marx, G. T. (2006) 'Varieties of personal information as influences on attitudes towards surveillance'. In Ericson, R., and Haggerty, K. (eds.) *The new politics of surveillance and visibility*. Toronto: Toronto University Press, pp. 79–110.
Mathiesen, T. (1997) 'The viewer society: Michel Foucault's Panopticon revisited'. *Theoretical Criminology*, 1(2), pp. 215–234.
Matringe, N., and Power, M., 2024. 'Memories lost: A history of accounting records as forms of projection'. *Accounting, Organizations and Society*, 112, https://doi.org/10.1016/j.aos.2023.101514.
Mayer, A. (2009) 'Online social networks in economics'. *Decision Support Systems*, 47(3), pp. 169–184.
Mazmanian, M., and Beckman, C. M. (2018) '"Making" your numbers: Engendering organizational control through a ritual of quantification'. *Organization Science*, 29(3), pp. 357–379.
McCloskey, D. N. (2016) *Bourgeois equality: How ideas, not capital or institutions, enriched the world* (Vol. 3). Chicago: University of Chicago Press.
McConnell, A., and Drennan, L. (2006) 'Mission impossible? Planning and preparing for crisis'. *Journal of Contingencies and Crisis Management*, 14(2), pp. 59–70.
McDaid, E., Andon, P., and Free, C. (2023) 'Algorithmic management and the politics of demand: Control and resistance at Uber'. *Accounting, Organizations and Society*, 109, https://doi.org/10.1016/j.aos.2023.101465.
McGivern, G., and Ferlie, E. (2007) 'Playing tick-box games: Interrelating defences in professional appraisal'. *Human Relations*, 60(9), pp. 1361–1385.
McKinlay, A., and Starkey, K. (1998) 'Managing Foucault: Foucault, management and organization theory'. In McKinlay, A., and Starkey, K. (eds.), *Foucault, management and organization theory*. London: Sage, pp. 1–13.
McMillan, K. P. (1998) 'The science of accounts: Bookkeeping rooted in the ideal of science'. *Accounting Historians Journal*, 25(2), pp. 1–33.
Mennicken, A., and Espeland, W. N. (2019) 'What's new with numbers? Sociological approaches to the study of quantification'. *Annual Review of Sociology*, 45, pp. 223–245.
Mennicken, A., and Kornberger, M. (2021) 'From performativity to generativity: Valuation and its consequences in the context of digitization', *KZfSS Kölner Zeitschrift für Soziologie und Sozialpsychologie*, 73, pp. 451–478.
Mennicken, A., and Miller, P. (2014) 'Michel Foucault and the administering of lives'. in Adler, P. S., du Gay, P., Morgan, G., and Reed, M. (eds.), *The Oxford handbook of sociology, social theory, and organization studies: Contemporary currents*. Oxford: Oxford University Press, pp. 11–38.
Mentzer, J. T., DeWitt, W., Keebler, J. S., Min, S., Nix, N. W., Smith, C. D., and Zacharia, Z. G. (2001) 'Defining supply chain management'. *Journal of Business Logistics*, 22(2), pp. 1–25.
Merconi, R. (2003) 'On auditing audit trail'. *Security Watch*, 46(1), pp. 17–20.
Merleau-Ponty, M. (1968) *The visible and the invisible: Followed by working notes*. Evanston: Northwestern University Press.

Meyer, J. W. (1986) 'Social environments and organizational accounting'. *Accounting, Organizations and Society*, 11(4–5), pp. 345–356.

Meyer, J. W., and Jepperson, R. L. (2000) 'The "actors" of modern society: The cultural construction of social agency'. *Sociological Theory*, 18(1), pp. 100–120.

Meyer, J. W., and Rowan, B. (1977) 'Institutionalized organizations: Formal structure as myth and ceremony'. *American Journal of Sociology*, 83(2), pp. 340–363.

Mikes, A., and Power, M. (2020) 'The switch: Negotiating between normality and crisis.' Oxford Answers, May 5. https://www.sbs.ox.ac.uk/oxford-answers/switch-negotiating-between-normality-and-crisis#.XrKSAhCRonk.linkedin.

Miller, P. (1991) Accounting innovation beyond the enterprise: Problematizing investment decisions and programming economic growth in the UK in the 1960s. *Accounting, Organizations and Society*, 16(8), pp. 733–762.

Miller, P. (1992) 'Accounting and objectivity: The invention of calculating selves and calculable spaces'. *Annals of Scholarship*, 9(1–2), pp. 61–86.

Miller, P. (1998) 'The margins of accounting'. *European Accounting Review*, 7(4), pp. 605–621.

Miller, P. (2001) 'Governing by numbers: Why calculative practices matter'. *Social Research*, 68(2), pp. 379–396.

Miller, P. (2021) 'Afterword: Quantifying, mediating and intervening: The R number and the politics of health in the twenty-first century'. In Mennicken, A., and Salais, R. (eds.), *The new politics of numbers, executive politics and governance*. London: Palgrave Macmillan, pp. 465–476.

Miller, P., and O'Leary, T. (1987) 'Accounting and the construction of the governable person'. *Accounting, Organizations and Society*, 12, pp. 235–265.

Miller, P., and Power, M. (2013) 'Accounting, organizing, and economizing: Connecting accounting research and organization theory'. *The Academy of Management Annals*, 7(1), pp. 557–605.

Miller, P., and Rose, N. (1990) 'Governing economic life'. *Economy and Society*, 19(1), pp. 1–31.

Millo, Y., Spence, C., and Xu, R. (2024) 'Algorithmic self-referentiality: How machine learning pushes calculative practices to assess themselves'. *Accounting, Organizations and Society*, 113, https://doi.org/10.1016/j.aos.2024.101567.

Min, S., Levina, N., and Lifshitz, H. (2024) Technology-centric contestation over symbolic and social boundaries: The social justice implications of COVID-19 contact tracing technologies. *MIS Quarterly*, 48(4), pp. 1745–1770.

Mintz, S. W. (1986) *Sweetness and power: The place of sugar in modern history*. London: Penguin.

Mirowski, P. (2002) *Machine dreams: Economics becomes a cyborg science*. Cambridge: Cambridge University Press.

Mökander, J. (2023) 'Auditing of AI: Legal, ethical and technical approaches'. *Digital Society*, 2(49), https://doi.org/10.1007/s44206-023-00074-y.

Mökander, J., Schuett, J., Kirk, H. R., and Floridi, L. (2023) 'Auditing large language models: A three-layered approach'. *AI and Ethics*, 4, pp. 1085–1115, https://doi.org/10.1007/s43681-023-00289-2.

Mol, A. (2008) 'I eat an apple: On theorizing subjectivities'. *Subjectivity*, 22(1), pp. 28–37.

Monteiro, E., Pollock, N., Hanseth, O., and Williams, R. (2013) 'From artefacts to infrastructures'. *Computer Supported Cooperative Work (CSCW)*, 22(4), pp. 575–607.

Morgan, M. S. (2012) *The world in the model: How economists work and think*. Cambridge: Cambridge University Press.

Morley, D., and Robins, K. (1995) *Spaces of identity*. London: Taylor & Francis.

Mouritsen, J., Larsen, H. T., and Bukh, P. N. (2001) 'Intellectual capital and the "capable firm": Narrating, visualising and numbering for managing knowledge'. *Accounting, Organizations and Society*, 26(7–8), pp. 735–762.

Muirhead, J., and Porter, T. (2019) 'Traceability in global governance'. *Global Networks*, 19(3), pp. 423–443.

Munro, E. (2004) 'The impact of audit on social work practice'. *British Journal of Social Work*, 34(8), pp. 1075–1095.
Munro, E. (2010) 'Learning to reduce risk in child protection'. *British Journal of Social Work*, 40(4), pp. 1135–1151.
Murray, A., Rhymer, J., and Sirmon, D. G. (2020) 'Humans and technology: Forms of conjoined agency in organizations'. *Academy of Management Review*, 46(3), 552–571
Nafus, D. (ed.) (2016) *Quantified: Biosensing technologies in everyday life*. Cambridge, MA: MIT Press.
Napier, C. J. (1996a) 'Accounting and the absence of a business economics tradition in the United Kingdom'. *European Accounting Review*, 5(3), pp. 449–481.
Napier, C. J. (1996b) 'Academic disdain? Economists and accounting in Britain, 1850–1950'. *Accounting, Business & Financial History*, 6(3), pp. 427–450.
Napolitano, V. (2015) 'Anthropology and traces'. *Anthropological Theory*, 15(1), pp. 47–67.
Neff, G., and Nafus, D. (2016) *Self-tracking*. Cambridge, MA: MIT Press.
Newlands, G. (2021) 'Algorithmic surveillance in the gig economy: The organisation of work through Lefebvrian conceived space'. *Organization Studies*, 42(5), pp. 719–737.
Norreklit, H. (2000) 'The balance on the balanced scorecard a critical analysis of some of its assumptions'. *Management Accounting Research*, 11(1), pp. 65–88.
Nurmi, N., and Hinds, P. J. (2020) 'Work design for global professionals: Connectivity demands, connectivity behaviors, and their effects on psychological and behavioral outcomes'. *Organization Studies*, 41(12), pp. 1697–1724. https://doi.org/10.1177/0170840620937885.
Nyberg, D. (2009) 'Computers, customer service operatives and cyborgs: Intra-actions in call centres'. *Organization Studies*, 30(11), pp. 1181–1199.
Nyman, R., Kapadia, S., and Tuckett, D. (2021) 'News and narratives in financial systems: Exploiting big data for systemic risk assessment'. *Journal of Economic Dynamics and Control*, 127, https://doi.org/10.1016/j.jedc.2021.104119.
Olofsson, T. (2025) 'Predictions, uncertainty, and collective epistemic work: How projected futures informed and misinformed enactments of COVID-19'. *Social Studies of Science*, https://doi.org/10.1177/03063127251351336.
O'Malley, P. (2012) *Risk, uncertainty and government*. London: Routledge-Cavendish.
O'Regan, D. J. (2024) *The closing of the auditor's mind?: How to reverse the erosion of trust, virtue, and wisdom in modern auditing*. Boca Raton: CRC Press.
Orlikowski, W., and Scott, S. (2014) 'What happens when evaluation goes online? Exploring apparatuses of valuation in the travel sector'. *Organization Science*, 25(3), pp. 868–891.
Orlikowski, W. J., and Scott, S.V. (2008) 'Sociomateriality: Challenging the separation of technology, work and organization'. *The Academy of Management Annals*, 2(1), pp. 433–474.
Orlikowski, W. J., and Scott, S. V. (2023) 'The digital undertow and institutional displacement: A sociomaterial approach'. *Organization Theory*, 4(2), https://doi.org/10.1177/26317877231180898.
Orlikowski, W. J., and Yates, J. (2002) 'It's about time: Temporal structuring in organizations'. *Organization Science*, 13(6), pp. 684–700.
Ortiz, H. (2022) 'Political imaginaries of the weighted average cost of capital: A conceptual analysis'. *Valuation Studies*, 8(2), pp. 5–36.
Orton, J. D., and Weick, K. E. (1990) 'Loosely coupled systems: A reconceptualization'. *Academy of Management Review*, 15(2), pp. 203–223.
Pacchera, F., Correia, R. F., Venciūtė, D., and Sousa, B. M. (2023) 'The use of digital technologies for traceability: An analysis of consumer and firm perceptions'. In Correia, R.F., Venciūtė, D., and Sousa, B. M. (eds.), *The role of brands in an era of over-information*. Hershey, PA: IGI Global, pp. 123–145. https://doi.org/10.4018/978-1-6684-8351-0.ch006.
Padgett, J. F., and Powell, W. W. (2012) 'The problem of emergence'. In Padgett, J. F., and Powell, W. W. (eds.), *The emergence of organizations and markets*. Princeton: Princeton University Press, pp. 1–29.

Palermo, T. (2018) 'Accounts of the future: A multiple-case study of scenarios in planning and management control processes'. *Qualitative Research in Accounting & Management*, 15(1), pp. 2–23.

Palermo, T., Power, M., and Ashby, S. (2017) 'Navigating institutional complexity: the production of risk culture in the financial sector'. *Journal of Management Studies*, 54(2), pp. 154–181.

Palermo, T., Power, M., and Ashby, S. (2022) 'How accounting ends: Self-undermining repetition in accounting life cycles'. *Contemporary Accounting Research*, 39(4), pp. 2790–2824.

Pape, H. (2008) 'Searching for traces: How to connect the sciences and the humanities by a Peircean theory of indexicality'. *Transactions of the Charles S. Peirce Society*, 44(1), pp. 1–25.

Parfit, D. (1971) 'On "the importance of self-identity"'. *The Journal of Philosophy*, 68(20), pp. 683–690.

Parfit, D. (1984) *Reasons and persons*. Oxford: Oxford University Press.

Parker, R. H., and Harcourt, G. C. (eds.). (1969) *Readings in the concept and measurement of income*. Cambridge: Cambridge University Press

Pasquale, F. (2015) *The black box society: The secret algorithms that control money and information*. Cambridge, MA: Harvard University Press.

Pedersen, I., and Iliadis, A. (eds.). (2020) *Embodied computing: Wearables, implantables, embeddables, ingestibles*. Cambridge, MA: MIT Press.

Pedersen, M. A. (2014) 'The fetish of connectivity'. In Evans, G., Silva, E., and Thoburn, N. (eds.), *Objects and materials*. London: Routledge, pp. 215–225.

Peirce, C. S. (1957) *Essays in the philosophy of science*. Edited by V. Thomas. New York: Liberal Arts Press.

Pentland, B. T. (1993) 'Getting comfortable with the numbers: Auditing and the micro-production of macro-order'. *Accounting, Organizations and Society*, 18(7–8), pp. 605–620.

Pentland, B.T., Hærem, T., and Hillison, D. (2011) 'The (n)ever-changing world: Stability and change in organizational routines'. *Organization Science*, 22(6), pp. 1369–1383.

Pentland, B. T., and Rueter, H. H. (1994) 'Organizational routines as grammars of action'. *Administrative Science Quarterly*, 39, pp. 484–510.

Pflueger, D. (2016) 'Knowing patients: The customer survey and the changing margins of accounting in healthcare'. *Accounting, Organizations and Society*, 53, pp. 17–33.

Pflueger, D., Kornberger, M., and Mouritsen, J. A. N. (2022) 'What is blockchain accounting? A critical examination in relation to organizing, governance, and trust'. *European Accounting Review*, 33(4), pp. 1139–1164, https://doi.org/10.1080/09638180.2022.2147973.

Pflueger, D., Palermo, T., and Martinez, D. (2019) 'Thinking infrastructure and the organization of markets: The creation of a legal market for cannabis in Colorado'. In Kornberger, M., Bowker, G., Pollock, N., Miller, P., Mennicken, A., Randa Nucho, J., and Elyachar, J. (eds.), *Thinking infrastructures*. Research in the sociology of organizations. Bingley: Emerald Group Publishing, pp. 233–253.

Phillips, N., Lawrence, T. B., and Hardy, C. (2004) 'Discourse and institutions'. *Academy of Management Review*, 29(4), pp. 635–652.

Pickering, A. (1993) 'The mangle of practice: Agency and emergence in the sociology of science'. *American Journal of Sociology*, 99(3), pp. 559–589.

Pidgeon, N., Kasperson, R., and Slovic, P. (eds.). (2003) *The social amplification of risk*. Cambridge: Cambridge University Press.

Pistor, K. (2020) 'Rule by data: The end of markets?' *Law & Contemporary Problems*, 83 (2), pp. 101–124.

Pistor, K. (2019) *The code of capital: How law creates wealth and inequality*. Princeton: Princeton University Press.

Pitti, I. (2024) 'More than "crumbs": Emotional entanglements and situated ethical strategies in qualitative research'. *American Behavioral Scientist*, 68(5), pp. 678–695.

Plantin, J. C., Lagoze, C., Edwards, P. N., and Sandvig, C. (2018) 'Infrastructure studies meet platform studies in the age of Google and Facebook'. *New Media & Society*, 20(1), pp. 293–310.
Poell, T., Nieborg, D., and van Dijck, J. (2019) 'Platformisation'. *Internet Policy Review*, 8(4), pp. 1–13.
Pollock, N., and D'Adderio, L. (2012) 'Give me a two-by-two matrix and I will create the market: Rankings, graphic visualisations and sociomateriality'. *Accounting, Organizations and Society*, 37(8), pp. 565–586.
Pollock, N., and Williams, R. (2010) 'The business of expectations: How promissory organizations shape technology and innovation'. *Social Studies of Science*, 40(4), pp. 525–548.
Poovey, M. (1998) *A history of the modern fact: Problems of knowledge in the sciences of wealth and society*. Chicago: University of Chicago Press.
Popper, K. (2005 [1959]) *The logic of scientific discovery*. London: Routledge.
Porter, J. K., Baker, G. A., and Agrawal, N. (2011) 'The US produce traceability initiative: Analysis, evaluation, and recommendations'. *International Food and Agribusiness Management Review*, 14(3), pp. 45–66.
Porter, T. M. (1996) *Trust in numbers: The pursuit of objectivity in science and public life*. Princeton: Princeton University Press.
Powell, W.W., and Rerup, C. (2017) 'Opening the black box: Microfoundations of institutions'. In Greenwood, R., Oliver, C., Lawrence, T., and Meyer, R. (eds.), *The SAGE handbook of organizational institutionalism*. 2nd ed. Thousand Oaks, CA: Sage Publications, pp. 311–337.
Power, M. (1992) 'The politics of brand accounting in the United Kingdom'. *European Accounting Review*, 1(1), pp. 39–68.
Power, M. (1994a) 'From the science of accounts to the financial accountability of science'. *Science in Context*, 7(3), pp. 355–387.
Power, M. (1994b) *The audit explosion*. London: Demos.
Power, M. (1996) 'Making things auditable'. *Accounting, Organizations and Society*, 21(2–3), pp. 289–315.
Power, M. (1997) *The audit society*. Oxford: Oxford University Press.
Power, M. (2003) 'Auditing and the production of legitimacy'. *Accounting, Organizations and Society*, 28(4), pp. 379–394.
Power, M. (2004a) *The risk management of everything: Rethinking the politics of uncertainty*. London: Demos.
Power, M. (2004b) 'Academics in the accounting policy process: England and Germany compared'. In Leuz, C., Pfaff, D., and Hopwood, A. (eds.), *The economics and politics of accounting: International perspectives on trends, policy, and practice*. Oxford: Oxford University Press, pp. 376–392.
Power, M. (2005) 'Organizational responses to risk: The rise of the chief risk officer'. In Hutter, B., and Power, M. (eds.), *Organizational encounters with risk*. Cambridge: Cambridge University Press, pp. 132–148.
Power, M. (2007) *Organized uncertainty: Designing a world of risk management*. Oxford: Oxford University Press
Power, M. (2010) 'Fair value accounting, financial economics and the transformation of reliability'. *Accounting and Business Research*, 40(3), pp. 197–210.
Power, M. (2011a) 'Assurance worlds: Consumers, experts and independence'. *Accounting, Organizations and Society*, 36(4), pp. 324–326.
Power, M. (2011b) 'Preparing for financial surprise'. *Journal of Contingencies and Crisis Management*, 19(1), pp. 28–31.
Power, M. (2012) 'Accounting and finance'. in Knorr Cetina, K., and Preda, A. (eds.), *The Oxford handbook of the sociology of finance*. Oxford: Oxford University Press, pp. 293–314.
Power, M. (2013) 'The apparatus of fraud risk'. *Accounting, Organizations and Society*, 38(6–7), pp. 525–543.

Power, M. (2014) 'Risk, social theories, and organizations'. In Adler, P., Du Gay, P., Morgan, G., and Reed, M. (eds.), *The Oxford handbook of sociology, social theory, and organization studies: Contemporary currents*. Oxford: Oxford University Press, pp. 370–392.
Power, M. (2015) 'How accounting begins: Object formation and the accretion of infrastructure'. *Accounting, Organizations and Society*, 47, pp. 43–55.
Power, M. (2016) 'Postscript: On riskwork and auditwork'. in Power, M. (ed.), *Riskwork: Essays on the organizational life of risk management*. Oxford: Oxford University Press, pp. 274–284.
Power, M. (2018) 'Accounting, boundary-making, and organizational permeability'. In Ringel, L., Hiller, P., and Zietsma, C. (eds.), *Towards permeable boundaries of organizations? Research in the sociology of organizations*. Bingley: Emerald Publishing Group, pp. 31–53.
Power, M. (2019) 'Infrastructures of traceability'. In Kornberger, M., Bowker, G., Pollock, N., Miller, P., Mennicken, A., Randa Nucho, J., and Elyachar, J. (eds.), *Thinking infrastructures: Research in the sociology of organizations*. Bingley: Emerald Group Publishing, pp.115–130.
Power, M. (2021a) 'Modelling the microfoundations of the audit society: Organizations and the logic of the audit trail'. *Academy of Management Review*, 46(1), pp. 6–32.
Power, M. (2021b) 'The financial reporting system—what is it?' *Accounting and Business Research*, 51(5), pp. 459–480. https://doi.org/10.1080/00014788.2021.1932253.
Power, M. (2022) 'Theorizing the economy of traces: From audit society to surveillance capitalism'. *Organization Theory*, 3(1), pp. 1–19.
Prat, A. (2005) 'The wrong kind of transparency'. *American Economic Review*, 95(3), pp. 862–877.
Pratt, M. G., Kaplan, S. and Whittington, R. (2020) 'Editorial essay: The tumult over transparency: Decoupling transparency from replication in establishing trustworthy qualitative research'. *Administrative Science Quarterly*, 65(1), pp. 1–19.
Price, F. (2017) *Right first time: Using quality control for profit*. London: Routledge.
Puranam, P. (2025) *Re-humanize: How to build human-centric organizations in the age of algorithms*. Singapore: Penguin Business.
Purser, R. E. (2000) 'The coming crisis in real-time environments: A dromological analysis'. *Proceedings of the 2000 Academy of Management*, pp. F1–F6, https://doi.org/10.5465/apbpp.2000.5535615.
Qu, S. Q., and Cooper, D. J. (2011) 'The role of inscriptions in producing a balanced scorecard'. *Accounting, Organizations and Society*, 36(6), pp. 344–362.
Quattrone, P. (2015) 'Governing social orders, unfolding rationality, and Jesuit accounting practices: a procedural approach to institutional logics'. *Administrative Science Quarterly*, 60(3), pp. 411–445.
Quattrone, P. (2016) 'Management accounting goes digital: Will the move make it wiser?' *Management Accounting Research*, 31, pp. 118–122.
Quattrone, P. (2017) 'Embracing ambiguity in management controls and decision-making processes: On how to design data visualisations to prompt wise judgement'. *Accounting and Business Research*, 47(5), pp. 588–612.
Quattrone, P., and Hopper, T. (2005) 'A "time–space odyssey": Management control systems in two multinational organisations'. *Accounting, Organizations and Society*, 30(7–8), pp. 735–764.
Quattrone, P., Ronzani, M., Jancsary, D., and Höllerer, M. A. (2021) 'Beyond the visible, the material and the performative: Shifting perspectives on the visual in organization studies'. *Organization Studies*, 42(8), pp. 1197–1218.
Raffnsøe, S., Mennicken, A., and Miller, P. (2019) 'The Foucault effect in organization studies'. *Organization Studies*, 40(2), pp. 155–182.
Rahman, H. A., Karunakaran, A., and Cameron, L. D. (2024) 'Taming platform power: Taking accountability into account in the management of platforms'. *Academy of Management Annals*, 18(1), pp. 251–294.
Raisch, S., and Krakowski, S. (2021) 'Artificial intelligence and management: The automation-augmentation paradox'. *Academy of Management Review*, 46(1), pp. 192–210.

Ratner, H., and Plotnikof, M. (2022) 'Technology and dis/organization: Digital data infrastructures as partial connections'. *Organization Studies*, 43(7), pp. 1049–1067. https://doi.org/10.1177/01708406211053200.
Ray, C. (2017) 'Logical positivism'. In Newton-Smith, W. (ed.), *A companion to the philosophy of science*. Oxford: Blackwell, pp. 243–251.
Reason, J., Hollnagel, E., and Paries, J. (2006) 'Revisiting the Swiss cheese model of accidents'. *Journal of Clinical Engineering*, 27(4), pp. 110–115.
Reed, I. and Zald, M. (2014) 'The unsettlement of communities of inquiry'. In Swedberg, R. (Ed.) *Theorizing in social Science: The context of discovery. Stanford, CA*: Standford Social Sciences, pp. 85–105.
Reinecke, J., and Lawrence, T. B. (2023) 'The role of temporality in institutional stabilization: A process view'. *Academy of Management Review*, 48(4), pp. 639–658.
Rheinberger, H. J. (2011) 'Infra-experimentality: From traces to data, from data to patterning facts'. *History of Science*, 49(3), pp. 337–348.
Riles, A. (ed.). (2006) *Documents: Artifacts of modern knowledge*. Ann Arbor: University of Michigan Press.
Rindova, V. P., and Martins, L. L. (2022) 'Futurescapes: Imagination and temporal reorganization in the design of strategic narratives'. *Strategic Organization*, 20(1), pp. 200–224.
Rival, A., Montet, D., and Pioch, D. (2016) 'Certification, labelling and traceability of palm oil: Can we build confidence from trustworthy standards?' *OCL*, 23(6), DOI: 10.1051/ocl/2016042.
Roberts, J. (2009) 'No one is perfect: The limits of transparency and an ethic for "intelligent" accountability'. *Accounting, Organizations and Society*, 34(8), pp. 957–970.
Roberts, J. (2018) 'Managing only with transparency: The strategic functions of ignorance'. *Critical Perspectives on Accounting*, 55, pp. 53–60.
Roberts, J., and Scapens, R. (1985) 'Accounting systems and systems of accountability: Understanding accounting practices in their organisational contexts'. *Accounting, Organizations and Society*, 10(4), pp. 443–456.
Robinson, A. (2009) *Writing and script: A very short introduction* (Vol. 208). Oxford: Oxford University Press.
Robson, K. (1992) 'Accounting numbers as "inscription": Action at a distance and the development of accounting'. *Accounting, Organizations and Society*, 17(7), pp. 685–708.
Robson, K., and Bottausci, C. (2018) 'The sociology of translation and accounting inscriptions: Reflections on Latour and accounting research'. *Critical Perspectives on Accounting*, 54, pp. 60–75.
Robson, K., Humphrey, C., Khalifa, R., and Jones, J. (2007) 'Transforming audit technologies: Business risk audit methodologies and the audit field'. *Accounting, Organizations and Society*, 32(4–5), pp. 409–438.
Rochet, J. C., and Tirole, J. (2003) 'Platform competition in two-sided markets'. *Journal of the European Economic Association*, 1(4), pp. 990–1029.
Ronzani, M., and Gatzweiler, M. K. (2022) 'The lure of the visual: Multimodality, simplification, and performance measurement visualizations in a megaproject'. *Accounting, Organizations and Society*, 97, https://doi.org/10.1016/j.aos.2021.101296.
Rorty, R. (1980) *Philosophy and the mirror of nature*. Oxford: Blackwell.
Rorty, R. (1995) 'Habermas, Derrida and the functions of philosophy'. *Revue Internationale de Philosophie*, 49(194), pp. 437–459.
Rosa, H. (2010) *Alienation and acceleration: Towards a critical theory of late-modern temporality*. Aarhus, Denmark: Aarhus Universitetsforlag.
Rose, N. (1991) 'Governing by numbers: Figuring out democracy'. *Accounting, Organizations and Society*, 16(7), pp. 673–692.
Rose, N., O'Malley, P., and Valverde, M. (2006) 'Governmentality'. *Annual Review of Law and Social Science*, 2(1), pp. 83–104.

Rosenberg, D. (2013) 'Data before the fact'. In Gitelman, L. (ed.), *Raw data is an oxymoron*. Cambridge, MA: The MIT Press, pp. 15–40.

Rostain, M., and Huising, R. (2024) 'Vicarious coding: Breaching computational opacity in the digital era'. *Academy of Management Journal, 67*(2), pp. 359–381.

Rothaermel, F. T., Hitt, M. A., and Jobe, L. A. (2006) 'Balancing vertical integration and strategic outsourcing: Effects on product portfolio, product success, and firm performance'. *Strategic Management Journal*, 27(11), pp. 1033–1056.

Roth Smith, W. (2022) 'On relationality and organizationality: Degrees of durability, materiality, and communicatively constituting a fluid social collective'. *Organization Studies*, 43(11), pp. 1815–1837.

Rothstein, H., Huber, M., and Gaskell, G. (2006) 'A theory of risk colonization: The spiralling regulatory logics of societal and institutional risk'. *Economy and Society*, 35(1), pp. 91–112.

Rottenburg, R., Merry, S. E., Park, S. J., and Mugler, J. (eds.) (2015) *The world of indicators: The making of governmental knowledge through quantification*. Cambridge: Cambridge University Press.

Rouvroy, A., Berns, T., and Libbrecht, L. (2013) 'Algorithmic governmentality and prospects of emancipation'. *Réseaux* (1), pp. 163–196.

Rowbottom, N., Locke, J., and Troshani, I. (2021) 'When the tail wags the dog? Digitalisation and corporate reporting'. *Accounting, Organizations and Society*, 92, 101226, https://doi.org/10.1016/j.aos.2021.101226.

Royal Society (1992) *Risk: Analysis, perception and management: Report of a Royal Society Study Group*. London: Royal Society

Ruckenstein, M. (2014) 'Visualized and interacted life: Personal analytics and engagements with data doubles'. *Societies*, 4(1), pp. 68–84.

Ruppert, E., Law, J., and Savage, M. (2013) 'Reassembling social science methods: The challenge of digital devices'. *Theory, Culture & Society*, 30(4), pp. 22–46.

Ryle, G. (1949) *The concept of mind*. London: Routledge.

Samiolo, R., Spence, C., and Toh, D. (2024) 'Auditor judgment in the fourth industrial revolution'. *Contemporary Accounting Research*, 41(1), pp. 498–528.

Sanasi, S., and Ghezzi, A. (2024) 'Pivots as strategic responses to crises: Evidence from Italian companies navigating COVID-19'. *Strategic Organization*, 22(3), pp. 495–529. https://doi.org/10.1177/14761270221122933.

Sandberg, J., and Tsoukas, H. (2020) 'Sensemaking reconsidered: Towards a broader understanding through phenomenology'. *Organization Theory*, 1(1), pp. 1–34.

Sander, L. C., Bedner, M., Tims, M. C., Yen, J. H., Duewer, D. L., Porter, B., Christopher, S. J., Day, R. D., Long, S. E., Molloy, J. L., and Murphy, K. E. (2012) 'Development and certification of green tea-containing standard reference materials'. *Analytical and Bioanalytical Chemistry*, 402(1), pp. 473–487.

Sandvig, C., Hamilton, K., Karahalios, K., and Langbort, C. (2014) 'Auditing algorithms: Research methods for detecting discrimination on internet platforms'. *Data and Discrimination: Converting Critical Concerns into Productive Inquiry*, 22(2014), pp. 4349–4357.

Sauder, M., and Espeland, W. N. (2009) 'The discipline of rankings: Tight coupling and organizational change'. *American Sociological Review*, 74(1), pp. 63–82.

Savage, M. (2013) 'The "social life of methods": A critical introduction'. *Theory, Culture & Society*, 30(4), pp. 3–21.

Savage, M., and Burrows, R. (2007) 'The coming crisis of empirical sociology'. *Sociology*, 41(5), pp. 885–899.

Scally, G. (2024) 'COVID inquiry: The flaws that led to system failure'. *British Medical Journal*, 386, http://dx.doi.org/10.1136/bmj.q1865.

Schatzki, T. (2020) 'Timespace and the organization of social life'. In Shove, E., Trentmann, F., and Wilk, R. (Eds.) *Time consumption and everyday life*. London: Routledge, pp. 35–48.

Schatzki, T. R. (2005) 'Peripheral vision: The sites of organizations'. *Organization Studies*, 26(3), pp. 465–484.

Schatzki, T. R. (2006) 'On organizations as they happen'. *Organization Studies*, 27(12), pp. 1863–1873.
Scherer, A. G., and Neesham, C. (2023) 'Organized immaturity in a Post-Kantian perspective: Toward a critical theory of surveillance capitalism'. *Organization Theory*, 4(3), https://doi.org/10.1177/26317877231204083.
Schilling-Vacaflor, A. (2021) 'Integrating human rights and the environment in supply chain regulations'. *Sustainability*, 13(17), https://doi.org/10.3390/su13179666.
Schneider, N. (2019) 'Decentralization: an incomplete ambition'. *Journal of Cultural Economy*, 12(4), pp. 265–285.
Schuilenburg, M., and Peeters, R. (2020) *The algorithmic society*. London and New York: Routledge.
Schutz, A. (1976) *The phenomenology of the social world*. Translated by G. Walsh and F. Lehnert. London: Heinemann Educational Books.
Scott, J. C. (1998) *Seeing like a state: How certain schemes to improve the human condition have failed*. New Haven, CT: Yale University Press.
Scott, M. B., and Lyman, S. M. (1968) 'Accounts'. *American Sociological Review*, 33(1), pp. 46–62.
Scott, S. V., and Orlikowski, W. J. (2025) 'Exploring AI-in-the-making: Sociomaterial genealogies of AI performativity'. *Information and Organization*, 35(1), https://doi.org/10.1016/j.infoandorg.2025.100558.
Scott, S. V., and Orlikowski, W. J. (2012) 'Reconfiguring relations of accountability: Materialization of social media in the travel sector'. *Accounting, Organizations and Society*, 37(1), pp. 26–40.
Scribano, A. (2023) 'Towards a sociology of vestiges'. *American Sociologist*, 54(2), pp. 123–145. https://doi.org/10.1007/s12108-023-09571-6 (accessed 15 December 2024).
Seaver, N. (2019) 'Captivating algorithms: Recommender systems as traps'. *Journal of Material Culture*, 24(4), pp. 421–436.
SEC. (2005) *Roundtable discussion on implementation of internal control reporting provisions*. Washington, DC: United States Securities and Exchange Commission.
Sellars, W. (1963) 'Empiricism and the philosophy of mind'. In Sellars, W. (Ed.) *Science, perception and reality*. London: Routledge Kegan Paul, pp. 253–329.
Selznick, P. (1957) *Leadership in administration: A sociological interpretation*. Berkeley: University of California Press.
Selznick, P. (1996) 'Institutionalism "old" and "new"'. *Administrative Science Quarterly*, 41(2), pp. 270–277.
Servida, F., and Casey, E. (2019) 'IoT forensic challenges and opportunities for digital traces'. *Digital Investigation*, 28, pp. S22–S29.
Shannon, C. E. (1948) 'A mathematical theory of communication'. *The Bell System Technical Journal*, 27(3), pp. 379–423.
Shapin, S., and Schaffer, S. (2011) *Leviathan and the air-pump: Hobbes, Boyle, and the experimental life*. Princeton: Princeton University Press.
Shapiro, S. (1987) 'The social control of impersonal trust'. *American Journal of Sociology*, 93(3), pp. 623–658.
Sharon, T., and Zandbergen, D. (2017) 'From data fetishism to quantifying selves: Self-tracking practices and the other values of data'. *New Media & Society*, 19(11), pp. 1695–1709.
Shore, C., and Wright, S. (2018) 'Performance management and the audited self'. In Ajana, B. (ed.), *Metric culture*. Leeds: Emerald Publishing, pp. 11–35. https://doi.org/10.1108/978-1-78743-289-520181002.
Simmel, G. (1909) 'The problem of sociology'. *American Journal of Sociology*, 15(3), pp. 289–320.
Simmel, G. (1971 [1918]) 'The transcendent character of life'. In Levine, D. N. (ed.), *Georg Simmel on individuality and social forms*. Chicago: University of Chicago Press, pp. 353–374.

Simondon, G. (2020) *Individuation in light of notions of form and information.* Translated by T. Adkins. Minneapolis: University of Minnesota Press.
Singh, N., Lai, K. H., Vejvar, M., and Cheng, T. E. (2019) 'Data-driven auditing: A predictive modeling approach to fraud detection and classification'. *Journal of Corporate Accounting & Finance*, 30(3), pp. 64–82.
Smith, D. (1984) 'Textually mediated social organization'. *International Social Science Journal*, 36, pp. 59–75.
Smith, D. E. (2001) 'Texts and the ontology of organizations and institutions'. *Studies in Cultures, Organizations and Societies*, 7(2), pp. 59–198.
Snow, C. P. (1998) *The two cultures.* Cambridge: Cambridge University Press.
Solomons, D. (1983) 'The political implications of accounting and accounting standard setting'. *Accounting and Business Research*, 13(50), pp. 107–118.
Spicer, A., and Alvesson, M. (2024) 'Critical management studies: A critical review'. *Journal of Management Studies*, 61(1), 1–25.
Sprague, C. E. (1922) *The philosophy of accounts.* New York: Ronald Press.
Star, S. L. (1999) 'The ethnography of infrastructure'. *American Behavioral Scientist*, 43(3), pp. 377–391.
Stark, D., and Broeck, P.V. (2024) 'Principles of algorithmic management'. *Organization Theory*, 5(2), https://doi.org/10.1177/26317877241257213.
Stark, D., and Pais, I. (2021) 'Algorithmic management in the platform economy'. *Sociologica*, 14(3), pp. 47–72. https://doi.org/10.6092/issn.1971-8853/12221.
Steiner, G. (1989) *Real presences.* Chicago: University of Chicago Press.
Stevens, G. C. (1989) 'Integrating the supply chain'. *International Journal of Physical Distribution & Materials Management*, 19(8), pp. 3–8.
Stiegler, B. (1998) *Technics and time, 1: The fault of Epimetheus* (Vol. 1). Stanford, CA: Stanford University Press.
Stiegler, B. (2016) *Automatic society, volume 1: The future of work.* New York: John Wiley & Sons.
Stiles, P., and Taylor, B. (1993) 'Maxwell: The failure of corporate governance'. *Corporate Governance: An International Review*, 1(1), pp. 34–45.
Strang, D., and Meyer, J. W. (1993) 'Institutional conditions for diffusion'. *Theory and Society*, 22(4), pp. 487–511.
Strathern, M. (1995) *The relation: Issues in complexity and scale.* Cambridge, UK: Prickly Pear Press.
Strathern, M. (1997) '"Improving ratings": Audit in the British university system'. *European Review*, 5(3), pp. 305–321.
Strathern, M. (ed.) (2000a) *Audit cultures: Anthropological studies in accountability, ethics and the academy.* London: Routledge.
Strathern, M. (2000b) 'The tyranny of transparency'. *British Educational Research Journal*, 26(3), pp. 309–321.
Strathern, M. (2005) *Partial connections.* New York: Altamira Press.
Suchman, L. (1995) 'Making work visible'. *Communications of the ACM*, 38(9), pp. 56–64.
Scandinavian Journal of Information Systems, 14(2), pp. 91–105.
Suchman, L., and Suchman, L. A. (2007) *Human-machine reconfigurations: Plans and situated actions.* Cambridge: Cambridge University Press.
Suddaby, R., Cooper, D. J., and Greenwood, R. (2007) 'Transnational regulation of professional services: Governance dynamics of field level organizational change'. *Accounting, Organizations and Society*, 32(4–5), pp. 333–362.
Surowiecki, J. (2005) *The wisdom of crowds.* New York: Anchor.
Suzuki, T. (2007) 'Accountics: Impacts of internationally standardized accounting on the Japanese socio-economy'. *Accounting, Organizations and Society*, 32(3), pp. 263–301.
Swan, M. (2012) 'Sensor mania! The internet of things, wearable computing, objective metrics, and the quantified self 2.0'. *Journal of Sensor and Actuator Networks*, 1(3), pp. 217–253.

Swan, M. (2013) 'The quantified self: Fundamental disruption in big data science and biological discovery'. *Big Data*, 1(2), pp. 85–99.
Swedberg, R. (2014) 'From theory to theorizing'. In Swedberg, R. (ed.), *Theorizing in social science*. Stanford, CA: Stanford University Press, pp. 1–28.
Taylor, C. (2004) *Modern social imaginaries*. Durham, NC: Duke University Press.
Thaler, R. H. (2016) 'Behavioral economics: Past, present, and future'. *American Economic Review*, 106(7), pp. 1577–1600.
Thornton, P. H., Jones, C., and Kury, K. (2005) 'Institutional logics and institutional change in organizations: Transformation in accounting, architecture, and publishing'. In Jones, C., and Thornton, P. H. (eds.), *Transformation in cultural industries*. Research in the sociology of organizations, 23, pp. 125–170. Bingley: Emerald Group Publishing.
Thornton, P. H., Ocasio, W., and Lounsbury, M. (2012) *The institutional logics perspective: A new approach to culture, structure, and process*. Oxford: Oxford University Press.
Thylstrup, N. B., Archer, M., and Ravn, L. (2022) 'Traceability'. *Internet Policy Review*, 11(1), pp. 1–12. https://doi.org/10.14763/2022.1.1646.
Tomkins, C., and Groves, R. (1983) 'The everyday accountant and researching his reality'. *Accounting, Organizations and Society*, 8(4), pp. 361–374.
Tomlinson, J. (2007) *The culture of speed: The coming of immediacy*. Thousand Oaks, CA: Sage.
Torpey, J. C. (2018) *The invention of the passport: Surveillance, citizenship and the state*. Cambridge: Cambridge University Press.
Townley, B. (1993) 'Foucault, power/knowledge, and its relevance for human resource management'. *Academy of Management Review*, 18(3), pp. 518–545.
Townley, B. (1997) 'The institutional logic of performance appraisal'. *Organization Studies*, 18(2), pp. 261–285.
Tsoukas, H. (1997) 'The tyranny of light: The temptations and the paradoxes of the information society'. *Futures*, 29(9), pp. 827–843.
Turner, B. A. (1976) 'The organizational and interorganizational development of disasters'. *Administrative Science Quarterly*, 21(3), pp. 378–397.
Turner, D. (2022) 'Three lines of defence—is it the right model?' *Journal of Financial Compliance*, 5(3), pp. 237–247.
Turner, S. F., and Cacciatori, E. (2016) 'The multiplicity of habit. Implications for routines research'. In Howard-Grenville, J., Rerup, C., Langley, A., and Tsoukas, H. (eds.), *Organizational routines: How they are created, maintained, and changed*. Oxford: Oxford University Press, pp. 71–95.
Ulbricht, N., and Weiner, C. (2005) *Worldscope meets Compustat: A comparison of financial databases* (No. 2005-064). SFB 649 Discussion Paper.
Ulbricht, L., and Yeung, K. (2022) 'Algorithmic regulation: A maturing concept for investigating regulation of and through algorithms'. *Regulation & Governance*, 16(1), pp. 3–22.
Valiaho, P. (2014) *Biopolitical screens: Image, power, and the neoliberal brain*. Cambridge, MA: MIT Press.
Valk, J., Preda, A., and Xu, R. (2023) 'Blockchain imaginaries: Introduction to this special issue'. *Anthropology Today*, 39(4), p. 3.
Van der Wagen, W., and Pieters, W. (2015) 'From cybercrime to cyborg crime: Botnets as hybrid criminal actor-networks'. *British Journal of Criminology*, 55(3), pp. 578–595.
Van Dijck, J. (2014) 'Datafication, dataism and dataveillance: Big data between scientific paradigm and ideology'. *Surveillance & Society*, 12(2), pp. 197–208.
Van Maanen, J., and Pentland, B. (1994) 'Cops and auditors: The rhetoric of records'. In Sitkin, S., and Bies, R. (eds.), *The legalistic organization*. Thousand Oaks, CA: Sage, pp. 53–90.
Varoufakis, Y. (2023) *Technofeudalism: What killed capitalism*. London: The Bodley Head.
Vaughan, D. (1996) *The Challenger launch decision: Risky technology, culture, and deviance at NASA*. Chicago: University of Chicago Press.

Vaughan, D. (2005) 'Organizational rituals of risk and error'. In Hutter, B., and Power, M. (eds.), *Organizational encounters with risk*. Cambridge: Cambridge University Press, pp. 33–66.
Vaughan, D. (2021) *Dead reckoning: Air traffic control, system effects, and risk*. Chicago: University of Chicago Press.
Véliz, C. (2021) 'Moral zombies: Why algorithms are not moral agents'. *AI & Society*, 36(2), pp. 487–497.
Véliz, C. (2023) *The ethics of privacy and surveillance*. Oxford: Oxford University Press.
Verbeek, P. P. (2011) *Moralizing technology: Understanding and designing the morality of things*. Chicago: University of Chicago Press.
Vermeer, L. (2022) 'From diaries to data doubles: Self-tracking in Dutch diaries (1780–1940)'. *Life Writing*, 19(2), pp. 215–240.
Vertesi, J. A., Goldstein, A., Enriquez, D., Liu, L., and Miller, K. T. (2021) 'Pre-automation: Insourcing and automating the gig economy'. *Sociologica*, 14(3), pp. 167–193. https://doi.org/10.6092/issn.1971-8853/11657.
Vinnari, E., and Laine, M. (2017) 'The moral mechanism of counter accounts: The case of industrial animal production'. *Accounting, Organizations and Society*, 57, pp. 1–17.
Vollmer, H. (2007) 'How to do more with numbers: Elementary stakes, framing, keying, and the three-dimensional character of numerical signs'. *Accounting, Organizations and Society*, 32(6), pp. 577–600.
Vollmer, H. (2019) 'Accounting for tacit coordination: The passing of accounts and the broader case for accounting theory'. *Accounting, Organizations and Society*, 73, pp. 15–34.
Vollmer, H., Mennicken, A., and Preda, A. (2009) 'Tracking the numbers: Across accounting and finance, organizations and markets'. *Accounting, Organizations and Society*, 34(5), pp. 619–637.
Vom Brocke, J., van der Aalst, W., Grisold, T., Kremser, W., Mendling, J., Pentland, B., Recker, J., Roeglinger, M., Rosemann, M., and Weber, B. (2021) 'Process science: The interdisciplinary study of continuous change'. SSRN Working Paper, 3916817.
von Colbe, W. B. (1996) 'Accounting and the business economics tradition in Germany'. *European Accounting Review*, 5(3), pp. 413–434. https://doi.org/10.1080/09638189600000027.
Vormbusch, U. (2022) 'Accounting for who we are and could be: Inventing taxonomies of the self in an age of uncertainty'. In Mennicken, A., and Salais, R. (eds.), *The new politics of numbers*. London: Palgrave Macmillan, pp. 97–134.
Voronov, M., and Weber, K. (2016) 'The heart of institutions: Emotional competence and institutional actorhood'. *Academy of Management Review*, 41(3), pp. 456–478.
Wacquant, L. (2015) 'For a sociology of flesh and blood'. *Qualitative Sociology*, 38(1), pp. 1–11.
Wajcman, J. (2020) *Pressed for time: The acceleration of life in digital capitalism*. Chicago: University of Chicago Press.
Wajcman, J., and Rose, E. (2011) 'Constant connectivity: Rethinking interruptions at work'. *Organization Studies*, 32(7), pp. 941–961. https://doi.org/10.1177/0170840611410829.
Walsh, J. P., and Ungson, G. R. (1991) 'Organizational memory'. *Academy of Management Review*, 16(1), pp. 57–91.
Wang, D., and Mao, Z. (2021) 'A comparative study of public health and social measures of COVID-19 advocated in different countries'. *Health Policy*, 125(8), pp. 957–971.
Wang, W., Lumineau, F., and Schilke, O. (2022) *Blockchains: Strategic implications for contracting, trust, and organizational design*. Cambridge: Cambridge University Press.
Weyermann, C., and Ribaux, O. (2012) 'Situating forensic traces in time'. *Science & Justice*, 52(2), pp. 68–75.
Wheeler, S. (ed.). (1969) *On record: Files and dossiers in American life*. Piscataway, NJ: Transaction Books.
Whitcomb, C. G. (2020) 'Review of Shoshana Zuboff (2019) "The age of surveillance capitalism: The fight for a human future at the new frontier of power"'. *Postdigital Science and Education*, 2(2), pp. 484–488.

Whitley, E. A., and Hosein, I. R. (2008) 'Doing the politics of technological decision making: Due process and the debate about identity cards in the UK'. *European Journal of Information Systems*, 17(6), pp. 668–677.

Whitley, R. (1986) 'The transformation of business finance into financial economics: The roles of academic expansion and changes in U.S. capital markets'. *Accounting, Organizations and Society*, 11(3), pp. 171–192.

Whitson, J. R. (2013) 'Gaming the quantified self'. *Surveillance & Society*, 11(1–2), pp. 163–176.

Wijen, F. (2014) 'Means versus ends in opaque institutional fields: Trading off compliance and achievement in sustainability standard adoption'. *Academy of Management Review*, 39(3), pp. 302–323.

Wijen, F. (2015) 'Coupling, not decoupling, should be institutional theory's mantra: A rejoinder to Haack and Schoeneborn'. *Academy of Management Review*, 40(2), pp. 310–313.

Williams, J. W. (2013) 'Regulatory technologies, risky subjects, and financial boundaries: Governing 'fraud' in the financial markets'. *Accounting, Organizations and Society*, 38(6–7), pp. 544–558.

Willman, P., Fenton-O'Creevy, M., Nicholson, N., and Soane, E. (2006) 'Noise trading and the management of operational risk: Firms, traders and irrationality in financial markets'. *Journal of Management Studies*, 43(6), pp. 1357–1374.

Wiltshire, P. (2019) *Traces*. London: Bonnier Books UK.

Wittgenstein, L. (1976 [1958]) *Philosophical investigations*. Oxford: Blackwell.

Woolgar, S. (1990) 'Configuring the user: The case of usability trials'. *The Sociological Review*, 38(1 Suppl), pp. 58–99.

WWF. (2015) *Traceability principles for wild-caught fish products*. https://www.worldwildlife.org/publications/traceability-principles-for-wild-caught-fish-products (accessed 9 January 2018).

Xu, R., Millo, Y., and Spence, C. (2023) 'The mountains are high and the emperor is far away: Credit scoring and the infrastructure of surveillance capitalism in China'. *Contemporary Accounting Research*, 41(2), pp. 781–808.

Yeung, K. (2018) 'Algorithmic regulation: A critical interrogation'. *Regulation & Governance*, 12(4), pp. 505–523.

Young, J. J. (2006) 'Making up users'. *Accounting, Organizations and Society*, 31(6), pp. 579–600.

Yu, A. (2021) 'Accountability as mourning: Accounting for death in the time of COVID-19'. *Accounting, Organizations and Society*, 90, https://doi.org/10.1016/j.aos.2020.101198.

Zachariadis, M., Hileman, G., and Scott, S. V. (2019) 'Governance and control in distributed ledgers: Understanding the challenges facing blockchain technology in financial services'. *Information and Organization*, 29(2), pp. 105–117.

Zahavi, D. (2018) *Phenomenology: The basics*. London: Routledge.

Zajac, E. J., and Westphal, J. D. (2004) 'The social construction of market value: Institutionalization and learning perspectives on stock market reactions'. *American Sociological Review*, 69(3), pp. 433–457.

Ziewitz, M. (2016) 'Governing algorithms: Myth, mess, and methods'. *Science, Technology, & Human Values*, 41(1), pp. 3–16.

Zuboff, S. (2015) 'Big other: Surveillance capitalism and the prospects of an information civilization'. *Journal of Information Technology*, 30(1), pp. 75–89.

Zuboff, S. (2019) *The age of surveillance capitalism: The fight for a human future at the new frontier of power*. London: Profile Books.

Zuboff, S. (2022) 'Surveillance capitalism or democracy? The death match of institutional orders and the politics of knowledge in our information civilization'. *Organization Theory*, 3(3), https://doi.org/10.1177/26317877221129290.

Index

For the benefit of digital users, indexed terms that span two pages (e.g., 52–53) may, on occasion, appear on only one of those pages.

Note: Page numbers followed by '*f*' refer to figures; those by '*t*' refer to tables; and those by 'n' to the notes.

www.ingramcontent.com/pod-product-compliance
Ingram Content Group UK Ltd.
Pitfield, Milton Keynes, MK11 3LW, UK
UKHW041434160926
475595UK00019B/17

9 780197 681497